AutoCAD LT 2006:
The Definitive Guide

AutoCAD LT 2006:
The Definitive Guide

by Ralph Grabowski

Wordware Publishing, Inc.

Library of Congress Cataloging-in-Publication Data

Grabowski, Ralph
AutoCAD LT 2006: the definitive guide / by Ralph Grabowski.
   p. cm.
Includes index.
   ISBN-13: 978-1-55622-858-9 (pbk.)
   ISBN-10: 1-55622-858-9 (pbk.)

1. Computer graphics. 2. AutoCAD. I. Title.
T385.G6912 2005
620'.0042'0285536--dc22   2005009700
                                          CIP

ISBN-13: 978-1-55622-858-2
ISBN-10: 1-55622-858-9
10 9 8 7 6 5 4 3 2 1
0505

All inquiries for volume purchases of this book should be addressed to Wordware Publishing, Inc., at the above address. Telephone inquiries may be made by calling:
(972) 423-0090

Contents Summary

IV – Customizing AutoCAD LT

Appendices

Contents

Part I – Introduction to AutoCAD LT

Part II – Drafting with AutoCAD LT

8 Creating Block Libraries and Attributes 151

13 Practicing Safe Computing 251

Part IV – Customizing AutoCAD LT

21 Customizing Toolbars and Workspaces 387

22 Customizing Buttons, Shortcut Menus, and Tablets 401

23 Advanced Programming Issues 411

Appendices

Introduction

AutoCAD LT 2006 is Autodesk's software for creating two-dimensional designs used by 2.7 million drafters.

You made an excellent choice in acquiring AutoCAD LT. It is many times cheaper than AutoCAD 2006, yet allows you to do almost all the same 2D drafting tasks.

This book is designed to quickly get you started with AutoCAD LT. Once you have the software installed on your computer, I recommend that you work though the first seven chapters. These chapters are written so that you can complete each in an hour or less. In seven hours, you'll learn how to set up new drawings, add details, make changes, and then print the drawings.

(Don't worry if you have difficulty completing a chapter. The companion files, available at www.wordware.com/files/acadlt06, contain copies of the project drawing as it stands at the end of each chapter. That lets you start with an accurate copy at the start of the next chapter.)

Later chapters delve into advanced functions, such as creating block libraries and attribute data, isometric drafting, CAD management issues, and customizing AutoCAD LT.

Updated for AutoCAD LT 2006

This is the ninth edition of this book, which was first written for the original AutoCAD LT Release 1. Each time Autodesk releases a new version of AutoCAD LT, this book is updated to reflect changes in user interface, commands, and features.

For AutoCAD LT 2006, this book includes these new and updated features:

- New form of user interface called "dynamic input"
- New designs for the **Layer** dialog box, **MText** toolbar, and **Text** command
- Updated Tool Palettes window
- Grips added to arcs
- Creating and editing tables
- Coverage of dynamic blocks
- Inserting spreadsheet-like formulas
- Customize User Interface dialog box
- Workspaces
- Updated screen images

About the Author

Ralph Grabowski began writing about AutoCAD in 1985 when he joined *CADalyst* magazine as Technical Editor. In the next 20 years, he authored 85 books and hundreds of magazine articles on CAD. For Wordware Publishing, he has written more than a dozen books on AutoCAD, AutoCAD LT, and Visio.

Mr. Grabowski is the editor of *upFront.eZine*, the weekly e-newsletter for CAD users, and *iCommunique*, the monthly e-newsletter for Canadian AutoCAD users. You can visit his Web site at www.upfrontezine.com and his WorldCAD Access weblog at worldcadaccess.typepad.com.

Introduction to AutoCAD LT

Notes

Chapter 1

AutoCAD LT 2006 Quick Tour

In This Chapter

- Starting AutoCAD LT
- Becoming familiar with the user interface
- Drawing lines
- Understanding dynamic input
- Reversing mistakes
- Accessing online help

In this chapter, you learn how to start AutoCAD LT 2006, and tour the AutoCAD LT user interface. You also get your feet wet by placing a few lines in a new drawing.

Starting AutoCAD LT 2006

Before starting AutoCAD LT, your computer must be running Windows 2000 or XP. If AutoCAD LT is not yet set up on your computer, do so first.

To start AutoCAD LT, double-click the AutoCAD LT icon found on the Windows desktop.

AutoCAD LT
2006

Key Terms

Buttons — execute commands when clicked
Cursors — provide feedback from Windows and AutoCAD LT
Flipscreen — switches between the drawing and text windows
Flyouts — buttons that hide additional toolbars
Icons — pictorial representations of commands
Layouts — define how drawings are plotted
Pickbox — specifies the points being picked (selected)
Right-clicking — press right mouse button to display context-sensitive menus
Toolbars — collections of buttons

Abbreviations

Alt	Alt (or alternate) key
Ctrl	Ctrl (or control) key
F	Function keys
U	Undoes the last command or option
UCS	User-defined coordinate system

Commands

Command	Shortcut	Menu Selection
Help	? *or* F1	Help | Help*
Line	L	Draw | Line
Quit	Alt+F4	File | Exit
TextScr	F2	View | Display | Text Window
Undo	Ctrl+Z	Edit | Undo
UcsIcon	Alt+VLU	View | Display | UcsIcon

* The vertical bar separates menu selections. For instance, from the **Help** menu select the **Help** item.

Alternatively, click the taskbar's **Start** button, and select **Programs**, followed by **Autodesk**, the **AutoCAD LT** group, and then **AutoCAD LT**.

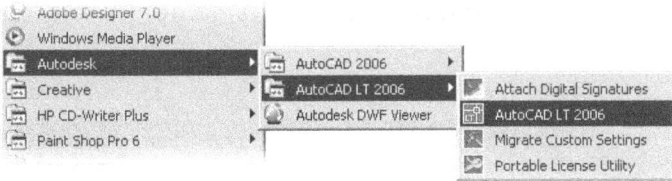

Depending on the speed of your computer, it can take from 10 to 60 seconds to load AutoCAD LT. During this time, a "splash screen" appears, and then the AutoCAD LT window appears.

The AutoCAD LT Window

After AutoCAD LT begins to appear, it displays the New Features Workshop. Its purpose is to provide tutorials on features new to the current release.

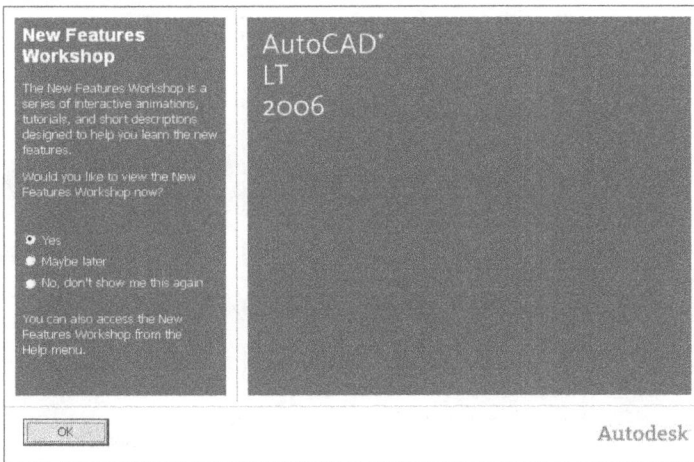

It presents you with three options:

> **Yes** — runs the New Features Workshop.
>
> **Maybe later** — closes the window after you click **OK**, but reappears the next time you start AutoCAD LT.
>
> **No, don't show me this again** — closes the window, and prevents it from appearing automatically. To see it at some time in the future, select **New Features Workshop** from AutoCAD LT's **Help** menu.

Select **Maybe later** or **No**, and then click **OK**.

The AutoCAD LT window consists of a graphical drawing area with areas of information arranged on four sides.

Along the top, you see the title bar, menu bar, and several toolbars.

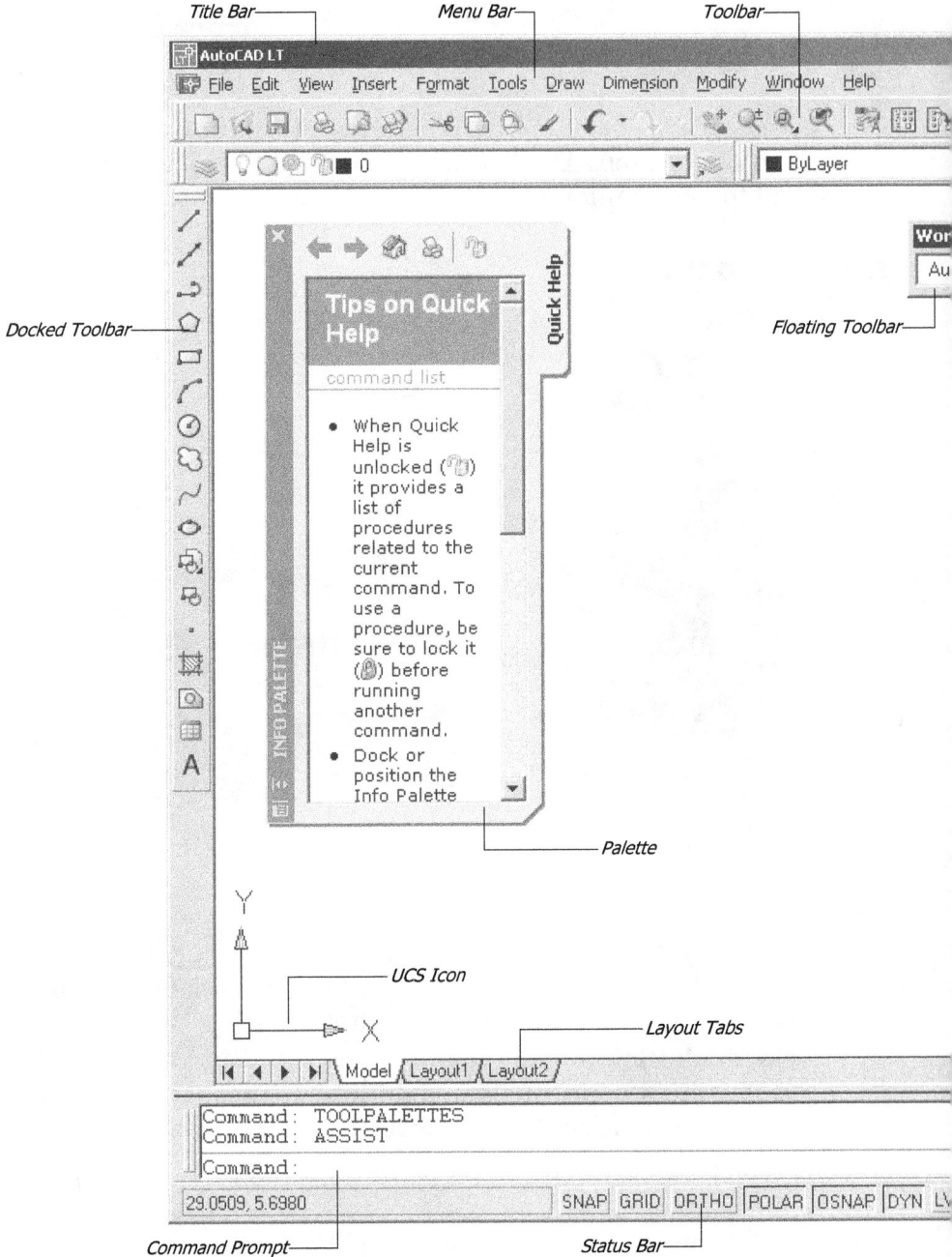

Title Bar — Menu Bar — Toolbar —

Docked Toolbar — Floating Toolbar —

Tips on Quick Help

command list

- When Quick Help is unlocked (⊕) it provides a list of procedures related to the current command. To use a procedure, be sure to lock it (🔒) before running another command.
- Dock or position the Info Palette

Palette —

UCS Icon —

Layout Tabs —

Command: TOOLPALETTES
Command: ASSIST
Command:

29.0509, 5.6980   SNAP GRID ORTHO POLAR OSNAP DYN LV

Command Prompt — Status Bar —

In the middle, you see the crosshair cursor with its pickbox and the UCS icon with its x, y axes. Floating in the drawing area are a toolbar and two palettes — the Info (Quick Help) and Tool palettes. For now, click the **x**

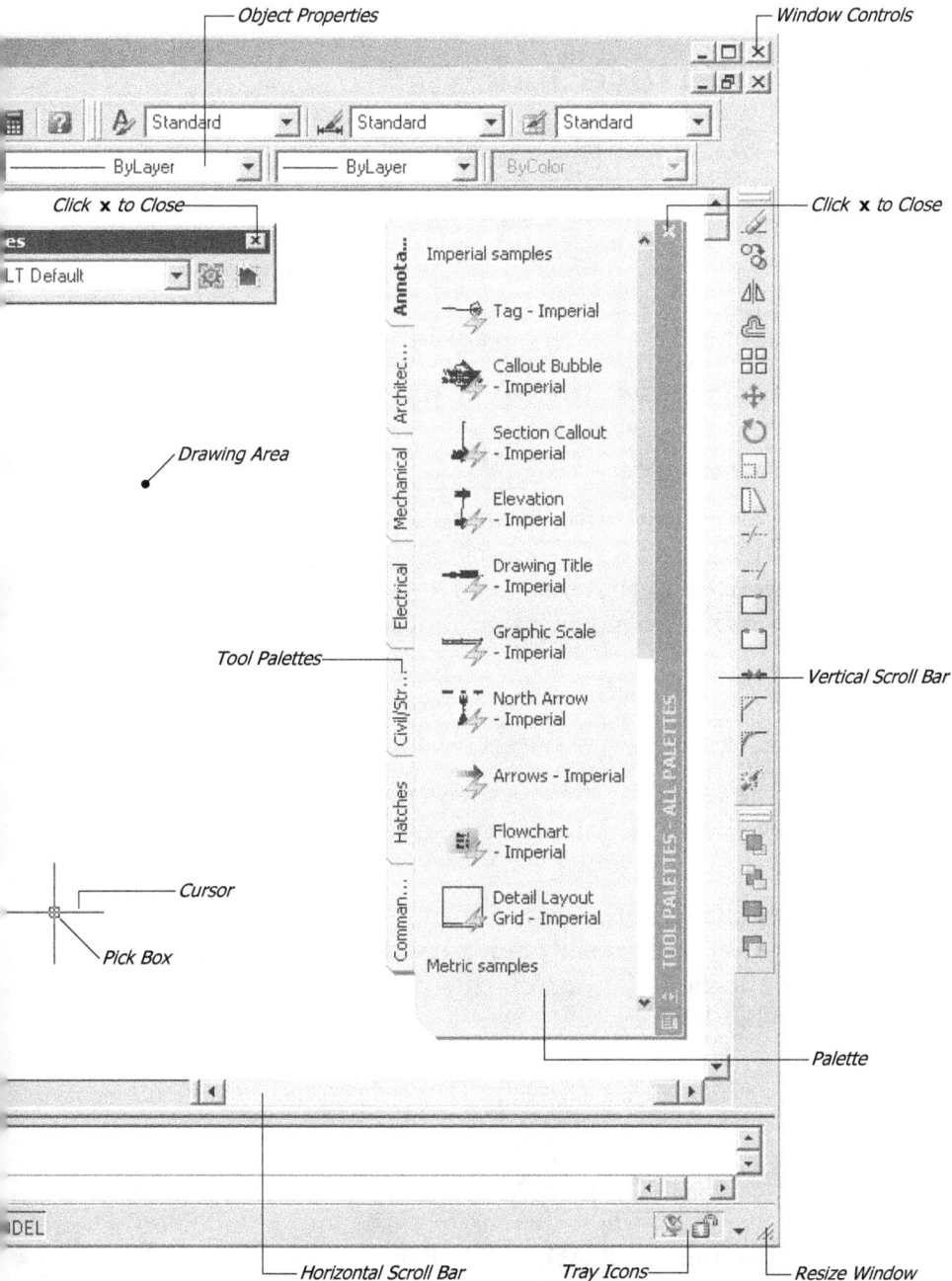

Object Properties

Window Controls

Click **x** to Close

Click **x** to Close

LT Default

Drawing Area

Tool Palettes

Vertical Scroll Bar

Cursor

Pick Box

Imperial samples

Tag - Imperial

Callout Bubble - Imperial

Section Callout - Imperial

Elevation - Imperial

Drawing Title - Imperial

Graphic Scale - Imperial

North Arrow - Imperial

Arrows - Imperial

Flowchart - Imperial

Detail Layout Grid - Imperial

Metric samples

Palette

Horizontal Scroll Bar

Tray Icons

Resize Window

button in the upper-right corner of the toolbar and the two palettes; you return to them later in the book.

Additional toolbars are docked to the left and right of the drawing. At the bottom are the layout tabs, command prompt area, and the status bar.

Basic User Interface Tour

The many aspects of AutoCAD LT's user interface can be daunting to learn all at once, so let's first look at just a few items:

- Crosshair and arrow cursors
- Menu bar
- Command line
- UCS icon

Chapter 2 provides a more detailed look at AutoCAD LT's user interface.

Crosshair and Arrow Cursors

The cursor gives you feedback from AutoCAD LT, Windows, and other software. While in the AutoCAD LT drawing area, the cursor is a crosshair that shows where you are in the drawing. Try moving the cursor around the AutoCAD LT window by moving your mouse.

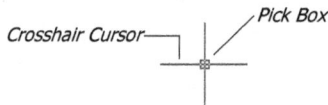

Crosshair Cursor —— / Pick Box

The small box in the center of the crosshairs is called the *pickbox*, which shows you the point you are picking. You use the cursor pickbox in Chapter 5, "Adding Details to Drawings."

When you move the crosshair out of the drawing area, the cursor changes to an arrow shape. You are probably familiar with the arrow cursor from other Windows applications. The arrow cursor lets you make menu selections and pick toolbar buttons.

The cursor changes to other shapes, which you learn about in the coming chapters. For example, when the cursor turns into a double-ended cursor, you can resize the AutoCAD LT window.

TIPS   The size of the crosshair cursor can be changed through the **Options** command: select the **Display** tab, and then look for **Crosshair size**.

The default value is **5**, which means the length of the crosshair is about 5% of the screen size. When set to **100**, the cursor stretches across the entire drawing area.

The size of the pickbox can be changed with the **Selection** tab's **Pickbox size** slider. Its size ranges from 0 to 50 pixels; the default size is 3 pixels.

Many other user interface options can be changed with the Options dialog box, accessed by the **Options** command.

Menu Bar

AutoCAD LT's menu bar is similar to the menu bar used by other Windows programs. Some of the words found on the menu bar are the same, such as File, Edit, View, Insert, Format, Tools, Window, and Help. The other menu items, such as Draw, Dimension, and Modify, are unique to AutoCAD LT.

Here is how menus work:

1. Move the computer's mouse so that the cursor touches the menu bar.

2. Move the mouse left or right until the cursor is over the word **View**. Notice View becomes highlighted.

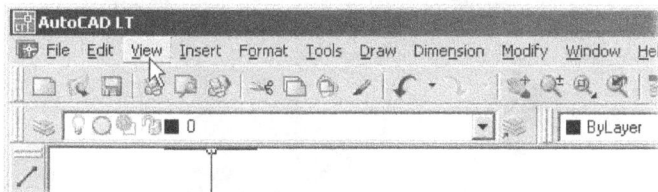

3. To select the **View** menu, press the first mouse button (the left button on the mouse). Instantly, the menu pops down.

    Notice that it lists many (but not all) of AutoCAD LT's view options: Redraw, Regen, Regen All, Zoom, Pan, Aerial View, and others.

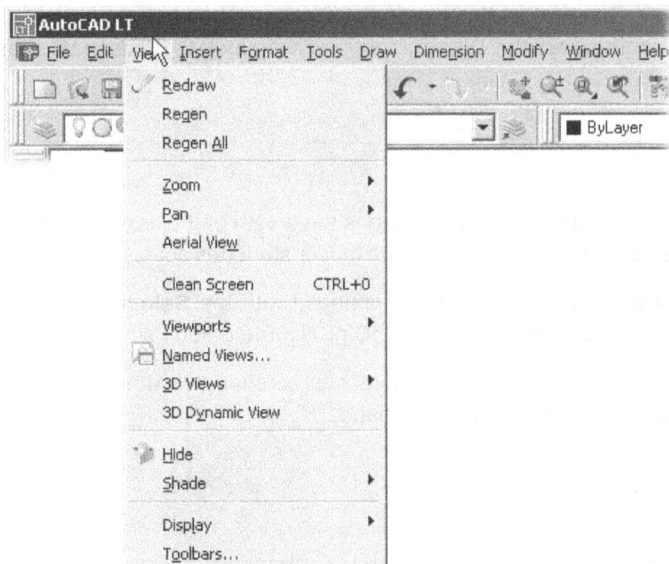

TIP If you pick a menu item accidentally, you can "unselect" it by picking it a second time.

4. Move the cursor down the menu, then pause over a menu item, such as **Redraw**. Notice that the menu item is highlighted.

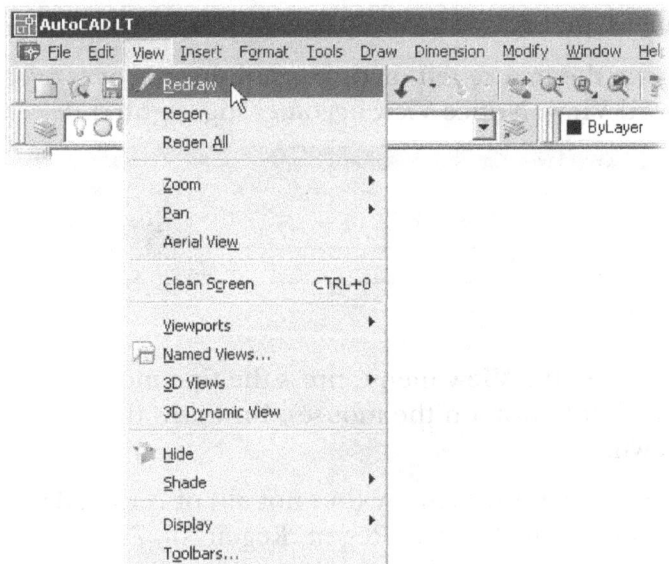

Look at the status line (at the bottom of the AutoCAD LT window). There you can read a one-sentence description of the command. This is helpful when you are not sure of a command's purpose.

For example, the **Redraw** command displays "Refreshes the display of the current viewport: REDRAW."

5. Continue moving the cursor down until you arrive at **3D Views**, located about halfway down the menu. A *submenu* appears, listing Viewpoint Presets, Viewpoint, Plan View, and so on.

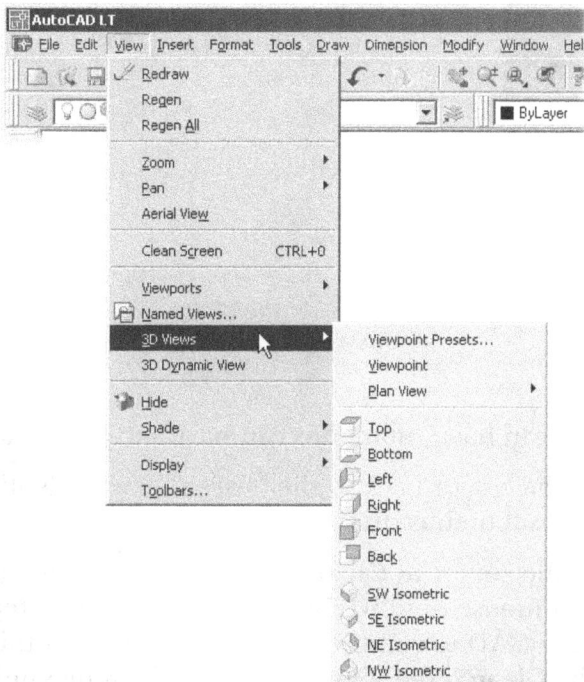

Just as menus group similar commands together, submenus group together command options and very closely related commands. This submenu lists methods of viewing drawings from different angles in 3D.

6. Move the cursor over to the submenu, and select **Plan View**. Notice that a second submenu appears.

Menus can have submenus can have sub-submenus!

7. Move the cursor back to the "parent" menu. Notice that the two submenus disappear.

8. Move the cursor to **Clean Screen**, and then *click* (press the left mouse button). By selecting the menu item, you tell AutoCAD to run the related command. In this case, it's the **CleanScreenOn** command, which maximizes the drawing area.

9. To return AutoCAD LT to normal, go back to the **View** menu, and then select **Clean Screen** again.

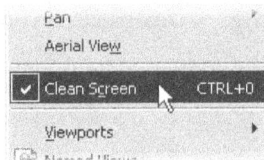

Notice the check mark in front of Clean Screen. This is an example of a *toggle*, where the menu items turn an option on (check mark) and off (no check mark.)

Also notice **CTRL+0** to the right of Clean Screen. This is an example of a *keystroke shortcut*. Instead of selecting items from menus, you can hold down the **Ctrl** key and press a second key. Some users find using the keyboard faster than the menu.

The check mark and the keystroke shortcut are examples of the symbols used by menus to indicate special meanings:

Menu Symbol	Example	When Selected...
(none)	Redraw	Executes command
... *(ellipses)*	Named Views...	Displays dialog box
▶ *(arrowhead)*	3D Views ▶	Displays submenu
✓ *(check mark)*	✓ Clean Screen	Turns on command

Or indicates the state of commands:

Menu Symbol	Example	Indicates That...
+	CTRL+N	Ctrl shortcut keystrokes
_ *(underline)*	New	Alt shortcut keystrokes
(black text)	Plot Style	Command is available
(gray text)	Plot Style	Command is not available and cannot be selected

TIP   You can access the menu without the mouse. Here's how:

1. Hold down the **Alt** key. On the menu bar, notice that each word has a different letter underlined, such as **View**.

2. Press the **v** key to drop the View menu. Again, notice that every menu item has a different letter underlined.

3. Press the **c** key to execute the **Clean Screen** command.

Command Area

Along the bottom of the AutoCAD LT window is the command prompt area. Here you type AutoCAD LT commands, if you (like me) prefer typing over making menu selections. Typing command names and options is a fast way to draw and edit when you are a touch typist, but it is slow if you're not.

The command area is also where AutoCAD LT prompts you for additional information it might need to complete a command.

In addition, AutoCAD LT 2006 adds an on-screen input area, known as "heads-up drafting." First, we'll look at the traditional prompt area, and then we'll examine the new interface.

Command Prompts

When you see the 'Command:' prompt by itself, like this:

Command:

it means AutoCAD LT is ready for you to enter a command.

(If you want to enter a command but there is text after 'Command:', press the **Esc** key once or twice to clear the command line.)

Try drawing a few lines now:

1. Enter the Line command, as follows:

    Command: **line** *(Press **Enter**.)*

    Type the word **line**, and then press the **Enter** key. Pressing Enter tells AutoCAD LT you have finished entering the command name.

2. AutoCAD LT changes the prompt from 'Command:' to:

    Specify first point:

    AutoCAD LT is asking you where the line should start. As you move the mouse, you see the crosshair cursor move about the drawing portion of the screen.

3. Pick a point on the screen by pressing the first button (the left button) on your mouse, also known as the "pick button." AutoCAD LT changes the prompt to read:

    Specify next point or [Undo]: *(Pick another point.)*

    Notice that a "rubberband" line stretches from the point you picked as you move the mouse around.

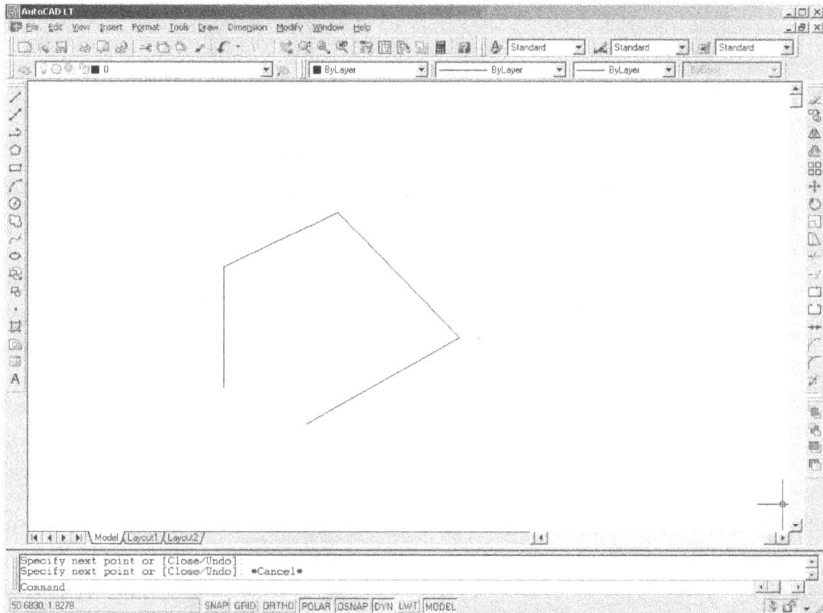

4. Move the mouse some more, and then press the pick button again. You have drawn your first line in AutoCAD LT!

5. Continue drawing lines by moving the mouse and pressing the pick button.

6. You end the **Line** command by pressing the **Enter** key, pressing the **Esc** key, or pressing the right mouse button, as follows:

    Specify next point or [Undo]: *(Press **Esc**.)*

    Pressing **Esc** cancels *any* AutoCAD LT command; some commands may need a couple of presses of **Esc**.

TIP   When you use the Line command, pressing the **Enter** key has three different effects, depending on the prompt:

*   At the 'From point:' prompt, pressing **Enter** causes AutoCAD LT to continue drawing from the last point, whether a line or an arc. This is a great way to ensure that a line is drawn perfectly tangent to the end of an arc.

*   At the 'To point:' prompt, pressing **Enter** terminates the Line command.

*   At the 'Command:' prompt, pressing **Enter** repeats the last command, which in this case would be the Line command.

7. To erase the lines you drew, type **U** at the 'Command:' prompt to undo the lines, as follows:

   Command: **u**

   You can also select the undo icon from the toolbar, select **Undo** from the **Edit** menu, or press **Ctrl+Z**.

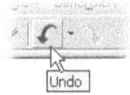

As you can see from this example, AutoCAD LT provides several different ways to perform actions. You will probably find yourself using a combination of keyboard typing, toolbar icons, menu picks, and keyboard shortcuts — whichever you find most convenient.

> **TIP** Right-click in the drawing area at any time to display shortcut menus. These menus are *context-sensitive*, meaning that their display changes depending on where the cursor is located at the time the right mouse button is pressed. During commands, for example, the shortcut menu displays the command's options. When commands are not active, the shortcut menu displays commonly used commands.

Dynamic Input

A second way to enter commands is to type directly in the drawing, something that will be new to you if you are used to older releases of AutoCAD LT. It feels a bit weird at first:

1. Move the cursor into the drawing area.

2. Type **line**. Notice that the word appears in a small rectangle.

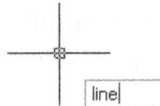

3. Press **Enter**. Notice that the Line command's prompt appears on the screen, as well as the x and y coordinates of the cursor's position. As you move the cursor, the coordinates update.

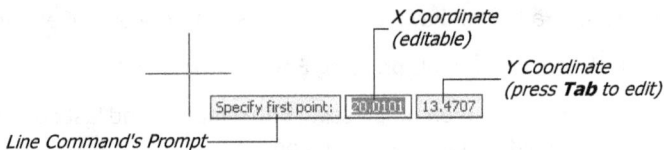

4. Now you have these options:

    • Pick a point in the drawing by pressing the left mouse button. AutoCAD LT places the point and prompts for the next point.

    • Enter numbers on the keyboard, such as **2.5**. AutoCAD LT takes those to be the value of the x coordinate, because it is the one that is highlighted (in blue).

    Press **Tab** to enter a value for the y coordinate.

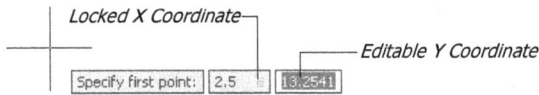

    Locked X Coordinate—

    Editable Y Coordinate

    Specify first point: | 2.5 | 13.2541

    (Notice the x coordinate has a padlock icon, indicating it is fixed in place. You can press **Tab** repeatedly to switch between editing and locking the x and y coordinates.)

    Press the left mouse button to place the point in the drawing.

5. For the next point, AutoCAD LT displays a different set of coordinates on the screen. They show the length and angle of the line, and are similar to *relative coordinates* entered at the 'Command:' prompt.

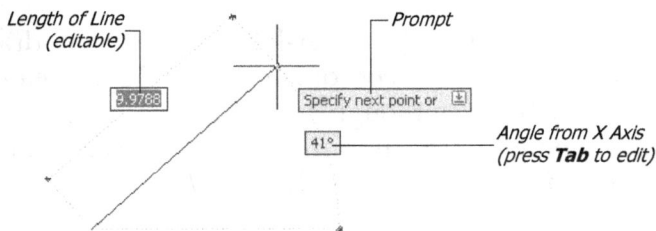

    Length of Line (editable)

    Prompt

    3.9788

    Specify next point or

    41°

    Angle from X Axis (press **Tab** to edit)

    Length — measured from the previous point. It is shown like a dimension, which AutoCAD LT calls a "dynamic dimension."

    Angle — measured from the x axis. It is shown as an arc. As you move the cursor, the length and angle values update. Again, you can press **Tab** to switch between editing the length and arc values.

6. The prompt displays a new icon, a downward pointing arrow. Press the down arrow on the keyboard.

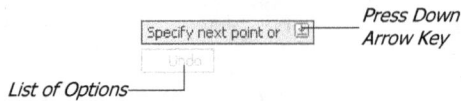

AutoCAD LT lists the options for this prompt. In this case, there is only the **Undo** option. You will encounter longer lists of options for other commands and prompts.

To select the option, move the cursor to the option and then click.

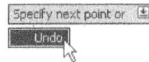

7. Continue drawing lines, and then press **Esc** to exit the command.

> **TIP** To change the colors of the dynamic input tooltips, use the **Option** command's Drafting tab. Click the **Settings** button under **Drafting Tooltip Appearance**. There you can change the color, size, and transparency of tooltips.

UCS Icon

UcsIcon
View | Display | UCS Icon | On

The UCS icon is located in the lower-left corner of the drawing area. *UCS* is short for "user-defined coordinate system." It is meant primarily to help you draw in 3D, even though AutoCAD LT is not meant for creating 3D models. Some drafters find the UCS icon useful in locating the origin and indicating the rotation of the x,y-plane.

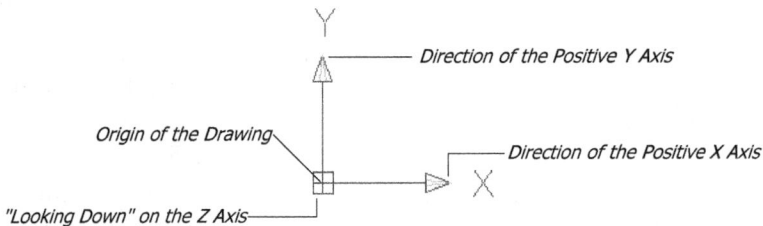

The X and Y arrows point in the direction of the positive x and y axes. Their intersection is usually (but not always) located at the origin of the drawing, where x=0 and y=0. The square around the origin means you are "looking down" the z axis straight onto the x,y-plane.

Because AutoCAD LT is not meant for 3D drawing, and the UCS icon gets in the way of 2D drafting, I recommend turning it off. From the **View** menu, select **Display | UCS Icon | On**. The vertical bars (|) separate menu picks.

> **TIP** You can change the look of the UCS icon with the **UcsIcon** command's **Properties** option. AutoCAD LT displays the UCS Icon dialog box.

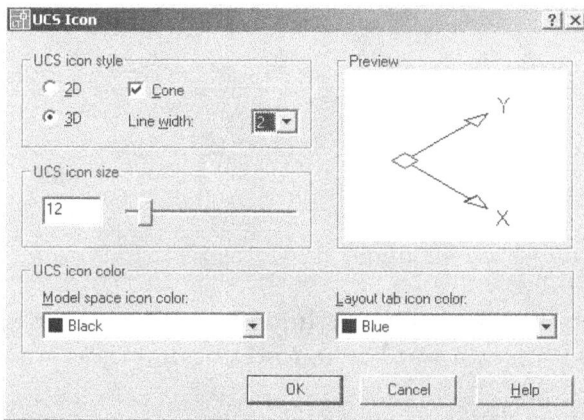

Online Help

Help | Help

Autodesk provides a myriad of methods for accessing help when using AutoCAD LT — perhaps *too* many.

To peruse specific subjects, select **Help** from the **Help** menu, and then select one of the tabs, such as **Contents** or **Search**.

Context-Sensitive Help

At any time while using commands, you can call up help on using AutoCAD LT by pressing **F1**. The help system is context-sensitive, meaning that the helpful information displayed is related to the current command.

Here's an example using the **Line** command:

1. Type the **Line** command, then press the **F1** function key. Pressing F1 invokes context-sensitive help, as follows:

Command: **line**
Specify first point: *(Press F1.)* '_help *(The Help window is displayed.)*

AutoCAD LT displays helpful information about using the Line command.

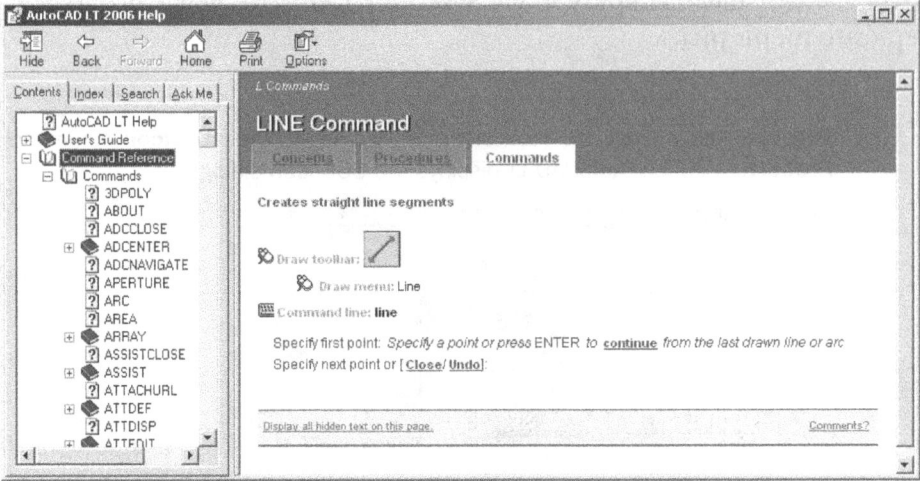

Whenever you see underlined text, click it to display the definition of a word or to find out more about an option.

2. You can continue using the Line command.

Resuming LINE command
From point:

Info Palette Window

Help | Info Palette

The Info Palette window appears when AutoCAD LT starts or when you enter the **Assist** command. It continually displays a couple of paragraphs of help for the command currently in effect. (This window was called "Active Assistance" in earlier releases of AutoCAD LT.)

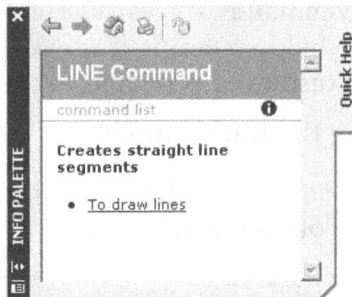

Electronic Documentation

You may not have noticed, but during the installation of AutoCAD, there is an option to access electronic documentation. (On the AutoCAD LT CD, double-click the **setup.exe** file, and then select **Documentation**.)

The documents are in PDF format, and so your computer must have Adobe Acrobat installed before you can read them. Titles include:

- *Stand-alone Installation Guide*
- *Stand-alone Licencing Guide*
- *Getting Started*
- *Network Administrator's Guide*

Exiting AutoCAD LT

File | Exit

To exit AutoCAD LT, use the **Quit** command. When AutoCAD LT asks if you want to save the drawing, click **No**.

Alternatively, press **Alt+F4** or **Ctrl+Q**, or select **Exit** from the **File** menu.

Notes

Navigating the AutoCAD LT Interface

In This Chapter
- Working with toolbars
- Finding out about right-click shortcut menus
- Understanding palettes

In this chapter, we continue the tour of AutoCAD LT's user interface, looking at each piece in greater detail. Later chapters describe nuances, such as entering aliases and working with relative coordinates.

At the top of the AutoCAD LT window are several lines of information. From top to bottom, these are:

Title bar — reports the program name and current drawing file name, as in "AutoCAD LT - [Drawing1.dwg]."

Menu bar — contains the pull-down menus, such as File, Edit, and View.

Toolbars — contain buttons labeled with icons (miniature pictures) and sometimes flyouts and list boxes.

Let's examine each of these to understand their function. The following figure "explodes" the elements to illustrate them more clearly.

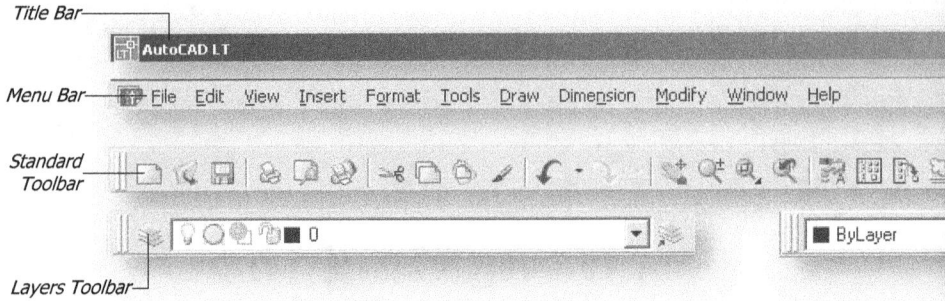

Title Bar — AutoCAD LT

Menu Bar — File   Edit   View   Insert   Format   Tools   Draw   Dimension   Modify   Window   Help

Standard Toolbar

Layers Toolbar — ☐ 0   ■ ByLayer

Title Bar

The title bar displays the name of the AutoCAD LT program and the drawing you are working with. It also contains a rarely used menu and three buttons that control the size and position of the window.

The title bar performs other important tasks of which some users are unaware:

- To maximize the AutoCAD LT window, double-click the title bar. To restore the window, double-click the title bar a second time.
- To quickly open another drawing, drag its .dwg file name from the Windows Explorer onto AutoCAD LT's title bar. AutoCAD LT opens the drawing in a new window.

  (If you drag the drawing's file name into the current drawing, AutoCAD LT inserts it as a block.)

Menu Bar

The menu bar is described in the previous chapter. Advanced users may be interested in customizing it with the **CUI** command; see Part IV of this book, "Customizing AutoCAD LT."

Toolbars

Below the menu bar are several toolbars. Each consists of a row of buttons and/or list boxes.

Toolbars can stick to any side of the drawing area and float anywhere on the desktop. AutoCAD LT has 23 toolbars, of which you currently see only seven: four along the top and three along the edges.

AutoCAD LT
Window Controls

Drawing Window
Controls

Styles Toolbar

ByLayer ByLayer ByColor

Object Properties Toolbar

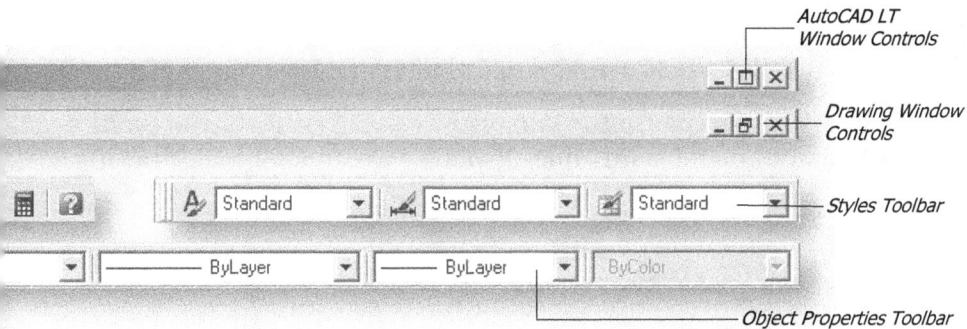

To see the complete list of toolbar names, right-click any toolbar: AutoCAD LT displays a shortcut menu that lists the names of the toolbars. Those names prefixed with a check mark are displayed. Toggle the display of toolbars by selecting their names.

AutoCAD LT lets you change the look of the icons displayed by all toolbars, the function of the icons, and even the shape of the toolbar. These operations are described in Part IV of this book.

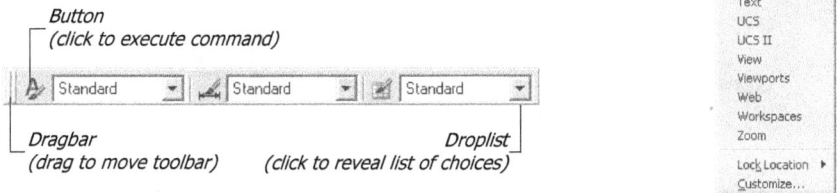

Dimension
✓ Draw
✓ Draw Order
Group
Inquiry
Insert
✓ Layers
Layouts
✓ Modify
Modify II
Object Snap
✓ Properties
Reference
✓ Standard
✓ Styles
Text
UCS
UCS II
View
Viewports
Web
Workspaces
Zoom

Lock Location ▶
Customize...

Button
(click to execute command)

Standard Standard Standard

Dragbar
(drag to move toolbar)

Droplist
(click to reveal list of choices)

Toolbar Buttons and Macros

Buttons have small pictures called "icons." *Icons* are pictorial representations of commands. For example, the first icon on the first toolbar shows a blank sheet of paper: this represents the **QNew** command for creating new drawings quickly.

Because icons are pictures, their meaning is not always clear. For this reason, word descriptions are displayed in several places. For instance, pass the cursor over an icon, then wait for a second. A small yellow tag, called a "tooltip," appears.

QNew

At the same time, look at the status line (at the very bottom of the AutoCAD LT window). It displays a one-sentence description of the button's meaning.

For example, when you pause the cursor over the New icon, the tooltip displays "QNew" and the status line displays "Creates a blank drawing file: QNEW."

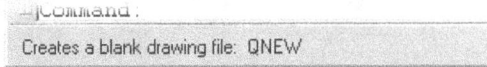

Clicking buttons executes AutoCAD LT commands or short macros. (A *macro* is a series of commands that executes automatically.) Macros are described in detail in Part IV of this book.

The Standard Toolbar

The topmost toolbar has buttons that you are probably familiar with from other Windows applications, plus several unique to AutoCAD LT. This toolbar is called the "Standard" toolbar, because it is standard to most Windows applications. From left to right, the buttons on the Standard toolbar have these meanings (with the related AutoCAD LT command in brackets):

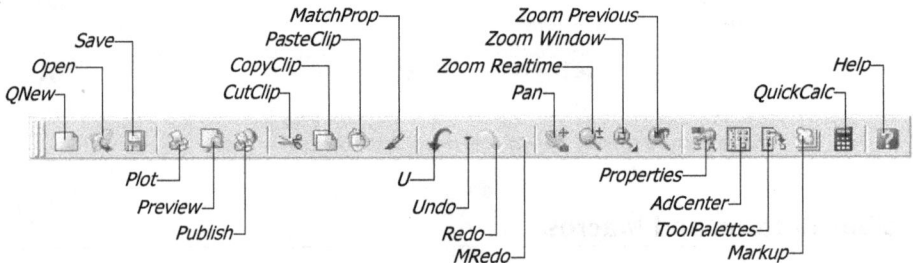

Creates new drawing files (**QNew** command)
Opens existing drawing files (**Open**)
Saves the current drawing (**QSave**)

Prints drawings to printers, plotters, or files (**Plot**)
Shows how drawings will look when they are printed or plotted (**Preview**)
Publishes drawings to DWF files (**Publish**)

Copies objects to the Windows clipboard and removes the objects from the drawing (**CutClip**)
Copies objects to the Windows clipboard (**CopyClip**)
Inserts data from the Windows clipboard (**PasteClip**)

Applies the properties of a selected object to other objects (**MatchProp**)

Undo (**U**)
Multiple Undo (**Undo**)
Redo (**Redo**)
Multiple Redo (**MRedo**)

Moves the view in the current viewport (**Pan**)

Zooms to increase or decrease the apparent size of objects in the current viewport (**Zoom Realtime**)

Zooms to display an area specified by a rectangle window (**Zoom Window**)

Zooms to display the previous view (**Zoom Previous**)

Controls properties of existing objects (**Properties**)

Manages and inserts contents, such as blocks, xrefs, and hatch patterns (**AdCenter**)

Shows or hides the Tool Palettes window (**ToolPalettes**)

Displays the details of markups and allows you to change their status (**Markup**)

Shows or hides the calculator (**QuickCalc**)

Displays online help (**Help**)

Flyouts

Look carefully at the Zoom Window button; notice it contains a tiny triangle in the lower-right corner.

Flyout Symbol

The triangle indicates that the button contains a *flyout*, which is a sub-toolbar containing two or more additional buttons "hidden" underneath.

To see how a flyout works, move the cursor over the Zoom Window button, then hold down the left button. Notice that a column of buttons flies out.

To select a flyout button, move down the cursor and let go of the mouse button. Notice that the button you select now appears on the toolbar.

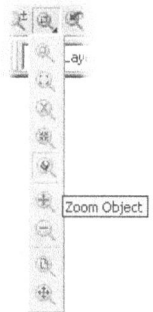

Layer and Object Properties Toolbars

The most important toolbars in AutoCAD LT are the Layers and Object Properties toolbars. They have several droplists that provide immediate feedback on the objects you are working with. *Droplists* display lists of options, such as colors and plot styles.

Layers Toolbar

From left to right, the toolbar's buttons and droplist have these meanings:

Layer Property Manager — displays the dialog box for creating and managing layers.

Layer droplist — displays the name and status of the current layer. When an object is selected, its layer name is displayed. Selecting a name from the layer list causes AutoCAD LT to set that layer name as the current layer.

Make Object's Layer Current — sets the *current* (working) layer by selecting an object. That object's layer becomes the current layer (**Ai_Molc** command).

TIP   New drawings, such as this one, have just one layer named "0," which can never be erased or renamed. Each layer name is prefixed by five symbols (from left to right):

Lightbulb — turns layers on and off.
Sun/snowflake — thaws and freezes layers in all viewports.
Sun on page — thaws and freezes layers in the current viewport only.
Padlock — unlocks and locks layers.
Square — specifies the color assigned to objects on layers.

More on layers in later chapters.

Object Properties Toolbar

The Object Properties toolbar reports the properties of the drawing and selected objects:

- When no objects are selected, the toolbar reports the default settings for the drawing.
- When one object is selected, the toolbar reports the properties of the object.

- When two or more objects are selected, the toolbar's droplists go blank for those properties that differ between objects.

The toolbar can be used to change the properties of objects. Select one or more objects, and then from the droplists select the properties to change, such as color or linetype.

Color Control — lists a selection of colors. Although just nine colors are listed here, AutoCAD LT works with as many as 255 colors.

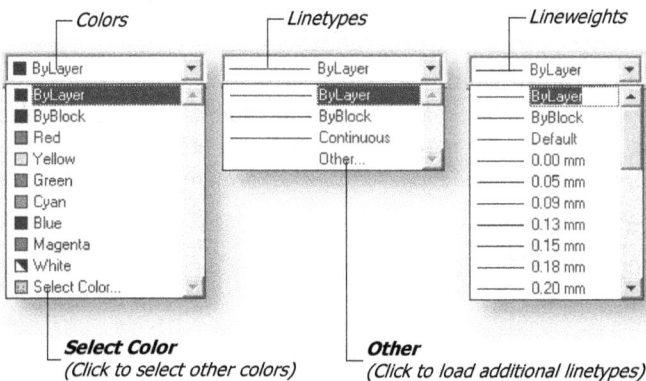

Select Color
(Click to select other colors)

Other
(Click to load additional linetypes)

To select other colors, click **Other** (found at the end of the list), and then pick a color from the Select Color dialog box. The color you picked is added to the list.

TIP It is good CAD drafting practice to assign colors and layers through layers, and not to override them with these droplists. The colors and linetypes named ByLayer and ByBlock have special meaning in AutoCAD LT:

ByLayer — objects take the color and linetype defined by the layer they reside on.
ByBlock — objects take the color and linetype defined by the block to which they belong.

Linetype Control — lists the names and descriptions of line-types in the drawing. New drawings like this one have three linetypes: Continuous, ByLayer, and ByBlock.

To load other linetypes, select **Other**, which displays the Linetype Manager dialog box. Select a linetype to set that pattern as the current linetype.

Linetypes can be customized.

Lineweight Control — lists line widths (weights). Drawings have a fixed set of widths, ranging from 0 to 2.11mm (0.083"). Selecting a lineweight causes AutoCAD LT to set that width as current.

Lineweights cannot be customized.

Plot Style — lists plot styles defined for this drawing. *Plot styles* define how objects in drawings should be plotted.

The plot style droplist is normally gray, meaning you cannot use it. To create new drawings that use named plot styles, follow these steps: From the **Tools** menu, select **Options | Plotting**, then select the **Use Named Plot Styles** option. Plot styles come into effect with the next new drawing you start.

TIPS Toolbars can be dragged around the AutoCAD LT window. If your computer has two monitors, you may want to drag the toolbars to the second monitor, creating a larger drawing area. AutoCAD LT remembers toolbar placement.

Toolbars can sometimes move accidentally. To lock them into place, right-click any toolbar and then select **Lock Location**.

Layout Tabs

Under the drawing area are three tabs, labeled Model, Layout1, and Layout2. You may have seen tabs in other Windows software, such as page tabs in Excel.

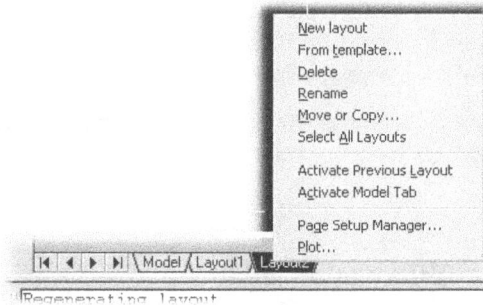

In AutoCAD LT, tabs switch between *layouts*. Layouts allow you to define how drawings will be plotted. You can create and rename layouts, as well as specify different plot settings. Right-click any layout tab for a shortcut menu of choices.

Layouts are discussed in greater detail later in this book.

Scroll Bars

Next to the layout tabs is a scroll bar. When it is dragged back and forth, the drawing view "pans," which is to say it moves from side to side. This is useful when the drawing is zoomed in (enlarged) and you want to see adjacent details.

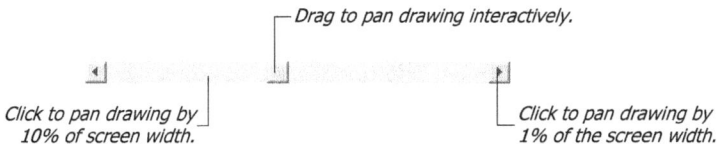

Drag to pan drawing interactively.

Click to pan drawing by 10% of screen width.

Click to pan drawing by 1% of the screen width.

The vertical scroll bar moves the drawing view up and down. Alternatively, you can use the **Pan** command to move the drawing view.

Status Bar

Below the command prompt area is the status line, which reports the status of the drawing:

2D X,Y Coordinates

Tray

Tray Settings

-13.8497, 0.0796   SNAP GRID ORTHO POLAR OSNAP DYN LWT MODEL

Drawing Setting Toggles (right-click for settings)

Resize Window

From left to right, the status line displays:

X,Y Coordinates — 2D coordinates of the cursor's current location in the drawing, as in –13.8497,0.0798. Click the coordinate area to change the display:

- **Absolute** updates the coordinates continuously.
- **Off** updates coordinates only when points are picked.
- **Relative** shows the distance and angle from the last point.

Right-click the coordinates to display a shortcut menu with the same options.

Drawing Settings — reports the status of drawing settings:

- SNAP — snap distance
- GRID — grid display
- ORTHO — orthographic drawing mode
- POLAR — polar snapping
- OSNAP — object snapping
- DYN — dynamic input

- LWT — lineweights
- MODEL — model/paper modes

Each word is an on/off button called a "toggle." When the button looks like it is sticking out, the mode is turned off, as in SNAP in the previous figure. Click the button to turn on the mode; the button appears pressed in, as in the POLAR item.

> **TIP** You can right-click any of the buttons (except MODEL) to display a shortcut menu. Most have the same options: On, Off, and Settings. The Settings option is a shortcut to the dialog box that regulates the modes. For example, to change the settings for lineweight, right-click **LWT** and then select **Settings**; AutoCAD LT displays the Lineweight Settings dialog box.

Help Text

As described earlier, when the cursor is paused on a toolbar button or a menu item, the status bar displays a line of helpful text describing the command.

Tray

The *tray* is located at the right end of the status bar. It reports the status of AutoCAD LT by displaying icons. Expect to see icons appear and disappear, as well as yellow alert balloons with additional information.

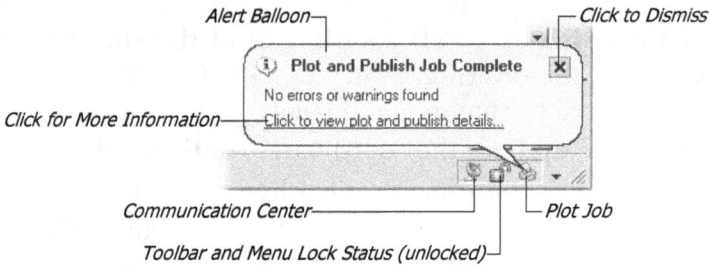

The Communication Center checks with Autodesk's Web site periodically for updates and other information. The padlock icon indicates whether toolbars and menus are locked into place. The printer icon shows that plotting is underway. Other icons indicate whether xref drawings need updating, and so on.

Right-click each icon for a shortcut menu or dialog box specific to its purpose. Click the small black down arrow, and then select **Tray Settings** for options related to the tray.

Text Window

When you need to see more than three lines of the command prompt area, switch to the text screen by pressing function key **F2**. A second AutoCAD LT window appears on the screen, labeled "AutoCAD LT Text Window."

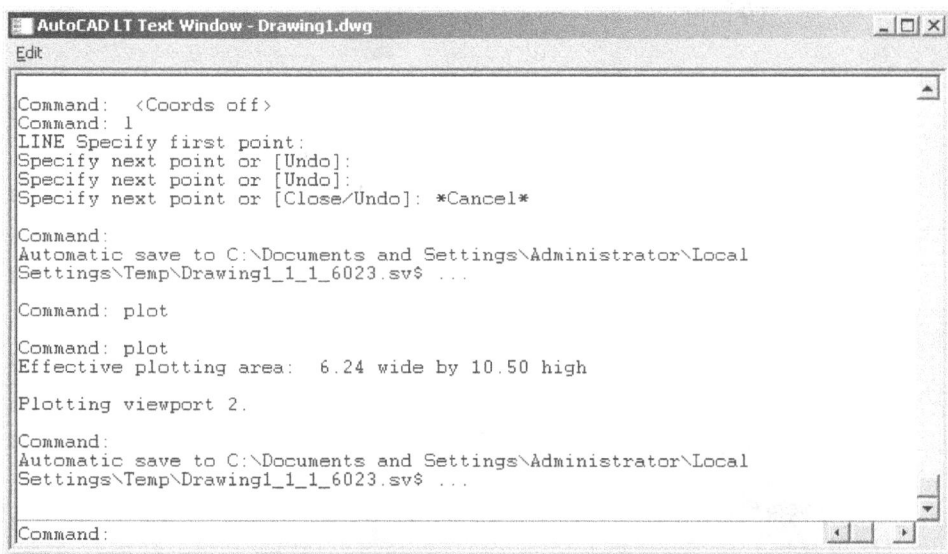

```
AutoCAD LT Text Window - Drawing1.dwg                              _□ ×

Edit

Command:  <Coords off>
Command: 1
LINE Specify first point:
Specify next point or [Undo]:
Specify next point or [Undo]:
Specify next point or [Close/Undo]: *Cancel*

Command:
Automatic save to C:\Documents and Settings\Administrator\Local
Settings\Temp\Drawing1_1_1_6023.sv$ ...

Command: plot

Command: plot
Effective plotting area:   6.24 wide by 10.50 high

Plotting viewport 2.

Command:
Automatic save to C:\Documents and Settings\Administrator\Local
Settings\Temp\Drawing1_1_1_6023.sv$ ...

Command:
```

The text screen displays the most recent 1,500 lines of command text. You scroll back to earlier text by clicking on the vertical scroll bar at the right edge of the window.

Right-click the text window to copy all or part of the text to the Windows clipboard.

Return to the drawing screen by pressing **F2** again.

Palettes

Palettes are a relatively recent user interface innovation to AutoCAD LT. While the concept is not new, their design is unique to Autodesk software products.

The drawback to dialog boxes is that they must be dismissed before you can work with other commands. Palettes are like *modeless* dialog boxes that are always displayed, no matter which command is underway.

Most share a similar arrangement, as illustrated in the following figure.

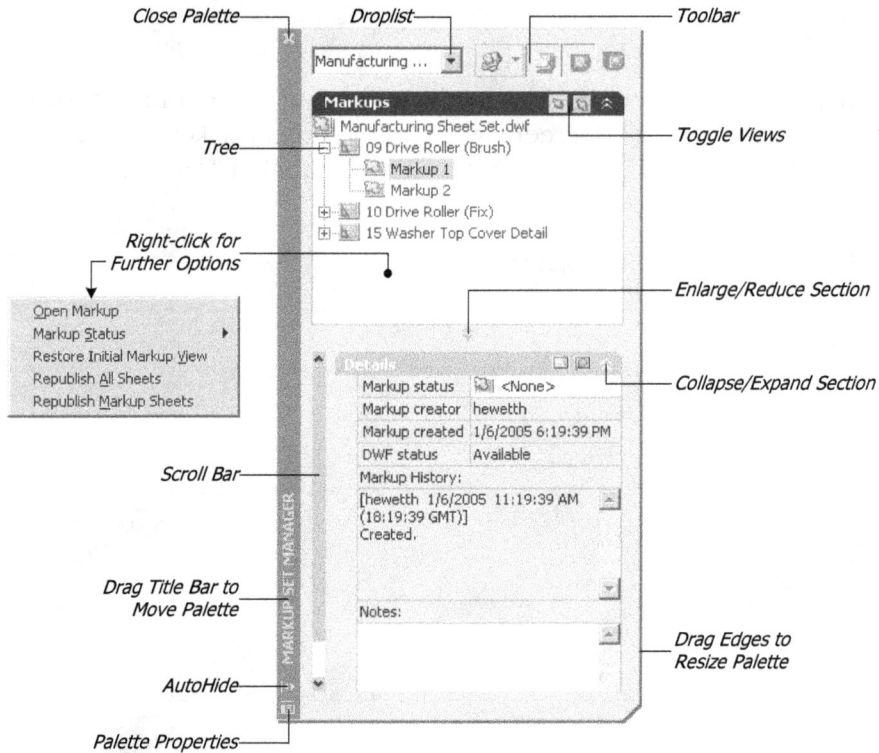

Close Palette —
Droplist —
Toolbar —

Manufacturing ...

Markups

Manufacturing Sheet Set.dwf

Tree —
09 Drive Roller (Brush)
Markup 1
Markup 2
10 Drive Roller (Fix)
15 Washer Top Cover Detail

Toggle Views —

Right-click for
Further Options

Open Markup
Markup Status
Restore Initial Markup View
Republish All Sheets
Republish Markup Sheets

Enlarge/Reduce Section —

Details

Markup status   <None>
Markup creator   hewetth
Markup created   1/6/2005 6:19:39 PM
DWF status   Available
Markup History:

Collapse/Expand Section —

Scroll Bar —

[hewetth 1/6/2005 11:19:39 AM
(18:19:39 GMT)]
Created.

Drag Title Bar to
Move Palette

MARKUP SET MANAGER

Notes:

AutoHide —

Drag Edges to
Resize Palette

Palette Properties —

Summary

In this chapter you learned more about AutoCAD LT's user interface.
With the next chapter, you begin to start working with AutoCAD LT.

Chapter 3

Setting Up
New Drawings

In This Chapter
- Preparing a drawing for first-time use
- Understanding how layers organize the drawing
- Saving the drawing
- The importance of automatic backups

In this chapter, you learn how to prepare the CAD environment for creating new drawings. By the end of the chapter, you will know how to save your work to disk and how to exit AutoCAD LT.

Before You Begin

To learn how to use AutoCAD LT, you will work with a drawing based on a yard plan. The example used for the drafting portion of this book creates and modifies a drawing of the yard around a house.

Before beginning this tutorial, you may want to measure your yard and locate major features, such as the house, driveway, and garden areas.

If you'd rather not measure your yard or you don't have a yard, you can follow along with the following sketch, which is the drawing used in the next several chapters.

Key Terms

File names — computer names for drawings and other documents
Grid — visual guide that consists of an array of dots
Layers — method of organizing drawings by segregating common elements
Limits — specify nominal limits of drawing and constrains the range of grid marks
Snap — constrains cursor movement to discrete distances
Units — units of measurement, such as metric, architectural, and engineering
Zoom — enlarges and reduces the visual size of drawings

Abbreviations

'	Feet
"	Inches
in	Inches
ANSI	American National Standards Institute
DWG	Portion of file names that identify them as AutoCAD drawings
BAK	Backups of AutoCAD drawing files

Commands

Command	Shortcut	Menu Selection
Layer	la	Format | Layer
New	Ctrl+N	File | New
Options	op	Tools | Options
SaveAs	Alt+FA	File | Save As

Preparing for Drawing the Yard

Before creating the drawing of the yard or any other new drawing, you must prepare AutoCAD LT for new drawings by:

- Naming the drawing
- Selecting the units of measurement
- Setting snap and grid spacings
- Specifing the drawing limits
- Naming the layers

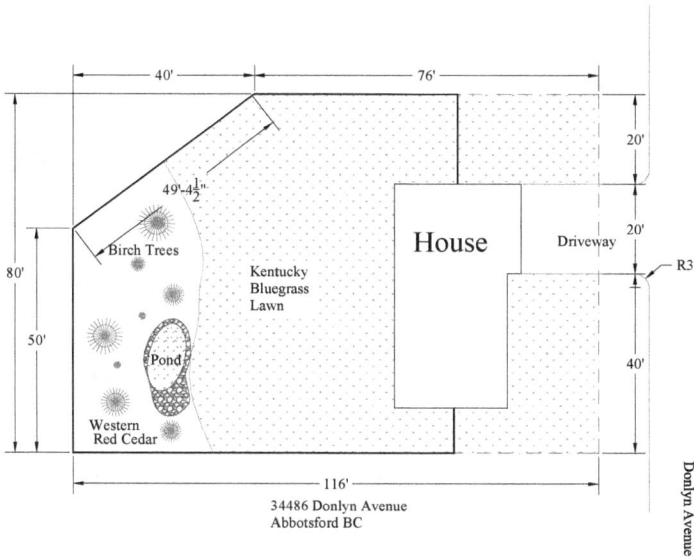

34486 Donlyn Avenue
Abbotsford BC

Starting New Drawings

When you start new drawings in AutoCAD LT, you can start it "from scratch" or you can enlist the services of a software "wizard." (A *wizard* is a series of dialog boxes that take users through the steps needed to set up new drawings, such as units and scale factors.) In this tutorial, we'll work through the wizard.

The difference between the two approaches — from scratch or by wizard — is controlled by the setting of the Startup system variable. (*System variables* hold settings that control many aspects of AutoCAD LT; there are hundreds of system variables, some of which you will encounter from time to time in this book.)

1. If AutoCAD LT is not running, start it now by double-clicking its icon on the Windows desktop.

2. After AutoCAD LT appears on the screen, enter the **Startup** system variable, as follows:

   Command: **startup**

3. The current value of **Startup** is 0, as shown in the angle brackets below. This means that the **New** command starts new drawings from template files ("from scratch"); change the value to **1**, which means that the **New** command will display the Create New Drawing wizard.

   Enter new value for STARTUP <0>: **1**

4. Enter the **New** command. AutoCAD LT displays the Create New Drawing dialog box, because of the setting stored in the **Startup** system variable.

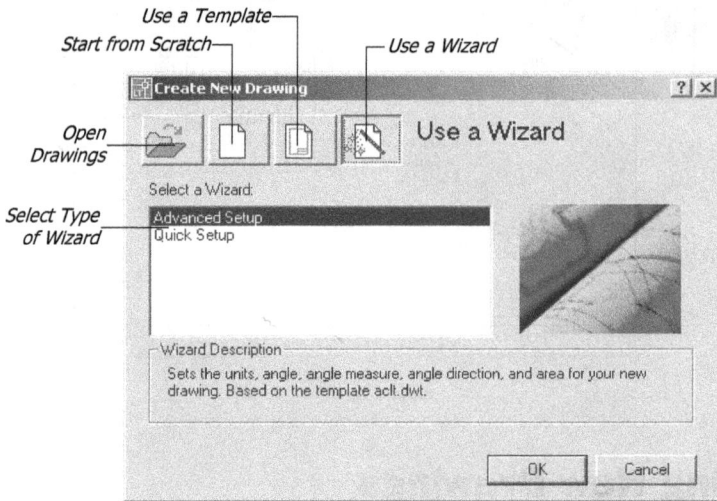

The dialog box has four buttons:

Open Drawings — lists the names of drawings previously opened in AutoCAD LT. If this is the first time you are using LT 2006, the list is empty. When you have opened drawings, their names are stored in this list.

Start from Scratch — starts empty new drawings based on either imperial or metric units.

Use a Template — starts new drawings based on templates.

Use a Wizard — creates new drawings based on settings selected from a series of dialog boxes.

TIP The only reason to set **Startup** to **1** is to access the wizard. The Start from Scratch and Use a Template options are available when **Startup** is set to **0**, which causes the **New** command to display the Select Template dialog box.

• To start with a template, select one from the dialog box.
• To start from scratch, click the arrow button next to **Open** to reveal the no-template choices, as illustrated below.

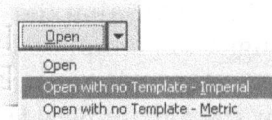

5. Select the **Use a Wizar**d button.

6. Under Select a Wizard, notice the two choices: Quick Setup and Advanced Setup.

    Select **Advanced Setup**, and then click **OK**. Notice that AutoCAD LT displays the Advanced Setup wizard. The dialog box has five stages: Units, Angle, Angle Measure, Angle Direction, and Area.

Units

AutoCAD LT displays measurement units in a variety of styles, including fractional and decimal inches, decimal units (used for metric drawings), and exponential (used to express very large numbers).

After selecting a measurement style, AutoCAD LT displays all measurements in that style. But don't worry: you may, at any time during the drawing, switch the measurement style with the **Units** command.

7. When you measured your yard, you probably measured the distances in feet and inches. For this reason, you should click the circle (called a "radio button") next to **Architectural**.

    (If you measured your yard in meters and centimeters, click the radio button next to **Decimal**.)

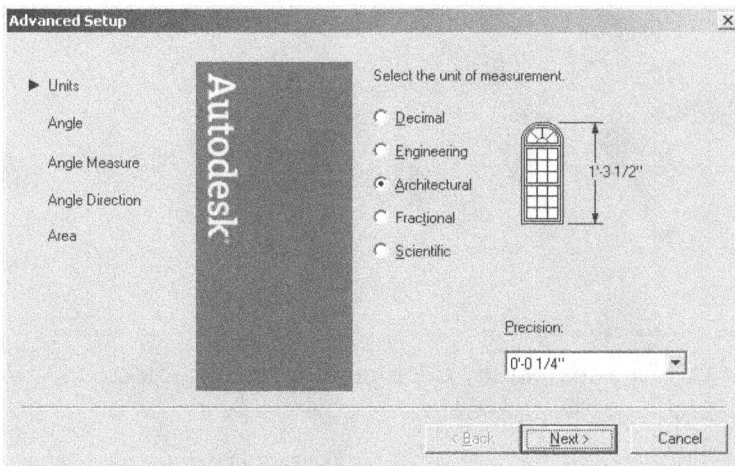

8. Measurements made to the nearest 1/4-inch are accurate enough for this project.

Under **Precision**, click the down arrow and then select **0'-0 1/4"**. (If necessary, click on the vertical scroll bar until 0'-0 1/4" is visible.)

You are free to enter distances more accurate than 1/4-inch; AutoCAD LT remembers distances to full accuracy. When AutoCAD LT displays coordinates, however, they are rounded to the nearest 1/4".

9. Click **Next**, and AutoCAD LT displays the settings for angles.

Angle, Measure, and Direction

The Angle dialog box displays the five formats of angular units that AutoCAD LT can work with: decimal degrees, degrees/minutes/seconds, grads, radians, and surveyor's format. (There are 400 grads and 2*pi radians in a 360-degree circle.)

If we were real land surveyors, we would use Surveyor format, which looks like N 45d23'10.9 W), but since we're not, we'll stick with the more familiar decimal degrees.

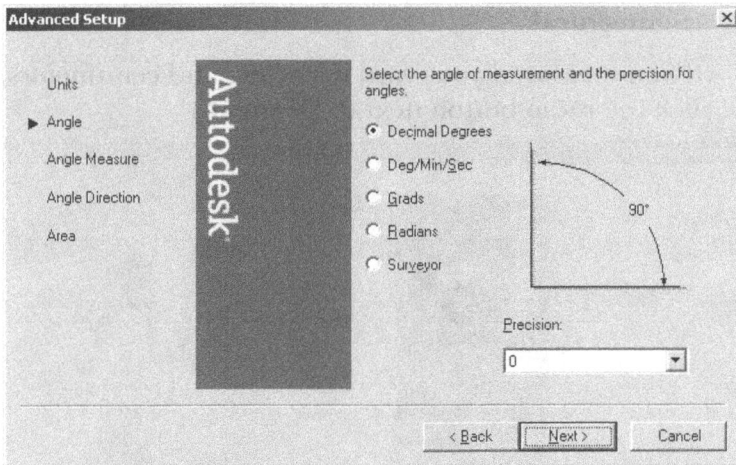

10. Ensure the default, **Decimal Degrees**, is selected for the angle of measurement.

11. The default **Precision** of 0 degrees is adequate for our project.

12. Click **Next**, and AutoCAD LT displays the Angle Measure dialog box.

Angle Measure

By default, AutoCAD LT measures 0 degrees starting in the direction to the east (the positive x-direction).

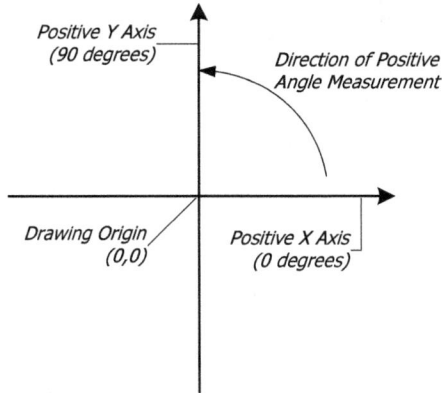

Positive Y Axis
(90 degrees)

Direction of Positive
Angle Measurement

Drawing Origin
(0,0)

Positive X Axis
(0 degrees)

13. Accept the default setting by clicking **Next**.

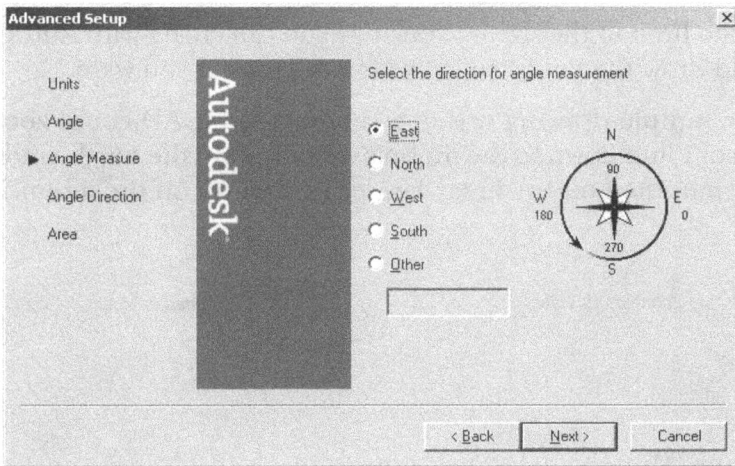

Notice that AutoCAD LT displays the Angle Direction dialog box.

Angle Direction

By default, positive angles are measured counterclockwise in AutoCAD LT. Ignore the misleading image in the following dialog box, which seems to show that angles are measured from 210 degrees.

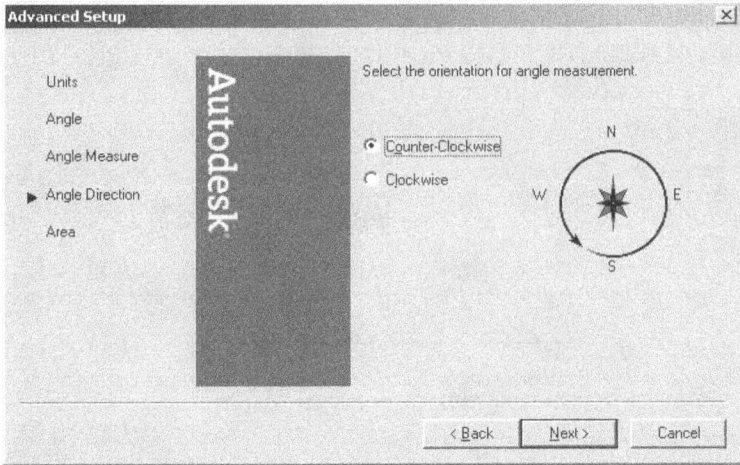

14. Accept the default setting by clicking **Next**. Notice that AutoCAD LT displays the Area dialog box.

Area

There is no limit to the size of drawings you can create with AutoCAD LT. You could draw the entire solar system full size, if you want.

(An early sample drawing was exactly that: AutoCAD could zoom from the orbit of Pluto down to the moon's orbit around the Earth, and then to a plaque mounted on the lunar lander in a crater on the moon.)

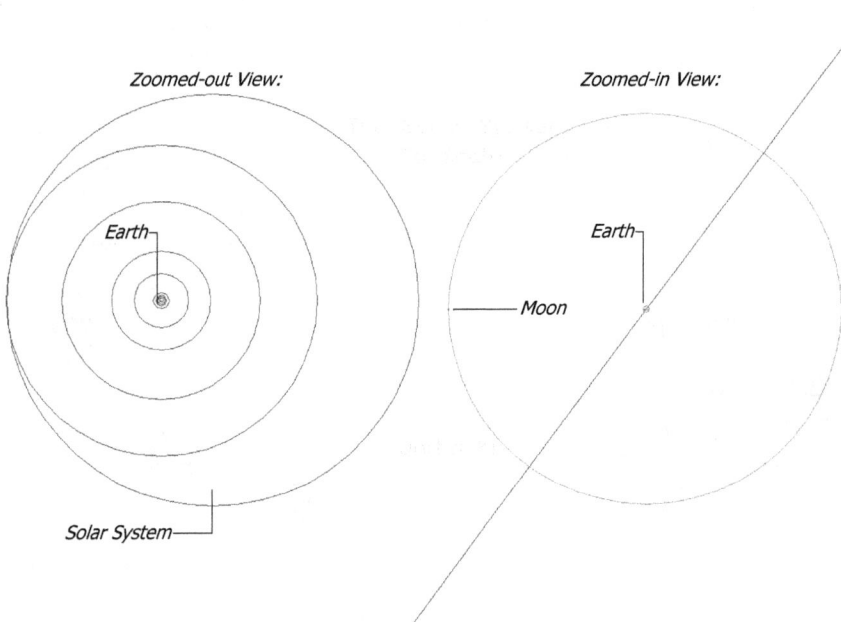

When it comes time to printing drawings, however, your drawing is constrained by the size of paper the printer can handle, often just 8-$\frac{1}{2}$" x 11" — a far sight smaller than the entire solar system, or even your yard.

The Area dialog box sets *limits*, which are useful for showing the nominal area of drawings. (Limits perform two other functions: constraining the limits of the grid marks and the **Zoom** command's **All** option. More on these later.)

15. Examine the size of the yard in the sketch. Leaving a bit of "breathing room" around the plan, the drawing will need about 130 feet of width and 100 feet of height.

    In the **Width** text box, enter **130'**.

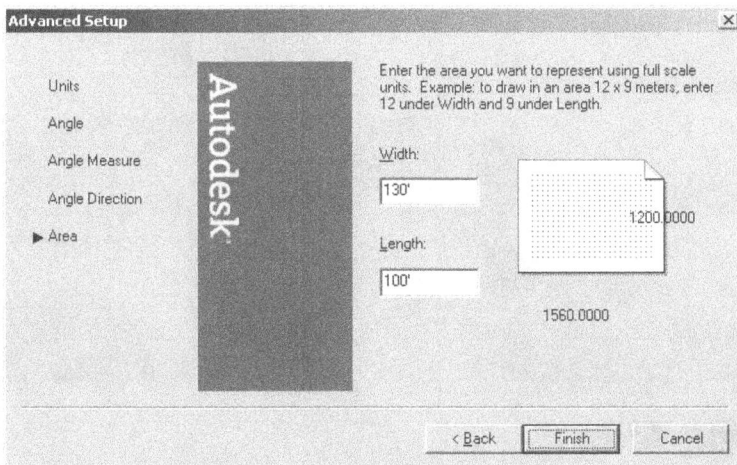

16. In the **Length** text box, enter **100'**.

    Notice that the preview of the paper updates itself to show the drawing as 1200 x 1560 inches.

WARNING It is important to type the apostrophe ('), because that tells AutoCAD LT you are entering the measurement in *feet*. If you leave out the apostrophe, AutoCAD LT assumes you typed 130 *inches*, which it translates into 10'-10".

TIP When entering text and numbers in a dialog box, pressing the **Tab** key is a quicker way to get to the next field. *Fields* are buttons, text entry boxes, list boxes, and other dialog box elements that you can change. To return to previous fields, press **Shift+Tab** (hold down the **Shift** key, and then press **Tab**).

17. Click **Finish**.

The Advanced Setup wizard is complete, and AutoCAD LT displays a
drawing that appears blank to you.

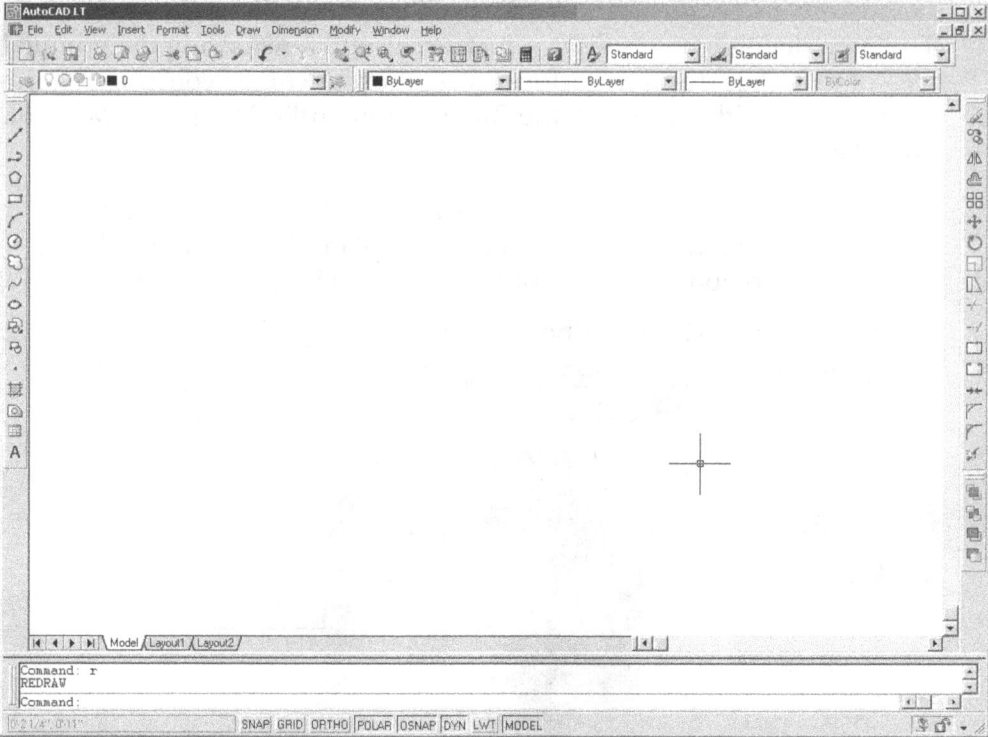

Drawing Aids

Tools | Drafting Settings

One great advantage to drawing with CAD is that it permits you to create
very accurate drawings. AutoCAD LT has several features that help you
draw with perfect accuracy.

One such feature is called "snap mode." AutoCAD LT's snap can be
thought of as setting the drawing resolution.

Another is called "grid," which helps you visualize distances. You learn
about other accuracy aids in later chapters of this book.

Setting the Snap and Grid

Follow these steps to set the snap and grid spacing:

1. From the **Tools** menu, select **Drafting Settings**.
   AutoCAD LT displays the Drafting Settings dialog box.
   If the Snap and Grid options are not visible, click on the
   namesake tab.

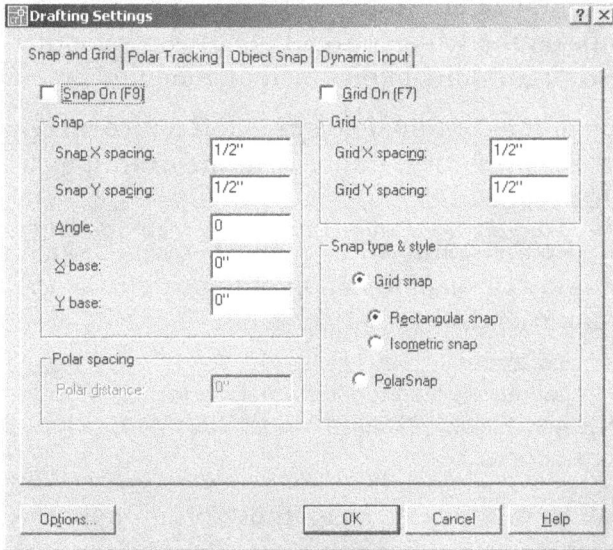

2. To draw everything to an accuracy of one inch, click the
   white square (called a "check box") next to **Snap On
   (F9)**. (The F9 is a reminder that you can turn the snap
   on and off by pressing function key F9.)

3. Change the snap distance of **Snap X spacing** and **Snap
   Y spacing** to 1".

   Leave other snap settings at their default values (Angle
   = 0; X and Y base = 0).

4. As a visual guide, turn on the grid (an array of dots) by
   clicking the **Grid On (F7)** check box. (Again, the F7 is a
   reminder that the grid can be turned on and off at any
   time by pressing F7.)

5. The grid is meant to guide you; the default spacing of
   1/2" would get in the way because it is closely spaced. (In
   fact, AutoCAD LT will not display the grid when it is too
   closely spaced.) Change the spacing to 10 feet by changing the value of **Grid X spacing** to **10'**.

TIP   A grid distance of 0" has a special meaning in AutoCAD LT. It means that the
grid spacing matches the snap spacing, 1" in our case.

6. Press **Tab**, and AutoCAD LT automatically sets the grid's y-spacing to 10'.

7. Click **OK**. The dialog box disappears.

8. Move your mouse around and note how the cursor jumps on the screen instead of moving smoothly. The cursor is jumping in one-inch increments.

   Look at the coordinate display and notice it is changing by the nearest inch, rather than the nearest quarter-inch, as set earlier.

9. Now use the **Zoom All** command to see the grid, which gives you a visual indication of the extents of the draw-ing limits, as follows:

   Command: **zoom**
   Specify corner of window, enter a scale factor (nX or nXP), or
   [All/Center/Dynamic/Extents/Previous/Scale/Window] <real time>: **a**
   Regenerating drawing.

   Don't be intimidated by all those prompt options; for the most part, we use just a couple throughout this book.

TIP For many options in AutoCAD LT's commands, you need only type the first letter of the option. Above, you typed "a" as the abbreviation for the "All" option. When two options begin with the same letter, you need to type the first two char-acters of the option.

When you began, AutoCAD LT displayed an area of one foot by nine inches; now AutoCAD displays an area of 130 feet by 100 feet. Thus, the **Zoom** command lets you see the "big picture," as well as zooming in for a detailed look.

Create Layers

Format | Layers

If you have worked with overlay drafting, then you are familiar with the concept of *layers*. In overlay drafting, you draw the base plan on one clear sheet of Mylar (plastic drawing media), the electrical on another sheet, and the structural on a third. Since the Mylar is transparent, you can overlay the three drawings to create a single blueprint.

Layers in CAD operate in a similar manner. You draw parts of the drawing on different layers. Then, you can turn layers off and on to display the drawing in different ways. For example, the electrical contractor would be interested in seeing only the base plan layer with the electrical layer.

While it is possible to create hundreds and thousands of layers in drawings, it is more common to work with a few dozen layers; in this book, we work with a mere half-dozen layers to segregate items like the text, the yard, the road, and so on.

A further advantage to CAD layers is that global properties can be applied to objects. For example, all objects on a layer called grass could be colored green (or maybe brown, depending on the time of year). Changing the color of the layer instantly changes the color of all objects assigned to that layer.

Naming Layers

Layers are specified by name. AutoCAD LT lets you give layers names up to 255 characters long. One way to start setting up new layers is to click the **Layer Properties Manager** button on the toolbar.

1. Click the **Layer Properties Manager** button (the one that looks like three stacked sheets of paper on the left end of the toolbar). AutoCAD LT displays the Layer Properties Manager dialog box; be patient, it may take several seconds to appear. This dialog box lets you control almost every aspect of AutoCAD LT's layers.

Layer Properties Manager

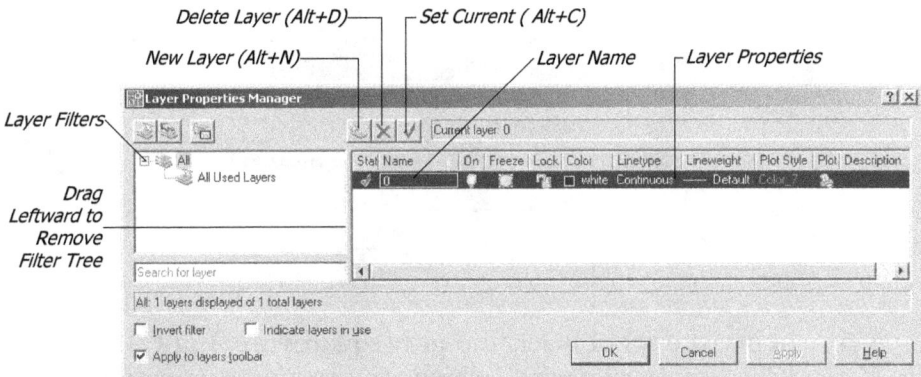

(For now, we'll ignore the Layer Filters section of the dialog box. You can remove it from the dialog box by dragging the separator bar to the left.)

Notice that the drawing already has one layer: 0. Every new AutoCAD LT drawing has one layer, called "0", which you can never remove. Layer 0 has special properties that affect the creation of blocks, as discussed in greater detail later in this book.

2. Create a layer by clicking the **New Layer** button. Notice that AutoCAD LT creates a new layer called "Layer1."

3. Change the name by clicking **Layer1**, and then typing in **Lot**.

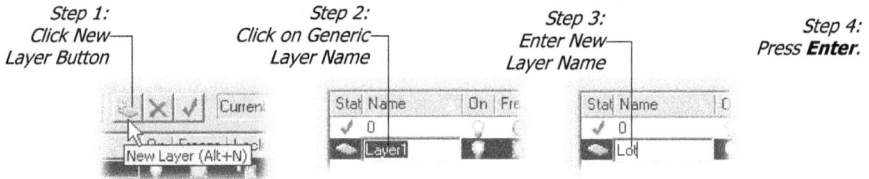

Step 1: Click New Layer Button

Step 2: Click on Generic Layer Name

Step 3: Enter New Layer Name

Step 4: Press **Enter**.

4. Assigning a color to each layer makes it easier to determine which lines belong to which layers. Change the color of the Lot layer to blue, as follows:

   Click the black square under the **Color** column across from the layer name Lot. The Select Color dialog box appears, displaying 255 colors. Which one to choose?

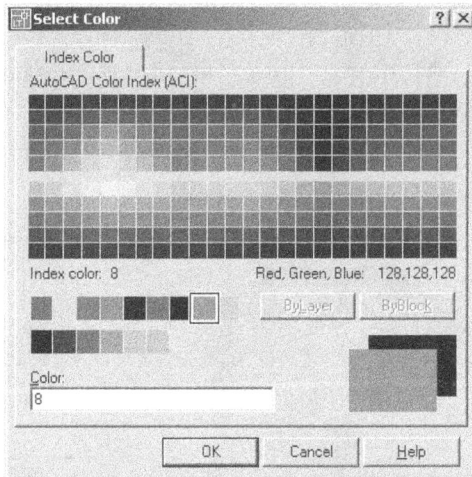

5. Above the set of black and gray squares are AutoCAD LT's "standard colors," which are the most-commonly used ones. Select the dark gray square. The number "8" appears in the **Color** text box, because this is color number 8.

6. Click **OK** to exit the Select Color dialog box. The color of the square across from layer Lot changes to gray.

7. Add the remaining layer names and colors, using the following table as a guide:

Layer Name	Layer Color
House	White (black)
Road	Red (color 1)
Lawn	Cyan (light blue)
Plants	Green
Pond	Blue

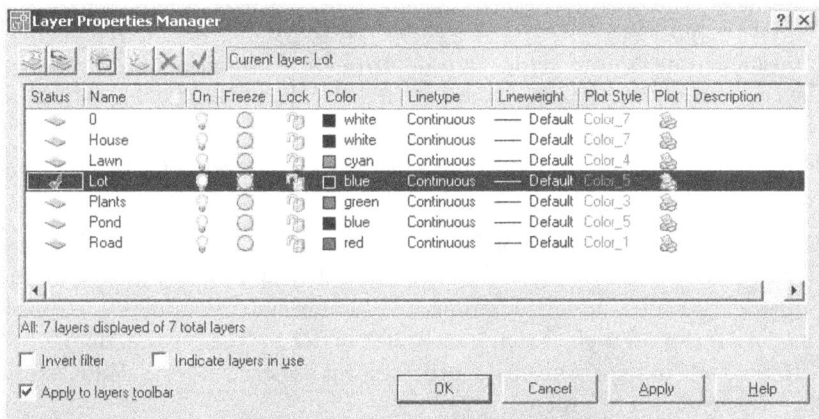

If you make a spelling mistake, just click the layer name and type the correction.

TIPS There can be some confusion over the color "white" — or is it black? AutoCAD LT switches white and black depending on the background color of the drawing area. When the background is black, AutoCAD LT displays white lines; when white, AutoCAD LT displays black lines. So, white can be black — at least in the world of AutoCAD LT.

To set the background color in AutoCAD LT, from the **Tools** menu, select **Options**. In the Options dialog box, click the **Display** tab, and then click the **Colors** button. Select the window element (such as **Background**), and then select the color.

8. When you finish assigning colors to layer names, pick the Lot layer name, then click **Current**. From now on, the drawing takes place on the Lot layer — until you select another name as the current layer.

About Layers in AutoCAD LT

AutoCAD LT provides great control over layers. Every layer has the following properties, as displayed by the header bar in the Layer Properties Manager dialog box:

Status	Name	On	Freeze	Lock	Color	Linetype	Lineweight	Plot Style	Plot	Description
✓	0				■ white	Continuous	—— Default	Color_7		
	Lot				■ blue	Continuous	—— Default	Color_5		

Status — used by AutoCAD LT to report the status of layers: current, in use, empty, or a filter.

Name — names can be up to 255 characters long. You can use numbers, letters, and some punctuation: dollar sign ($), hyphen (-), underline (_), and spaces. Two layers cannot have the same name in the same drawing. There is no limit to the number of layers in drawings.

On — when layers are on, the object can be seen and edited; when off, you cannot see objects nor will they be plotted.

Freeze — when layers are not frozen, objects can be seen and edited; when frozen, they cannot be seen, edited, or plotted, and they are not included when AutoCAD LT performs drawing regenerations and hidden-line operations. (To *thaw* layers means to turn off their frozen status.) It is better to freeze layers than turn them off; the "off" state is a historical artifact from the early days of AutoCAD LT, before freeze was invented.

Lock — when layers are locked, you can see objects but not edit them. (To *unlock* layers means to make the objects available for editing.)

Color — specifies the color for objects placed on the layer. The default color is 7, which is displayed as white or black, depending on the background color. Objects drawn on the layer are displayed in this color, but the object color can be overridden with the **Color** command.

Linetype — specifies the linetypes for objects placed on the layer. The default is Continuous (solid lines). Before other linetypes can be used, their definitions must be loaded into the drawing.

Lineweight — specifies the line widths for objects on the layer. The default is 0.00mm; the maximum is 2.11mm (about 0.08", or 6 points wide).

Plot Style — objects drawn on the layer are plotted with the named plot style, which defines colors, widths, and percentages of black during plotting. This option is not available for drawings created with color-dependent plot styles.

Plot — plots layers; when off, does not plot layers.

Description — allows you to add explanatory text to each layer. Right-click the layer, and then select **Change Description** from the shortcut menu.

Layout Mode Properties

When drawings are in layout mode (paper space), this dialog box displays two more columns:

Active VP Freeze — independently freezes or thaws layers for every viewport displayed in the layout. (VP is short for "viewport.")
New VP Freeze — freezes or thaws new viewports created in paper space.

Controlling Layer Display

To provide control over drawings with many layers, the Layer Properties Manager dialog box lets you sort layers and display selected groups of layers.

To sort layers alphabetically, click headers such as Name, On, and Freeze. Click the headers a second time to sort in reverse order (Z to A).

Erasing Layers

To erase one or more layers from the drawing, select them and then press the **Del** key. As an alternative, you can use the **Purge** command to remove all empty layers from the drawing. (Empty layers are those that have no layers assigned to them.)

Note that you can only erase layers that are empty, not current, not part of externally referenced drawings, and not layer 0. If you try, AutoCAD LT displays a warning dialog box.

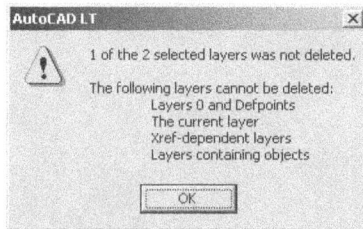

9. To exit the Layer Properties Manager dialog box, click **OK** at the bottom of the dialog box.

   Notice that the name of the layer on the Object Properties toolbar changes from 0 to Lot. The color has changed from black to blue.

Saving Drawings

File | Save

Finally, save this important work you have done with the **Save** command.

1. Click on the icon that looks like a diskette (tooltip = Save).

2. Because this drawing has the generic name "Drawing1.Dwg," AutoCAD LT displays the Save Drawing As dialog box. By default, AutoCAD LT stores drawings in the My Documents folder.

1. Select a Folder and Drive

2. Enter File Name   *3. Click Save*

Type the name **Yard** in the **File name** text entry box.

3. Click the **Save** button, and AutoCAD LT saves the drawing with the name **yard.dwg**. From now on, you and AutoCAD LT refer to this drawing as "Yard."

About the SaveAs Command

The Save As dialog box lets you save drawings in several dialects of AutoCAD. Newer versions of AutoCAD (such as LT 2006) can always read drawings created by older versions of AutoCAD (such as LT 98).

Some versions of AutoCAD LT can read a newer version of drawing file. AutoCAD LT 2006, 2005, and 2004 read each other's .dwg files without translation. In most cases, however, older versions of AutoCAD LT cannot read drawing files created by newer versions. For example, AutoCAD LT 2002 cannot read a drawing file created by AutoCAD LT 2006. For this reason, you must explicitly save the drawing in an earlier format for the earlier software to read the drawing:

AutoCAD LT 2004 Drawing (*.dwg) — saves the drawing in the DWG format read by AutoCAD LT 98, LT 97, and AutoCAD Release 14.

AutoCAD LT 2000 Drawing (*.dwg): — saves the drawing in the DWG format read by AutoCAD LT 2000, 2000i, and 20002. *Warning!* AutoCAD erases and alters some objects when it translates a drawing to earlier formats of DWG.

Drawing Template File (*.dwt) — saves drawings in .dwt template format.

DXF — the drawing interchange format read by many CAD and other programs. AutoCAD LT imports DXF files with the undocumented **DxfIn** command. AutoCAD LT has the capability to translate the drawing in one other file format.

Use the **File | Export** command to save the drawing in WMF (Windows metafile) format, used by the Windows operating system as its default vector format. AutoCAD LT imports WMF files with the **WmfIn** command.

Automatic Backups

Tools | Options

For speed, AutoCAD LT keeps drawings in the computer's memory (RAM). The drawback is that when Windows crashes or when the power is cut to the computer, you lose your work. Because Windows crashes are common, it is an excellent idea to save drawings every 10 or 15 minutes.

AutoCAD LT lets you set a time to save the drawing automatically without needing to use the **Save** command. The default setting is 10 minutes, which is good enough.

If you want to ensure that automatic backups are enabled, here's how to do it:

1. From the **Tools** menu, select **Options**. AutoCAD LT displays the Options dialog box.

2.   Select the **Open and Save** tab.

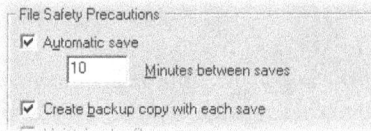

File Safety Precautions

☑ Automatic save

   10   Minutes between saves

☑ Create backup copy with each save
---

3.   If necessary, click the check box next to **Automatic save**
     to turn it on.

     The **Minutes between saves** box specifies how much time
     elapses before AutoCAD LT saves the drawing. Don't set
     this number too low, or the computer spends so much time
     saving to disk that other work cannot be done.

     If it isn't already, you might want to turn on **Create
     backup copy with each save**. This means that AutoCAD
     LT makes a copy of the drawing file.

4.   Click **OK**. Although AutoCAD LT automatically saves
     drawings, it is still a good idea for you to save your work
     after finishing a significant amount of editing.

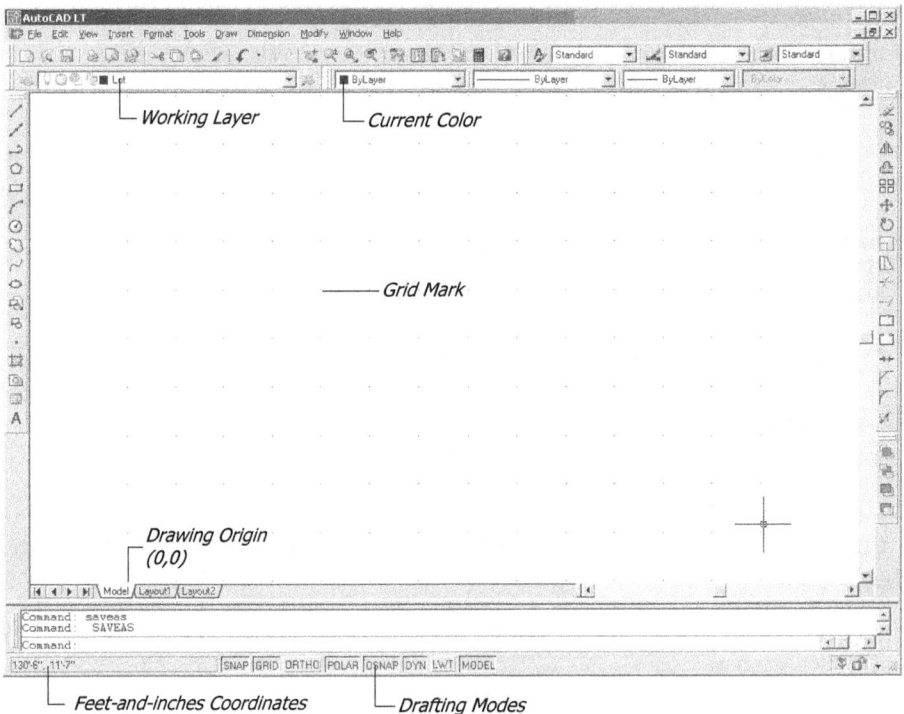

Working Layer — Current Color

Grid Mark

Drawing Origin
(0,0)

Feet-and-inches Coordinates — Drafting Modes

> **TIP** Automatic saves and backups are not made to the original files. During automatic saves, AutoCAD LT saves drawings with the extension of .sv$ and backed up files with .bak.

5. If you need to take a break at this point, use **File | Exit**. AutoCAD LT closes its window and you find yourself back at the Windows desktop.

Summary

Let's review the drawing to this point. Although you haven't drawn anything yet, the drawing file contains a fair amount of information.

On the toolbar, you see the color of the current layer is blue and its name is Lot. On the status line, you see that the coordinates are displaying in feet and inches; and that drafting modes, like snap, grid, and model, are turned on. The figure on the previous page shows you where the origin (0,0) is located.

The automatic backup feature saves your drawing six times an hour.

Notes

Drafting with AutoCAD LT

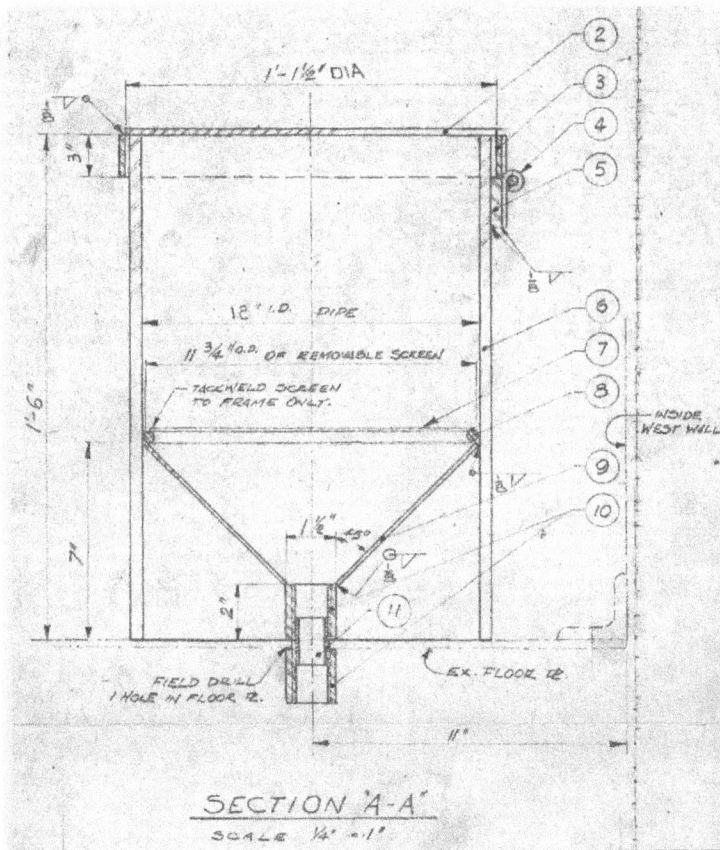

SECTION 'A-A'
SCALE ¼" = 1"

Notes

Chapter 4

Creating Your First Drawing

In This Chapter

- Drawing with lines and polylines
- Understanding absolute and relative distances
- Using polar coordinates
- Modifying objects
- Plotting (printing) drawings

In the last chapter, you learned how to start AutoCAD LT, set up new drawings, and save drawings to the computer's hard drive. In this chapter, you learn how to draw lines accurately, make simple changes to drawings, and produce copies of drawings on your printer.

Bringing Back the Yard Drawing

File | Open

If you exited AutoCAD LT at the end of the last chapter, you need to restart AutoCAD LT, and load the Yard drawing. Here's how:

1. Be sure Windows is running.

   Start AutoCAD LT by selecting **AutoCAD LT** from the Windows Start menu. (Alternatively, double-click the AutoCAD LT icon on the Windows desktop.)

Key Terms

Absolute coordinates — measurements made relative to the drawing origin
Aperture — area at the cursor where AutoCAD LT searches for objects to snap to
Direct distance entry — method of entering points by moving the mouse in a direction, then entering the distance
Extents — invisible rectangle that encompasses all objects in drawings
Fillets — rounded corners
Mirror — mirrored copy of objects, except for text
Object snaps — snap cursor to geometric features, such as ends of lines
Origin — located at 0,0 and usually at the lower-left corner of drawings
Ortho — constrains cursor movement to the vertical and horizontal; short for "orthographic"
Pick cursor — area where AutoCAD LT searches for objects to select
Polar coordinates — measurements specified by distances and angles
Relative coordinates — measurements made relative to the last point

Abbreviations

@   Specifies relative coordinates, such as @2,3
\#   Specifies absolute coordinates, such as #4,5
<   Specifies angles, such as 10<45
-      Hyphen prefix forces AutoCAD LT to use the command-line version of a command, such as **-layer**
[*option*]   Square brackets indicate command options, such as [Undo]
<*value*>   Angle brackets indicate the default (current) value, such as <LOT>
x   X coordinate, along the horizontal axis
y   Y coordinate, along the vertical axis

Commands

Command	Shortcut	Menu Selection
Cancel	Esc	...[1]
Fillet	f	Modify | Fillet
Mirror	mi	Modify | Mirror
Move	m	Modify | Move
Open	op *or* Ctrl+O	File | Open
OSnap	F3 *or* Ctrl+F	Tools | Drafting Settings
PLine	pl	Draw | Polyline
Plot	p *or* Ctrl+P	File | Plot
QSave	Ctrl+S	File | Save
Zoom	z	View | Zoom

[1] ... indicates no menu selection.

2. After AutoCAD LT appears, click the **Open a Drawing** button to display the list of recently opened drawings.

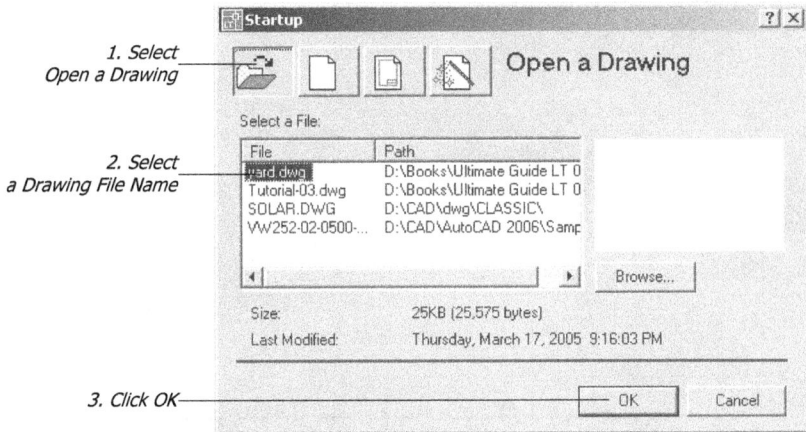

If the Startup dialog box does not appear, select the **File** menu. The names of recently opened drawings are listed at the bottom of the menu, as illustrated below.

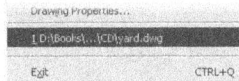

Alternatively, use the **Open** command in the **File** menu.

3. Select **yard.dwg**.

4. Click **OK** to open the drawing.

The drawing should look exactly the same as when you last saw it, that is to say, blank, except for the grid.

Drawing the Lot Boundary

Draw | Line

Let's get some lines on the screen! To orient yourself, the first thing to do is to draw the boundary of the yard. That helps you see the extents of the drawing.

The lines making up the lot boundary are drawn with the **Line** command. You begin drawing the lot lines at the lower-left corner, the origin (0,0), then work counterclockwise around the lot boundary, as shown in the following illustration.

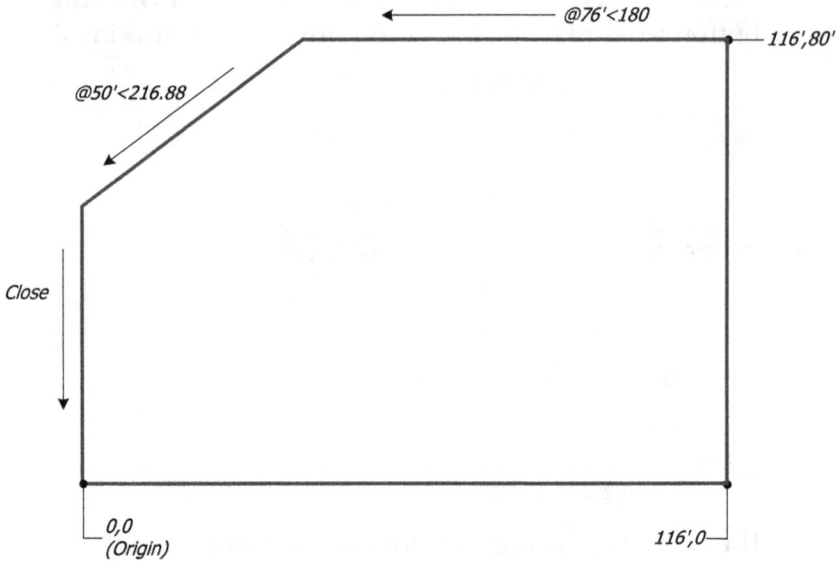

1. From the **Draw** menu, select **Line**. Alternatively, select the **Line** button from the Draw toolbar.

   As confirmation, AutoCAD LT prints "_line" at the command line.

2. Respond to the 'Specify first point:' prompt by typing the coordinates of the origin:

   Command: _line Specify first point: **0,0**

3. To draw the lower 116'-long boundary line, you need to tell AutoCAD that the other end of the line is located at the x,y coordinates of 116',0:

   Specify next point or [Undo]: **116',0**

   Notice the word [Undo] in square brackets. The square brackets indicate that Undo is an *option* of the **Line** command. If you were to type "undo," AutoCAD LT would undraw the last line segment. Later, you will see a second option, named "Close."

4. The next line is 80 feet north. Its endpoint is located at coordinates 116',80':

   Specify next point or [Undo]: **116',80'**

Remember to include the apostrophe (') with each distance. The apostrophe indicates *feet*; if you were to leave it out, AutoCAD LT would interpret the numbers as *inches*, and you would end up with a very small yard!

5. You drew the first two lines with *absolute coordinates*, where you calculated the coordinates based on measurements relative to the origin (at 0',0'). AutoCAD LT can, however, do these calculations for you.

    When you use *relative coordinates*, AutoCAD LT draws a line from the current point relative to the last point.

    AutoCAD LT can also work with *polar coordinates*, which specify distances and angles. Continue drawing the lot boundary using both relative and polar coordinates combined, as follows:

    Specify next point or [Close/Undo]: **@76'<180**

TIPS   When you tell AutoCAD LT to draw a line with the above relative polar coordinates, you enter a special notation that has the following meaning:

Notation	Meaning
@	Use relative coordinates
76'	Distance is 76 feet from the current point
<	Draw the line at an angle...
180	...of 180 degrees

Line are drawn relative to the current point; the angle, however, is measured in absolute degrees using the East-is-0-degrees convention. Using relative polar coordinates makes sense when you have many angled lines to draw.

6. Enter the coordinates for the next endpoint:

    Specify next point or [Close/Undo]: **@50'<216.88**

    With all that punctuation, entering @50'<216.88 can feel like quite a typing chore. I'm getting you to type the coordinates here so that you can better appreciate other methods later.

    In the meantime, if you make a mistake entering the coordinate notation, simply use the **Undo** option (type **U** at the prompt) and re-enter the coordinates.

7. To finish the lot boundary, you use a shortcut. Type **c** (short for "Close") instead of typing the final coordinates (0,0), as follows:

Specify next point or [Close/Undo]: **c**

AutoCAD LT automatically draws a line from the current endpoint to the beginning of the first line.

As mentioned earlier, square brackets surround the options of a command prompt. Here, [Close/Undo] means you have two options: close the polygon or undo the last line segment.

8. To give some space around the drawing, use the **Zoom** command, as follows:

Command: **zoom**
Specify corner of window, enter a scale factor (nX or nXP), or [All/Center/Dynamic/Extents/Previous/Scale/Window/Object] <real time>: **0.9x**

This zooms the drawing 90% smaller.

Instead of drafting on paper, you have created your first digital drawing! More importantly, you have drawn it full size (even if it looks small on your computer screen).

This is one of the most powerful aspects of CAD: everything is drawn full size. There is no need for a scale ruler or to divide distances by a scale factor as in manual drafting.

Planning the Next Steps

The next step is to draw the outline of the house. The lower-right corner of the house is located 10' up and 20' in from the lot corner.

There are several ways in AutoCAD LT to locate one object relative to another, in this case the corner of the house:

- Calculate the coordinates of the house's corner.
- Use the **XLine** command to draw a pair of construction lines, then start drawing from their intersection.
- Use the **From** option to start drawing from an offset from the lot corner.
- Use *tracking* to offset the starting point (described in a later chapter).
- Draw the house in the corner of the lot, then move the house into position.

We'll use the last method in demonstrating two of AutoCAD LT's most powerful commands, **PLine** and **Move**.

Changing Layers

-Layer

Before you draw the house, you need to change the layer to House. Keep in mind that many of AutoCAD LT's commands, including the **Layer** command, can be carried out in more than one way.

In the previous chapter, you used the Layer Properties Manager dialog box to create new layers and to set the Lot layer as the current (or working) layer. Earlier in this chapter, you started the **Line** command via the toolbar or the menu.

This time, try executing commands by typing at the keyboard: type the **-Layer** command at the 'Command:' prompt. The hyphen (-) in front of Layer forces the command to display its prompts in the command area, located at the bottom of the AutoCAD LT window.

```
Command: -layer
Current layer:  "0"
Enter an option [?/Make/Set/New/ON/OFF/Color/Ltype/LWeight/Plot/Freeze/Thaw/LOck/Unlock/stAte]: s
```

1. To set the House layer, enter the **-Layer** command:

    Command: **-layer**
    Current layer: "Lot"

AutoCAD LT reminds you of the name of the current layer.

2. The **-Layer** command has more than a dozen options, most of which you ignore for now, as follows:

Enter an option
[?/Make/Set/New/ON/OFF/Color/Ltype/LWeight/Plot/Freeze/Thaw/LOck/
Unlock/stAte]: **s**

Enter **s** to invoke the **Set** option.

TIP For many of its commands, AutoCAD LT presents lists of options. To select an option, you need only type its first character, such as **S** for the **Set** option.

When two (or more) options begin with the same first letter — such as the **Ltype** and **LWeight** options — you sometimes type the first two or three characters (**LT** and **LW**). Other times, you sometimes type a character in the middle of the option name, such as **A** for the **stAte** option. AutoCAD LT shows you the characters to enter by capitalizing them.

3. AutoCAD LT prompts you to enter the name of the layer. To change the working layer to House, type **house** and then press **Enter**.

Enter layer name to make current <Lot>: **house**

Notice that AutoCAD LT lists the current layer name in angle brackets — <Lot>. This is the default name, which lets you retain the current layer by simply pressing the **Enter** key.

4. The -Layer command repeats its 12-option prompt. Press **Esc** to cancel the command and return to the 'Command:' prompt.

Enter an option
[?/Make/Set/.../LOck/Unlock]:(Press **Esc**.)
Command:

TIP You can cancel commands at any time by pressing **Esc**. Sometimes, however, you may need to press **Esc** two or even three times in commands that have large numbers of suboptions, such as the **PEdit** command.

5. Look at the toolbar to confirm that AutoCAD LT has changed the working layer from layer Lot to layer House.

Drawing the House Outline

Ortho
Draw | Polyline
Object Snap

Earlier in this chapter, you drew the lot boundary with the **Line** command. You created what looks like a *polygon*: one continuous line made of several segments. In fact, each line segment is independent; they only look connected. That can make it difficult to select the entire lot boundary at once.

To remedy this, AutoCAD LT has a special kind of line called the "polyline." As the prefix "poly" suggests, *polylines* are lines made up of many features — lines and arcs, or splines of varying widths — all connected together as a single object, as illustrated below.

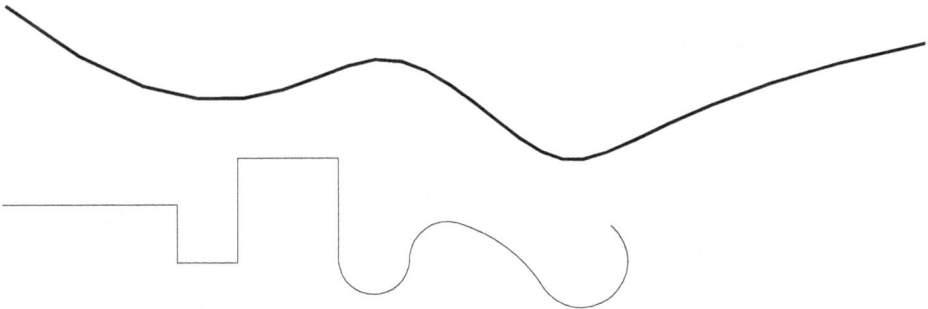

The figure on the following page gives the x,y coordinates for the house outline.

1. Because the lines describing the house are all at right angles, I recommend using *ortho* mode. It constrains cursor movement to the horizontal and vertical directions.

    Turn on ortho mode by clicking the **ORTHO** button on the status bar.

    GRID ORTHO POLAR

    In confirmation, AutoCAD LT reports:

    Command: <Ortho on>

Object Snap Modes

AutoCAD LT has 11 object snaps that look for specific geometric features on objects.

Mode	Object Snap	Snaps to...
cen	CENter	Center of arcs, circles, and polyarcs
end	ENDpoint	Either end of lines, arcs, and other open objects
ins	INSertion	Insertion points of blocks and text
int	INTersection	Intersections of lines, arcs, circles, and other objects
app	APParent	Apparent intersections of two objects
mid	MIDpoint	Middle of lines, arcs, and other open objects
nea	NEArest	Nearest point on the nearest object
nod	NODe	Point objects
per	PERpendicular	Perpendicular to lines, arcs, and other objects
qua	QUAdrant	The 0-, 90-, 180-, and 270-degree points on arcs, circles, and polyarcs
tan	TANgent	Tangents of arcs and circles

These icons indicate the type and location of object snaps:

☐ Endpoint   ⊑ Insertion

△ Midpoint   ⊥ Perpendicular

○ Center   ⊙ Tangent

⊠ Node   ⋉ Nearest

◇ Quadrant   ⊠ Apparent intersection

✕ Intersection

AutoCAD LT uses a collection of on-screen aids, called AutoSnap, to assist with object snapping. The "magnetic" *icon* jumps to the location of the nearest object snap. The *tooltip* reports the type of object snap. The *aperture* shows the area in which AutoCAD LT searches for geometry to snap to.

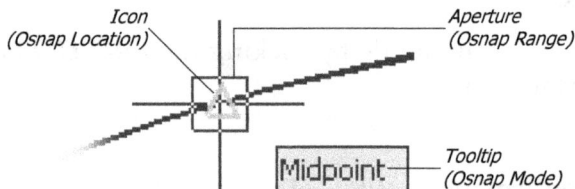

The display of these visual aids can be toggled in the Drafting tab of the Options dialog box.

2. Draw the house outline as a polyline. Select **Draw | Polyline**.

   (When you see two words separated by a vertical line, such as **Draw | Polyline**, it means to select **Draw** from the menu bar, then select **Polyline** from the **Draw** menu.)

   As with the **Line** command, AutoCAD LT prompts you for the point from which to begin drawing the polyline:

   Command: _pline

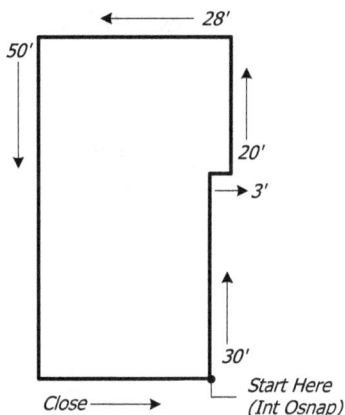

3. Instead of specifying a coordinate, you ask AutoCAD LT to find a geometric feature by using object snap:

   Specify start point: **int**

   When you enter **int** (short for "intersection"), a square appears around the crosshair cursor. The square is called the "aperture," and shows the area in which AutoCAD LT hunts for the object snap geometry.

   AutoCAD LT attempts to snap to the nearest intersection, rather than snapping to the nearest 1" you specified with the snap mode. Because the intersection snap overrides the 1"-snap, this is sometimes referred to as "object snap override."

4. AutoCAD LT then curtly prompts you with "of." It is asking you to position the aperture cursor near the intersection of the two lines.

   of: *(Pick lower-right corner of lot.)*

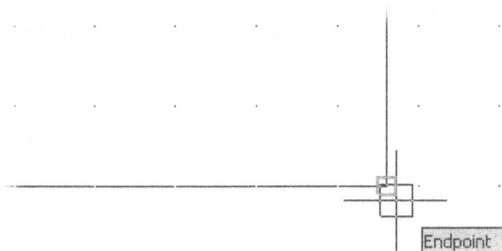

Move the cursor until the aperture is over the lower-right corner of the lot boundary, and then click (press the left mouse button).

5. The **PLine** command's prompt reports that the polyline currently has no width (0'-0").

Current line-width is 0'-0"

That does not mean the line is invisible. Rather, zero width in AutoCAD LT means that the line is drawn as narrow as possible on the screen and by the printer (usually one pixel wide).

The second line of the prompt displays (just) seven of the PLine command's 22 options.

Specify next point or [Arc/Close/Halfwidth/Length/Undo/Width]:

Don't let it intimidate you; for now, you ignore all options except the default, 'Specify next point.' Move the cursor up (or in the positive y direction or North or at 90 degrees). On the keyboard, type 30' and then press **Enter**.

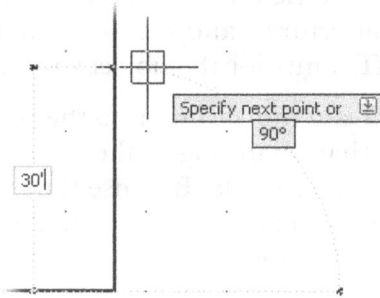

This system of drawing that combines cursor movement with keyboard entry is called "direct distance entry." Moving the cursor is quicker than typing the values for the angles — and more intuitive, too.

6. Draw the remainder of the house outline by moving the cursor in the appropriate direction, and then entering the distances:

Cursor Direction	Distance
East	3'
North	20'
West	28'
South	50'

Options of the PLine Command

The **PLine** command has the following options for drawing polylines:

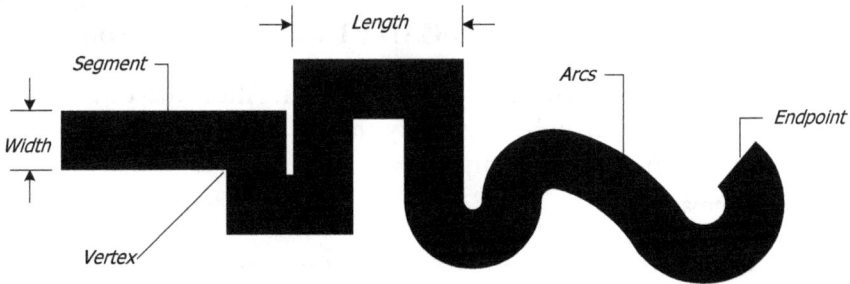

Endpoint of line — specifies the locations of polyline *vertices* (the endpoints of polyline segments)

Arc — draws polyarcs; you can switch between lines and arcs when drawing polylines

Close — joins the last endpoint with the starting point

Halfwidth — specifies the width of polylines by the distance from their centerline to their outside edge

Length — draws a specific distance, in the manner of direct distance entry

Undo — undoes the last polyline drawing operation

Width — specifies the width of polyline segments; allows independent starting and ending widths for creating tapered polylines

Esc — exits the **PLine** command

---

7. Complete the polyline with the **C** option, as you did with the Line command.

When Lot was the working layer, the lines you drew showed up in blue. You changed the layer to House, and AutoCAD LT automatically drew the lines in black instead of blue. Notice that the lines take on the color specified by their layer. (You can, if you need to, change colors on-the-fly with the Color command.)

Moving the House into Position

Modify | Move

Now that you've drawn the outline of the house, you need to move it into position. You move objects in AutoCAD LT with the **Move** command.

1. Select **Move** from the **Modify** toolbar. Alternatively, select **Move** from the **Modify** menu, or enter **Move** at the 'Command:' prompt.

   Command: _move

   AutoCAD LT first asks you *what* you want to move:

   Select objects:

   At the same time, AutoCAD LT changes the crosshair cursor into a small square cursor, called the pick cursor.

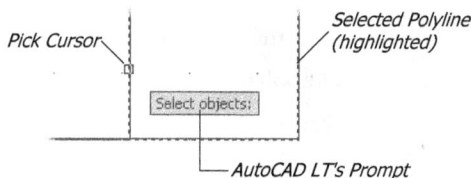

   Pick Cursor — | Selected Polyline (highlighted)

   Select objects:

   —AutoCAD LT's Prompt

2. Move the cursor to any part of the polyline making up the outline of the house, and then press the pick button.

   Select objects: *(Pick house outline.)*

   The entire house outline is highlighted. The highlighting shows as a dotted line, which is how AutoCAD LT lets you know it found the object you picked.

3. AutoCAD LT lets you make several selections, if need be, and so the prompt repeats itself:

   Select objects: *(Press **Enter** to exit object selection.)*

   Because just one polyline is being moved, press **Enter** to end the object selection process.

4. Just as when drawing lines, the **Move** command needs to know a from-point and a to-point. But here the from-point is called the "base point," as follows:

   Specify base point or [Displacement] <Displacement>: **0,0**

5. Now AutoCAD LT wants to know where you want to move the selected objects. The **Move** command calls the to-point the "second point," as follows:

Specify second point or <use first point as displacement>: **-20',10'**

The coordinates (–20',10') tell AutoCAD LT to move the house *left* by 20 feet (x = –20') and *up* by ten feet (y = 10'). AutoCAD LT instantly relocates the house much faster than a house mover. The **Move** command shows you a powerful aspect of CAD: no eraser dust!

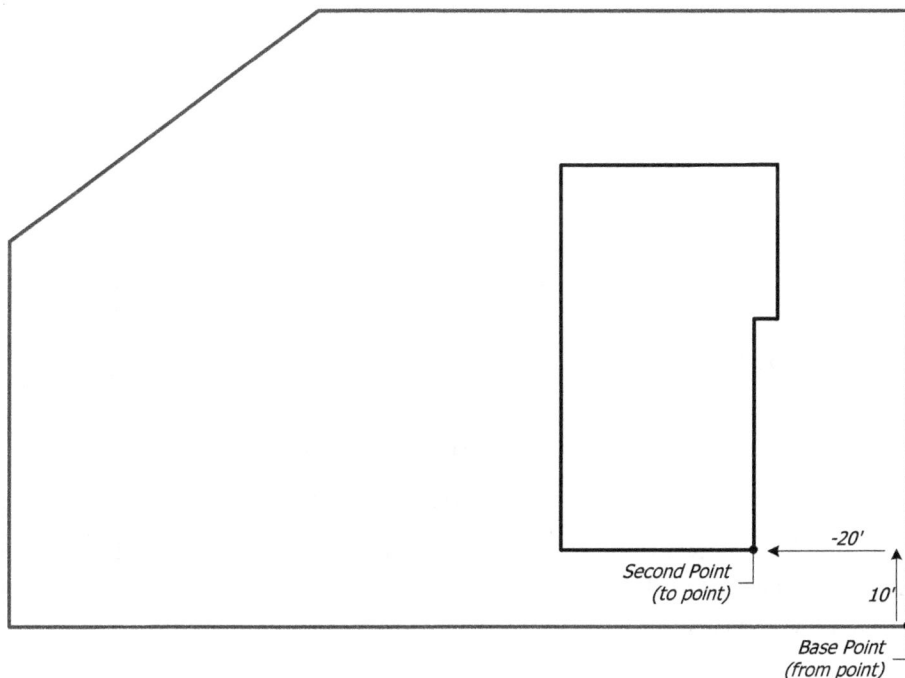

Second Point (to point)

-20'

10'

Base Point (from point)

6. It's a good idea to regularly save your work. Press **Ctrl+S**, and AutoCAD silently saves the drawing to disk. The only indication is that "Command: _qsave" appears on the command line.

Alternatively, you can click the diskette icon on the toolbar, enter the **QSave** command, or select **Save** from the **File** menu.

Starting on the Driveway

The final drafting project in this chapter is the driveway and street. Before drawing them, change the layer to Road, as follows:

1. On the toolbar, click on the House layer name.

2. When the list box appears, select **Road**. AutoCAD LT changes the layer name from House to Road and the working color from black to red.

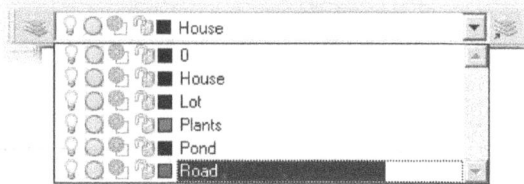

With the layer set correctly, draw the driveway and street outlines. After drawing the upper roadwork, you duplicate it with a single command to create the lower driveway and street outline.

3. Ensure that ortho mode is still on by glancing at the status bar. The **ORTHO** button should look pressed in.

4. Select the **Line** icon from the **Draw** toolbar.

Draw the upper driveway and street line using direct distance entry, as follows:

```
Command: _line
Specify first point: int
of: (Pick upper-right corner of house.)
Specify next point or [Undo]: (Move cursor to the right.) 28'
Specify next point or [Undo]: (Move cursor upward.) 40'
Specify next point or [Close/Undo]: (Press Enter to end the command.)
```

Recall that if you leave out the apostrophe ('), such as entering 40 instead of 40', the line is drawn only 40 inches long. You can "back up" and undraw the incorrect line with the **u** option (short for "Undo"), as follows:

```
Specify next point or [Undo]: @40<0
Specify next point or [Undo]: u
Specify next point or [Undo]: @40'<0
```

From Point: *int*

40'

28'

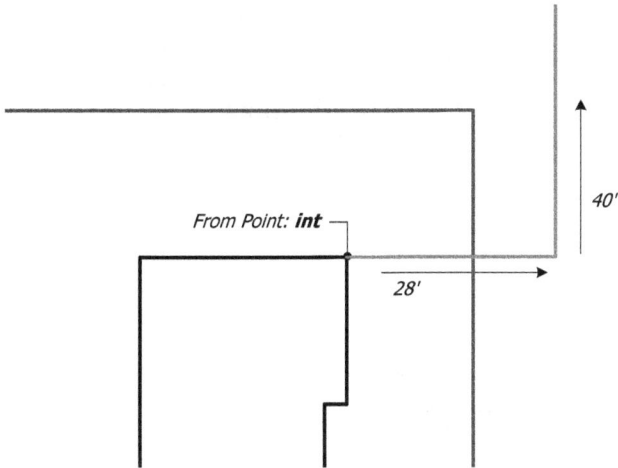

Finishing the Driveway

Modify | Fillet
Modify | Mirror

To add the *curb return* — the arc joining the driveway and street — use AutoCAD LT's **Fillet** command. It draws arcs between intersecting lines. The lines don't have to physically meet; AutoCAD LT takes care of extending (or trimming) the lines so that the arc is drawn between them.

You use the **Fillet** command by specifing the radius of the arc and then applying the fillet.

1. To start the command, select the **Fillet** button on the Modify toolbar. (It's the second to last button. As an alternative, select **Fillet** from the **Modify** menu, or do as I do: just type **fillet** at the 'Command:' prompt.)

2. Select the radius option by typing **R** and then pressing **Enter**:

   Command: _fillet
   Current settings: Mode = TRIM, Radius = 0'-0"
   Select first object or [Undo/Polyline/Radius/Trim/Multiple]: **r**

3. Enter the fillet radius of three feet:

   Specify fillet radius <0'-0">: **3'**

4. With the fillet radius set to three feet, perform the filleting, as follows:

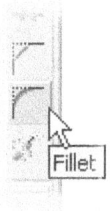

Select first object or [Undo/Polyline/Radius/Trim/Multiple]: *(Pick one line.)*
Select second object or shift-select to apply corner: *(Pick another line.)*

AutoCAD LT automatically shortens the two lines to fit the 3-foot arc between them.

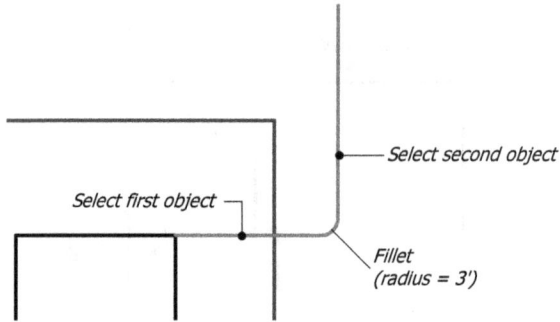

You needed the **Line** command and an application of the **Fillet** command to create part of the driveway and street. One of the most important concepts behind computer-aided anything is that you should never have to draw the same line twice.

To illustrate the power of this concept, use the **Mirror** command to duplicate the lower driveway and street line without having to draw them! The **Mirror** command creates mirrored copies of objects.

5. Select **Modify | Mirror** from the menu. (Or pick the Mirror button on the Modify toolbar.)
   Command: _mirror

6. AutoCAD LT asks you to select the objects you want to mirror. Use the cursor to pick the line and arc segments, as follows:
   Select objects: *(Pick the driveway line.)*
   Select objects: *(Pick the curb return.)*
   Select objects: *(Pick the street line.)*
   Select objects: *(Press **Enter** to end object selection.)*

7. AutoCAD LT needs you to specify the *mirror line*, an imaginary line about which it mirrors the objects you just picked:
   First point of mirror line: **mid**
   of: *(Pick center of garage entrance.)*
   Second point: **per**
   of: *(Pick right-hand lot boundary.)*

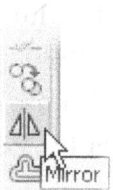

The length of the mirror line is not important, but its angle is crucial. For this reason, you used two new object snap modes: **mid** to find the *mid*point of the garage entrance and **per** to ensure the mirror line is *per*pendicular to the lot boundary, as shown in the following figure.

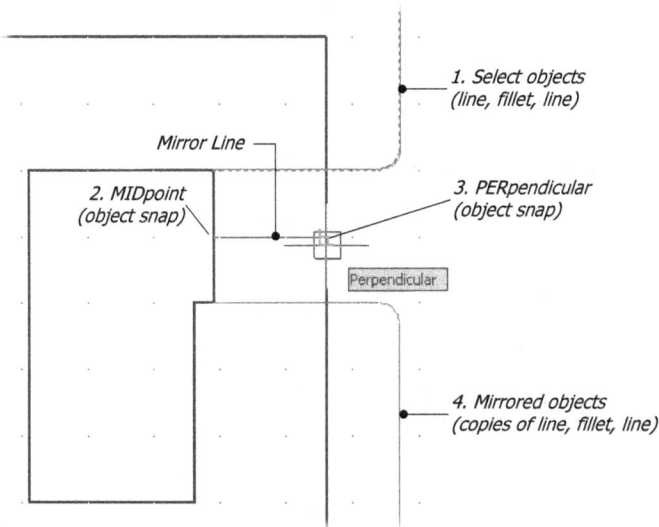

Mirror Line

1. Select objects (line, fillet, line)

2. MIDpoint (object snap)

3. PERpendicular (object snap)

Perpendicular

4. Mirrored objects (copies of line, fillet, line)

8. At this point, AutoCAD LT gives you the option of erasing the old objects — the two lines and arc you picked. In most cases, as in this case, you don't want them erased:

    Delete old objects? <N> **n**

AutoCAD LT draws the lower driveway and street outline as a perfect mirror image of the upper set.

You have now drawn the outline of the lot, house, and driveway. The work you have done is valuable and it is important that you save the drawing to disk. Use the **QSave** command to store the drawing on disk.

Putting Drawings to Paper

File | Plot

While it is efficient (and environmentally aware) to create and store drawings on computers and share them electronically via email or Web sites, you may want to print copies on paper. That lets you mark up the drawing with notes or show off your progress to friends and family!

The **Plot** command sends the drawing to printers, plotters (oversize printers), and files. The following series of dialog boxes assumes you have a printer compatible with Windows attached to your computer.

1. Press **Ctrl+P**, and AutoCAD LT displays the Plot - Model dialog box.

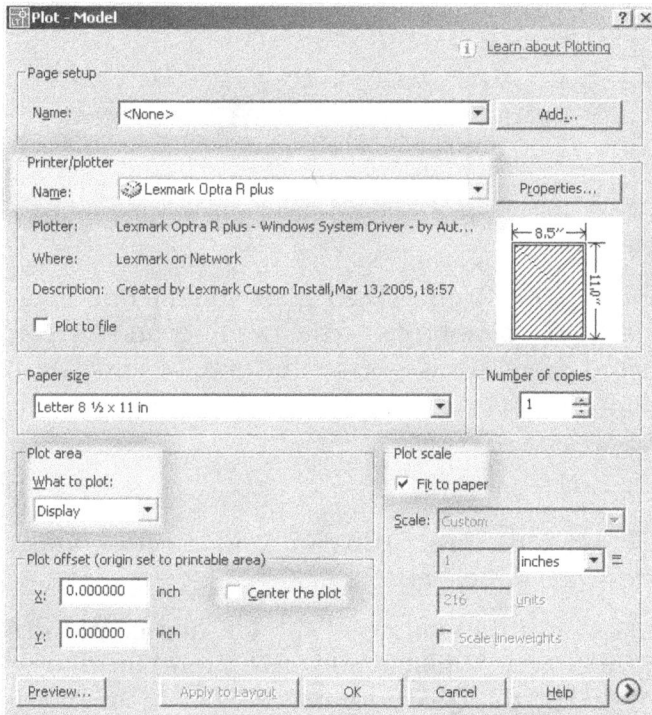

2. The dialog box has a confusing array of options. (Autodesk has attempted to make plotting easier by redesigning this dialog box every couple of releases.) Fortunately, you can ignore most options, except for these:

Printer/plotter — select a printer from the **Name** droplist.

Plot area — select Extents from the **What to plot** droplist. The Extents option ensures everything in your drawing is plotted on the paper.

Plot scale — check that **Fit to Paper** is selected. This ensures the entire drawing will be plotted, and that it won't be too large or too small.

Plot offset — select **Center the plot** to turn on the option. This nicely centers the drawing on the paper.

3. The *orientation* of the paper doesn't match that of the drawing. The paper is tall but the drawing is wide. To change the orientation of the paper, follow these steps:

    Click the **More Options** button.

    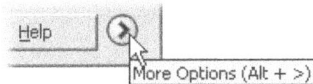

    Notice that the dialog box widens to accommodate even more options!

    In the Drawing Orientation area, select **Landscape**.

    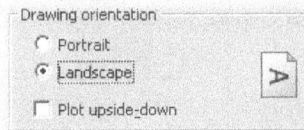

4. To check that the drawing fits the paper, click the **Preview** button. The drawing appears on a simulated sheet of paper. (See figure on next page.)

5. Press **Esc** to exit full preview mode.

6. When the Plot-Model dialog box reappears, click the **OK** button.

    AutoCAD LT calculates the area the drawing takes up on the paper and sends the drawing to the printer:

    Effective plotting area: 6.24 wide by 10.50 high
    Plotting viewport 2.

A dialog box displays the progress of the plot. AutoCAD LT converts its vector drawing to the format required by the printer.

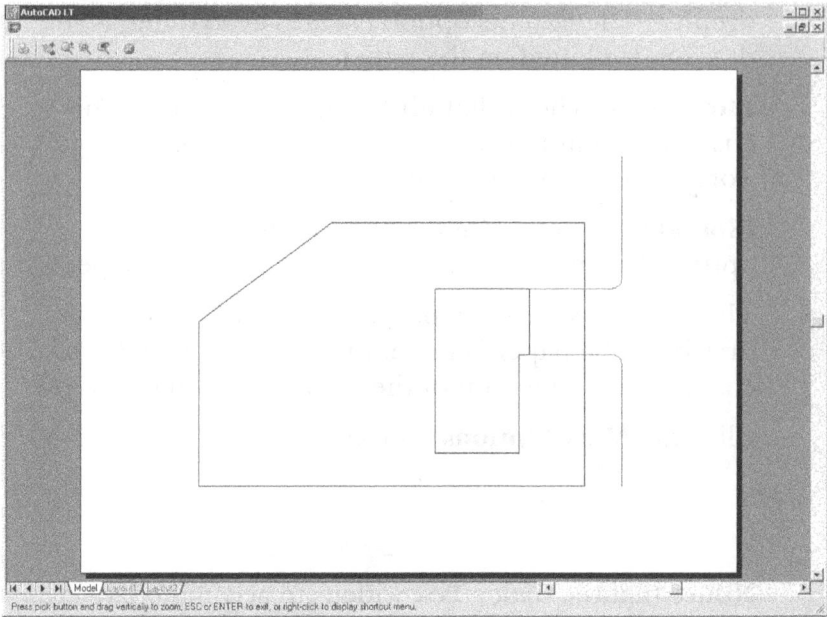

7. When done, AutoCAD LT returns the 'Command:' prompt and displays an information balloon in the tray at the end of the status bar.

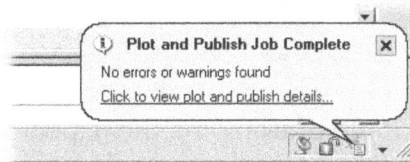

Click the **x** to dismiss the balloon.

Or click the blue underlined text to view the Plot and Publish Details dialog box, which reports on the success (or failure) of plots.

Summary

Congratulations! You've drafted your very first drawing using a computer. You can save the drawing as a memento of your introduction to computer-aided drafting.

Chapter 5

Adding Details to Drawings

In This Chapter
- Drawing circles and ellipses
- Editing with grips
- Applying hatch patterns to areas
- Creating arrays of objects
- Creating parallel offsets of objects
- Creating symbols (blocks)
- Real-time zooming and panning

In the last chapter, you created the outlines of the lot, the house, and the driveway. In this chapter, you add details to the yard, such as the lawn, trees, and a pond. You learn to use some of AutoCAD LT's intermediate commands, such as creating ellipses, offsets, arrays, and blocks.

Dividing the Lot

The yard has a lawn and a garden area. In this section, you draw the boundary between the two areas with a polyline, then smooth it with the **PEdit** (polyline edit) command.

If AutoCAD LT is not running, start it now.

Key Terms

Drag — hold down the mouse button while moving the object
Grips — squares that indicate the editing points of objects
Hatch patterns — repeating patterns that indicate the material of objects
Modal editing — starts editing commands, and then selects objects
Non-modal editing — selects objects, and then applies editing commands
Palettes — windows that provide continuous information about AutoCAD LT

Abbreviations

L	last (object selection)
W	window (object selection and zooming)

Commands

Command	Shortcut	Menu Selection
Array	ar	Modify | Array
BHatch	h	Draw | Hatch
Block	b	Draw | Block | Make
Circle	c	Draw | Circle
DsViewer	ds	View | Aerial View
Ellipse	el	Draw | Ellipse
Insert	i	Insert | Block
Offset	o	Modify | Offset
Pan	p	View | Pan | Realtime
PEdit	pe	Modify | Object | Polyline
Zoom Window	z w	View | Zoom | Window

(If you were unsuccessful in completing the previous chapter, open the tutorial-04.dwg file found on book's resource page on the book's resource page.)

1. Before starting the **PLine** command, take these steps:

   Turn off ortho mode by clicking **ORTHO** on the status bar.

   Change the working layer to Lawn by selecting layer **Lawn** from the Layers toolbar; the color should be cyan (light blue).

2. Select **Polyline** from the **Draw** menu.

    Command: _pline
    Specify first point:

3. Hold down the **Shift** key on the keyboard, press the right mouse button, then let go of the **Shift** key.

    A new menu pops up on the screen. This shortcut menu lists all of AutoCAD LT's object snap modes. Move the cursor down to **Midpoint**. Notice that AutoCAD LT prints a brief description of the Midpoint object snap on the status line: "Snaps the midpoint of an arc or line: mid."

    Click the mouse button on **Midpoint**. AutoCAD LT reports:

    Specify first point: _mid

⌖	Tracking
⌐	From
	Mid Between 2 Points
	Point Filters ▸
⌀	Endpoint
⌀	Midpoint
✕	Intersection
✕	Apparent Intersect
⊙	Center
◈	Quadrant
○	Tangent
⊥	Perpendicular
∘	Node
⊙	Insert
⋏	Nearest
▨	None
∏	Osnap Settings...

4. Move the cursor to any point on the diagonal portion of the lot line, and then pick it.

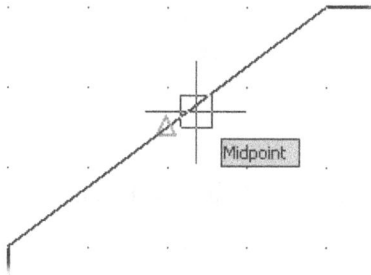

of (Pick diagonal lot line.)

AutoCAD LT snaps the start of the polyline to the precise midpoint of the diagonal lot line.

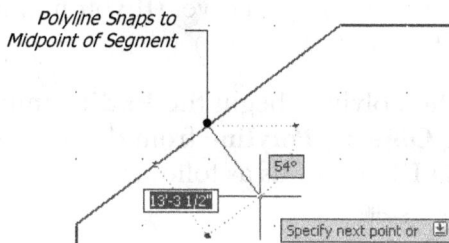

5. Pick a few more points at roughly 10' to 20' intervals, moving your way down toward the bottom yard line.

> **TIP** If you cannot tell how far 10 feet is, keep an eye on the distance displayed by the dynamic dimension tooltip. Alternatively, turn on relative coordinates on the status bar.

6. When you get to the bottom lot line, press **Shift**+right mouse button. From the shortcut menu, select **Nearest**.

7. Pick anywhere the line crosses the cursor's aperture box. Again, AutoCAD LT snaps the polyline precisely to the lot line.

8. Press **Esc** to end the **PLine** command.

Smoothing Polylines

Modify | Object | Polyline

Here is the reason for creating the boundary as a polyline: you now use the **PEdit** command (short for "polyline edit") to smooth the crooked polyline segments into a flowing curve. (If you had used the **Line** command, you couldn't smooth the lines.)

1. To edit the polyline, begin the **PEdit** command by selecting **Object | Polyline** from the **Modify** menu. AutoCAD LT responds as follows:

    Command: _pedit
    Select polyline or [Multiple]:

Options of the PEdit Command

The **PEdit** command performs the following polyline editing functions:

Close — closes an open polyline; a segment is drawn between the starting and ending vertices of the polyline (this prompt is only displayed when an open polyline is selected).

Open — opens a closed polyline; the last segment drawn is erased (this prompt is only displayed when a closed polyline is selected).

Join — joins another polyline, line, or arc connected to this polyline to form a single polyline. This option fails when there is even a slight gap between the objects to be joined.

Width — changes the width of the polyline. This option applies a uniform width to all segments making up the polyline; variable width is not possible.

Edit vertex — edits the width and position of individual vertices; also allows you to insert and remove vertices.

Fit — applies a curve fit to the polyline.

Spline — applies a Bezier spline to the polyline.

Decurve — reverts a curve-fit or splined polyline to its original form.

Ltype gen — toggles linetype generation. When on, the linetype is stretched from the starting point to the ending point of the polyline. When off, the linetype stretches from vertex to vertex.

Undo — undoes the last polyline editing operation.

eXit — exits the command.

---

2. Pick the polyline.

3. The **PEdit** command has many, many options. Its purpose is to change the look of polylines. Use the **Spline** option to smooth the straight lines into a flowing curve, as follows:

   Enter an option [Close/Join/Width/Edit vertex/Fit/Spline/Decurve/Ltype gen/Undo]: **s**

   The straight lines disappear and are replaced by a smooth curve. (Technically, AutoCAD LT redrew the line segments as a *cubic Bezier curve* based on the polyline frame.)

Original Polyline (frame)

Splined Polyline (cubic Bezier curve)

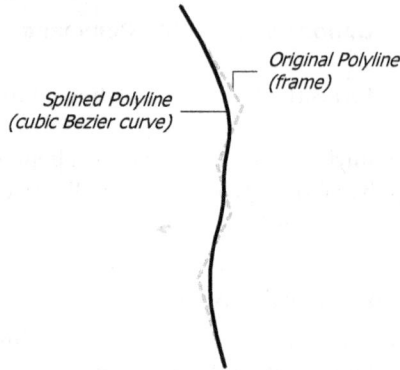

4.   Exit the **PEdit** command by pressing **Esc**.

Grips Editing

Earlier, you began the **PEdit** command, then selected the polyline to edit. This is called "verb-noun editing," or *modal* editing. The *verb* is the command (**PEdit**), followed by the *noun* — the object (the polyline). Modal editing means that you first enter a *mode* (the **PEdit** command mode) before performing the action, such as selecting the polyline and editing it.

AutoCAD LT has the option of first selecting objects and then editing them. This is called "noun-verb editing," or *non-modal* editing. Autodesk gives it yet another name: grips editing.

Grips editing can be a faster way to edit, but not all editing commands lend themselves to it. Here we use grips editing to change the shape of the splined polyline that separates the garden from the lawn.

1.   First though, enlarge the view of the splined polyline. Select the **Zoom Window** icon (looks like a magnifying glass with a square in the center) from the toolbar. AutoCAD LT launches the Zoom command with the Window option:

```
Command: '_zoom
Specify corner of window, enter a scale factor (nX or nXP), or
[All/Center/Dynamic/Extents/Previous/Scale/Window/Object] <real time>:_w
Specify first corner: (Pick a point.)
```

Editing with Grips

Grips editing is interactive: select an object, select a grip, and manipulate it.

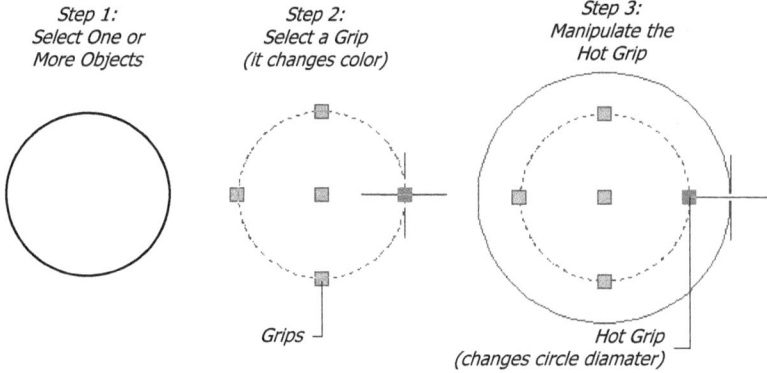

Step 1: Select One or More Objects	Step 2: Select a Grip (it changes color)	Step 3: Manipulate the Hot Grip

Grips ⌐

Hot Grip ⌐
(changes circle diamater)

Most grips look the same, so you cannot determine their function until you start to drag them. The exception are triangular grips on arcs.

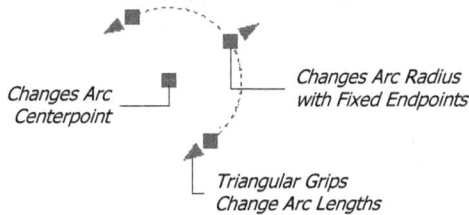

Changes Arc Centerpoint

Changes Arc Radius with Fixed Endpoints

Triangular Grips Change Arc Lengths

AutoCAD LT employs six editing commands during grips editing: Stretch, Move, Rotate, Scale, and Mirror, as well as Copy. These commands operate identically to their non-grips equivalent. To see the commands, press the Spacebar repeatedly. Each time you do, AutoCAD LT displays a different set of prompts:

```
** STRETCH **
<Stretch to point>/Base point/Copy/Undo/eXit:
** MOVE **
<Move to point>/Base point/Copy/Undo/eXit:
** ROTATE **
<Rotation angle>/Base point/Copy/Undo/Reference/eXit:
** SCALE **
<Scale factor>/Base point/Copy/Undo/Reference/eXit:
*** MIRROR ***
<Second point>/Base point/Copy/Undo/eXit:
```

After ** MIRROR **, AutoCAD LT repeats the cycle. Other non-modal editing options are:
- **Base point** — specifies a base point other than the hot grip.
- **Reference** — specifies a reference point other than the hot grip.
- **Undo** — undoes the last editing operation.
- **eXit** — exits non-modal editing mode (or press **Esc**).

2. The Window option lets you pick a rectangular area on the screen to magnify. When you pick points for the first and other corners, you specify the two opposite corners of the rectangle, as shown in the following figure.

    Specify opposite corner: *(Pick another point.)*

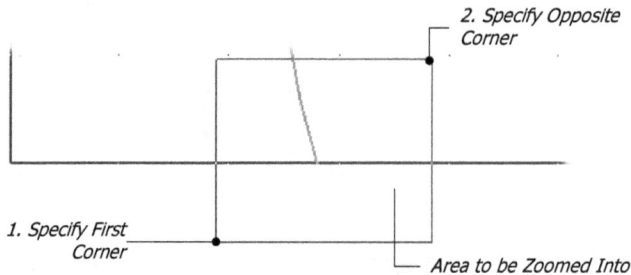

    2. Specify Opposite Corner

    1. Specify First Corner

    Area to be Zoomed Into

TIP If floating toolbars obscure the polyline, use the scroll bar to move the polyline into view. Grab the horizontal scroll bar and drag it until you clearly see the polyline.

3. In an earlier chapter, I pointed out the small square at the center of the crosshair cursor. It is called the "pickbox." When AutoCAD LT displays the pickbox, you can pick objects without first starting editing commands.

    Pick the polyline. The polyline changes from solid to dashed. Notice the small blue squares that appear on the polyline, including at its ends. The blue squares are called "grips," because they let you grip objects.

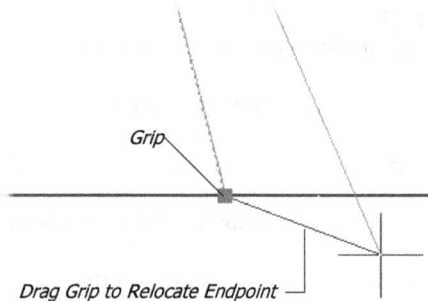

    Grip

    Drag Grip to Relocate Endpoint

4. Pick the blue square at the bottom end of the polyline. It turns solid red. The red square is called a "hot grip," because editing commands affect it (not the "cold" blue grips). In addition to the solitary red square, a new prompt appears in the command area:

** STRETCH **
<Stretch to point>/Base point/Copy/Undo/eXit: **nea**
to *(Pick lot line.)*

5.   Enter the NEAr object snap mode, and then move the cursor. As you do, the last segment of the polyline curves and arcs to follow you. (The NEAr object snap ensures the polyline ends precisely at the lot line.)

6.   Click along the lot line where you want the end of the polyline to move to.

7.   Now go ahead and interactively reshape the rest of the polyline, segment by segment. The blue grips indicate the vertices of the straight polyline segments you originally drew, before splining it with **PEdit**.

8.   When you are finished reshaping the polyline, press **Esc** twice to exit modeless editing.

9.   Select the **View | Zoom | Previous** command from the menu bar to see the entire drawing again.

Hatching the Lawn

Draw | Hatch

You created the boundary between the lawn and garden, but how do you show the difference between grassy areas and the areas of earth? One way is to add symbols that indicate grass. In AutoCAD LT, this is done with the **Hatch** command.

1.   First, switch back to the Lawn layer via the toolbar.

2.   Select **Draw | Hatch** to start the **Hatch** command. Notice the Hatch dialog box:

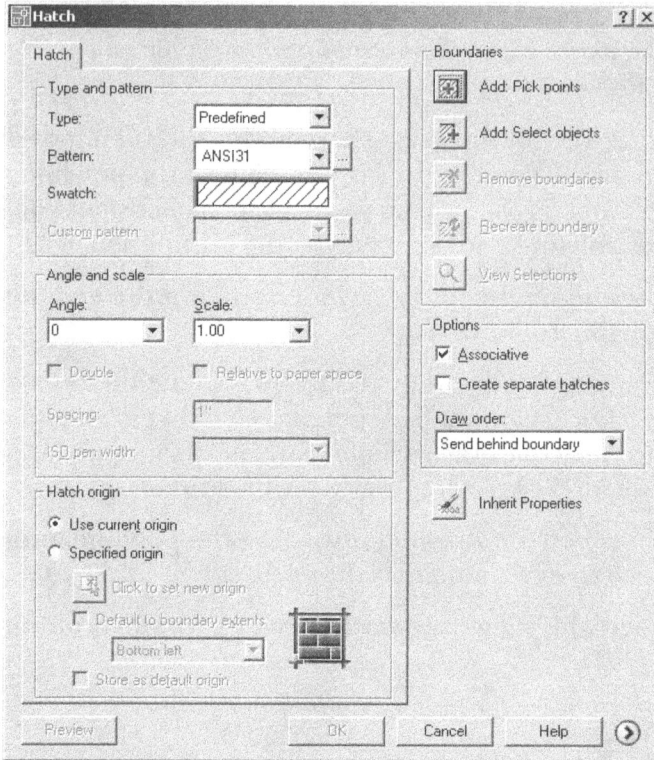

3. To find the grass hatch pattern, click the **...** button (next to **Pattern: ANSI31**).

4. AutoCAD LT displays the Hatch Pattern Palette dialog box.

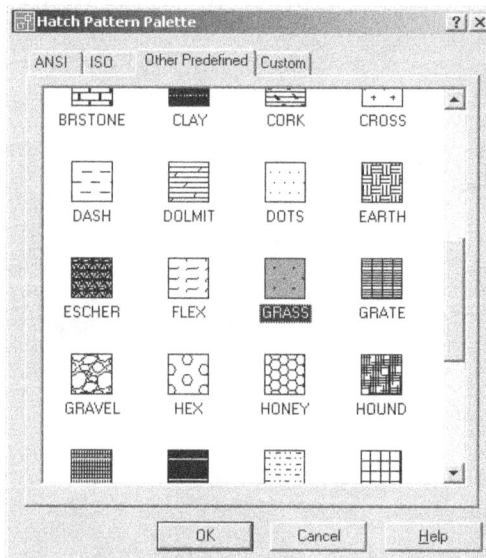

Click the **Other Predefined** tab, scroll down the list, and then select **Grass**.

5. Click **OK** to return to the Hatch dialog box.

6. In the Angle and Scale section, change **Scale** to **25**. (When the scale factor is too small, AutoCAD LT refuses to draw the hatch pattern and complains, "Hatch spacing too dense, or dash size too small.")

7. AutoCAD LT has a useful feature that searches a contiguous area, no matter how many different borders the area has. To employ this feature, click **Add: Pick points**.

The dialog box disappears and AutoCAD LT prompts:

Pick internal point or [Select objects/remove Boundaries]: *(Pick a point inside the lawn area.)*

8. Pick a point anywhere in the lawn area. AutoCAD LT spends a few moments reflecting upon your selection:

Selecting everything...
Selecting everything visible...
Analyzing the selected data...
Analyzing internal islands...

And then highlights the objects that make up the boundary.

9. Press **Enter** to return to the dialog box:

Pick internal point or [Select objects/remove Boundaries]: *(Press Enter.)*

AutoCAD LT draws the boundary out of a polyline, although you cannot see it.

10. After you press **Enter**, the Hatch dialog box reappears. A hatch pattern applied at the wrong scale can cause you grief:

Scale too large — hatch pattern seems invisible

Scale too small — hatch pattern looks black and takes a longer time to display

To help you out, AutoCAD LT includes a preview feature. Click **Preview**.

AutoCAD LT quickly hatches the lawn area. It looks like the scale factor is good enough. Note how precisely the hatch pattern is applied, and how it is automatically clipped along boundaries. Try doing a hatch pattern that neatly and that quickly by hand!

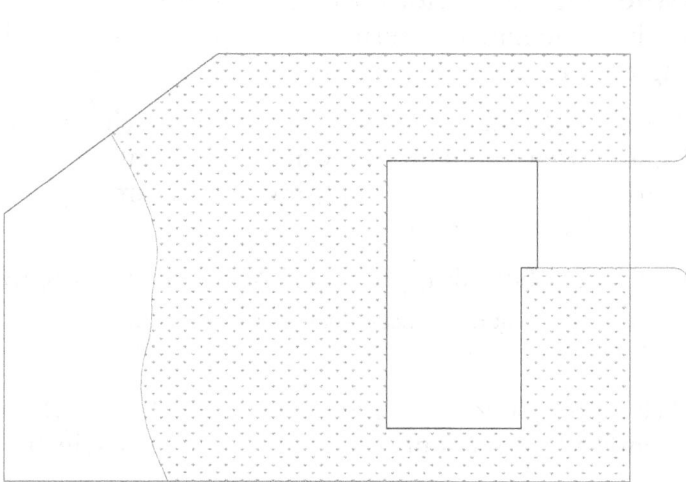

11. Press **Enter** to end the preview and return to the dialog box:

    Pick or press Esc to return to dialog or <Right-click to accept hatch>: (Press *Enter*.)

12. The Hatch dialog box reappears. Click on the **OK** button. The dialog box disappears one last time, and the hatch pattern is in place.

With all this hard work on your drawing, it's a good idea to save the drawing to the computer's hard disk with the **Save** command... right now!

TIP   Once hatch patterns are in place, they are not cast in stone. You can change them in several ways.

Double-click the hatch object and AutoCAD LT brings up the Edit Hatch dialog box. (Double-clicking other objects brings up other dialog boxes appropriate for editing them or the Properties window.) You can change the pattern, scale factor, rotation angle, and so on.

Move (or stretch) objects that make up the boundary of the pattern, and the hatching automatically updates itself.

The hatch does not need to stay in place. You can move it, copy, erase, and so on.

Creating Symbols

You've given the lawn area its grass. Now add trees and shrubs to the garden area. Instead of trying to draw things as complex as trees, landscape architects typically draw simple representations, such as a circle with radiating lines.

In this section, you learn how to create tree symbols. After creating one tree symbol, you add many more with just a single command.

Drawing Circles

Draw | Circle
View | Regen

1. Before starting on the first tree, make sure the working layer is set to Plants. (Select layer **Plants** from the toolbar.)

2. Select **Draw | Circle | Center, Radius** to draw a six-inch radius circle, as follows:

    Command: _circle
    Specify center point for circle or [3P/2P/Ttr (tan tan radius)]:
    (Pick a point anywhere in garden area.)
    Specify radius of circle or [Diameter]: **6**

    With a radius of 6, AutoCAD LT draws the circle with a one-foot diameter. (Recall that the radius is half the diameter.)

3. The one-foot circle looks very small on the screen. The **Zoom** command lets you see your work more clearly. Select **View | Zoom | Realtime.**

    Command: '_zoom
    All/Center/Extents/Previous/Scale(X/XP)/Window/<Realtime>:

    To exit, press **Esc** or **Enter,** or right-click to activate a shortcut menu.

    The cursor changes to a magnifying glass. Drag the cursor over the circle.

Methods of Drawing Circles

AutoCAD LT provides several methods for drawing circles:

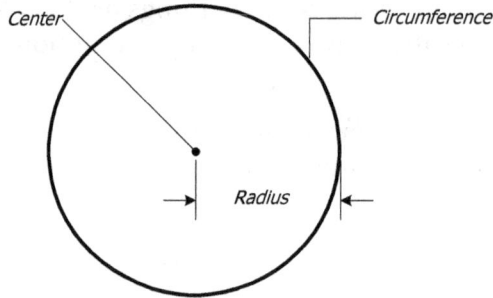

Center, Radius — pick the center point, and then specify the radius.

Center, Diameter — pick the center point, and then specify the diameter.

2 Points (2P) — pick two points to define the diameter.

3 Points (3P) — pick three points to define the circumference.

Tan, Tan, Radius (TTR) — pick two points of tangency (to other objects), and then specify the radius.

Tan, Tan, Tan — pick three points of tangency to other objects.

As you move the mouse forward and backward, AutoCAD LT dynamically increases and decreases the zoom. (As an alternative, if you have a wheelmouse, roll the wheel forward to zoom in.)

NOTE   To *drag* means to hold down the left mouse button, move the mouse, and then let go of the mouse button.

4. If you find the tree going off the edge of the screen, click the scroll bars to pan the drawing. Move the tree-circle to the center of the drawing area.

5. When the tree-circle is at a satisfactory size, press **Esc** to get out of real-time pan-and-zoom mode:

   Press Esc or Enter to exit, or right-click to display shortcut menu. *(Press **Esc**.)*

6. Oops! What happened to the circle? If the circle looks like an octagon, select **View | Regen** to clean it up, as follows:

   ```
   Command: _regen
   Regenerating drawing.
   ```

   Now that the circle looks rounder and larger, it is easier to work with.

Creating Arrays

Modify | Array

To draw arrays of lines (that represent the branches), you draw one line, then use the **Array** command to create the radiating lines. This command creates three types of arrays: rectangular, polar rotated, and polar non-rotated.

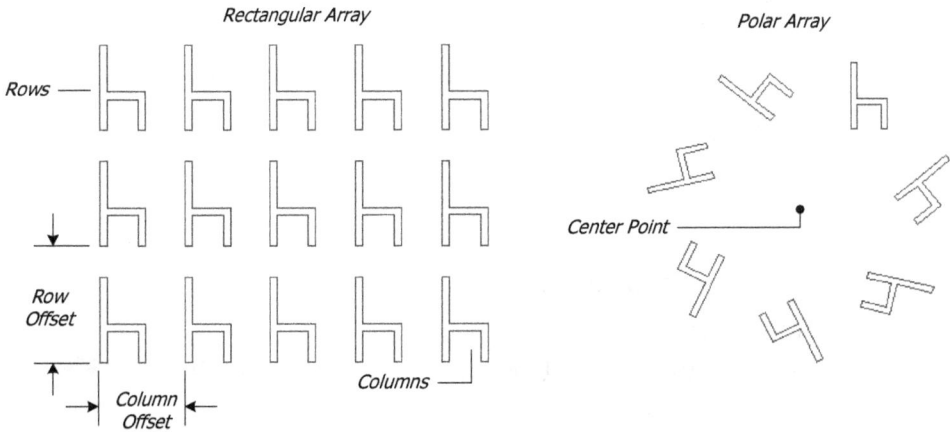

Rectangular Array

Polar Array

Rows

Row Offset

Column Offset

Columns

Center Point

1. Select the **Line** icon from the **Draw** toolbar, and proceed as follows:

   ```
   Command: _line
   Specify first point: cen
   of (Pick center.)
   Specify next point or [Undo]: (Pick point anywhere outside of circle.)
   Specify next point or [Undo]: (Press Enter.)
   ```

   Here the CENter object snap begins the line at the precise center of the circle. The other end of the line extends beyond the edge of the circle.

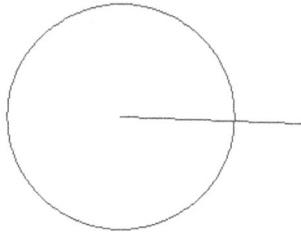

2. From the **Modify** menu, select **Array**. Notice the Array dialog box. (The **Rectangular Array** option creates linear, square, and rectangular arrays of objects.)

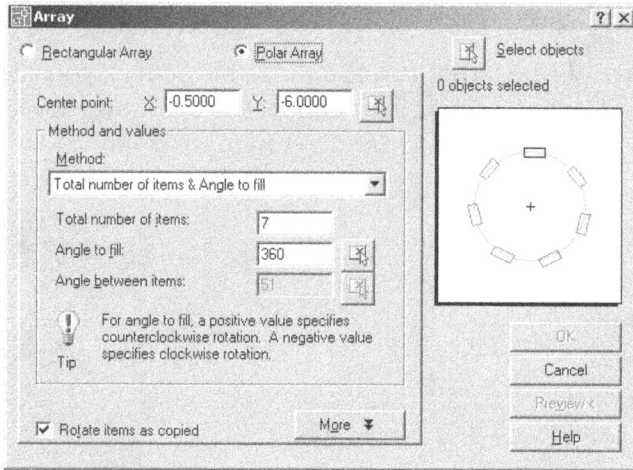

3. Click the **Polar Array** radio button.

4. This dialog box can look intimidating with its many buttons and fields. The process you go through is:

   a. Select objects to array.
   b. Specify the centerpoint of the array.
   c. Define the array method.
   d. Take care of any other options.
   e. Preview to make sure it looks right.
   f. And commit!

   Select the line to array by clicking the **Select objects** button. The dialog box disappears so you can see the screen.

5. AutoCAD LT displays:

   Select objects: **L**
   I found

   Type **L** to select the line, then press **Enter**.

TIP The letter **L** is short for "last," and is shorthand notation for selecting the last object drawn still visible on the screen. After you select one or more objects, AutoCAD LT reports the number selected: "1 found."

6. Press **Enter** to end object selection and return to the dialog box:

   Select objects: *(Press **Enter** to end object selection.)*

7. Click the **Pick Center Point** button, located across from the **Center point** fields. Notice that the dialog box disappears (again) so that you can see the screen.

8. Use ENDpoint object snap to select the end of the line at the center of the circle:

   Specify center point of array: **end**
   of *(Pick line at center of circle.)*

   Although you are using a dialog box to construct this array, note that you still need to watch the command prompt area from time to time! After picking the center of rotation, the Array dialog box immediately returns.

9. Now you need to tell AutoCAD LT how you want the array constructed. You use the default method **Total number of items & Angle to fill**.

   In the **Total number of items** field, erase **4** and type **25**.

   The **Angle to fill** field reads **360**, which is what you want (items are arrayed around a full circle).

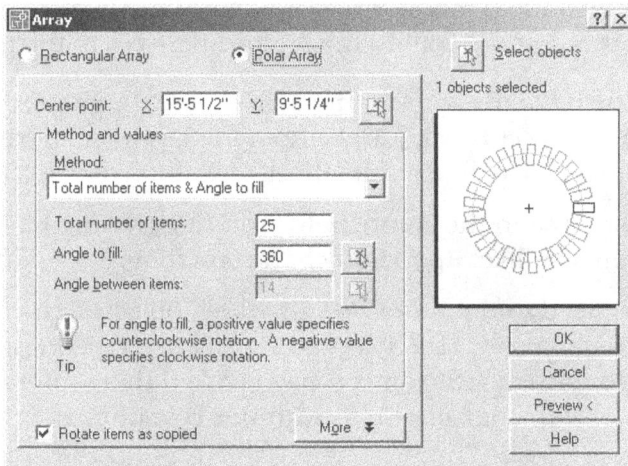

10. At the bottom of the dialog box is one more option: **Rotate items as copied**. Click the check box to make the lines radiate.

11. With all the parameters (hopefully) set up correctly, click **Preview**. AutoCAD LT quickly draws 24 more lines around the circle, completing the tree symbol.

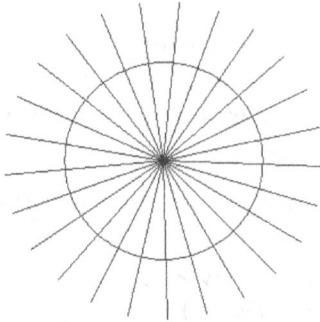

12. Since the array looks correct, click **Accept**.

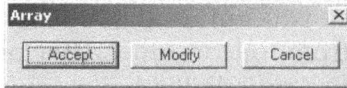

The array is left as is; unlike the Hatch command, the Array dialog box does not reappear.

Making Blocks

Draw | Block | Make

CAD draws symbols more quickly and accurately than you could by hand. The key is to turn the symbols into *blocks*, and then *insert* the blocks into drawings. In this section, you do this by adding trees to the garden area.

1. To turn the tree symbol into a block, use the **Block** command. Select **Block | Make** from the **Draw** menu bar. AutoCAD LT displays the Block Definition dialog box.

2. Type **Tree** in the Name field. You can give the block any name you like, up to 255 characters long.

3. You need to tell AutoCAD LT which objects to turn into a block. AutoCAD LT lets you select objects several different ways. So far, you have picked them (one at a time) with your mouse or with the **L** option.

Block Definition ? X

N_a_me:
tree

Base point
Pick point

X: 0.0000
Y: 0.0000
Z: 0.0000

Objects
Select objects

C Retain
(•) Convert to block
C Delete
⚠ No objects selected

Settings

Block unit:
Inches

☐ Scale uniformly
☑ Allow exploding

Description:

Hyperlink...

OK   Cancel   Help

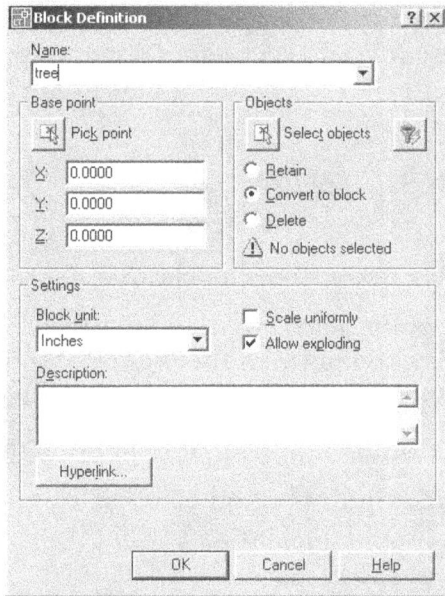

Just as you windowed the zoomed-in view, you can window the objects you want to select with the **W** option (short for "Window").

Click the **Select objects** button. The dialog box disappears, and AutoCAD LT prompts:

Select objects: **w**
Specify first corner: *(Pick one corner.)*
Specify opposite corner: *(Pick another corner.)*
26 found Select objects: *(Press **Enter** to end object selection)*

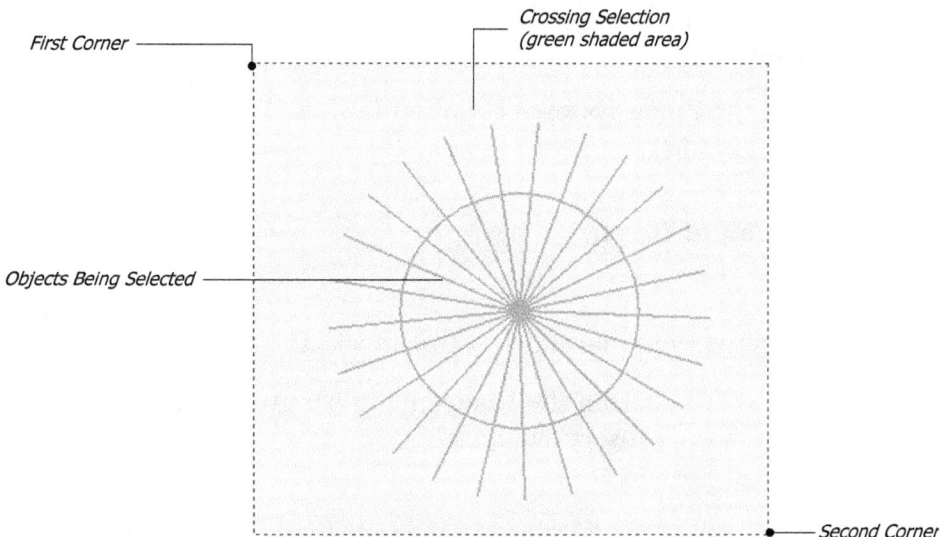

First Corner

Crossing Selection
(green shaded area)

Objects Being Selected

Second Corner

You pick the two corners of a rectangle that encompasses the circle and 25 lines making up the tree symbol. (The green shaded area is new to AutoCAD LT 2006.)

The dialog box reappears and reports:

26 found.

4.   Click **Delete** to turn on the feature.

5.   The **Base point** fields are used later by the **Insert** command. It is also known as the "insertion point": the point where the block is placed in the drawing.

The center of the tree symbol is a logical insertion point.

Click the **Pick point** button. The dialog box disappears and AutoCAD LT prompts:

Specify insertion base point: **cen**
of (Pick the circle.)

Using the CENter object snap ensures a precise selection. The dialog box reappears with the x,y,z coordinates of the base point filled in.

6.   For the **Description** field, type anything you like up to 255 characters long:

Basic 1'-dia Tree Symbol

7.   Click the **OK** button.

AutoCAD LT removes the dialog box, erases the old tree symbol, and records it as a block.

8.   Use the **Zoom Extents** command to see the entire yard.

Adding Many More Trees

Insert | Block

With the bigger view in place, insert tree blocks in the drawing.

1.   Select **Block** from the **Insert** menu bar. AutoCAD LT displays the Insert dialog box.

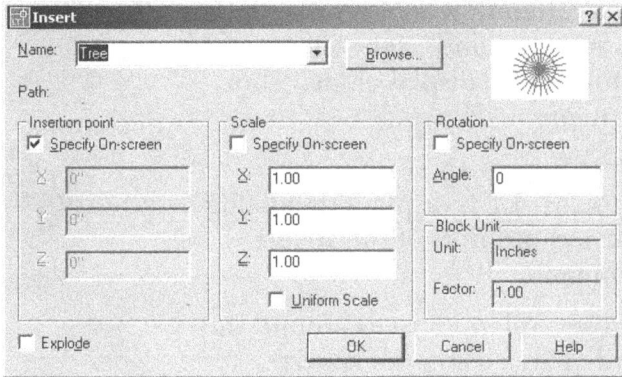

2. The Tree block name should be shown in the **Name** field.

    You can ignore everything else in the dialog box, other than to ensure that the following options are turned on (check marks show):

Insertion Point: Specify On-screen	✓(*on*)
Scale: Specify On-screen	✓(*on*)
Uniform Scale	✓(*on*)

3. Click **OK**. AutoCAD LT prompts you to pick a spot to place the block:

    Specify insertion point or [Basepoint/Scale/Rotate/PScale/PRotate]: *(Pick a point in the garden area.)*

4. When you supply an X-scale factor, AutoCAD LT draws the block larger or smaller than the original symbol.

    Specify scale factor < 1 >: **5**

    By specifying an X-scale factor of **5**, AutoCAD LT draws the block five times larger. Because you drew the original symbol one foot in diameter, the newly inserted tree is five feet in diameter. You can see that it makes sense to draw a symbol to *unit size* (to the nearest inch or foot); that makes it easier to scale the block during insertion.

    (If you want to stretch or squeeze the block, the command allows you to specify a different Y-scale factor. This is useful for inserting rectangles, such as different-sized lumber, based on a unit square.)

5. Try a different way of repeating the **Insert** command: right-click and AutoCAD LT displays a new short-cut menu.

   Select **Repeat INSERT**, and AutoCAD LT redisplays the dialog box and prompts of the **Insert** command.

6. Add several more trees around the garden area using the **Insert** command and different X-scale factors, such as 6.0, 4.0, 2.0, and 1.5. Use the **Mirror** command to double the number of trees.

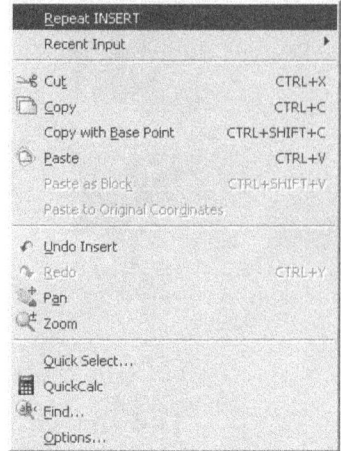

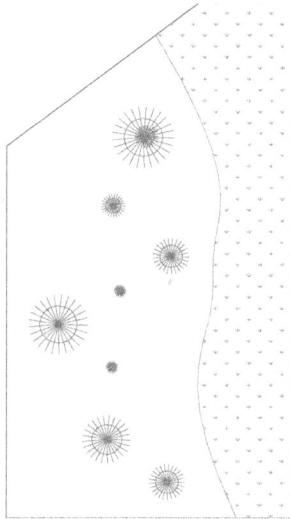

Repeat INSERT	
Recent Input	▶
Cut	CTRL+X
Copy	CTRL+C
Copy with Base Point	CTRL+SHIFT+C
Paste	CTRL+V
Paste as Block	CTRL+SHIFT+V
Paste to Original Coordinates	
Undo Insert	
Redo	CTRL+Y
Pan	
Zoom	
Quick Select...	
QuickCalc	
Find...	
Options...	

Drawing the Pond

Draw | Ellipse
Modify | Offset

Drawing the garden pond illustrates another pair of AutoCAD LT commands: **Ellipse** (for drawing the oval-shaped pond) and **Offset** for adding the pond's edging.

1. Switch to the Pond layer via the toolbar.

Methods of Drawing Ellipses

AutoCAD LT provides three methods for drawing ellipses (ovals):

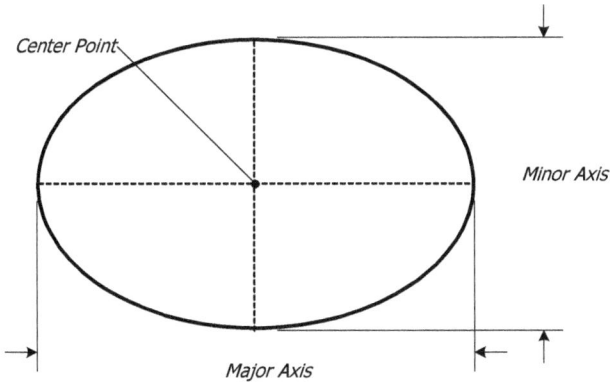

Center — specifies the ellipse's center point and the endpoints of the major and minor axes.

Axis, End — specifies the endpoints of the ellipse's major and minor axes.

Arc — draws elliptical arcs.

In addition, the **Ellipse** command draws *isocircles*, which are isometric circles, as described in a later chapter. This option is available only when isometric drawing mode is turned on through the **Snap** or **DSettings** commands.

2. The pond is an oval 15 feet long and five feet wide. Draw the pond with the **Ellipse** command by selecting **Ellipse | Center** from the **Draw** menu.

    Command: _ellipse
    Specify axis endpoint of ellipse or [Arc/Center]: *(Pick a point.)*

    Pick the starting point of the ellipse anywhere in the garden area.

3. The other end of the pond is 15 feet away. Use direct distance entry by moving the cursor down and right:

    Specify other endpoint of axis: *(Move the cursor.)* **15'**

4. And the pond is five feet wide:

    Specify distance to other axis or [Rotation]: **5'**

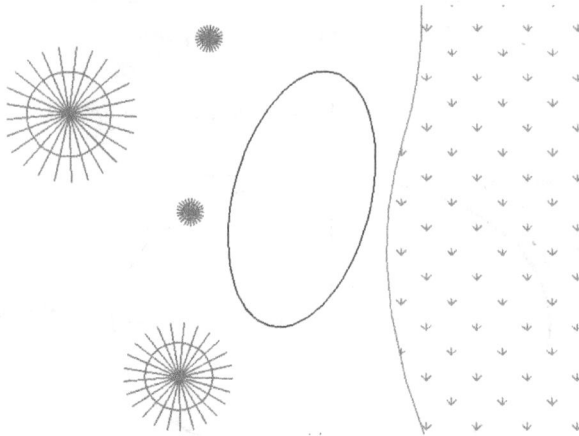

5. You could draw the rock edging of the pond by repeat-
    ing the **Ellipse** command. An alternative method is to
    use the **Offset** command, which creates offset lines and
    concentric ellipses.

    Select **Offset** from the **Modify** menu, and then follow
    the prompts:

    ```
    Current settings: Erase source=No  Layer=Source
    OFFSETGAPTYPE=0
    Specify offset distance or [Through/Erase/Layer] <Through>: I'
    Select object to offset or <exit>: (Pick the ellipse.)
    Specify point on side to offset: (Pick outside the ellipse.)
    Select object to offset or <exit>: (Press Enter.)
    ```

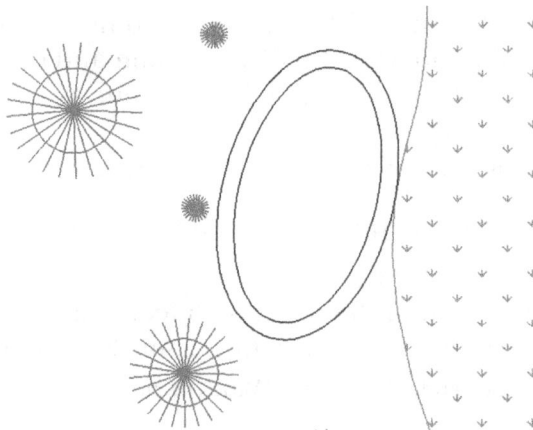

The **Offset** command also creates parallel lines, parallel polylines, and
concentric circles and arcs.

If you wish, add the Gravel hatch pattern to the pond edging.

Your drawing should look similar to the following:

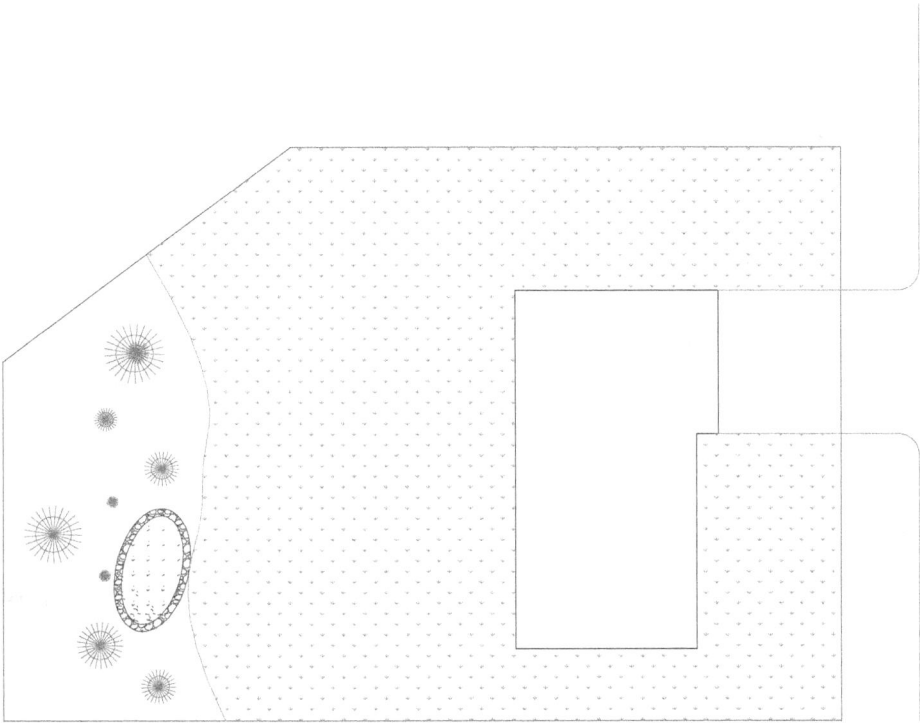

Summary

Remember to save your work with the **Save** command. To see the progress you are making in learning AutoCAD LT, plot your drawing with the **Plot** command by clicking on the printer icon on the toolbar.

Notes

Chapter 6

Making Changes to Drawings

In This Chapter
- Modifying properties of objects
- Applying scaled linetypes to objects
- Filtering selection sets of objects
- Changing the length of open and closed objects
- Finding information about objects in drawings
- Positioning the cursor with tracking

In the last chapter, you added details to the drawing, such as the lawn, trees, and a pond. In this chapter, you learn how to change parts of the drawing and how to get information out of it.

Changing the Look of Lines

Format | Linetype
Modify | Properties

When you drew the lot lines in an earlier chapter, they showed on the screen as solid lines. Lot lines are, however, usually shown by a dashed pattern. Just as AutoCAD LT comes with several hatch patterns, it also includes a number of line patterns called *linetypes*.

Key Terms

Extend — extends open objects to boundaries that are defined by other objects
Filters — create specified subsets of objects based on their properties
Linetypes — line patterns made of dashes, dots, gaps, and symbols
Properties — listings of all characteristics of objects
Tracking — moves the cursor during drawing and editing commands
Trim — cuts objects at cutting edges that are defined by other objects

Abbreviations

ISO   International Organization for Standardization
.lin   Linetype definition file

Commands

Command	Shortcut	Menu Selection
Dist	di	Tools | Inquiry | Distance
Lengthen	len	Modify | Lengthen
Linetype	Alt+FN	Format | Linetype
List	li	Tools | Inquiry | List
Properties	Ctrl+1	Modify | Properties
QSelect	Alt+TQ	Tools | Quick Select
Stretch	s	Modify | Stretch
Tracking	tk	...

It takes two steps to change a line from solid (named "Continuous" by AutoCAD LT) to dashed: first, you load the linetype, and then you change the line to the new linetype.

Start AutoCAD LT, and then open your copy of yard.dwg. If necessary, you can open the Tutorial-05.dwg file from the book's resource page.

1. First, use the **Zoom** command's **All** option so that you see the entire drawing on the screen.

    Follow that by an 80% zoom that adds some breathing space around the drawing:
    ```
    Command: zoom
    Specify corner of window, ...  <real time>: 0.8x
    ```

2. The linetype definitions are stored in files separate from AutoCAD LT and the drawing. You can recognize the files by the .lin extension at the end of their file names. Before you can use linetypes, however, you must load their definitions into the drawing.

   From the **Format** menu, select **Linetype**.

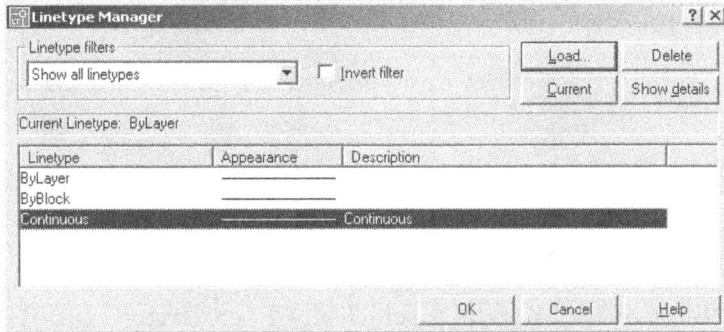

   Notice that AutoCAD LT displays the Linetype Manager dialog box that lists the three linetypes found in all new drawings:

   ByLayer — lines take on the linetype assigned to the layer.
   ByBlock — lines take on the linetype of the block.
   Continuous — lines are solid.

   TIP Although AutoCAD LT refers to linetypes and lineweights, these apply to all objects in drawings and not just to lines.

3. Click the **Load** button.

   Notice that AutoCAD LT displays the Load or Reload Linetypes dialog box.

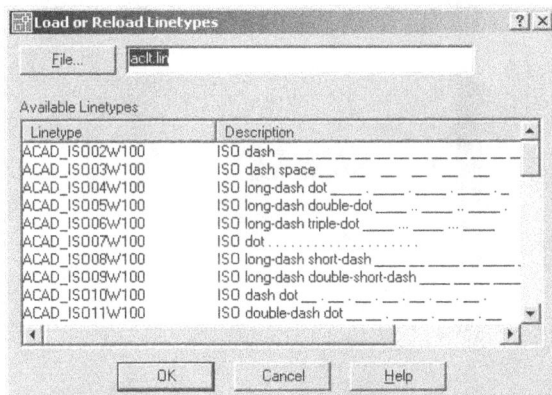

This dialog box lists in alphabetical order the names of all linetype definitions stored in the aclt.lin file. Scroll through the list to see what is available:

- Linetype names prefixed with ACAD_ISO are compliant with ISO (International Organization for Standardization).
- Linetype names postfixed with X2 are double scale.
- Linetype names postfixed with 2 are half size (0.5x scale).

4. To load the Border linetype, select it, then click **OK**.

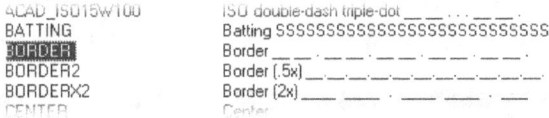

```
ACAD_ISO15W100      ISO double-dash triple-dot __ __ ... __ __ .
BATTING             Batting SSSSSSSSSSSSSSSSSSSSSSSSSSSS
BORDER              Border __ __ . __ __ . __ __ . __ __ .
BORDER2             Border (.5x) __ __ . __ __ . __ __ . __ __ .
BORDERX2            Border (2x) ____ ____ . ____ ____ . ____
CENTER              Center
```

5. Back in the Linetype Manager dialog box, ensure that the Border linetype is selected. Click **Current**, and then click **OK** to dismiss the dialog box.

On the Object Properties toolbar, notice that the linetype changes to Border.

6. The **Properties** command is handy for changing several properties of one or more objects. You use it now to change the lot lines from Continuous to Border.

From the **Modify** menu, select **Properties**. Notice that the Properties window opens.

(As an alternative, press **Ctrl+1** to open and close the window. *Windows* differ from dialog boxes in that windows can be left open while you continue to work on the drawing.)

7. At the 'Command:' prompt, AutoCAD LT does not ask you to select the objects you want to change (as it would with the **Change** and **ChProp** commands). Instead, you can just pick the five blue lot lines.

   As you pick the lot lines, notice that AutoCAD LT highlights them: they are shown as dashed lines, with blue grip squares appearing on each line. Over in the Properties window, notice that the list box reports Line (5), indicating that five lines have been selected.

TIP   Sometimes it can be too difficult to pick objects or take too long to pick many objects in large, crowded drawings. The Properties window includes a **Quick Select** button that lets you select objects based on their properties. In our case, for example, we want all lines in layer Lot. To select them in the Quick Select dialog box, make these changes to the settings:

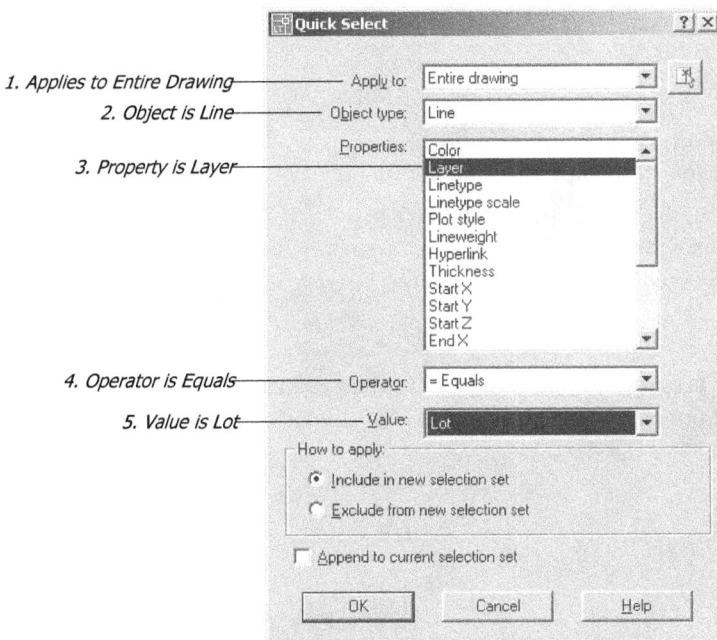

You can read the above as "in the **entire drawing**, we want **lines** whose **layer** property is **equal** to **Lot**." Click **OK** and AutoCAD LT selects the five lines.

About Properties

Properties describe objects, and include color, linetype, starting and ending coordinates, thickness, and so on. The Properties window displays information in several different ways:

No objects selected — Properties window displays the current settings, repeating some of the information displayed by the Object Properties toolbar when nothing is selected.

Single object selected — Properties window displays everything AutoCAD LT knows about the object. The list of properties varies, depending on the object selected.

Two or more objects selected — Properties window displays only those properties in common. Naturally, the list of properties displayed varies, depending on which kinds of objects are selected. The more different objects are selected, the fewer properties are displayed.

When two or more objects are selected, you can have the Properties window display subsets.

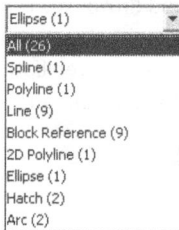

The Properties window does more than display the properties of selected objects. It allows you to change the value of individual properties:

Can be changed — displayed in black text.
Cannot be changed — displayed in gray text.
Not yet been assigned — shown blank.

There are three ways to change property values:
• Enter new values by typing them in.
• Select preset values from droplists (when available).
• Click buttons (when available) to select values from drawings or dialog boxes.

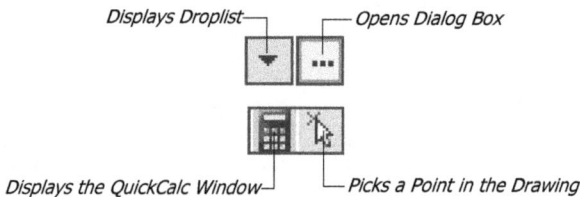

Displays Droplist — — Opens Dialog Box

Displays the QuickCalc Window — — Picks a Point in the Drawing

8. In the Properties window, click **ByLayer** next to
    Linetype. Notice that AutoCAD LT displays a list of the
    linetypes loaded in the drawing: ByLayer, ByBlock,
    Continuous, and Border.

9. Select the Border linetype by clicking its name.

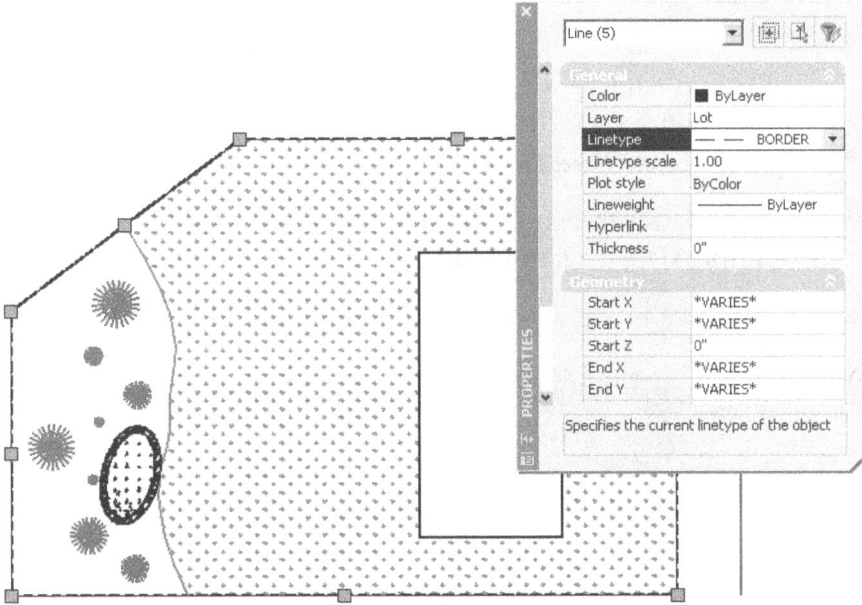

10. Press **Esc** to clear the grips.

11. Looking at the drawing, it may be difficult to tell that
    the lines have changed. In the next section, you find out
    how to fix this problem.

Changing the Linetype Scale

Tools | Quick Select

The reason the Border linetype looks continuous is that linetypes are
sensitive to scale. Until you change their scale factor, all linetypes start
with a scale factor of 1.0, which can be too small to display the pattern of
dots and dashes.

> **WARNING**   Setting linetype scale is one of the trickiest aspects of AutoCAD LT.
> Linetypes look continuous when the scale is too large or too small.

One method is to use the older **LtScale** command. Another method is to reuse the Properties window and its **Linetype scale** option.

1. In the Properties window, click the **Select Objects** button.

2. At the 'Command:' prompt, AutoCAD LT asks you:

   Select objects: **p**

   Enter **p** (short for "previous") to reuse the previous selection set, the five blue lines on layer Lot.

   Select objects: *(Press **Enter**.)*

3. Press **Enter** to exit object selection. Notice that AutoCAD LT again highlights the five blue lot lines.

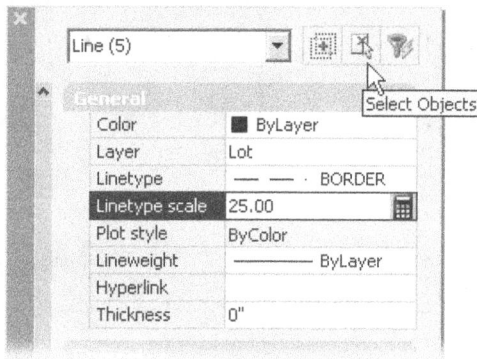

4. In the Properties window, click the text entry field next to **Linetype scale**.

5. Change 1.0 to **25**, and press **Enter**.

6. To see the linetypes more clearly, press **Esc**.

TIP In addition to **Quick Select** and **Select Objects** buttons, the Properties window has one more button on its toolbar. The **Toggle PickAdd** button toggles the value of the PickAdd system variable:

On (icon shows a +) — each object you select is added to the selection set.

Off (the icon shows a 1) — hold down the **Shift** key to add objects to the selection set, which mimics the Windows selection style.

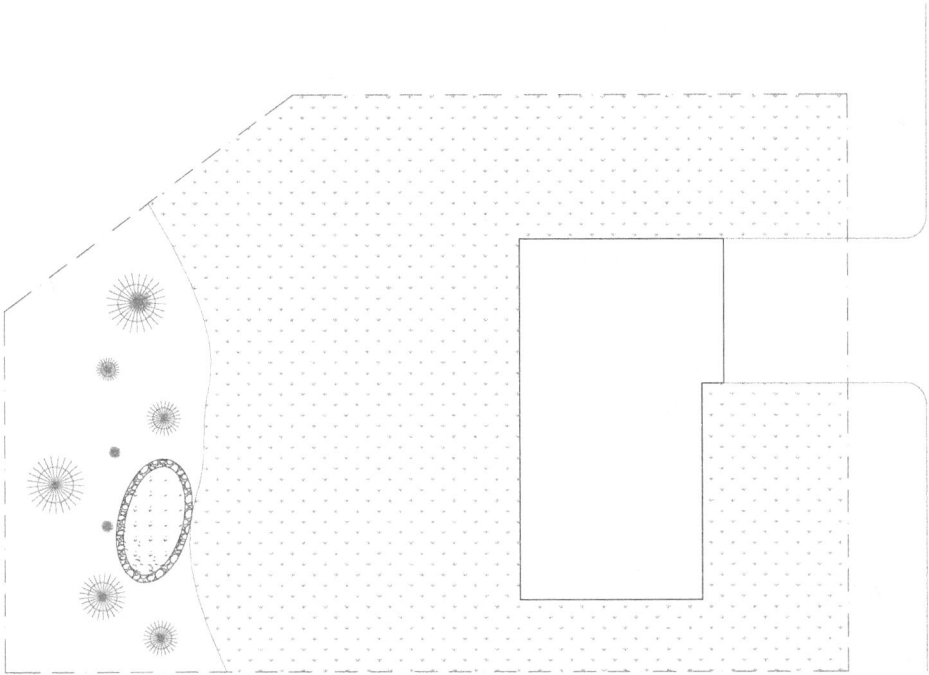

Changing Line Lengths

Modify | Lengthen

As an example of how the **Lengthen** command changes the length of an object, extend the edge of the street to the bottom of the screen. You may want to zoom in on the area around the pond first.

1. Select **Lengthen** from the **Modify** menu.

2. Pick the lower road line, as follows:

   Command: _lengthen
   Select an object or [DElta/Percent/Total/DYnamic]: *(Pick line.)*
   Current length: 37'-0"

3. AutoCAD LT reports that the line is currently 37 feet long. Select the **DYnamic** option:

   Select an object or [DElta/Percent/Total/DYnamic]: **dy**

4. When prompted, pick the line again:

   Specify new end point.
   Select an object to change or [Undo]: *(Pick line again.)*

About Lengthen

The **Lengthen** command provides you with the following options for changing the length (longer or shorter) of open objects, such as lines, arcs, and polylines:

Angle — changes the arc's angle; default = 0 degrees. (Available for arcs only.)

DElta — changes the length to an absolute amount where you show the delta by picking a point the required distance from the endpoint; default = 0 units. (*Delta* is the Greek word used by mathematicians to indicate "change.")

DYnamic — changes the length by interactive dragging.

Percent — changes the length relative to 100%. Less than 100%, such as 50%, shortens the object, and more than 100%, such as 200%, lengthens the object.

Total — changes the length to an absolute amount; default = 1 unit.

Undo — undoes the last change.

As is common in AutoCAD LT, there is more than one way to change the length of lines and other open objects:

Change command — changes the length of a group of lines to a common endpoint.
Extend command — extends a line to a boundary object.
Trim command — cuts back a line to a cutting edge object.

---

5. As you move the cursor up and down, AutoCAD LT lengthens and shortens the line. Move the cursor to the bottom of the screen, and click.

Select an object to change or [±] [12'-11 1/2"] [< 282°]

6. Press **Enter** to end the command.

Select an object to change or [Undo]: *(Press **Enter**.)*

Changing the Look of the Pond
Modify | Stretch

So far, you have used several editing commands to change objects: **PEdit** to modify polylines; grips editing to stretch the sketch line; **Properties** to change linetype and scale; and **Lengthen** to alter the length of lines.

One of AutoCAD LT's most powerful editing commands is **Stretch**. This command lets you take parts of objects and stretch them wider and thinner.

Here you apply it to change the shape of the pond. You may find it helpful to zoom in on the area around the pond.

1. Select **Stretch** from the **Modify** menu bar.

    Command: _stretch
    Select objects to stretch by crossing-window or crossing-polygon...

2. Select objects with a crossing-window selection mode, as follows:

    Select objects: _c
    Specify first corner: *(Pick a point.)*
    Specify opposite corner: *(Pick another point.)*

    C is short for "crossing," an object selection mode similar to the window mode you used earlier with the **Zoom** command. In this case, AutoCAD LT selects all objects within the selection rectangle *and* all objects crossing or touching the rectangle. You may find crossing mode somewhat faster than window mode since you don't have to draw as large a rectangle.

3. After picking two corners of a rectangle that covers part of the pond, press **Enter**:

    Select objects: *(Press **Enter** to end object selection.)*

TIPS If the pond were entirely inside the object selection rectangle, the **Stretch** command would only *move* the pond, not stretch it.

If you accidentally select objects other than the pond, type the **R** option (short for "remove from selection set"), and then select the objects to remove.

Specify First Corner

Crossing Area
(dashed rectangle
and green area)

Specify Other Corner

Specify opposite corner:

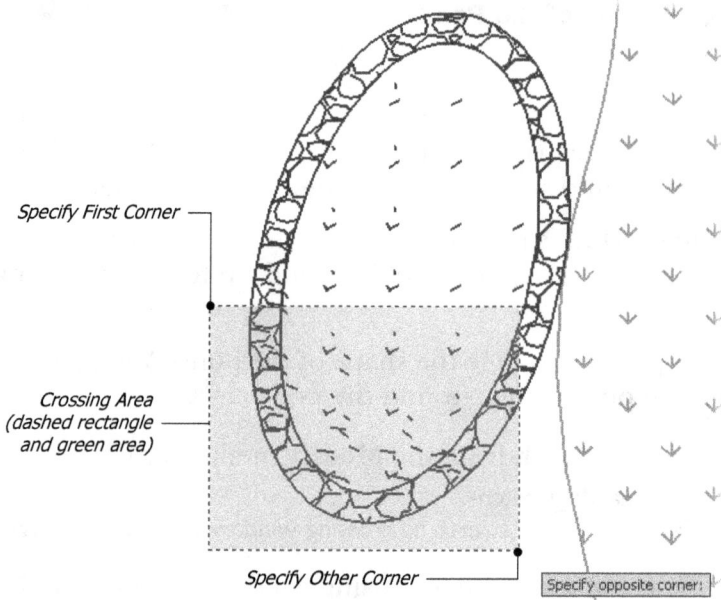

4. To tell AutoCAD LT how much you want the pond stretched, pick two points that indicate the distance:

Specify base point or [Displacement]: *(Pick a point near the pond.)*
Specify second point: *(Pick a point away from the pond.)*

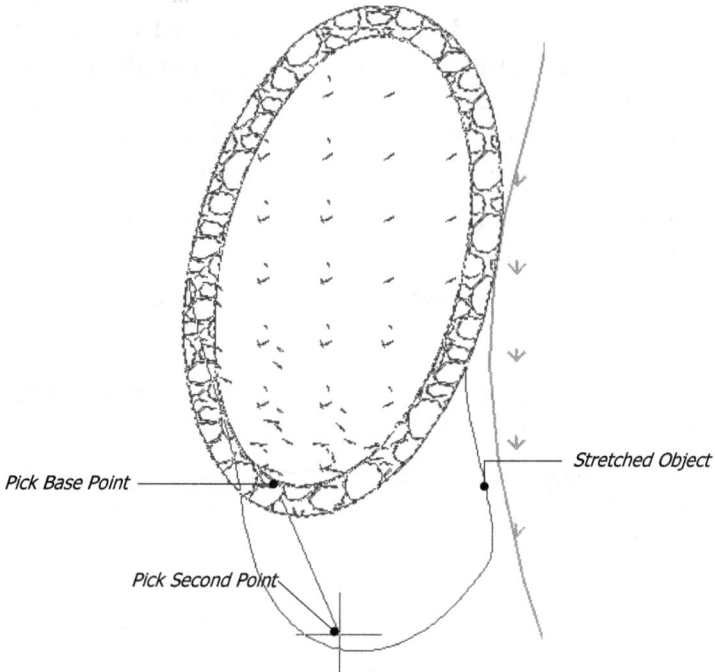

Stretched Object

Pick Base Point

Pick Second Point

5. You have now created a whole new look to your pond! If you don't like it, you can undo the stretch with the U command, as follows:

Command: **u**
U: STRETCH

... and try stretching the pond again.

(Your pond will look different from the one illustrated in this book.)

6. If the pond isn't exactly where you want it, you can relocate it with the **Move** command. Move the pond, as follows:

Command: **m**

Here you used another of AutoCAD LT's shortcuts. **M** is the abbreviation for the Move command.

7. Continue the **Move** command, as follows:

MOVE Select objects: **c**
Specify first corner: *(Pick a point near the pond.)*
Specify opposite corner: *(Pick another point to encompass the pond.)*
Select objects: *(Press **Enter** to end object selection.)*

Specify base point or [Displacement] <Displacement>: *(Pick edge of pond.)*
Specify second point or <use first point as displacement>: *(Pick new location for pond.)*

8. Clean up the screen with the **Redraw** command, as follows:

Command: **r**
REDRAW

9. Save your work.

TIP AutoCAD LT lets you specify commands by typing just one or two letters at the 'Command:' prompt. *Shortcut keystrokes* are listed at the start of each chapter. The complete list of command name abbreviations (called "aliases") is stored in the file aclt.pgp and is provided in Appendix A, "AutoCAD LT Command Reference."

Adding the Fence

Tracking
List
Dist

Say you've decided to add a fence to the backyard. You can use AutoCAD LT to help plan the materials needed. After drawing the fence as a polyline, you can find out from AutoCAD LT how long that fence is.

1. First, switch the working layer to House by selecting its name from the toolbar.

   Use the **Zoom Previous** command to see the full drawing.

2. If you turned off the **INTersection** object snap, turn it back on:

   a. On the status bar, right-click **OSNAP**.
   b. From the shortcut menu, select **Settings**.
   c. In the Drafting Settings dialog box, select the **Object Snap** tab.
   d. Click **Clear All**, select **Intersection**, and then click **OK**.

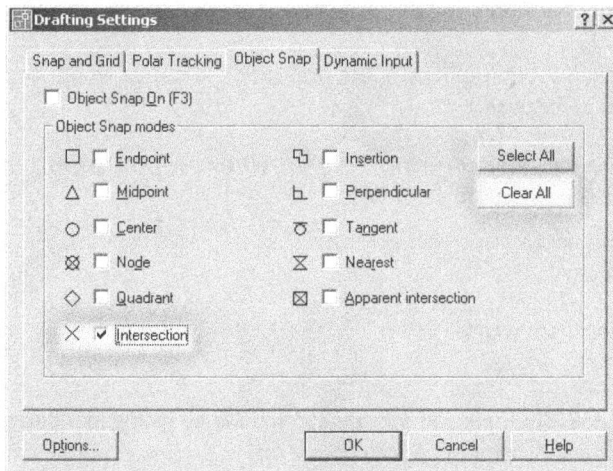

3. The fence is drawn as a 4"-wide polyline. Along the way, you'll use a variety of object snap modes and tracking mode. Begin the **PLine** command by selecting **Draw | Polyline**.

4. Start the polyline at the middle of the upper house line (#1 in the following figure). Use the **MIDdle** object snap override to precisely locate the polyline's starting point, as follows:

   Command: _pline
   Specify start point: **mid**
   of *(Pick upper house line.)*
   Current line-width is 0'-0"

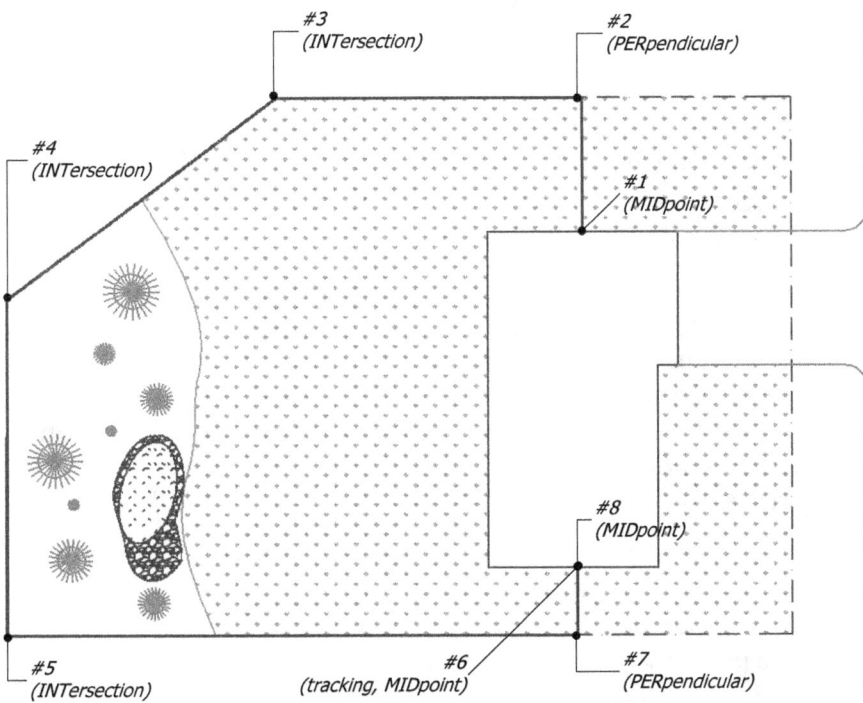

5. To change the width of the polyline from zero to four inches, use the w option, as follows:

   Specify next point or [Arc/Close/Halfwidth/Length/Undo/Width]: **w**
   Specify starting width <0'-0">: **4"**
   Specify ending width <0'-4">: *(Press **Enter** to accept the default.)*

   (You can specify a different starting and ending width to produce tapered polylines.)

6. Now that the starting point and width are set, continue drawing the fence. Follow the path shown by the numbers in the figure above.

Specify next point...: **per**
to *(Pick upper lot line, #2.)*
Specify next point...: *(Pick upper-right of diagonal, #3.)*
Specify next point...: *(Pick lower-left of diagonal, #4.)*
Specify next point...: *(Pick lower-left corner of lot, #5.)*
Pause the picking action here.

7. When you get to the bottom of the house, you get into a bit of tricky geometry. You want the fence to end at the same relative location as its starting point. You're not sure of the x coordinate, which is located somewhere along the bottom line of the lot. Fortunately, you can find that point with tracking.

    Enter **tk** (the abbreviation for "tracking"), as follows:

    Specify next point...: **tk**
    First tracking point: **per**
    of *(Pick lower house line, #6.)*

    Tracking lets you position the next endpoint of a line. When in tracking mode, you move the cursor (to indicate direction), then pick a point (to specify a distance). AutoCAD LT constrains cursor movement by turning on ortho mode automatically. This means you move the cursor in the vertical or horizontal direction only.

8. Indicate the other tentative point, then press **Enter** to exit tracking mode:

    Next point (Press ENTER to end tracking): **per**
    to *(Pick lot line below house, #7.)*
    Next point (Press ENTER to end tracking): *(Press **Enter** to exit tracking mode.)*

9. Complete the fence by drawing the last polyline segment **PERpendicular** to the lower house line (#7), and exit the **PLine** command, as follows:

    Specify next point...: **per**
    to *(Pick lower house line, #8.)*
    Specify next point...: *(Press **Enter** to exit the command.)*

10. Now that you've drawn the fence, you can use the **List** command to tell you the length. Select the **List** icon from the toolbar:

    Command: _list
    Select object: *(Pick fence polyline.)*

Select objects: *(Press **Enter** to end object selection.)*

AutoCAD LT flips to the Text Window and lists lines of information.

```
AutoCAD LT Text Window - D:\Books\Ultimate Guide LT 05 - Feb 05\CD\yard.dwg        _□×
Edit

Command: list

Select objects: 1
1 found

Select objects:
                LWPOLYLINE  Layer: "House"
                        Space: Model space
                Color: BYLAYER    Linetype: "BORDER"
                Handle = 8c6
           Open
  Constant width    0'-4"
          area    888549.2 square in. (6170.481 square ft.)
        length    259'-2"

        at point  X=   85'-0"  Y=   60'-0"  Z=    0'-0"
        at point  X=   85'-0"  Y=   80'-0"  Z=    0'-0"
        at point  X=   40'-0"  Y=   80'-0"  Z=    0'-0"
        at point  X=    0'-0"  Y=   50'-0"  Z=    0'-0"
        at point  X=    0'-0"  Y=    0'-0"  Z=    0'-0"
        at point  X=   84'-2"  Y=    0'-0"  Z=    0'-0"
        at point  X=   84'-2"  Y=   10'-0"  Z=    0'-0"

Command:
```

The **List** command tells you every piece of information about the polyline (technically called an "lwpolyline") that AutoCAD LT has stored in its database. Most of the information is about the vertices ("at point").

The total length of the polyline is shown in the middle of the listing:

length   259'-2"

Roughly 259 feet. You now know how much fencing you would need.

Press function key **F2** to flip back to the graphics window.

11. You can measure distances directly on the drawing with the **Dist** command (short for "distance"). Find the shortest distance from the house to the pond with the **Dist** command.

From the **Tools** menu bar, select **Inquiry | Distance**:

Command: _dist
Specify first point: **nea**
to *(Pick inside edge of pond.)*
Specify second point: **per**
to *(Pick house wall.)*

Distance = 46'-1 1/4", Angle in XY Plane = 0, Angle from XY Plane = 0
Delta X = 46'-1 1/4", Delta Y = 0'-0", Delta Z = 0'-0"

The beeline distance from house to pond is just over 46 feet. The value on your drawing may differ, depending on where you located the pond.

> **TIP** The Properties window also reports area and length information, albeit with less detail than the **Area** command. For example, **Properties** reports the area only of closed polylines, and does not report the area of length of more than one object.
>
> The place to find length and area information is to click the **Categorized** tab, then look under the **General** section.

New to AutoCAD LT 2006 is the ability to report the area of hatch patterns. Use the Properties command to find the area of lawn.

1. Select the lawn hatch pattern. Notice the single grip in the pattern's center.

2. Right-click and select Properties from the shortcut menu.

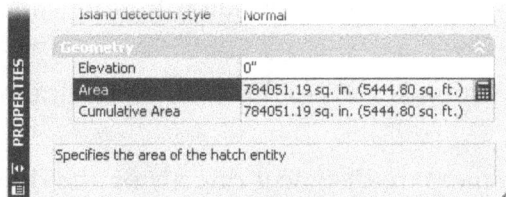

3. In the Geometry area, notice that the **Area** is 5444.80 sq. ft.

   (Cumulative Area is used when multiple areas are hatched at once.)

Now you know that you need enough fertilizer and lime for about 5,500 square feet.

About Selection Set Options

AutoCAD LT has 17 options for selecting objects, as shown in the following table. I find that I use only a few of the options, such as pick, W, C, L, P and Enter.

Mode	Abbreviation	Meaning
Object	[pick]	Selects a single object.
Window	W	Selects all objects within a rectangular window.
Window Polygon	WP	Selects all objects within a polygonal window.
Crossing	C	Selects objects crossing and within a rectangular window.
Crossing Polygon	CP	Selects all objects crossing and within a polygon.
Fence	F	Selects objects along a fence polyline.
Box	B	Switches to W or C mode, depending on cursor movement.
Automatic	AU	Allows a single pick, or switches to W or C mode, depending on the pick point and cursor movement.
Single	SI	Selects first object encountered.
Last	L	Selects the most-recently created object visible on the screen.
Previous	P	Selects most recently selected object.
Multiple	M	Delays database scanning.
Undo	U	Removes most recent selection group.
Remove	R	Enters remove-objects mode.
Add	A	Enters add-objects mode.
End	[Enter]	Ends object selection.
Cancel	[Esc]	Cancels object selection.

Summary

You've done a lot of editing in this chapter. Remember to save the work you have done on the drawing. You may also want to plot out the drawing.

In the next chapter you add text and dimensions to the drawing.

Notes

Chapter 7

Adding Notes
and Dimensions

In This Chapter
- Understanding drawing scales
- Placing text in drawings
- Defining styles and justification modes for text
- Modifying and rotating text
- Toggling text and quick text
- Attaching a variety of dimensions to objects in the drawing

In the last chapter, you changed parts of the yard and learned how to get some information out of the drawing. In this chapter, you add the finishing touches by adding callouts and dimensions to the drawing.

Before starting the exercises in this chapter:

1. Start AutoCAD LT, and then open the **Yard.dwg** file.

    (If you were unable to complete the exercises of previous chapters, open the **Tutorial-06.dwg** file from the book's resource page.)

2. Do a **Zoom All** to make the full drawing visible.

3. Create a new layer, and then name it **Text**.

    Assign color **White** to the layer, and then make the layer current by clicking the **Current** button.

Key Terms

Associative — objects, such as dimensions and hatches, that update automatically when associated objects are updated
Bounding box — invisible rectangles that determines the word wrap of paragraph text
Callouts — text that describes parts of drawings
Dimensions — indicate measured distances, usually consisting of lines, arrowheads, and text
Justification — determines the relative positioning of text, such as right, left, and centered
Layouts — editable print previews

Abbreviations

dims	Dimensions
dimvars	Dimension variables

Commands

Command	Shortcut	Menu Selection
DdEdit	ed	Modify | Object | Text | Edit
DimAligned	dal	Dimension | Aligned
DimBaseline	dba	Dimension | Baseline
DimContinue	dco	Dimension | Continue
DimLinear	dli	Dimension | Linear
DimRadius	dra	Dimension | Radius
JustifyText	...	Modify | Object | Text | Justify
MText	t	Draw | Text | Multiline Text
QText	qt	...
Rotate	ro	Modify | Rotate
ScaleText	...	Modify | Object | Text | Scale
Style	st	Format | Text Style
Text	dt	Draw | Text | Single Line Text

Adding Notes to Drawings

Draw | Text | Multiline Text

With the plan largely complete, you now add *callouts* (text) to describe the different parts of the yard.

1. In AutoCAD LT, callouts are added with the **MText** command (short for "multiple-line text"). Select **Text | Multiline Text** from the **Draw** menu.

    Command: _mtext
    Current text style: "Standard" Text height: 1/4"

    AutoCAD LT displays the status of MText: the current text style and height.

    Text styles define the global properties of text, such as the font, its size, and orientation — like a word processing style. You learn more about text styles later in this chapter. The text style "Standard" is the default style found in all new AutoCAD LT drawings.

    The height of the text should be large enough to be legible when you plot the drawing. This drawing is 130 feet wide but needs to fit a sheet of paper that's just 11 inches wide. Text at 1/4" height would be printed 0.0002" tall. Clearly (or otherwise), that's not going to work. The text needs to be taller; we'll work that out later.

2. To place a note within the house outline, pick a starting point there:

    Specify first corner: (*Pick a point within the house outline.*)

3. As you drag the cursor, notice the rectangle being formed. Pick a second point:

    Specify opposite corner or [Height/Justify/Line spacing/Rotation/Style/Width]: (*Pick a second point.*)

The rectangle forms a *boundary box* that constrains the text within its width. The box is visible only when the MText command is active; otherwise, it is neither displayed nor printed.

AutoCAD LT uses the top of the boundary to determine where the text begins. The two sides of the boundary determine where to wrap the text.

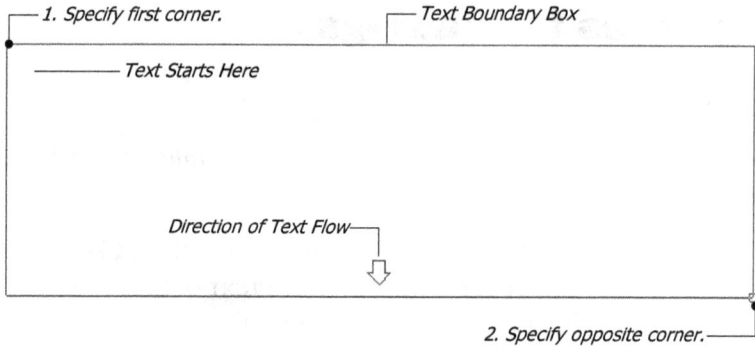

1. Specify first corner.

Text Boundary Box

Text Starts Here

Direction of Text Flow

2. Specify opposite corner.

The bottom of the boundary is ignored; text flows down as far as necessary. This is very similar to using frames in desktop publishing software.

Determining the Size of Text

Here we have to do some multiplication and division to work out the height of the text. The standard size for text in drawings is 3/8" tall. If the text were placed at that size, it would be nearly invisible in the drawing; after all, 3/8" is tiny next to a 50'-long house!

We want the text to be legible when printed, which means it must be scaled up (made larger). To figure out how much larger, read the adjacent box, "Calculating Text Heights." We need to specify a text height of 53".

1. After picking the second point, AutoCAD LT displays the Text Formatting toolbar and boundary box, where you enter the text.

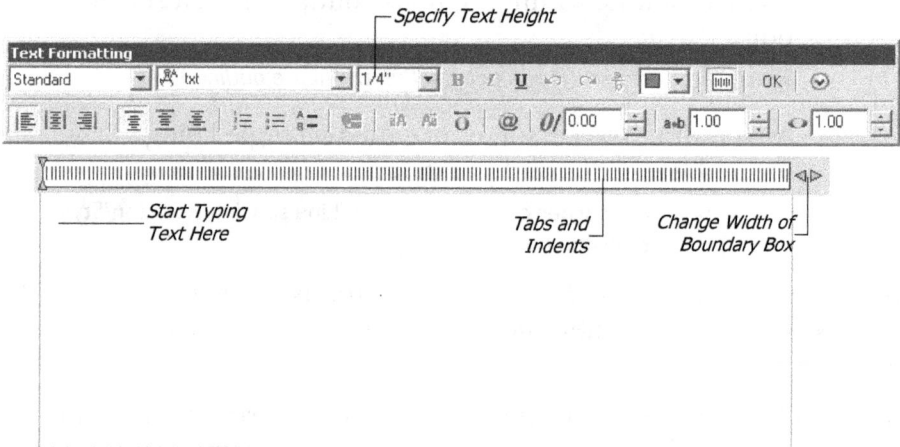

Specify Text Height

Start Typing Text Here

Tabs and Indents

Change Width of Boundary Box

Calculating Text Heights

Here are the steps to calculating the height of text appropriate for drawings:

Step 1: Work out the related drawing and paper widths, which will specify the scale factor:

$$\frac{\text{Width of drawing}}{\text{Width of paper}} = \frac{130 \text{ ft.}}{11 \text{ in.}}$$

Step 2: To make the units consistent, convert the feet to inches:

$$\frac{130 \text{ ft} \times 12 \text{ in/ft}}{11 \text{ in.}} = \frac{1{,}560 \text{ in.}}{11 \text{ in.}}$$

Step 3: Determine the scale factor by dividing:

$$\frac{1{,}560 \text{ in.}}{11 \text{ in.}} = 142$$

The scale factor is 142. That means text in the drawing should be about 140 times taller to plot big enough to be legible on the page. The standard for text heights in drawing is 3/8".

Step 4: Multiply the standard text size by the scale factor:

$$3/8" \times 142 = 53"$$

In AutoCAD LT's **MText** and **Text** commands, specify a text height of **53"**.

Although the dialog box has many options, just change the text height for now. In the **Text Height** box, enter **53"**, and then press **Enter**. AutoCAD LT converts it to 4'-5" and makes the cursor larger to match.

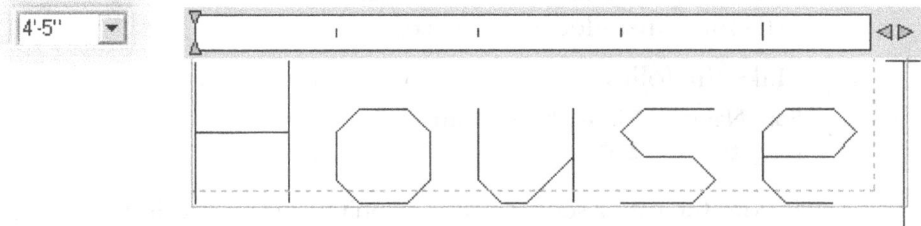

> **NOTE** The Multiline Text Editor has an Import button. If you want to place text in the drawing from an external file created by a word processor or spreadsheet, click the Import button to load the file. The file must be in ASCII format and must be 16KB or smaller.

2. Type **House**, and then click **OK**. AutoCAD LT places the word "House" in the drawing.

   If necessary, zoom in on the word "House" to get a closer look. Use the **Object** option, which zooms to the selected objects:

   Command: **zoom**
   Specify corner of window, enter a scale factor (nX or nXP), or [All/.../Object] <real time>: **o**
   Select objects: *(Pick House.)*
   Select objects: *(Press **Enter**.)*

Hmmm... The text looks kinda ugly, like a computer created it! This is the basic font, called TXT, found in every AutoCAD LT drawing. Fortunately, AutoCAD LT comes with a large number of TrueType fonts that look better than this one. In the following section, you change the font.

> **TIP** To change the size of the boundary, select the text. Four handles appear, one at each corner of the boundary. You can drag the boundary wider and narrower to change the word wrap.

Creating Text Styles

Format | Text Style

Just as hatch patterns and linetypes must be loaded into AutoCAD drawings before you can use them, text fonts other than TXT must also be loaded into drawings. This is done through the **Style** command.

1. Select **Text Style** from the **Format** menu. The Text Style dialog box appears on the screen. AutoCAD LT comes with a large collection of fonts, and can read TrueType (.ttf) fonts installed on your computer.

2. Make the following changes to the dialog box:
   Font Name: **Times New Roman**
   Height: **2'3"**

   Ignore the other settings, as we don't want the text to print backward, upside-down, or vertically — at least for now.

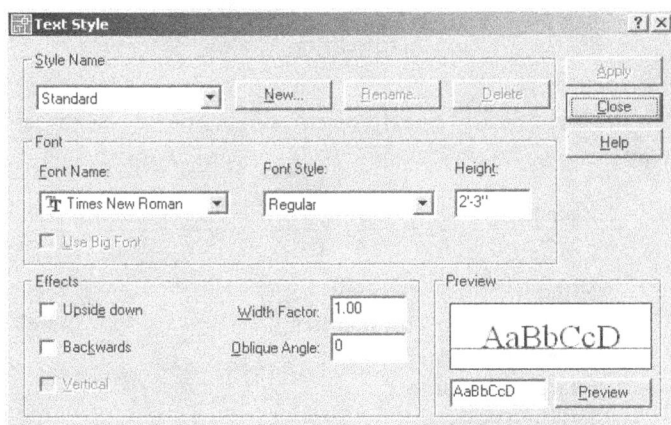

From now on, all text you place uses the Times New Roman font, 2'-3" tall — text that is half as tall as before.

3. Click **Apply**, then **Close**. Notice that the word "House" is updated automatically and appears in the new font.

Text Alignment

Draw | Text | Single Line Text

AutoCAD LT has a second command for placing text. The **Text** command places single lines of text at a time. In some ways, it is easier to use than the **MText** command. To try the **Text** command, first zoom in on the pond.

1. Now that you see the pond area more clearly, start the **Text** command with **Draw | Text | Single Line Text**.

   Command: _text
   Current text style: "Standard" Text height: 2'-3"

   Notice that the text is preset to the height you defined in the Text Style dialog box. (The height of 0" has special meaning: the text height is not predefined and can be specified during the **Text** command.)

2. Use one of AutoCAD LT's 15 justification modes by specifying the **Justify** option:

   Specify start point of text or [Justify/Style]: **j**
   Enter an option [Align/Fit/Center/Middle/Right/TL/TC/TR/ML/MC/MR/ BL/ BC/BR]: **a**

Text Justification Modes

AutoCAD LT can specify justification (alignment) for text in many different ways:

Justification	Meaning
Start point	Baseline left.
Align	Fitted between two points.
Fit	Fitted with constant text height.
Center	Baseline center.
Middle	Exact center of text.
Right	Baseline right.
TL	Top left.
TC	Top center.
TR	Top right.
ML	Middle left.
MC	Middle center (equivalent to Middle).
MR	Middle right.
BL	Baseline left (equivalent to Start point).
BC	Baseline center (equivalent to Center).
BR	Baseline right (equivalent to Right).

3. Select the **Align** justification, which places the text fitted between two points that you pick:

    Specify first endpoint of text baseline: *(Pick one end of the pond.)*
    Specify second endpoint of text baseline: *(Pick other end of the pond.)*

    Because the **Align** option's pick points define the width and angle of the text, AutoCAD LT doesn't ask for the height or rotation angle.

Text Boundary Box

Start Typing Text Here

Pool

First Endpoint of Text Baseline

Second Endpoint of Text Baseline

4.   The **Text** command goes straight to the prompt:

Text: **Pool**

Notice that the word "Pool" is drawn with the Times New Roman text font specified by the style.

5.   Press **Enter** twice to exit the **Text** command.

Text: *(Press **Enter**.)*
Text: *(Press **Enter**.)*

Changing Existing Text

Modify | Object | Text | Edit

Oops! "Pool" should be "Pond." When you need to change the wording of text, you use the **DdEdit** command. While you could select **Object | Text | Edit** from the **Modify** menu, there is a much faster way to access the text editor.

1.   Double-click the word **Pool**.

2.   Press the **Backspace** key, and then type **Pond**.

3.   Press **Enter** twice to exit the text editor.

> **TIP**   Double-clicking *any* text displays the appropriate text editor — whether the text was placed by **MText**, **Text**, or **AttDef**.

Placing Rotated Text

Now add some more text, such as the street name written sideways. First, perform a **Zoom All** to see the entire drawing, and then restart the **Text** command.

1.   Select **Draw | Text | Single Line Text**:

Command: _text
Current text style: "Standard" Text height: 2'-3"
Specify start point of text or [Justify/Style]: *(Pick point on street.)*

2. Specify a rotation angle of 90 degrees, and then enter the text:

Specify rotation angle of text <0>: **90**
Text: **Donlyn Avenue**
Text: *(Press **Enter**.)*
Text: *(Press **Enter**.)*

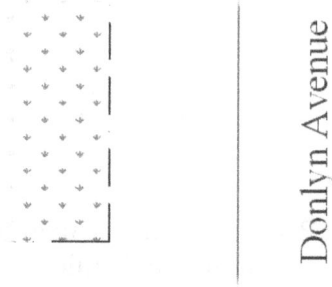

By specifying a rotation angle of 90 degrees, AutoCAD LT draws the text sideways. You can, of course, place text at any angle — from 0 degrees to 359 degrees.

3. If you picked the wrong rotation angle, you can rotate the text after the fact. Use the **Zoom Window** command to take a closer look, and then pick the text, as follows:

Command: *(Pick text.)*

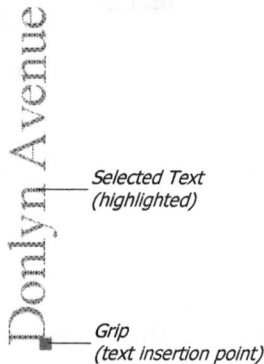

Selected Text
(highlighted)

Grip
(text insertion point)

Notice that a small blue box — a grip — appears at the text's insertion point.

4. Click the blue box. Notice that it turns solid red.

5. Select the rotate option by pressing the Spacebar until ** ROTATE ** shows up in the command prompt area. Then specify an angle of 180 degrees, as follows:

** STRETCH **
Specify stretch point or [Base point/Copy/Undo/eXit]: *(Press Spacebar.)*
** MOVE **
Specify move point or [Base point/Copy/Undo/eXit]: *(Press Spacebar.)*
** ROTATE **
Specify rotation angle or [Base point/Copy/Undo/Reference/eXit]: **180**

6. AutoCAD LT draws the text flipped over. Press **Esc** to exit grips editing.

Adding More Text

Place more callouts throughout the drawing. First, though, **Zoom All** to see the entire drawing.

1. Use the **Text** command to add more callouts to the drawing.

   Command: _text
   Current text style: "Standard" Text height: 2'-3"
   Specify start point of text or [Justify/Style]: *(Pick near bottom of drawing.)*

2. Remember to change the rotation angle back to 0 degrees.

   Specify rotation angle of text <90>: **0**
   34486 Donlyn Avene *(Press **Enter**.)*

   Misspell "Avene" as shown; we correct it next.

3. When you press **Enter** at the end of "Avene," the cursor jumps to the next line. Now that you've noticed the spelling mistake in "Avene," you backspace with the **Backspace** key and type the correction, as follows:

   *(Press **Backspace** twice.)* **ue** *(Press **Enter**.)*

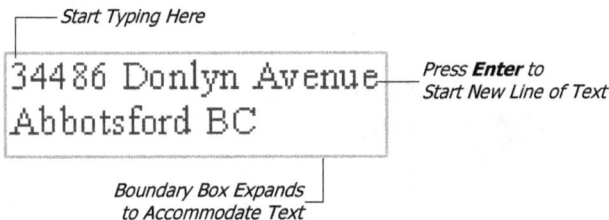

   ───── *Start Typing Here*

   ```
   34486 Donlyn Avenue
   Abbotsford BC
   ```

   *Press **Enter** to*
   Start New Line of Text

   Boundary Box Expands
   to Accommodate Text

4. Type the next line:

   Abbotsford BC *(Press **Enter**.)*

5. Add labels to trees, such as Birch, Aspen, Yellow Pine, Western Red Cedar, and so on.

At this point, it is a good idea to save your work using the **Save** command.

Text Background Color

The lawn is heavily hatched; any text placed there would be hard to read. The **MText** command has an option that creates a color background for the text.

1. Start the **MText** command, and pick two points in the lawn area.

2. Right-click, and from the shortcut menu select **Background Mask**.

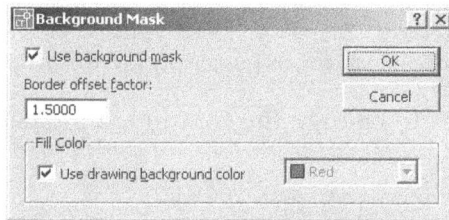

3. In the Background Mask dialog box, select these options:

    Use Background Mask: ✓ (on)
    Use Drawing Background Color   ✓ (on)

    Click **OK**.

4. Enter text for the lawn, such as **Kentucky Bluegrass Lawn**, and then click **OK**.

Notice that the text has a white area around it, and that the hatch does not interfere with the words.

Reducing Text Display Time

QText

A lot of text in drawings can slow the display speed. If you find that happening, AutoCAD LT has a special command, **QText** (short for "quick text"), that changes text into rectangular outlines.

1. Change the text into outlines with the **QText** command:

    Command: **qtext**
    ON/OFF <OFF>: **on**

    The callouts look no different! AutoCAD LT doesn't change the text until the next regeneration.

2. Force a screen regeneration with the **Regen** command. Select **View | Regen** and the text turns into rectangles.

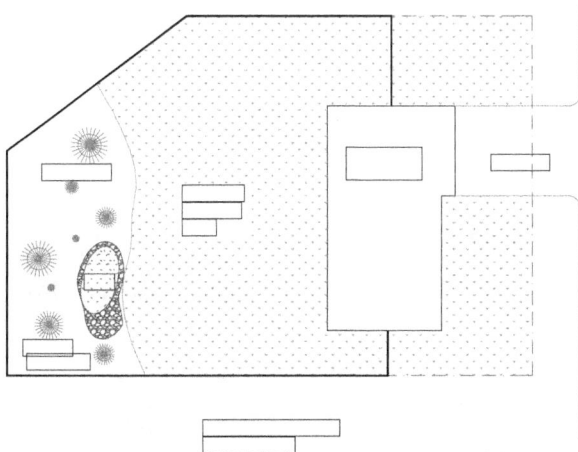

3. Change the outlines back to text, this time typing the **QText** command followed by the **Regen** command, as follows:

    Command: **qtext**
    Enter mode [ON/OFF] <OFF>: **off**
    Command: **regen**
    Regenerating drawing.

Global Text Modifications

Over several releases of AutoCAD LT, Autodesk added more tools to make it easier to make *global* changes to text. "Global" means that changes can be made to all text at once. (Older versions of AutoCAD LT allowed changes to individual lines of text only.)

The Properties window makes some global changes easier than the command line-oriented **Change** command, while the **ScaleText** and **JustifyText** commands perform global changes to text size and justification.

You may find it helpful to select the text with the **QSelect** option of the Properties window. Note, however, that the Quick Select dialog box treats **Text** and **MText** differently; use the **Append to current selection set** option to combine the two types of text into a single selection set.

Searching and Replacing Text

Edit | Find

To find text and replace it with different text, use the **Find** command (Edit | Find).

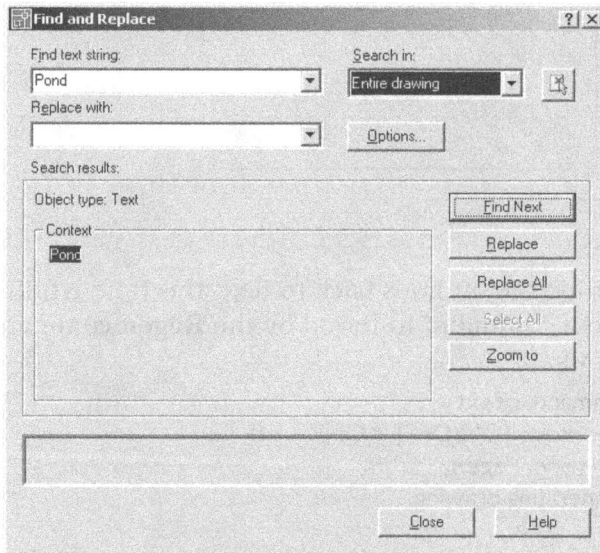

AutoCAD LT can search and replace text in:

- **Regular text** — text, mtext, and field text
- **Table text** — cells, headers, and titles
- **Dimension text** — including leaders

- **Attribute text** — found in blocks
- **Hyperlink text** — URLs and hyperlink descriptions

Changing Text Size

Modify | Object | Text | Scale

To change the size of text throughout the entire drawing, use the **ScaleText** command (Modify | Object | Text | Scale).

At the 'Select objects:' prompt, you can enter **All**, and AutoCAD LT filters out non-text objects automatically.

Specify the base point from which scaling takes place; press **Enter** to use the existing insertion point.

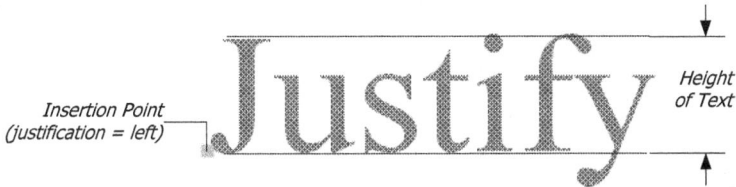

Insertion Point
(justification = left)

Height
of Text

You have three options for specifying the new size of the text:

Specify new height — enter a value for the new size. Entering 2, for example, redraws the text 2 units tall.

Match object — pick another text object, and AutoCAD LT copies its height measurement, applying it to all other text.

Scale factor — enter a value to scale to the new size. Entering 2, for example, redraws the text twice as tall; enter 0.5 to redraw the text half as tall.

NOTE AutoCAD LT calls *text size* a variety of terms, including "height" and "scale."

Changing Text Justification

Modify | Object | Text | Justify

Just as text size can be changed globally, so can the justification through the **JustifyText** command (Modify | Object | Text | Justify).

Again, at the 'Select objects:' prompt, you can enter **All**, and AutoCAD LT filters out non-text objects automatically. Then, specify the new justification option.

TIP The JustifyText command relocates the insertion point, not the text itself. Subsequent edits may cause the text to relocate relative to its insertion point.

Setting Properties for Plotted Text

Tools | Wizards | Add Plot Style Table

1. To turn on the plot style feature for a new drawing, select **Tools | Options** to display the Options dialog box.

2. Select the **Plotting** tab, and select **Use named plot styles**. You can specify the default plot style for layers and objects. Click **OK**.

3. To convert existing drawings to use plot styles, enter the **ConvertPStyles** command, and then select a named plot style table. Sample .stb files are stored in AutoCAD LT's \Plot Styles folder.

4. To create new plot styles, select **Tools | Wizards | Add Plot Style Table**.

NOTE Plot styles can be assigned to layers and to objects. Plot style options include dithering, grayscale, pen numbers, screening, linetype, lineweight, fill style, and line end styles.

Converting Text to Other Formats

Modify | Explode

Use **Modify | Explode** to convert text.

- **MText** — converted to text objects
- **Attribute text** — converted to attribute definitions

TIPS Text objects cannot be exploded within AutoCAD.

It is poor CAD practice to change the color of objects independent of their layer. Always use the **Layer** command to change the color of the layer (and hence the color of objects assigned to that layer), unless you have a good reason for using the **Color** command.

AutoCAD LT cannot change the linetype and lineweight of text. While AutoCAD LT goes through the motions of allowing you to make changes and the **List** command shows the changes, the text itself is unchanged in appearance.

Placing Dimensions in Drawings

DimScale

With callouts placed on the drawing, let's turn to dimension the lot with the commands that start with **Dim** (short for "dimensioning"). The bad news is that there are dozens and dozens and dozens of settings for dimensions in order to adhere to international standards. The good news is that AutoCAD LT comes preconfigured with most variables set to reasonable values.

These settings are called *dimensioning variables*, or "dimvars" for short. (If you ever need to change dimvars, select **Style** from the **Dimension** menu. When AutoCAD LT displays the Dimension Style Manager dialog box, click **Modify**.) The elements of linear dimensions are illustrated below.

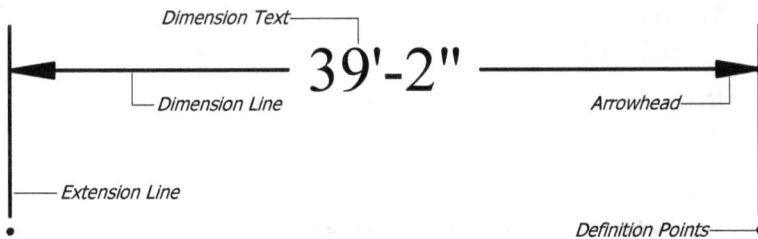

Dimension Text

39'-2"

Dimension Line   Arrowhead

Extension Line

Definition Points

Before applying dimensions, set the scale.

1. Like text, hatch patterns, and linetypes, the scale of dimensions is relative to the printed size. Otherwise, the arrowheads and text will be too small to read.

   Set the dimension scale with the **DimScale** command. Use the same scale factor you calculated for text, 142.

   Command: **dimscale**
   Enter new value for DIMSCALE <0'-1">: **142**

   TIP The size of dimension text is controlled by **Style** and is unaffected by the **DimStyle** scale factor.

2. Create a new layer called **Dims** (black, continuous), and then make it current. Freeze unnecessary layers, such as Text, Lawn, Plants, and Pond.

3. Because dimensioning often takes place at intersections, turn on **INTersection** object snap mode, as follows:

   Command: **osnap**
   Object snap modes: **int**

Dimensioning the Yard

DimLinear
DimContinue

Let's begin dimensioning!

1. To begin dimensioning the drawing, select **Linear** from the **Dimension** menu.

   Command: _dimlinear

   The **DimLinear** command draws horizontal, vertical, and rotated linear dimensions, depending on how you move the cursor:

   Horizontal — select two points roughly horizontal, and AutoCAD LT draws a horizontal dimension.

   Vertical — select two points roughly vertical, and AutoCAD LT draws a vertical dimension.

   Rotated — enter **R** at the prompt to force rotated dimensions.

2. Dimension the lower lot line, as follows:

   Specify first extension line origin or <select object>: *(Pick intersection near #1.)*
   Specify second extension line origin: *(Pick #2.)*

   Specify dimension line location or [Mtext/Text/Angle/Horizontal/Vertical/Rotated]: *(Pick below the lot line at #3.)*
   Dimension text = 116'

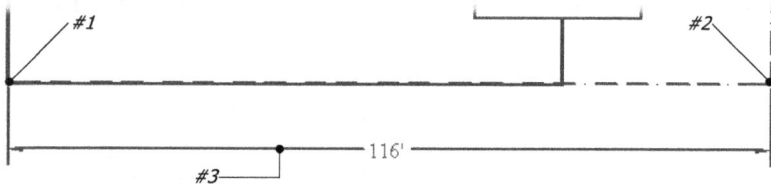

AutoCAD LT knows the length of the line, and places it for you.

TIPS AutoCAD LT automatically draws all the components of dimensions: the two extension lines, the dimension line, the arrowheads, and the dimension text.

Dimensions are attached to geometric features on objects. The *dimpoints* (short for "dimension points") are no longer used, nor is layer "DimPoints."

3. Try another horizontal dimension. This time, use AutoCAD LT's *object* dimensioning. In this method, you pick the object (the top lot line), and AutoCAD LT dimensions it. The method uses just two picks instead of three.

    Press the Spacebar to repeat the **DimLinear** command:

    Command: *(Press Spacebar to repeat command.)* _dimlinear
    Specify first extension line origin or <select object>: *(Press **Enter** to select object.)*
    Select object to dimension: *(Pick property line at #4.)*

    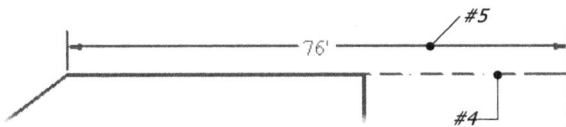

    Specify dimension line location or
    [Mtext/Text/Angle/Horizontal/Vertical/Rotated]: *(Pick #5.)*
    Dimension text = 76': *(Press **Enter** to accept the distance calculated by AutoCAD LT.)*

4. Continue the horizontal dimension with the **DimContinue** command. From the **Dimension** menu, select **Continue**.

    Command: _dimcontinue
    Specify a second extension line origin or [Undo/Select] <Select>: *(Pick #6.)*
    Dimension text = 40' *(Press **Enter** to accept the calculated distance.)*
    Specify a second extension line origin or [Undo/Select] <Select>: *(Press **Enter** to end the command.)*

    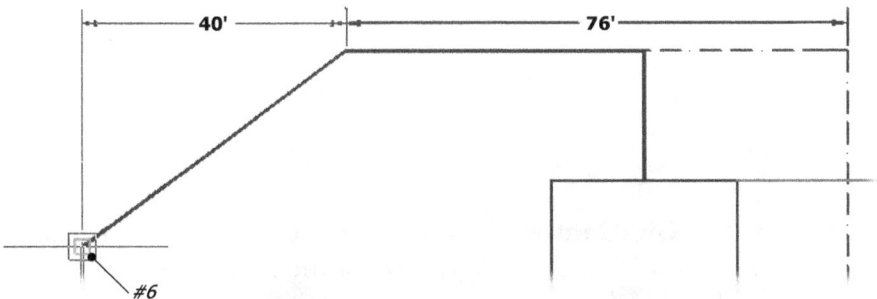

Because AutoCAD LT knows where the last extension line was, it only needs to know the location of the next extension line to draw in the second dimension.

Vertical and Baseline Dimensions

DimBaseline

As noted earlier, the **DimLinear** command draws vertical dimensions in addition to horizontal dimensions. When you move the cursor in a vertical direction, AutoCAD LT knows to draw the dimension vertically.

1. To draw vertical dimensions, select **Dimension | Linear**.

   Command: _dimlinear
   Specify first extension line origin or <select object>: *(Pick #7.)*
   Specify second extension line origin: *(Pick #8.)*

   Specify dimension line location or [Mtext/Text/Angle]: *(Pick #9.)*
   Dimension text = 20'

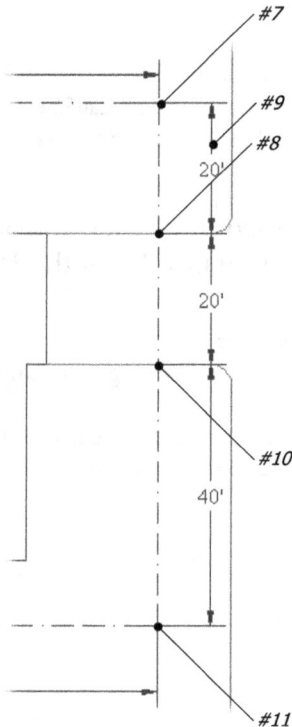

2. Use the **DimContinue** command to continue the vertical dimensions along the right side of the lot at points 10 and 11.

   Command: **dimcontinue**
   Specify a second extension line origin or [Undo/Select] <Select>: *(Pick #10.)*

Dimension text = 20'
Specify a second extension line origin or [Undo/Select] <Select>: *(Pick #11.)*
Dimension text = 40'
Specify a second extension line origin or [Undo/Select] <Select>: *(Press Enter.)*

3.   A variation on the **DimContinue** command is the **DimBaseline** command. Rather than continue a dimension from the previous extension line, **DimBaseline** dimensions from the original extension line.

   To see how it works, first place a vertical dimension:
   a. Place the first extension line at #12.
   b. Place the second extension line at #13.
   c. Place the dimension line at #14.

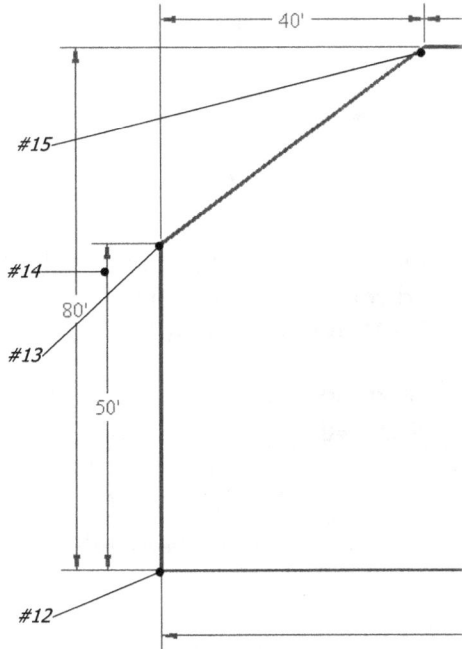

4.   Now try the **DimBaseline** command. From the **Dimension** menu, select **Baseline**.

   Command: _dimbaseline
   Specify a second extension line origin or [Undo/Select] <Select>: *(Pick #15.)*
   Dimension text = 80'
   Specify a second extension line origin or [Undo/Select] <Select>: *(Press Enter.)*

Pressing **Enter** exits the command. The **DimBaseline** and **DimContinue** commands work with all linear and angular dimensions.

TIPS The **Text** option of dimensioning commands lets you modify or replace the dimension text.

The **MText** option lets you substitute paragraphs of text for the dimension text. When you select the option, it displays the same mtext editor shown earlier in this chapter.

AutoCAD highlights the measured dimension text. You can add other text in front and behind it. You could, for instance, add **Fence length =** and AutoCAD LT places **Fence length = 20'** as the dimension text.

Finally, the **Angle** option allows you to rotate dimension text. For example, enter:

Specify angle of dimension text: **45**

AutoCAD LT rotates the dimension text by 45 degrees.

Aligned and Radial Dimensions

DimAligned
DimRadius

So far, you have dimensioned the straight and angled portions of the lot line with horizontal and vertical dimension commands. To dimension an angled line, you use the **DimAligned** command.

1. From the **Dimension** menu, select **Aligned**.

   Command: _dimaligned
   Specify first extension line origin or <select object>: *(Pick #16.)*
   Specify second extension line origin: *(Pick #17.)*

   Specify dimension line location or [Mtext/Text/Angle]: *(Pick #18.)*
   Dimension text = 49'-4$^1/_2$"

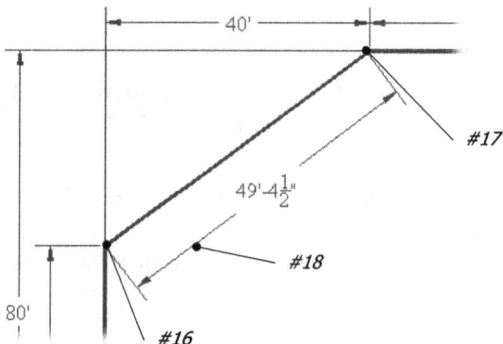

The dimension in your drawing may be different, depending on how the angled line was drawn.

2. So far, all dimensioning commands have presented pretty much the same prompts. Now try one that's a bit different.

    The **DimRadius** command dimensions arcs and circles. From the **Dimension** menu, select **Radius**. (Zoom in for a closer look, if necessary.)

    Command: _dimradius
    Select arc or circle: *(Pick #19.)*
    Dimension text = 3'
    Specify dimension line location or [Mtext/Text/Angle]: *(Pick #20.)*

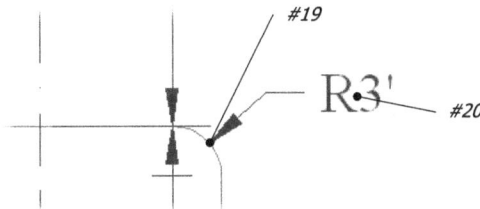

    The **DimRadius** command gives you some flexibility as to where you want to place the dimension text. As you move the cursor, AutoCAD LT ghosts in the leader and text.

3. Save your work, and then print out a copy.

Summary

This chapter showed how to add text and dimensions to drawings — completing the tutorial. The following chapters describe other topics in greater details, including block libraries, attribute data, isometric drafting, and 2D regions.

Notes

Chapter 8

Creating Block Libraries and Attributes

In This Chapter

- Creating libraries of blocks (symbols)
- Defining attributes (data)
- Attaching attributes to blocks
- Understanding DesignCenter and tool palettes
- Creating drawings made of (mostly) blocks
- Manipulating dynamic blocks

Earlier in this book, you learned how to draw and edit accurate drawings, including creating blocks to quickly place many symbols. In this chapter, you learn how AutoCAD LT can create custom blocks with embedded data (called "attributes"). In addition, you work with the AutoCAD DesignCenter to manage libraries of blocks.

There are two reasons for using blocks in drawings:

- Blocks make you a faster drafter; if you are a faster drafter, you complete more work in the same amount of time — or finish work sooner.
- Blocks store attributes, which consist of customized data.

(AutoCAD LT uses the term "block" for symbols. Other CAD software calls them "components," "cells," "shapes," or "parts.")

Key Terms

Attributes — text data attached to blocks
Blocks — Autodesk's term for symbols
Donut — solid-filled circles
Insertion points — specify where blocks are inserted in drawings
Prompts — attribute prompts displayed by AutoCAD LT during block insertions
Tags — identify attributes by name
Unit size — blocks drawn to fit a 1x1-unit area
Values — default values of attribute data

Commands

Command	Shortcut	Menu Selection
AdCenter	Ctrl+2	Tools | DesignCenter
Arc	a	Draw | Arc
AttDef	at	Draw | Block | Define Attributes
Donut	do	Draw | Donut
DSettings	ds	Tools | Drafting Settings
Rectangle	rec	Draw | Rectangle
ToolPalettes	Ctrl+3	Tools | Tool Palettes Window

As this and previous chapters show, it is much faster to add blocks to drawings than it is to draw symbols from scratch each time you need one.

You could use the **Copy** command to repeat symbols, but it is more efficient to insert blocks than to copy them. A drawing that uses blocks takes up less disk space.

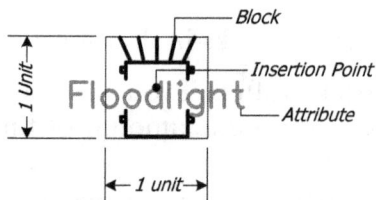

Later in this chapter, you learn how to create attributes, add them to the blocks, and store the blocks on disk. When it comes time to produce bills of material in the next chapter, you'll see how AutoCAD LT produces lists of all blocks in drawings; you can't do that with the **Copy** command!

Before You Begin

The example in the chapter creates a drawing of part of the electrical schematic of an antique automobile. If you have repair manuals and other schematic drawings handy, you can use them to reproduce your own schematics with AutoCAD LT.

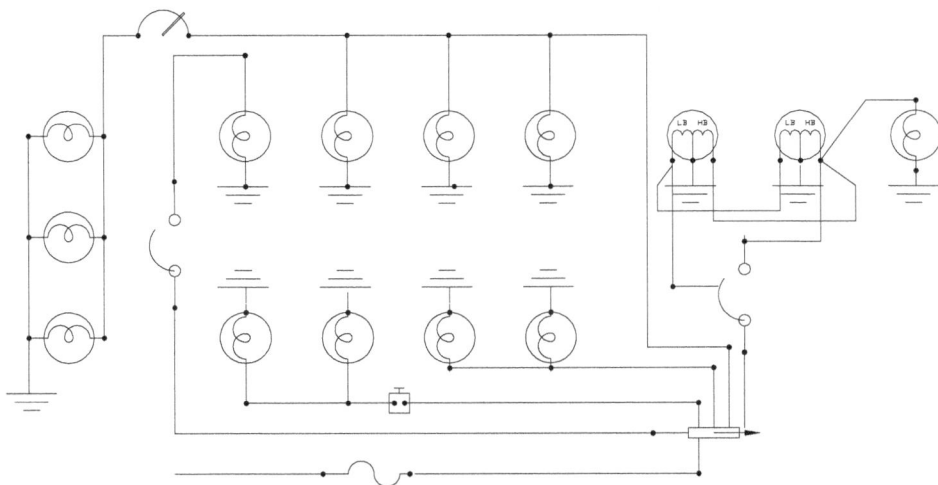

If you'd rather not, follow along with the schematic sketch above, the drawing used by this book.

(Wondering about the automobile this is from? It's adapted from a 1965 Volkswagen Beetle.)

Preparing the Drawing for Blocks

It takes three steps to create drawings that contain custom blocks: creating the custom blocks, saving the blocks to disk, and then creating the drawings by inserting the blocks.

1. Start AutoCAD LT from the Windows **Start** menu, or by double-clicking on its icon in the Windows desktop.

    (If the Start Up dialog box appears, click the **Start from Scratch** button and click **OK**.)

2. Because you will be drawing these blocks to an accuracy of 0.1 units, it makes sense to change the snap spacing.

From the **Tools** menu, select **Drafting Settings**. In the Snap and Grid tab, make these changes:

Snap On (F9)   ✓ (on)
Snap X spacing   **0.1**
Snap Y spacing   **0.1**
Grid On (F7)   ✓ (on)
Grid X spacing   **0.0**
Grid X spacing   **0.0**

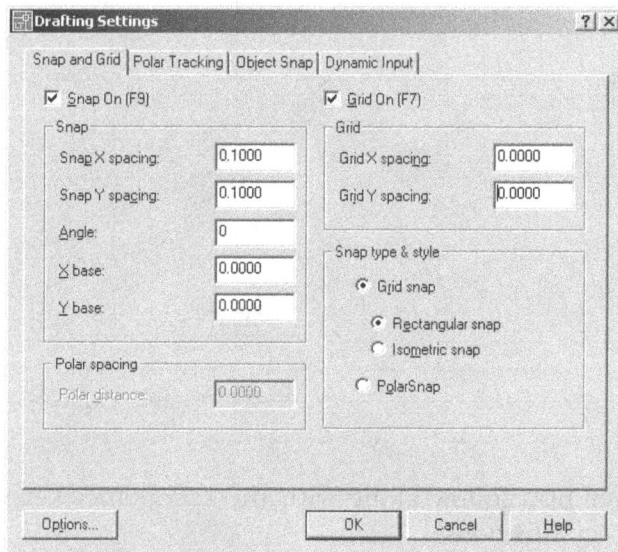

3. Click **OK** when done.

   Notice that the screen fills with a fine grid of dots. (Recall that the limits determine the extents of the grid display.)

4. The blocks have many straight lines, so turn on ortho mode by clicking **ORTHO** on the status bar.

   There is no need for the UCS icon, so turn it off by selecting (paradoxically) **View | Display | UCS Icon | On**.

5. Perform a **Zoom All** to center the drawing on the screen.

6. Use the **Save** command to save the new drawing with the name **Symbols**.

Selecting the Parts

Before drawing the first block, look over the sketch of the schematic. Decide which parts should be converted into blocks. The light bulbs, for instance, are likely candidates, because there are so many of them. Other candidates are the headlamps and the ground symbols.

This is how a CAD drafter would think about the problem:

> Create a block of anything that would be listed in the bill of material, even if it appears just once.

Thus, blocks should also be created of the dome light switch, the fuse, the instrument light dimmer, the light switch, and the brake light switch — even the solder connections.

The following figure shows the blocks needed for the electrical schematic. The small black dots show the connection points for wires.

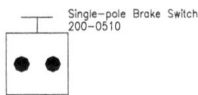

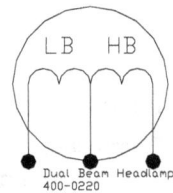

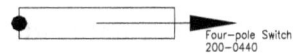

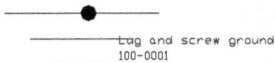

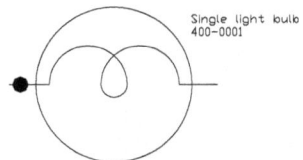

Single-pole Brake Switch
200-0510

Solder Connection
000-0000

Single-pole Dome Switch
200-0020

40 Amp Fuse
300-0040

Lug and screw ground
100-0001

LB   HB

Dual Beam Headlamp
400-0220

80 Ohm Dimmer
500-0080

Four-pole Switch
200-0440

Single light bulb
400-0001

Unit Size Blocks

With the drawing set up, start drawing the blocks.

With rare exceptions, blocks are always drawn at *unit size*. Unit size means that the entire component is drawn within a one-unit square boundary.

This makes it much easier to scale the component when it comes time to place it in the drawing.

Drawing the First Block

Draw | Donut

To create the block library, begin by drawing the easiest block: the symbol for solder connections. The block is a dot, which is best drawn with the **Donut** command, because it creates solid-filled and thick-walled circles.

1. From the **Draw** menu bar, select **Donut**.

2. The donut is 0.1 units in diameter. Solid filled donuts have an inside diameter of zero, as follows:

    ```
    Command: _donut
    Specify inside diameter of donut <0.5000>: 0
    Specify outside diameter of donut <1.0000>: 0.1
    ```

3. AutoCAD LT prompts you to place the donut, as follows:

    ```
    Specify center of donut or <exit>: (Pick anywhere in the screen.)
    Specify center of donut or <exit>: (Press Enter.)
    ```

    Notice that the **Donut** command repeats itself until you exit it by pressing **Enter**.

4. That 0.1-unit donut is tiny. Enlarge the drawing area with the **Zoom Object** command. If the donut has straight sides...

... then use the **Regen** command to smooth its edge.

Defining Attributes

Draw | Block | Define Attributes

With the solder connection block drawn as a donut, you now define the attributes. *Attributes* are customized data that describe blocks, such as the part number and the price. While the drawing shows you how to assemble the electrical system, the attribute list tells you how many parts are needed for the assembly.

In AutoCAD LT, attributes attach only to blocks. It is possible to add data to other kinds of objects, such as line and circles, but the process is difficult, because you have to work with *xdata* (extended entity data) and be familiar with programming languages.

Just as blocks are graphical descriptions, attributes are textual descriptions. A single block can contain one or more attributes. Graphical data, such as images or other blocks, cannot be included in attributes.

Attributes can describe the block's part number, manufacturer, price, and any other text-based information you want to include. These attributes can have descriptive labels, such as "Product name," "Manufacturer," "Model number," "Stock number," "Serial number," and "Material." You could include "Price" as an attribute field; but since prices tend to change, it is better to deal with the price later in the spreadsheet program. Instead, use a price code.

> **TIP** You may be familiar with database software, where each record has one or more fields. In AutoCAD LT, an *attribute* (or "field" in database terminology) has up to 255 characters. Each *block* (or "record" in databases) can store up to 255 attributes — to a maximum of 64KB of data. It is rare that you will ever need to take advantage of that much space.

1. Attributes are created with the **AttDef** command (short for "attribute definition"). From the **Draw** menu, select **Block | Define Attributes**. AutoCAD LT displays the Attribute Definition dialog box.

    Although the dialog box has a number of fields to fill in, you work with just five: the Attribute section, the Insertion Point, and Height.

2. Enter data in the Attribute section as follows:
    Tag: **Product**
    Prompt: **Product**
    Value: **Solder Connection**

3. Set the **Height** (of the text) to a small, unobtrusive value, such as **0.01**.

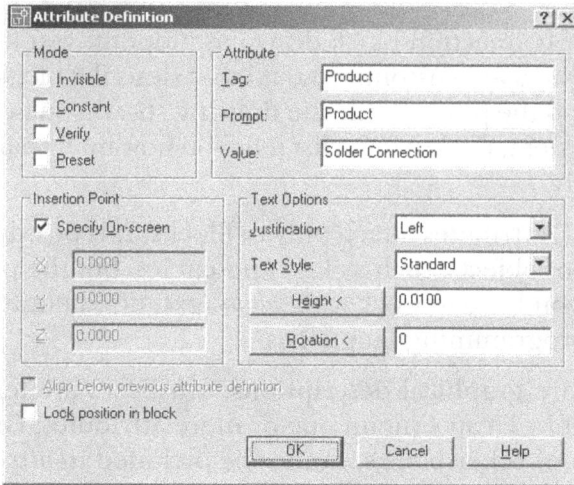

4. The *insertion point* is the spot in the drawing where the attribute text starts. On or near the block is a logical location.

   For the insertion point, click **Specify On-screen**. Later, after clicking OK, AutoCAD LT will prompt you for the location of the insertion point. Place the attribute data to the right of the connection block.

5. Click **OK**.

   AutoCAD LT prompts you to locate the attribute:

   Specify start point: *(Pick a point to the right of the donut.)*

   AutoCAD LT shows the attribute text in all uppercase letters.

Adding Additional Attributes

Add a second attribute directly below the first.

1. Press the Spacebar to repeat the **AttDef** command:

Terms Used with Attributes

AutoCAD LT uses three terms to define the parts of attributes: *tag*, *prompt*, and *value*.

Tags — identifiers used by AutoCAD LT (and you) to identify the attribute, such as "Price." (Think of baggage tags that identify your luggage.) The name of the tag can be up to 255 characters long but must contain no spaces.

Prompts — prompt text AutoCAD LT displays when you later place the block in drawings. It's a reminder of the attribute's purpose, such as "Enter price:." The prompt can be up to 255 characters long and may contain spaces for legibility. Do not include a colon (:) at the end, because AutoCAD LT adds it for you.

Values — default values displayed when you later place the block in the drawing. Values are typically common default values, thus saving you keystrokes upon inserting attributed blocks. Values can be up to 255 characters long, and are displayed by AutoCAD LT in angle brackets, such as:

> Price <0.00>:

The default value can be anything, from specific numbers to *filler* text. Fillers remind you (and other users) of the size and type for the field. For example, "99999" suggests a five-digit number, while "AAA-999" suggests three characters, a dash, and three digits.

```
Command: (Press Spacebar.)
_attdef
```

And the Attribute Definition dialog box reappears.

2. Click the check box next to **Align below previous attribute definition**. This ensures the second attribute lines up cleanly below the first.

> ☑ <u>A</u>lign below previous attribute definition

3. Fill in the following data in the Attribute section:

    Tag: **Stockno**
    Prompt: **Stock No.**
    Value: **000-0000**

    Ensure the tag name "Stockno" is a single word, with no spaces.

4. Click **OK**.

AutoCAD LT adds the second attribute directly below the first; no need to line it up manually!

PRODUCT
STOCKNO

Notice that the attributes are identified by their *tag* names "PRODUCT" and "STOCKNO." This changes when the attributes are combined with the donut to create a block, as we see next.

Combining Objects and Attributes into Blocks

You now have a donut and two attributes. The next step is to link the donut and attributes together in a single block. This is done with the **Block** command.

1. From the **Draw** menu, select **Block | Make**.

2. When the Block Definition dialog box appears, enter a name for the block:

   Name: **connect**

3. AutoCAD LT needs to know which objects will be part of the block.

   Click the **Select objects** button, and then select the donut and attributes using Crossing selection mode:

PRODUCT
STOCKNO

Select objects: **c**
Specify first corner: *(Pick a point.)*
Specify opposite corner: *(Pick another point.)*
3 found Select objects: *(Press **Enter** to return to the dialog box.)*

4.   The *base point* is the spot where the block will be inserted in drawings. When deciding on the base point for blocks, pick a convenient spot, such as the center of the block or a connecting point.

For this block, change the base point from the default (0,0,0) to the center of the donut.

In the Base Point section, click **Pick Point**, and then select the center of the donut:

Specify insertion base point: *(Pick center of donut.)*

5.   In the Objects section, turn on **Delete**. This erases the original objects from view but retains them (invisibly) in block form.

6.   Because the solder connections will always be round, turn on **Scale uniformly**.

If you wish, add text to **Description**, such as **Solder Connection**.

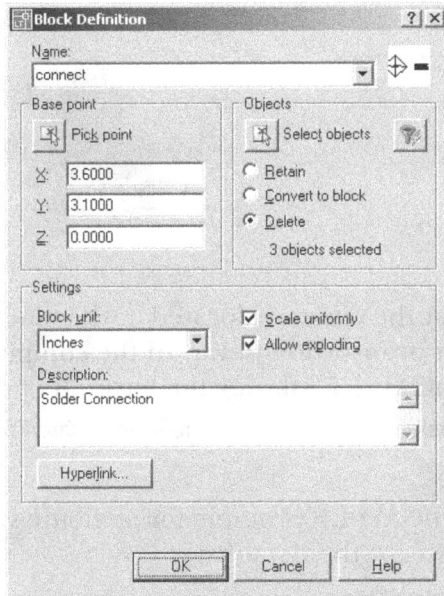

7.   Click **OK**, and then save the drawing with **Ctrl+S**.

Notice that the donut and attribute text disappear. Don't worry! AutoCAD LT has stored the donut as a *block definition* called "Connect" in the drawing's database. You bring it back later.

Inserting Blocks with Attributes

Insert | Block

Earlier in this book, you placed blocks with the **Insert** command. To see
how attributes work, use the command for the Connect block.

1. From the **Insert** menu, select **Block**

2. In the Insert dialog box, check that Name is "Connect."

    Turn on or off the following **Specify On-screen** options:

    Insertion point   ✓ *(on)*
    Scale   *(off; scale = 1)*
    Rotation   *(off; angle = 0)*

    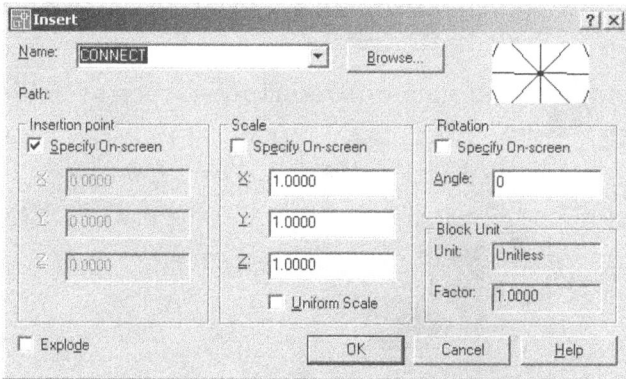

3. Click **OK**.

    Notice that the cursor is located at the block's center, its
    base point or insertion point. In the command prompt
    area, AutoCAD LT asks for the location of the block:

    Specify insertion point or [Basepoint/Scale/Rotate/PScale/PRotate]: *(Pick a
    point.)*

4. When AutoCAD LT prompts for attribute values, press
    Enter to accept the defaults:

    Enter attribute values
    Stock No. <000-0000>: *(Press **Enter**.)*
    Product <Solder Connection>: *(Press **Enter**.)*

    AutoCAD prompts for attributes in the reverse order
    that they appear in the drawing, strangely enough!

Solder Connection
000-0000

Notice that the attribute values appear next to the solder block.

Alternatives to the Insert Command

In addition to **Insert**, AutoCAD LT has several methods for placing blocks in drawings. The following involve *drag and drop*:

Windows Explorer — drag and drops .dwg files from Windows Explorer into the drawing. AutoCAD LT inserts them as blocks. (When the .dwg file is dragged onto AutoCAD LT's title bar instead, the file is opened as a new drawing.)

DesignCenter — accesses blocks from other drawings, and then drag and drops into drawings.

Tool Palettes — populates categorized palettes with blocks, and then drag and drops them into drawings.

In addition, there is the **-Insert** command, which prompts you for insertion options at the command line.

In the following sections, we look at how the DesignCenter and tool palettes work.

AutoCAD DesignCenter

Tools | DesignCenter

An alternative to the **Insert** command's dialog box is DesignCenter. It is a centralized window that allows sharing of blocks, linetypes, text styles, and other named objects between drawings, no matter their location — on your computer, other networked computers, and the Internet.

(DesignCenter's predecessor was known as "Content Explorer," and could place blocks and hatches only.)

Touring the DesignCenter GUI

To see what it looks like and how it works, open DesignCenter by selecting **DesignCenter** from the **Tools** menu. Alternatively, press **Ctrl+2** or enter the **adc** alias at the 'Command:' prompt. It may take a few seconds for the DesignCenter to appear. (To close the DesignCenter, press **Ctrl+2** a second time.)

DesignCenter displays data in an Explorer-like tree. It shows data from four (and sometimes five) sources: Folders, Open Drawings, History, DC Online, and optionally Custom Content. Click the tabs to display different views:

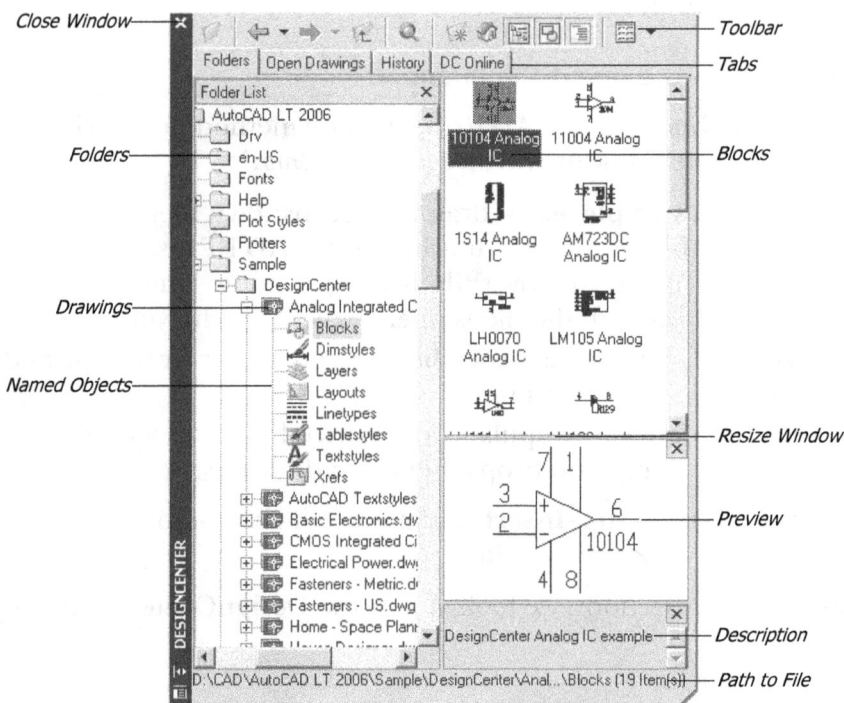

Desktop displays all drives, folders, and AutoCAD LT-related files on your computer. Like Explorer, DesignCenter can view drives and files located on other computers connected to yours through local networks and the Internet.

Open Drawings displays drawings and their content currently open in AutoCAD LT. Recall that AutoCAD LT can open more than one drawing at a time.

Custom Content is available only when certain ObjectARX applications are running; otherwise, you don't see the tab.

History displays up to 120 of the documents you most recently viewed with DesignCenter.

DC Online accesses Autodesk's Web site with block libraries that are free to download.

The toolbar performs these tasks:

Load displays a file dialog box for opening .dwg drawing and .pat hatch pattern files from your computer, the network, or the Internet.

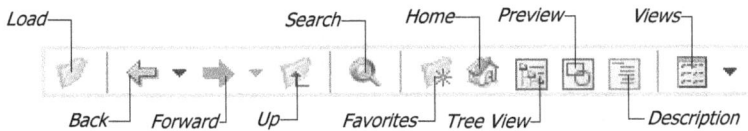

Load— Search— Home— Preview— Views—
Back— Forward— Up— Favorites— Tree View— —Description

Back returns DesignCenter to the previously accessed folder.

Forward returns to the previously, previously accessed folder.

Up moves up one level in the tree. For instance, if you are viewing blocks in a drawing, click this button to view the drawing itself.

Search searches for files on your computer and displays the Search dialog box.

Favorites accesses the \documents and settings\favorites\ autodesk folder, where you can store often-used files.

Home returns DesignCenter to the folder defined by the **AdcNavigate** command.

Tree View toggles the tree view (left-hand pane).

Preview toggles the preview area.

Description toggles the description area.

Views changes the display of icons in the palette; the choices are large icons, small icons, list, and details.

The large icon view is the most useful; the details view is useful only for drawings. In details view, you can click the headers — Name, File Size, and Type — to sort the list alphabetically; click a second time to sort in reverse order.

Shortcut Menus

The DesignCenter has a host of shortcut menus whose content differs depending on where you right-click. The most important shortcut menu is the one that appears when you right-click items in the right-hand pane, such as the names of blocks.

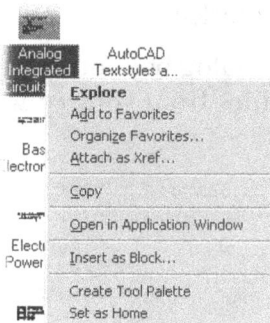

Explore opens the tree, giving you access to the drawing's blocks, dimstyles, layers, layouts, linetypes, text styles, and xrefs — if any.

Add to Favorites adds the drawing to the list of favorites.

Organize Favorites opens an Explorer-like window to the \favorites\autodesk folder, where you can move and delete shortcuts.

Attach as Xref displays the External Reference dialog box, which allows you to specify options for attaching the xref to the drawing.

Copy copies the selected items to the Windows clipboard. They can be pasted in another drawing with the Edit | Paste command.

Open in Application Window opens the drawing in its own AutoCAD LT window.

Insert as Block displays the Insert dialog box, which allows you to specify the block insertion parameters. This option appears only with blocks and xrefs. (You can also just drag blocks into the drawing; AutoCAD LT assumes default values.)

Create Tool Palette creates a palette of all blocks found in this folder or drawing.

Set as Home makes this the default folder for the **Home** button.

Inserting Blocks with DesignCenter

Use DesignCenter to insert the Connect block in the drawing. Start a new drawing, and then ensure DesignCenter is open.

1. Click the **Open Drawing**s tab.

2. Navigate to the symbols.dwg file.

3.   Open symbols.dwg by clicking the **+** sign.

4.   Select **Blocks**. Notice the Connect block.

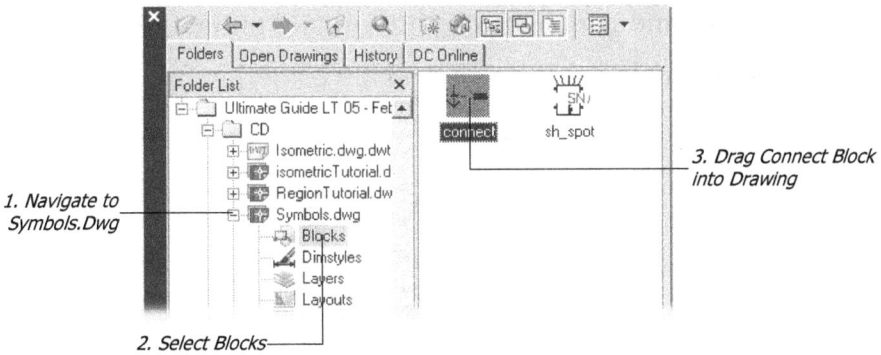

1. Navigate to Symbols.Dwg

2. Select Blocks

3. Drag Connect Block into Drawing

5.   Drag the Connect block into the drawing. Pick any convenient point on the screen, then let go of the mouse button.

6.   Notice that AutoCAD LT displays the Edit Attributes dialog box.

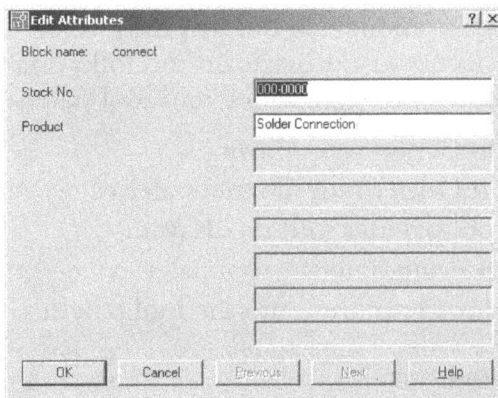

Click **OK** to accept the default attribute values — 000-000 and Solder Connection. Notice that AutoCAD LT draws the connection block accompanied by the words "Solder Connection" and "000-0000."

Tool Palettes

Tools | Tool Palettes Window

In addition to dragging objects from DesignCenter into drawings, you can also drag them to and from the Tool Palettes window. The word "palettes" refers to the numerous tabs on the window.

Tool palettes provide easy access to collections of often-used blocks, hatch patterns, and other drawing elements. To see the tool palettes, press **Ctrl+3**, or select **Tool Palettes Window** from the **Tools** menu. It comes populated with some sample hatch patterns and numerous blocks.

(To close the tool palettes, press **Ctrl+3** a second time.)

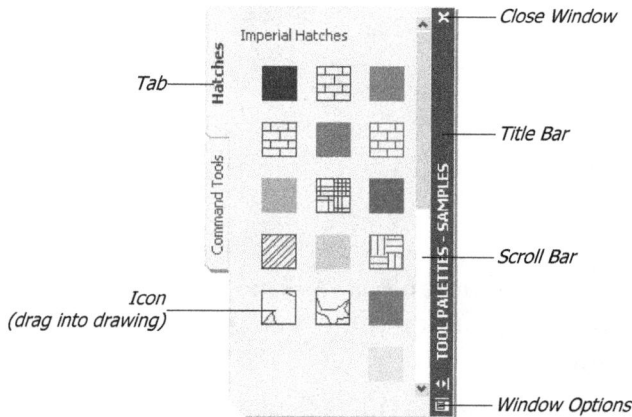

AutoCAD LT does not automatically add the blocks you create to tool palettes. But it is easy enough to do: just drag them from the drawing onto a palette. In fact, you can perform the following dragging operations between drawings, DesignCenter, and tool palettes:

- From DesignCenter into drawings
- From DesignCenter into the tool palettes
- From the tool palettes into the drawing
- From the drawing onto the tool palettes
- From Windows Explorer onto the tool palettes

Adding Blocks to Palettes

The advantage of tool palettes is that they display the same collection of blocks, patterns, etc., in every drawing that you work with. It makes sense to create a new palette for the blocks created in this chapter. Follow these steps to add blocks to new palettes:

1. To create new palettes, right-click a blank area carefully, as illustrated by the figure below.

2. From the shortcut menu, select **New Palette**.

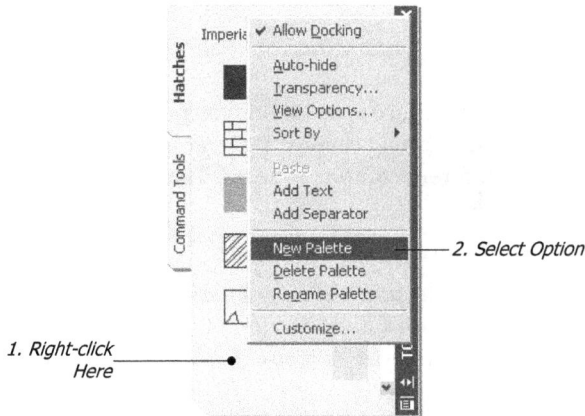

1. Right-click Here

2. Select Option

3. AutoCAD LT creates a new palette, and offers the opportunity to change its name from the uninspiring "New Palette."

    Change the name to **Auto Electrical**.

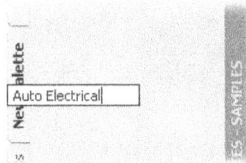

4. Drag the Connect block in a special manner:
    a. Select the block. Notice the highlighting and grips.
    b. Hold down the *right* mouse button.
    c. Drag the block onto the Tool Palette.

    Don't attempt to drag in the normal manner by holding down the left mouse button. AutoCAD may complain that you have to save the drawing first.

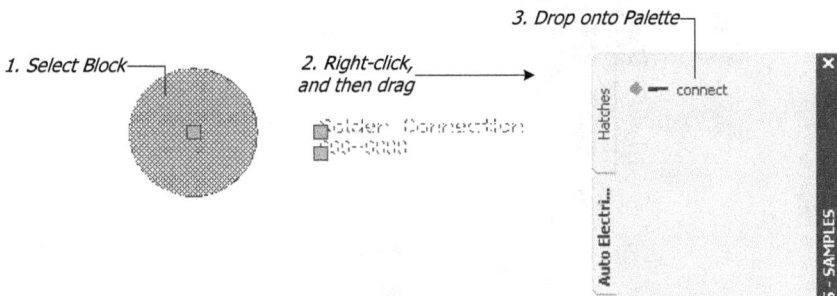

1. Select Block

2. Right-click, and then drag

3. Drop onto Palette

connect

    AutoCAD automatically saves the content of palettes, so no "Save" action is needed.

Organizing Tool Palettes

The tool palettes' user interface is too subtle for my liking, because all its options are "hidden" in shortcut menus. Depending on where you right-click, a shortcut menu with different content appears. That can make it difficult to find specific options.

Options that may be of interest to you include:

Transparency — changes the transparency of the Tool Palette, or keeps it opaque.
Properties — controls the look and function of icons on palettes.
View Options — changes the size of icons, and toggles icons and text.

AutoCAD LT allows you to create large numbers of palettes. But too many becomes unwieldy, and so AutoCAD LT allows you to create *groups* of palettes. Groups organize palettes, limiting the number that are displayed at a time.

The **Customize** command's dialog box creates and modifies groups of palettes.

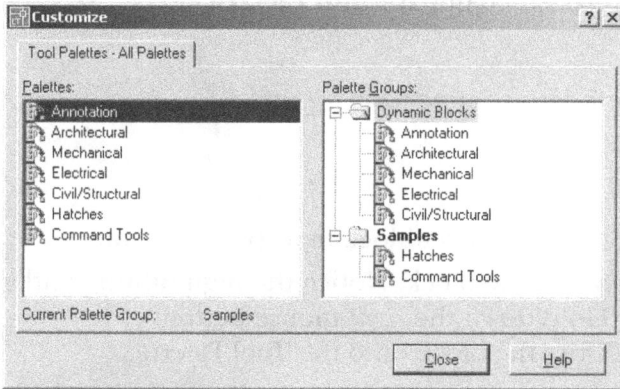

The left pane lists the name of palettes. In the right pane, you create new groups, and then drag palettes from the left pane into the group. When done, click **Close**.

To switch between groups, right-click the Tool Palettes title bar, and then select the group name to show or hide.

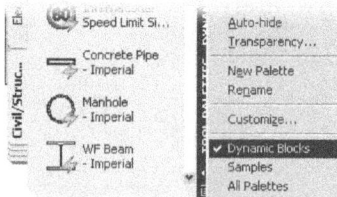

Inserting Blocks from Palettes

With the block on the palette, practice inserting it into drawings:

1. In the Tool Palettes, select the tab containing the blocks of interest.

2. Drag the block into the drawing, dropping it in the location you want it placed. It is helpful to have snap or osnap turned on for precise placements.

    (If the block has attributes, AutoCAD LT displays the Edit Attributes dialog box. Make the appropriate changes, and then click **OK**.)

    The block appears in the drawing. It's that easy. AutoCAD LT even figures out the correct scale.

Creating Additional Blocks

There are eight more blocks that need to be created for the automotive electrical schematic. Below, I've suggested their names and attributes, along with tips for drawing the bits and pieces. The most complex is the headlamp, which is drawn with circles, arcs, lines, and donuts (see illustration).

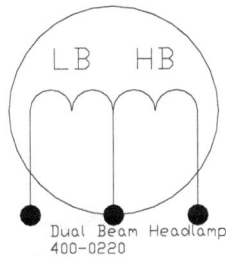

Dual Beam Headlamp
400–0220

Here is a way to draw the headlamp symbol:

1. Turn on ortho mode.

    Set snap and grid to **0.1**.

2. Draw a one-inch circle with the **Draw | Circle | Center, Radius** command, setting the radius to **0.5** inches.

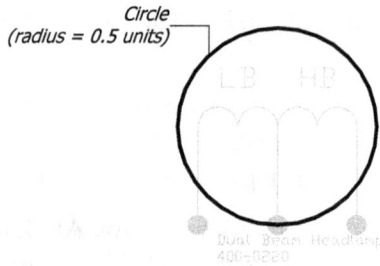

3. Draw one filament arc with the **Draw | Arc | Start, Center, End** command.

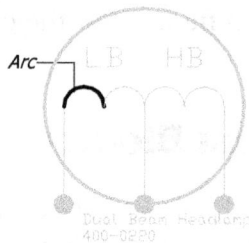

4. Use the **Draw | Line** command to extend one end of the filament to the base of the lamp.

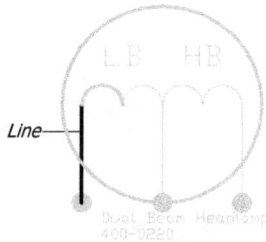

5. Place a **0.1** diameter donut at the end of the line with the **Draw | Donut** command.

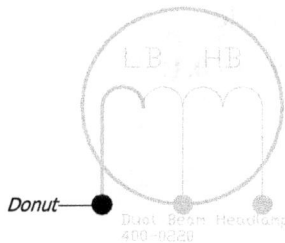

6. Use the **Modify | Mirror** command to make a mirrored copy of the line, donut, and arc to the left.

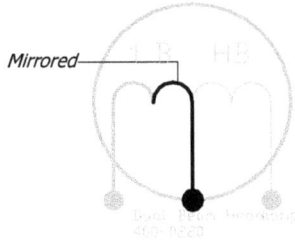

7. Repeat the **Mirror** command to make a second copy of the filament to the left.

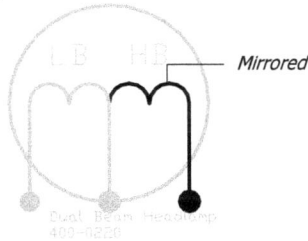

8. Use **Draw | Single Line Text** to add the **HB** (high beam) and **LB** (low beam) text. Use center justification and a text height of **0.1**.

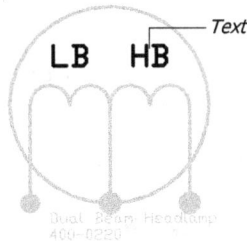

9. Use the **Draw | Block | Define Attributes** command to add the following attributes:

Tag #1:   **Product**
Prompt: **Product**
Value: **Dual Beam Headlamp**

Tag #2:   **Stockno**
Prompt: **Stock No.**
Value: **400-0220**

10. Finally, use the **Draw | Block | Make** command to convert the drawing into a block called **HLamp**.

Select the middle donut as the insertion point.

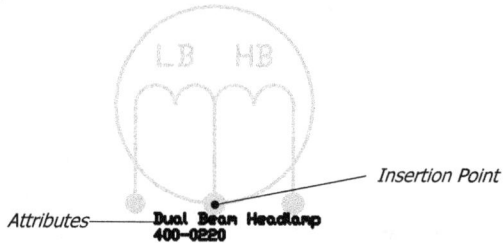

The Remaining Symbols

These instructions explain how to create the seven remaining symbols.

1. Draw the four-pole switch with the **Draw | Rectangle** command, 1" x 0.2" in size.

Add a line with the **Line** command.

Draw the 0.3-long arrowhead with the **PLine** command. Set the starting width to 0.0 and the ending width to 0.2.

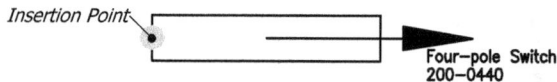

The block name and attributes are:

Block name: **Lswitch**

Tag #1:   **Product**
Prompt: **Product**
Value: **Four-pole Switch**

Tag #2:   **Stockno**
Prompt: **Stock No.**
Value: **200-0440**

2. Draw the single-pole brake switch with the **Rectangle** command, with sides 0.4 units long.

Finish with the **Line** and **Donut** commands.

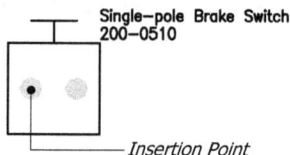

The block name and attributes are:

Block name: **Bswitch**

Tag #1:   **Product**
Prompt: **Product**
Value: **Single-pole Brake Switch**

Tag #2:   **Stockno**
Prompt: **Stock No.**
Value: **200-0510**

3.   Draw the 40-amp fuse with two arcs and two lines.

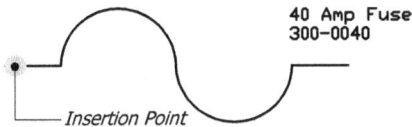

40 Amp Fuse
300-0040

Insertion Point

The block name and attributes are:

Block name: **Fuse40**

Tag #1:   **Product**
Prompt: **Product**
Value: **40 Amp Fuse**

Tag #2:   **Stockno**
Prompt: **Stock No.**
Value: **300-0040**

4.   Draw the single-pole dome switch with an arc, donut, two circles, and lines.

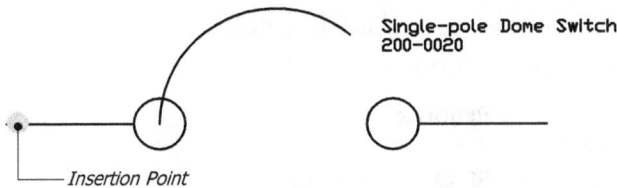

Single-pole Dome Switch
200-0020

Insertion Point

The block name and attributes are:

Block name: **DomeSw**

Tag #1:   **Product**
Prompt: **Product**
Value: **Single-pole Dome Switch**

Tag #2:   **Stockno**
Prompt: **Stock No.**
Value: **200-0020**

5. Draw the single light bulb with a circle, arcs, lines, and donut.

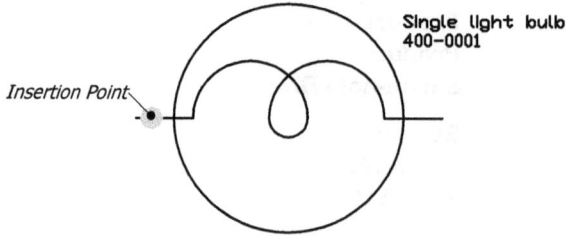

The block name and attributes are:

Block name: **LBulb**

Tag #1:   **Product**
Prompt: **Product**
Value: **Single light bulb**

Tag #2:   **Stockno**
Prompt: **Stock No.**
Value: **400-0001**

6. Draw the 80-ohm dimmer with an arc, rectangle, and donut.

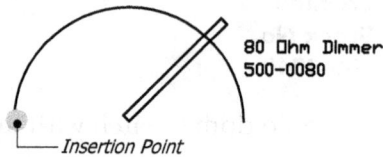

The block name and attributes are:

Block name: **Ldimmer**

Tag #1:   **Product**
Prompt: **Product**
Value: **80 Ohm Dimmer**

Tag #2:   **Stockno**
Prompt: **Stock No.**
Value: **500-0080**

7. Draw the lug and screw ground with three lines and a donut.

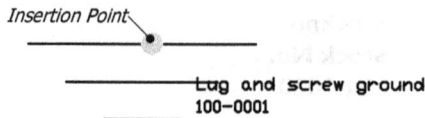

The block name and attributes are:

Block name: **Ground**

Tag #1: **Product**
Prompt: **Product**
Value: **Lug and screw ground**

Tag #2: **Stockno**
Prompt: **Stock No.**
Value: **100-0001**

8. Finally, save the Symbols drawing. For easy reference to your new symbol library, plot the drawing.

    (The symbols.dwg file is available on the book's resource page.)

Drawing the Electrical Schematic

With the electrical blocks stored on disk, you can create the drawing of the automobile electrical schematic.

1. With **File | New**, start a new drawing named **Electric**.

    Make sure ortho mode is turned on; set snap to **0.1** and grid to **0.5**.

2. Make sure the DesignCenter is open with the **Tools | DesignCenter** command.

    Click the **Symbols.dwg** icon. (The drawing should still be open in AutoCAD LT.)

3. Click **Blocks** to display the blocks in the Symbols drawing.

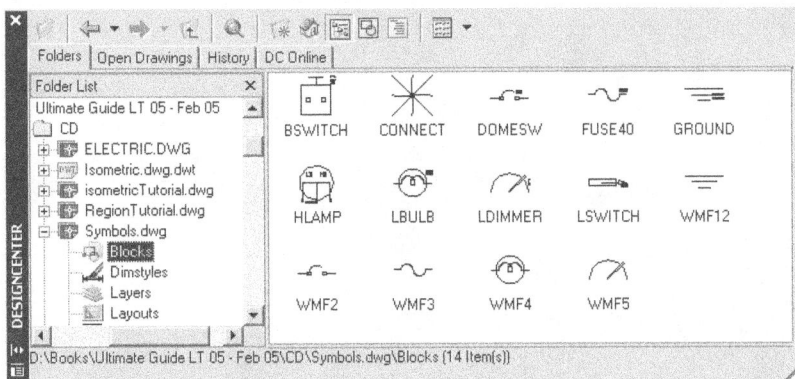

4. Drag blocks into the drawing, placing them in roughly the correct location. (For now, do not drag the Connect block into the drawing.)

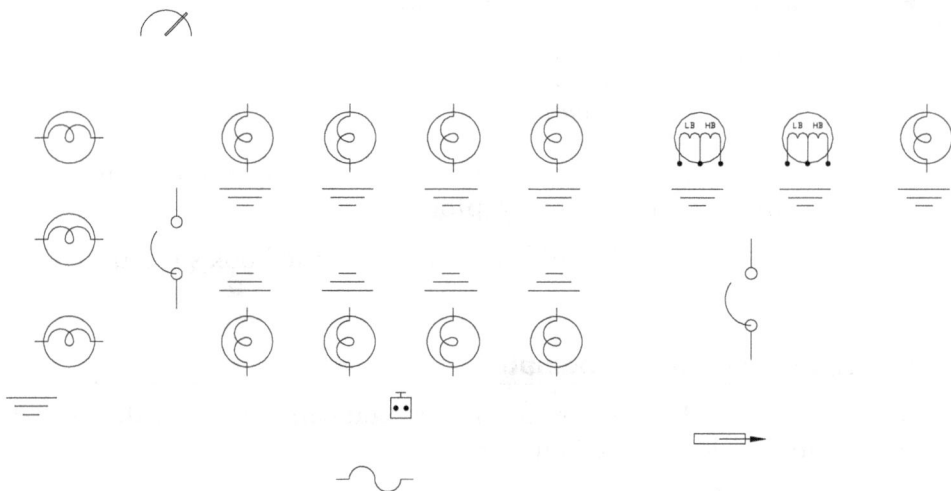

5. Once all the blocks are positioned, turn on **ENDpoint** object snap.

6. Use the **Draw | Line** command to connect the blocks, as shown below.

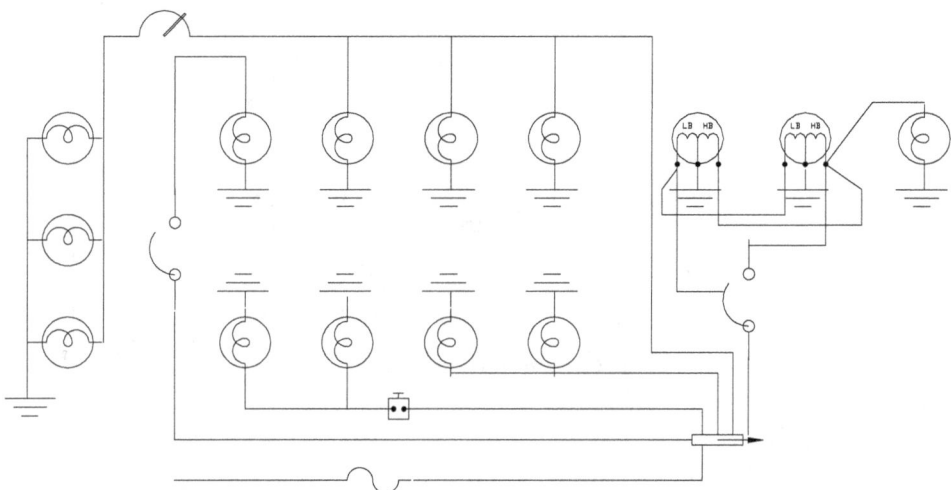

7. Complete the electrical connections by placing the Connect block.

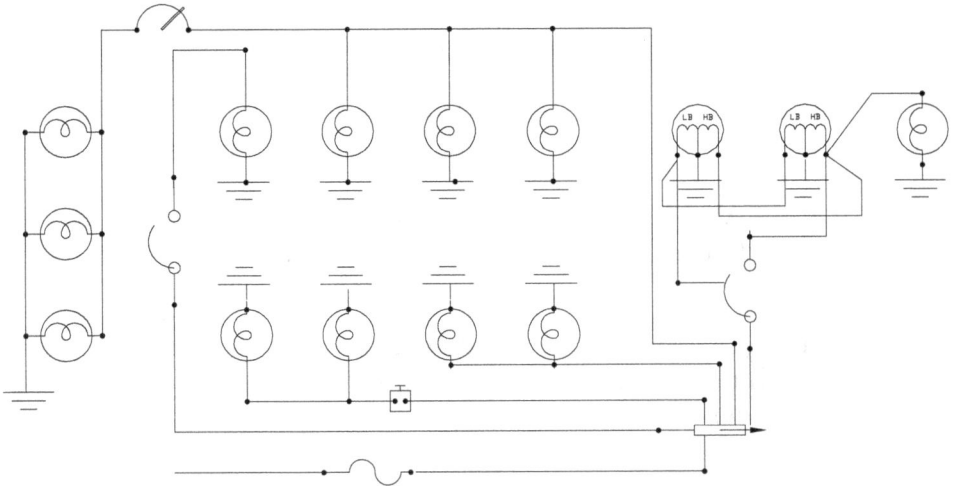

8. Add descriptive text to the schematic with the **Text** command.

9. Finally, save your work.

Dynamic Blocks

Dynamic blocks are an exciting form of block new to AutoCAD LT 2006. These are blocks that change in a predefined manner.

You can make some changes to normal blocks (which I'll call "static"): rotate at any angle, scale to any size, modify attributes, and so on. But dynamic blocks can limit rotation to specific angles, stretch to specific lengths, and even change shapes entirely.

But there's a problem with dynamic blocks: AutoCAD LT cannot create them. That is possible only in big brother AutoCAD 2006's Block Editor environment. AutoCAD LT can, however, work with dynamic blocks.

Working with Dynamic Blocks

Not all dynamic blocks have all capabilities; the functions are defined by the user. Dynamic blocks use grips with specific shapes to identify the permitted functions.

Grip	Name	Grip Manipulation
	Alignment	Aligns dynamic blocks with objects (within 2D planes)
	Flip	Flips dynamic blocks (mirrors)
	Linear	Moves dynamic blocks along defined directions or axes
	Lookup	Displays lists of items that change dynamic blocks
	Rotation	Rotates dynamic blocks about axes
	Standard	Moves dynamic blocks in any direction within 2D planes

Because AutoCAD LT cannot create dynamic blocks, let's look at some of the ones included as samples. Start a new drawing, and ensure the Tool Palettes is open.

1. Drag the **Aluminum Window** dynamic block from the Architectural palette into the drawing. (Dynamic blocks are identified by a lightning icon.)

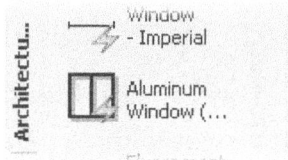

2. When the block is in the drawing, select it. Notice the two triangular grips. These stretch dynamic blocks by predefined increments.

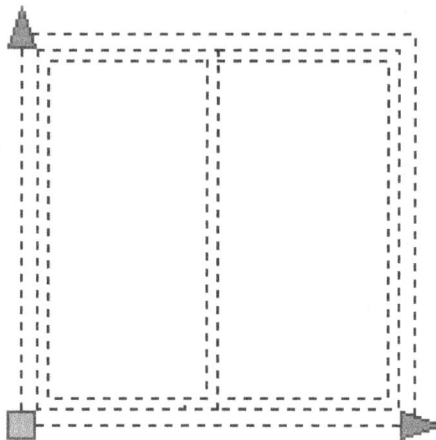

3. Click one of the triangle grips. Notice it turns red, and that increment markers appear. These indicate the predetermined sizes to which the dynamic block will stretch.

Stretch Grip⎯▲

Standard Grip⎯▣

Increment Indicators⎯|

Stretch Grip
Resizing Window

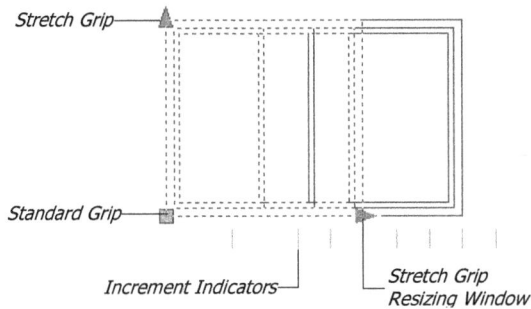

4. Drag the grip. Notice that the window changes its size in discrete increments. Notice also that you cannot stretch the window wider (or narrower) than preset limits allow.

5. As an example of a complex dynamic block, drag the **Door** symbol from the Architectural palette, and then select it. Notice that it has six special grips.

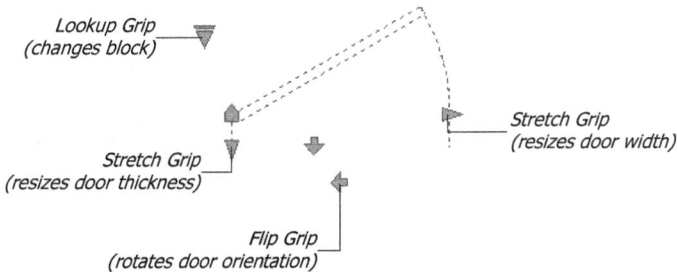

Lookup Grip
(changes block)

Stretch Grip
(resizes door thickness)

Stretch Grip
(resizes door width)

Flip Grip
(rotates door orientation)

6. Click the lookup grip. Notice the shortcut menu of choices.

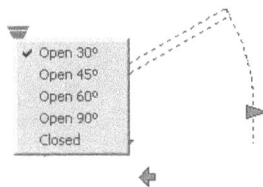

✓ Open 30°
Open 45°
Open 60°
Open 90°
Closed

7. Experiment with selecting different kinds of door openings.

Summary

In this chapter, you learned about adding attributes to blocks and numerous methods of inserting blocks into drawings.

The electrical schematic tutorial continues in the next chapter, where you learn how to extract the attribute data to a spreadsheet and then place it in the drawing as a table.

Notes

Chapter 9

Bills of Material

In This Chapter
- Exporting attributes from drawings to spreadsheets
- Creating templates for formatting attribute data
- Importing spreadsheets into drawings

In the last chapter, you learned how to create custom symbol libraries with AutoCAD LT. In this chapter, you learn how to extract the attribute information with AutoCAD LT's attribute extraction command.

Attribute Extraction

In the last chapter, you created the Electric drawing of an automobile electrical schematic. The drawing contains many components: headlamps, fuse, several light bulbs, and quite a few ground and solder connections. You could count the components by hand, but it's possible you would miscount them.

It's faster and more accurate to let AutoCAD LT do the counting. This process is called "attribute extraction."

Key Terms

Attribute extraction — exports attribute data to files
Template files — defines formats of attribute export files

Abbreviations

CDF	Comma-delimited format
DXF	Drawing interchange format
SDF	Space-delimited format
TXT	Extension for an ASCII text file
XLS	Excel spreadsheet file

Commands

Command	Shortcut	Menu Selection
AttDisp	ad	View | Display | Attribute Display | On
AttExt	Alt+TE	Tools | Attribute Extraction
PasteSpec	pa	Edit | Paste Special

In this chapter, you learn how to extract attributes from a drawing. The process proceeds in three steps:

Step 1. Template: Create an attribute extraction template file.

Step 2. Extract: Set up the AttExt command to extract attributes.

Step 3. Import: Bring the attribute data into a spreadsheet.

Extracting attributes, unfortunately, is one of the toughest areas to learn in AutoCAD LT. (The much easier method of attribute extraction found in AutoCAD is not available in LT.)

AttExt is the attribute extraction command, and it goes back to AutoCAD v2.0 for DOS. It remains unchanged since 1985, except for the addition of a dialog box front end. While other Windows programs boast "coaches" and "wizards" to step you through complicated procedures, AutoCAD LT provides no assistance in this important area of CAD.

Step 1: Creating Template Files

Before AutoCAD LT can extract attribute data, it needs to know two things: which data you want extracted and the format you want the data in.

Unfortunately, AutoCAD LT has no default values; you must create a *template* file, to which the **AttExt** command refers for guidance in these matters.

Here's how you create the template file:

1. Start the Notepad application, the handy little text editor that ships with every copy of Windows. From the taskbar, click **Start**, and then select **Programs | Accessories | Notepad**.

2. Enter the text shown below. Make sure you type the number 0 (zero) and not the letter O in the right column:

BL:NAME	C008000
BL:NUMBER	N003000
PRODUCT	C016000
STOCKNO	C016000

    There must be no blank lines in the file.

    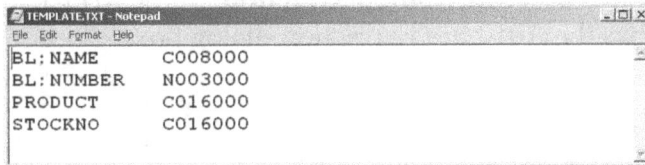

    The text in the template file has the following meaning:

Template Text	Meaning
BL:NAME	Extracts the name of all blocks found in the drawing.
BL:NUMBER	Counts the number of occurrences of each block.
PRODUCT, STOCKNO	Extracts the values of attributes with PRODUCT and STOCKNO tags.
C008000	Formats the data as characters (C), eight characters wide.
N003000	Formats the data as numbers (N), three places wide (003) and with zero decimal places (000).

3. Save the file as **Template.txt**, and then exit Notepad.

Step 2: Extracting Attribute Data

View | Display | Attribute Display | On
Tools | Attribute Extraction

1. Launch AutoCAD LT, and open the Electric.dwg file.

    (If you did not complete the drawing in the last chapter, open the Electric.dwg file from the book's resource page.)

2. To see the attribute text, use the **AttDisp** command. From the **View** menu, select **Display | Attribute Display | On**. This allows you to see *all* the attributes, including those that are invisible. (This step is not necessary for extracting attributes; AutoCAD LT extracts both visible and invisible attributes.)

    > **TIP**   The **AttDisp** command changes the way AutoCAD LT displays attribute text:
    >
    > **On** — displays all attribute text
    > **Off** — displays no attribute text
    > **Normal** — displays attribute text except that set to Invisible mode

3. Let's start the attribute extraction. From the **Tools** menu, select **Attribute Extraction**. AutoCAD LT displays the Attribute Extraction dialog box.

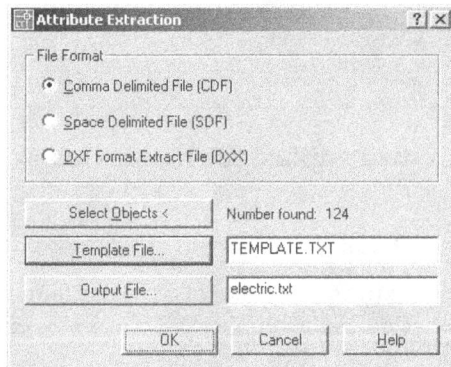

4. Under File Format, you have the choice of three output formats:

    CDF (short for "comma-delimited format") separates values by commas and is best suited for importing attribute data in spreadsheets and word processors.

SDF (short for "space-delimited format") separates values by spaces or tabs, and is best suited for importing data into database programs.

DXF (short for "drawing interchange format") exports data in AutoCAD's own DXF format and is best suited for programmers.

Make sure that the **CDF** radio button is selected.

5. Click **Select Objects**. When AutoCAD LT prompts you, select all objects, as follows:

Select objects: **all**
124 found
Select objects: *(Press **Enter** to return to dialog box.)*

When you specify **All**, AutoCAD LT selects all objects in the entire drawing. This is faster than using Window or Crossing modes. The number of objects listed for your drawing may differ, depending on how it was drawn.

6. Click **Template File**.

In the Template File dialog box, select Template.txt. (This file was created previously, and is also available on the book's resource page.)

7. Click **OK**. AutoCAD LT quickly searches through the drawing, counting each instance of every block. After a second or two, the results are deposited in the Electric.txt file.

8. Open the file with Notepad, as illustrated below:

```
ELECTRIC.txt - Notepad
File  Edit  Format  Help
'CONNECT',  1,'Solder Connectio','000-0000'
'CONNECT',  2,'Solder Connectio','000-0000'
'CONNECT',  3,'Solder Connectio','000-0000'
'CONNECT',  4,'Solder Connectio','000-0000'
'CONNECT',  5,'Solder Connectio','000-0000'
'CONNECT',  6,'Solder Connectio','000-0000'
'CONNECT',  7,'Solder Connectio','000-0000'
'CONNECT',  8,'Solder Connectio','000-0000'
'CONNECT',  9,'Solder Connectio','000-0000'
'CONNECT', 10,'Solder Connectio','000-0000'
'CONNECT', 11,'Solder Connectio','000-0000'
'CONNECT', 12,'Solder Connectio','000-0000'
```

For each block placed in the Electric drawing, AutoCAD LT lists the block's name, a sequential number, the product name, and the stock number. You've created a rudimentary bill of material, which can be printed out on your printer or imported to a spreadsheet.

Step 3: Importing Bills of Material into Excel

The steps shown here for importing the extracted attribute data (bill of material) into a spreadsheet is shown here for Open Office, a free collection of Office software available from www.openoffice.org. Other spreadsheet programs, such as Excel, have analogous steps.

1. Launch the spreadsheet program.

2. From the **File** menu, select **Open** to display the Open dialog box.

   In the **Files of type** droplist, scroll down to select **Text CSV (*.csv, *.txt)**.

   Navigate to the folder holding the Electric.txt file.

3. Select the **Electric.txt** file, and then click **Open**.

   Notice that Open Office displays the Text Import dialog box, which allows you to specify the format of files being imported.

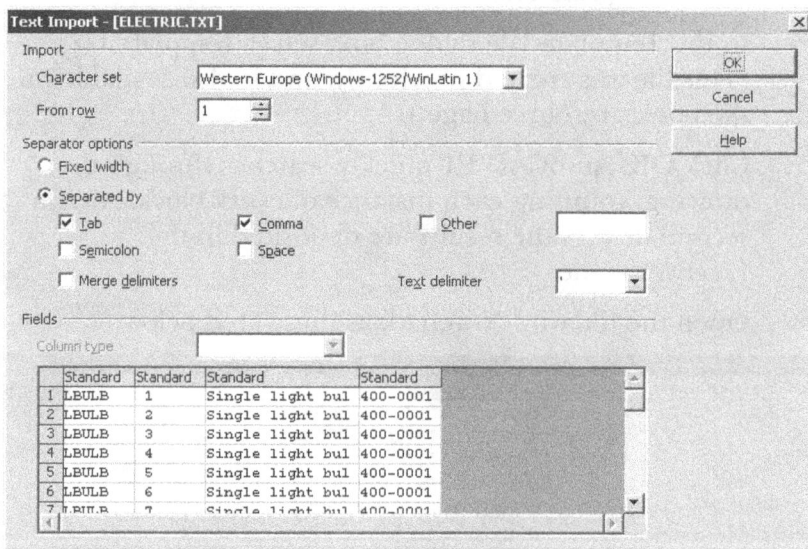

Specify the following options:

Import From row:	I
Separated by:	**Comma** (*turn off Tab*)
Text delimiter:	' (*single quote*)

4. Click **OK**.

Notice that Open Office loads the Electric.txt file, and then displays each field in its own column.

If it is necessary to adjust the column widths, select the four columns, then select **Format | Column | Optimal Width**.

5. If you wish, add price and extension fields, a totals row, and format the text for lovely output.

> **TIP** The spreadsheet formula to count the number of items in column B is:
>
> =count(B1:B70)

6. Remember to save the spreadsheet as an .xls file.

Importing Spreadsheet Data into AutoCAD LT

To bring the bill of material from the spreadsheet back into the AutoCAD LT drawing as a table, use the Windows clipboard.

1. In the spreadsheet program, select the rows you want to import into the drawing. You might want to select all the rows with data, or perhaps just the summary rows.

2. From the **Edit** menu, select **Copy** to copy the rows to the clipboard.

3. Switch to AutoCAD LT.

4. Reduce the size of the drawing to make some room for the incoming data. Try the **Zoom 0.5x** command.

About Paste Special

Why not just use the **Edit | Paste** command? Because spreadsheets place data in the clipboard in numerous formats, and because Paste gives you no choice over the best format for your needs. In contrast, the Paste Special dialog box lets you select which format would work best.

Depending on the spreadsheet software you use, the choices include:

Picture (Metafile or **Enhanced Metafile)** — spreadsheet looks exactly like the linked object version but is not linked back to the spreadsheet, which saves memory.

Device Independent Bitmap — graphical representation of the spreadsheet, pasted as a bitmap raster image.

Microsoft Excel Worksheet (linked object) — places an image of the spreadsheet in the drawing. Double-clicking the image loads the file back into Excel for further processing.

AutoCAD LT Entities — spreadsheet converted to AutoCAD LT text. While the formulae are lost, the text retains its formatting to a certain extent. The text can be edited with the **DdEdit** command.

Text — spreadsheet is placed as an mtext object, with greater loss of formatting than when placed as AutoCAD LT Entities. The text uses the Standard style.

Icon — the spreadsheet's icon is placed in the drawing, which redisplays faster than the actual spreadsheet but provides no useful information,

---

5. Select the **Edit | Paste Special** command. AutoCAD LT displays the Paste Special dialog box.

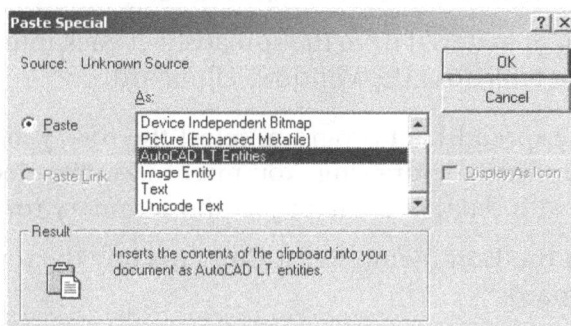

6. Decide on the format that best suits you. Select the format name.

7. Click **OK**. AutoCAD LT copies the spreadsheet from the clipboard and places it into the drawing.

> **WARNING!** The paste operation may fail when the amount of data in the clipboard is too large for AutoCAD LT to handle. The failure ranges from nothing happening to AutoCAD LT crashing.

Building Tables

Draw | Table

A second way to create bills of material is through the **Table** command. It acts like a simple spreadsheet within AutoCAD LT: rows, columns, and even simple formulae. But because Autodesk provides no method of importing data into tables, you have to construct them by hand.

(AutoCAD LT users are shortchanged further: while AutoCAD can export attribute data directly into tables, this very useful feature is missing from AutoCAD LT.)

Tables consist of cells defined by rows and columns. You can change the look of tables, including the color of lines and cells, the font, and the spacing.

Title		
Column Head	Column Head	Column Head
Data	Data	Data
Data	Data	Data
Data	Data	Data
Data	Data	Data
Data	Data	Data

Title Row, *Column Header Row*, *Data Rows* — *Columns*, *Cell*, *Borders*

Two rows at the top of the table are special. One is named the Title row and the one below is the Column Head row. These two are treated differently because they can have different styles.

Placing Tables

Let's see how to build tables.

1. In the Electric drawing, use the scroll bars to pan the schematic to the side — creating room for the table about to be built.

2. From the **Draw** menu, select **Table**. Notice the Insert Table dialog box.

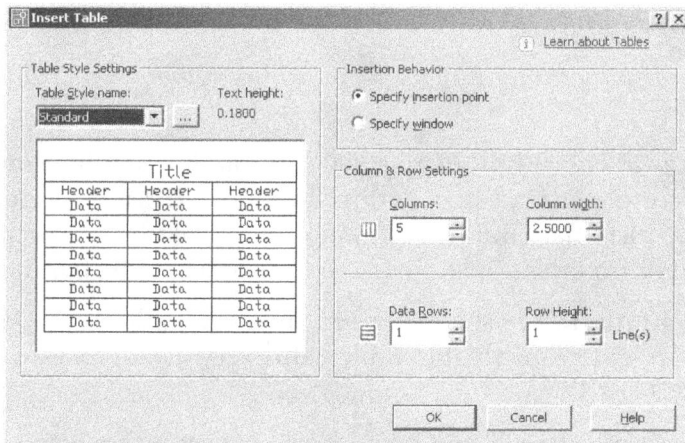

The purpose of the dialog box is twofold: to specify a table style and to specify the size of the table.

First, specify the style of the table.

3. Click the **...** button next to **Table Style Name**. Notice that the dialog box looks similar to that of the **DimStyle** command.

Click **Modify**.

4. The **Data** tab of the Modify Table Style dialog box allows you to specify the look of data rows.

For this tutorial, change only the font from TXT to something more legible, like Arial:

a. Click the **...** button next to **Text Style**.

b. Notice the Text Style dialog box. From the **Font Name** droplist, select **Arial**.

c. Click **Apply**, and then **Close.**

In the preview window, the sample text changes to Arial.

5. Make the column heads and title rows stand out from the data rows. Select the **Column Heads** tab.

   Notice that the content of this tab is near-identical to the previous tab; the only difference is the **Include Header Row** option. Change the **Text Color** and **Fill Color** options.

6. Select the **Title** tab and change the text color, as well. Notice that the preview window updates with every change.

7. Click **OK**, and then click **Close**.

8. Back in the Insert Table dialog box, it's time to work out the size of the table. The following illustration shows ten rows and six columns.

Component	Description	Stock No	Total	Price	Cost
CONNECT	Solder Connectio	000-0000	38	$0.02	
BSWITCH	Single-pole Brak	200-0510	1	$6.78	
DOMESW	Single-pole Dome	200-0020	2	$2.54	
FUSE40	40 Amp Fuse	300-0040	1	$1.23	
GROUND	Lug and screw gr	100-0001	12	$0.34	
HLAMP	Dual Beam Headla	400-0220	2	$9.45	
LBULB	Single light bul	400-0001	12	$2.21	
LDIMMER	80 Ohm Dimmer	500-0080	1	$4.32	
LSWITCH	Four-pole Switch	200-0440	1	$1.53	

Change the table size, as follows:

Columns   **6**
Data Rows   **9**

Note that the number of rows is for *data* rows only; AutoCAD automatically adds the column header and title rows if the **Include Header Row** option is turned on in the table style.

9. Click **OK**.

AutoCAD ghosts the table in the drawing, and prompts you:

Specify insertion point: *(Pick a point.)*

The point you pick becomes the upper-left corner of the table.

Populating the Table

TablEdit

After placing the empty table in the drawing, AutoCAD displays a text editor identical to that of the **MText** command.

1. Fill in the title row, and then press **Tab** to move the cursor to the next cell.

Text Formatting												
Standard ▾	𝔗 Arial ▾	0.2500 ▾	**B** *I* U		■ ▾		OK	⊙				

Automotive Electrical System - Bill of Materials

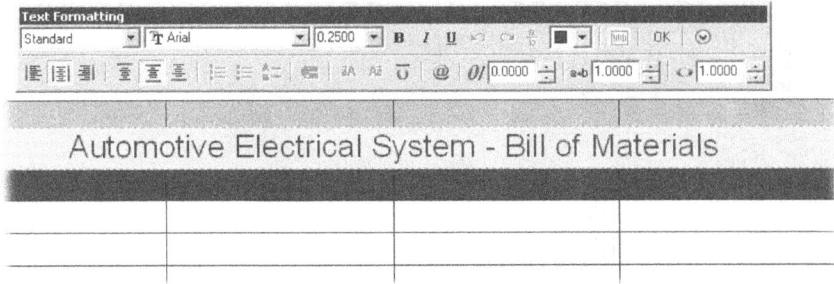

Move the cursor to the previous cell by pressing **Shift+Tab**. You can also move directly to cells by clicking in them.

2. Fill in the rest of the table data. (If you'd rather not, the table is available as Table.dwg on the book's resource page.)

Automotive Electrical System - Bill of Materials					
Component	Description	Stock No	Total	Price	Cost
CONNECT	Solder Connectio	000-0000	38	0.02	
BSWITCH	Single-pole Brak	200-0510	1	6.78	
DOMESW	Single-pole Dome	200-0020	2	2.54	
FUSE40	40 Amp Fuse	300-0040	1	1.23	
GROUND	Lug and screw gr	100-0001	12	0.34	
HLAMP	Dual Beam Headla	400-0220	2	9.45	
LBULB	Single light bul	400-0001	12	2.21	
LDIMMER	80 Ohm Dimmer	500-0080	1	4.32	
LSWITCH	Four-pole Switch	200-0440	1	1.53	

3. Column F is labeled "Cost." Its purpose is to determine the total cost of each part. This involves multiplication: the number of parts x the price of each.

For CONNECT, this is 38 x 0.02 = 0.76. Tables use the same formulae as spreadsheets, so the calculation looks like this:

= D3 * E3

where D3 is the cell at the intersection of column D and row 3, and the asterisk (*) is the symbol for multiplication.

Although AutoCAD LT does not support fields directly, you can still enter formulae in cells as you would any other text. Enter the formula in the appropriate cell.

m - Bill of Materi₂

	Total	Price	Cost
	38	0.02	=D3*E3

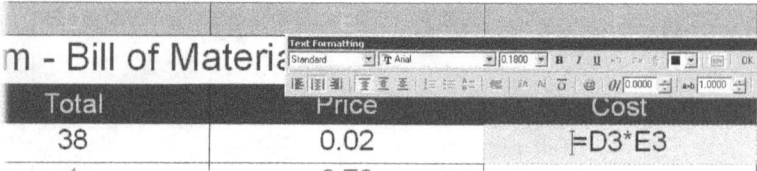

(Fields are like automatic text, text that updates itself when conditions in the drawing change. Fields are found in AutoCAD, but are lacking in AutoCAD LT.)

4.   After entering the formula text, press **Enter**. AutoCAD LT performs the calculation, and displays 0.760000. You cannot, unfortunately, format the number to display as the more reasonable $0.76.

5.   Enter similar formulae in the remaining cells:

    = D4 * E4
    = D5 * E5

    ... and so on.

Automotive Electrical System - Bill of Materials					
Component	Description	Stock No	Total	Price	Cost
CONNECT	Solder Connectio	000-0000	38	0.02	0.760000
BSWITCH	Single-pole Brak	200-0510	1	6.78	6.7800
DOMESW	Single-pole Dome	200-0020	2	2.54	5.0800
FUSE40	40 Amp Fuse	300-0040	1	1.23	1.2300
GROUND	Lug and screw gr	100-0001	12	0.34	4.0800
HLAMP	Dual Beam Headla	400-0220	2	9.45	18.9000
LBULB	Single light bul	400-0001	12	2.21	26.5200
LDIMMER	80 Ohm Dimmer	500-0080	1	4.32	4.3200
LSWITCH	Four-pole Switch	200-0440	1	1.53	1.5300

TIPS   The gray background to the text alerts you that this is field text.

To edit text in tables, double-click a cell.

6.   Now we need a grand total of the Cost column. That means adding another row to the bottom of the table.

    Select the last row in the table, and then right-click. From the shortcut menu, select **Insert Rows | Below**.

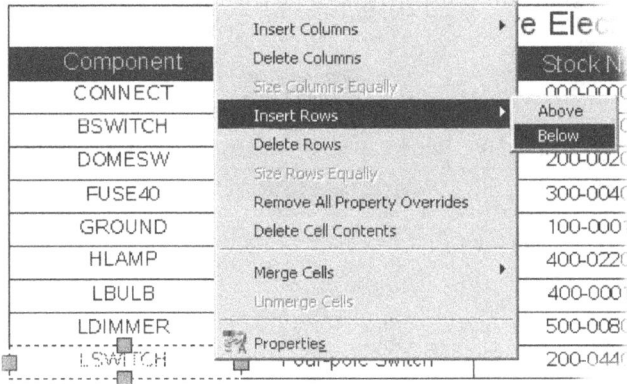

AutoCAD adds the empty row.

7. Use the **Sum** formula to add up the Cost column:
=sum(F3:F11)

Sum adds up all cells specified by the *range*. The colon
(:) indicates the range of cells — from cells F3 to F11.

8. The bottom row has several empty cells. You can ignore
them, or you can tidy them up as follows:

a. Select the empty cells.
b. Right-click, and then select **Merge Cells | All**.

AutoCAD LT makes one long cell out of the five.

9. In the new, long cell, enter the words **Total Cost**.

Click the **Right** justification button on the Text Formatting toolbar to force the text to the right end of the cell.

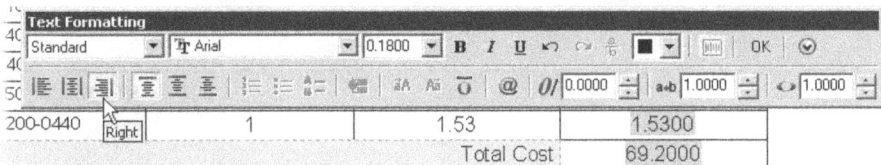

10. Click **OK** to exit the editor.

11. To resize the columns, select the table and then drag the grips.

Grip Moves Entire Table — Grips Change Column Width — Corner Grips Resize Entire Table

Automotive Electrical System - Bill of Materials

CONNECT	Solder Connectio	000-0000	38	0.02	0.760000
BSWITCH	Single-pole Brak	200-0510	1	8.78	8.7800
DOMESW	Single-pole Dome	200-0020	2	2.54	5.0800
FUSE40	40 Amp Fuse	300-0--	1	1.23	1.2300
GROUND	Lug and screw gr	100-0001	12	0.34	4.0800
HLAMP	Dual Beam Headla	400-0220	2	9.45	18.9000
LBULB	Single light bul	400-0001	12	2.21	26.5200
LDIMMER	80 Ohm Dimmer	500-0090	1	4.32	4.3200
LSWITCH	Four-pole Switch	200-0440	1	1.53	1.5300
				Total Cost	69.2000

12. Save your work.

Summary

In this chapter, you learned how to export attribute data to spreadsheets, and then bring formatted spreadsheet data back into AutoCAD LT. You also learned about creating, populating, and editing tables.

Chapter 10

Isometric Drafting

In This Chapter

- Understanding isometric drafting
- Setting up AutoCAD LT for isometric drafting
- Switching between the three isoplanes
- Creating isometric text and dimension styles

AutoCAD LT has a limited capability for drawing in three dimensions ("3D" for short). The limited 3D capabilities include:

- Inputting 3D coordinates to most drawing and editing commands.
- Using the **3dPoly** command to draw 3D polylines.
- Giving all objects an *elevation* (a height above the x,y-plane) and a *thickness* with the **Elev** and **Thickness** commands.
- Setting 3D viewpoints via the **DView** and **View** commands.
- Creating user-defined 3D coordinate systems with the **UCS** command.
- Viewing 3D solid and surface models created in AutoCAD, as well as editing them to a limited extent.
- Shading 3D models with the **Shade** command, and removing hidden lines with the **Hide** command.

Key Terms

Isometric — form of drafting that shows three sides of "3D" models; an equal projection
Isoplanes — three isometric drawing planes, situated at 120 degrees to each other
Oblique — slant angle of text

Abbreviations

2D   Two dimensions
3D   Three dimensions
Iso   Isometric

Command

Command	Shortcut	Menu Selection
Isoplane	F5 *or* Ctrl+E	...

In the days of manual drafting, it wasn't possible to create 3D drawings. To represent objects in 3D, manual drafters used visual tricks to create drawings that looked as if they were three-dimensional. You may be familiar with some of these, such as one- and two-point perspectives.

The most common visual trick is called "isometric" drafting, which shows the front, right, and top sides at the same time. To accomplish this, the sides are drawn at 120-degree angles to each other.

AutoCAD LT provides a little help for isometric drafting, limited to displaying isometric grid and cursor and drawing isometric circles. But that's all.

This chapter shows you how to draft isometric drawings, including creating the appropriate text and dimension styles.

> **TIP** Isometric drawings are not 3D drawings; they are an illusion created in 2D. For this reason, commands like **Hide** or **Shade** cannot be used on isometrics.

What Is Isometric Drafting?

Isometric drafting is a way to simulate 3D drawings. It shows three sides of objects, making them easier to visualize than standard 2D drawings. Isometric drawings are commonly used for piping layouts and assembly drawings.

Isometric means "equal projection," and is sometimes called "axonometric projection."

The front, top, and right sides of objects are drawn at 120 degrees to each other. To make isometric objects look "right," they must be drawn skewed. A square, for instance, is drawn as a rhombus. A circle is drawn as an ellipse. Arcs and fillets are drawn as elliptical arcs.

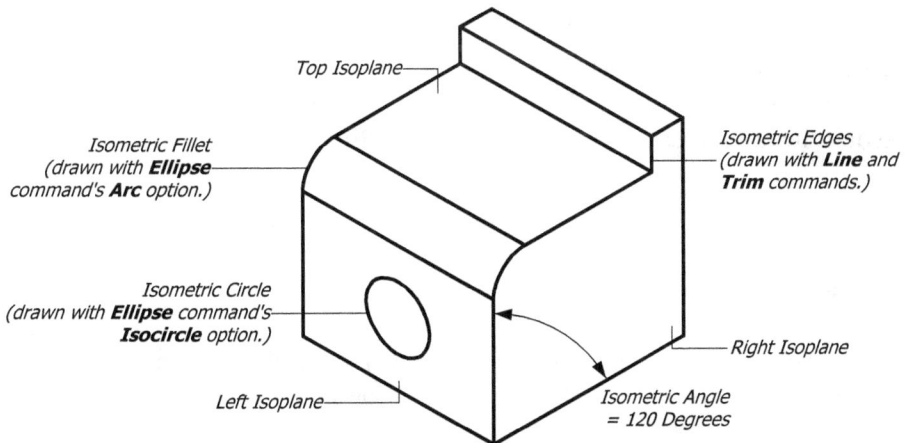

Top Isoplane

Isometric Fillet
(drawn with **Ellipse** command's **Arc** option.)

Isometric Edges
(drawn with **Line** and **Trim** commands.)

Isometric Circle
(drawn with **Ellipse** command's **Isocircle** option.)

Left Isoplane

Right Isoplane

Isometric Angle
= 120 Degrees

Text is slanted by 30 degrees. And all are drawn at a different skew for each of the three isometric planes — top, left, and right.

In addition to isometric drafting, there are two other forms of drafting that represent 3D and can be created in AutoCAD LT:

Oblique projection — front view is drawn first, and then the top and right sides are drawn at an angle, typically 30 or 45 degrees. Oblique drawings are drafted in LT using methods similar to that of isometric drafting.

Perspective projection — simulates the effect of objects decreasing in size the farther they are from your eye. One- and two-point perspective are commonly used for artist conception drawings, but cannot be used for construction because distances cannot be measured correctly. AutoCAD LT allows you to display drawings in perspective mode using the **DView** and **3dZoom** commands.

AutoCAD LT provides these tools to help create isometric drawings:

- Isometric grid and cursor for each of the three isometric planes. The **Snap** command's **Style** option turns on isometric mode, which then displays the isometric grid and cursor.
- Shortcut keys for switching between isometric planes mid-command. Press **Ctrl+E** or function key **F5** to switch between the three isometric planes: top, right, and left.
- Ellipses and elliptical arcs for drawing isometric circles and arcs in the appropriate isoplane. Use the **Ellipse** command's **Isocircle** option to draw isometric circles; use the **Ellipse** command's **Arc** option to draw isometric arcs.

On the minus side, AutoCAD LT does not provide isometric text styles or isometric dimension styles.

In the next section, you learn how to turn on iso mode and switch between isometric planes. In the sections following, you practice drawing isocircles and create isometric text and dimension styles.

Setting Up LT for Isometric Drafting

Tools | Drafting Settings
Isoplane

Start AutoCAD LT with a new drawing. To switch to isometric mode, use the Drafting Settings dialog box, as follows:

1. From the **Tools** menu, select **Drafting Settings**. Notice the Drafting Settings dialog box. If necessary, select the **Snap and Grid** tab.

2. In the Snap type & style area, select the **Isometric snap** radio button.

   Notice that the **Snap X spacing** and **Grid X spacing** fields turn gray. AutoCAD does not allow you to specify different spacing in the X and Y directions. You can, if you wish, rotate the isometric grid.

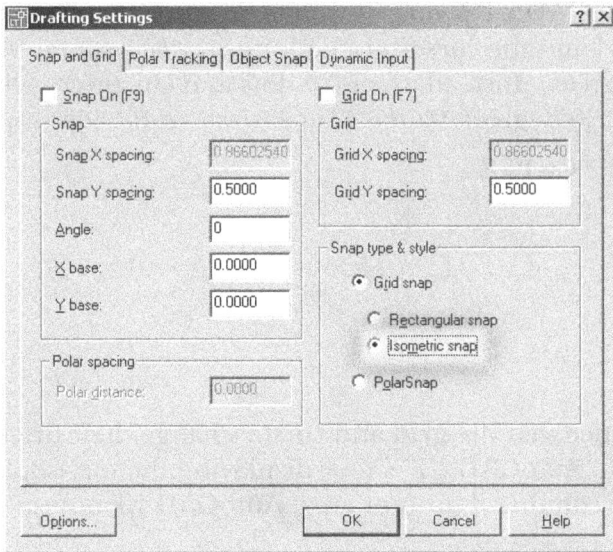

3. Click **OK**. If necessary, click the **GRID** button on the status bar to turn on the grid display.

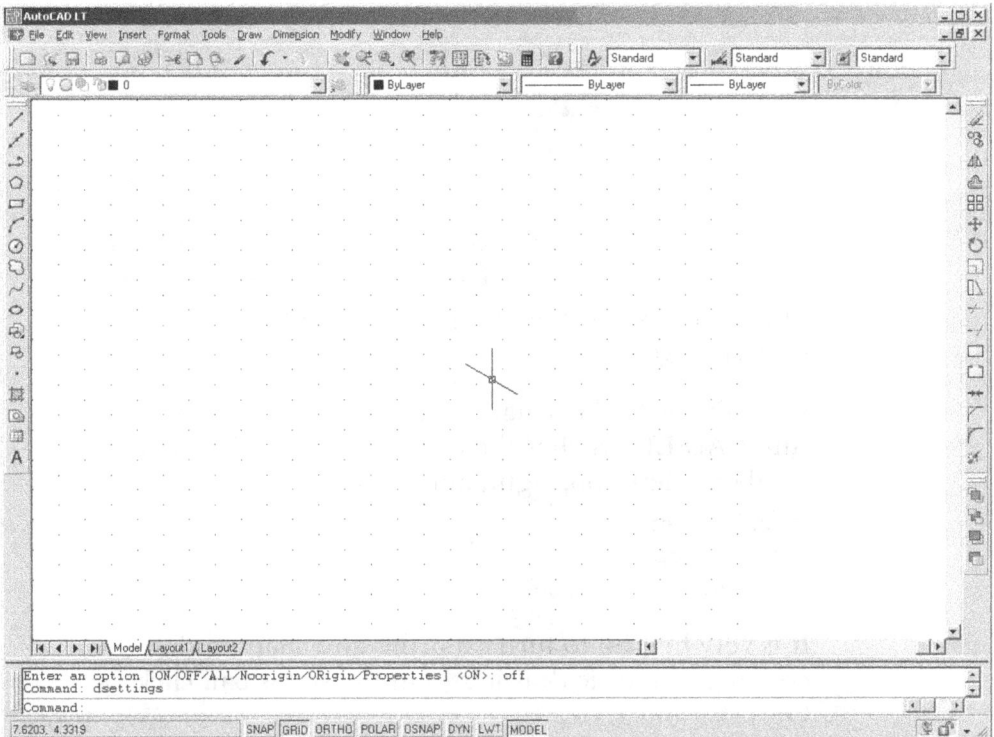

AutoCAD LT is now in isometric mode. Notice that the grid and the cursor are no longer *orthogonal* (at 90 degrees). Instead, the grid dots and cursor crosshairs are at 120 degrees. AutoCAD LT starts in the left isoplane.

4. Press **Ctrl+E**.

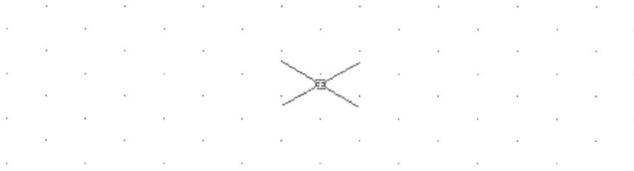

Notice that the grid and cursor change their orientation. AutoCAD LT is now displaying the top isoplane. In the command prompt area, AutoCAD LT notes:

<Isoplane Top>

5. Function key **F5** is an alternative to pressing **Ctrl+E** for changing the isoplane. Press **F5**.

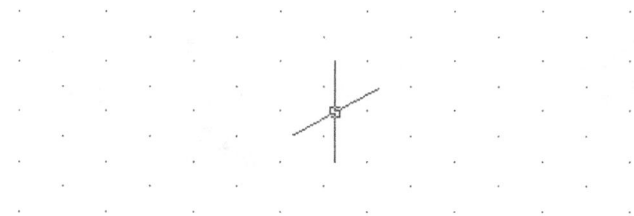

Notice again that the grid and the cursor change their orientation. AutoCAD LT is now displaying the right isoplane, as the command prompt notes:

<Isoplane Right>

6. Press **F5** (or **Ctrl+E**) again and again. As you do, AutoCAD LT switches the display between the three isoplanes: left, top, right, and back to left:

<Isoplane Left>
<Isoplane Top>
<Isoplane Right>

7. It is very helpful to turn on ortho and snap modes when creating isometric drawings. On the status bar, click **ORTHO** and **SNAP**.

8. Save the drawing as an isometric template drawing, as follows:

   a. From the **File** menu, select **Save As**.

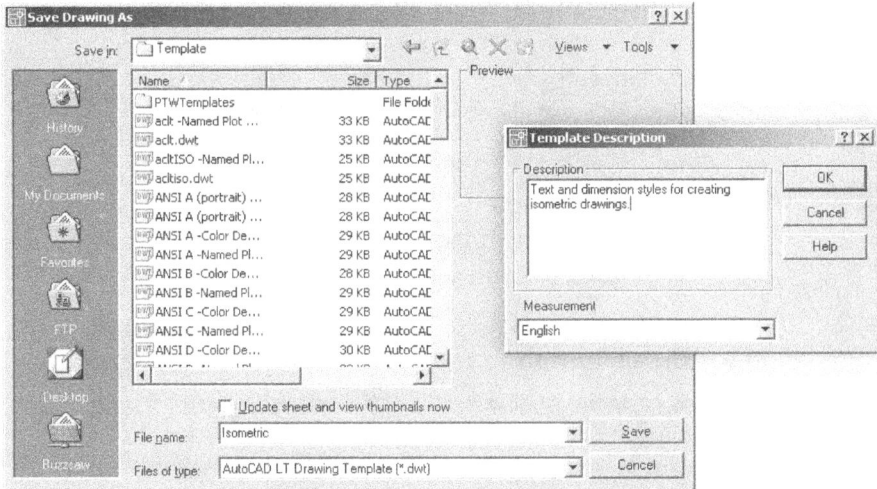

   b. When the Save Drawing As dialog box appears, select **Drawing Template File (*.dwt)** from the **Files of type** list. AutoCAD LT automatically selects the \templates folder.
   c. For the **File name**, type **Isometric**.
   d. Click **Save**. Notice that AutoCAD LT displays the Template Description dialog box.
   e. In the **Description** field, type something useful, such as:
      Text and dimension styles for creating isometric drawings.

   f. From the **Measurement** list box, select either **English** or **Metric**, whichever you prefer.
   g. Click **OK**.

You'll save this drawing again as you add more template style features throughout this chapter.

Drawing Isometric Circles and Arcs

Draw | Ellipse

Earlier I mentioned that all objects are drawn skewed in isometric drawings. AutoCAD LT provides a command to draw two such objects, the isometric circle and isometric arc; there are no similar commands for drawing isometric rectangles or other shapes basic to axonometric drafting.

To draw isometric circles and arcs, you use a "hidden" option of the **Ellipse** command. Here's how:

1. At the 'Command:' prompt, enter the **Ellipse** command:

    Command: **ellipse**
    Specify axis endpoint of ellipse or [Arc/Center/Isocircle]:

    Notice that AutoCAD LT adds an **Isocircle** option, which you haven't seen before. This option appears only when AutoCAD LT is in isometric mode. (You cannot access the **Isocircle** option from the menu bar.)

2. Type **I** to specify isocircles. When AutoCAD LT prompts you for the center and radius, click points on the screen:

    Specify axis endpoint of ellipse or [Arc/Center/Isocircle]: **i**
    Specify center of isocircle: *(Pick a point.)*
    Specify radius of isocircle or [Diameter]: *(Pick another point.)*

    Notice that AutoCAD LT draws an isocircle.

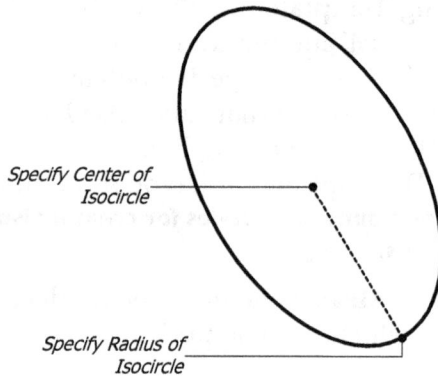

Specify Center of Isocircle

Specify Radius of Isocircle

3. Press **F5** to change to another isoplane.

    Repeat the **Ellipse** command. Notice that the isocircle is drawn in another orientation — top.

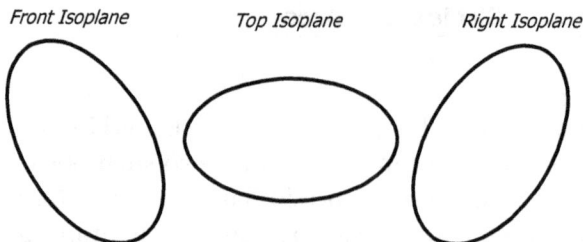

Front Isoplane   *Top Isoplane*   *Right Isoplane*

Press **F5** again, and repeat the **Ellipse** command. This time the isocircle is drawn in the third orientation — right.

4. To draw isometric arcs and fillets, use the **Arc** option of the **Ellipse** command, as follows:

    Command: **ellipse**
    Specify axis endpoint of ellipse or [Arc/Center/Isocircle]: **arc**
    Specify axis endpoint of elliptical arc or [Center/Isocircle]: **isocircle**
    Specify center of isocircle: *(Pick a point.)*
    Specify radius of isocircle or [Diameter]: *(Pick another point.)*
    Specify start angle or [Parameter]: **0**
    Specify end angle or [Parameter/Included angle]: **180**

    Like isocircles, AutoCAD LT draws isometric arcs appropriate to the current isoplane.

Text and Dimension Styles

Format | Text Style
Format | Dimension Style

As noted earlier, AutoCAD LT lacks the text and dimension styles appropriate for isometric drafting. Even if the text were rotated for isometric planes (+120 or –120 degrees), the text would look as if it were slanted; it would not look "correct," as illustrated below.

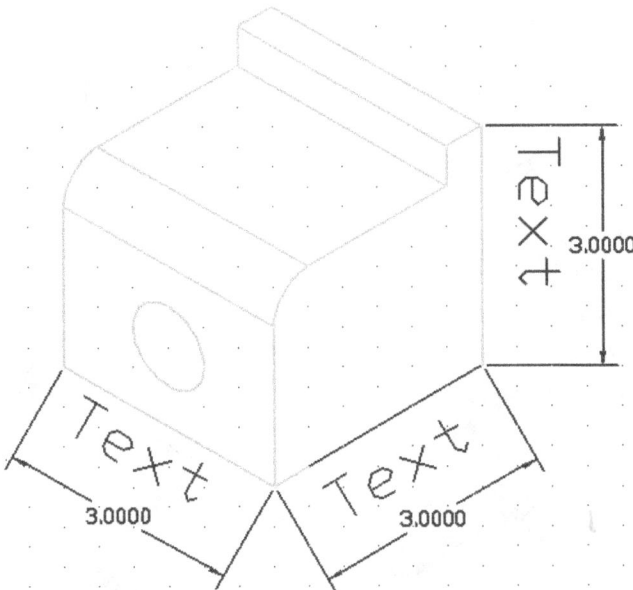

We have to fool the eye into thinking the text looks "natural." The solution is to also *oblique* (slant) the text by 30 degrees, as illustrated in the following figure.

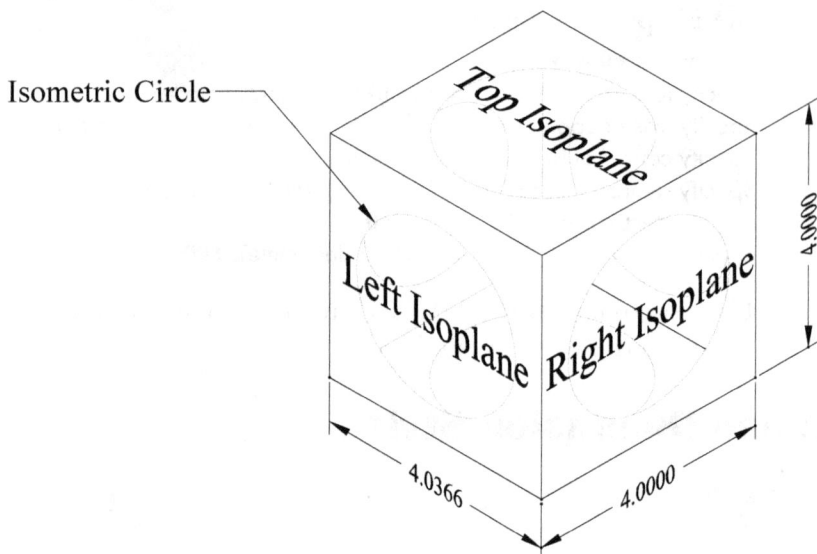

Isometric Circle

4.0366   4.0000

Because it is inconvenient to repeatedly angle and oblique text for each of the three isoplanes, we create *text styles* that do the work for us.

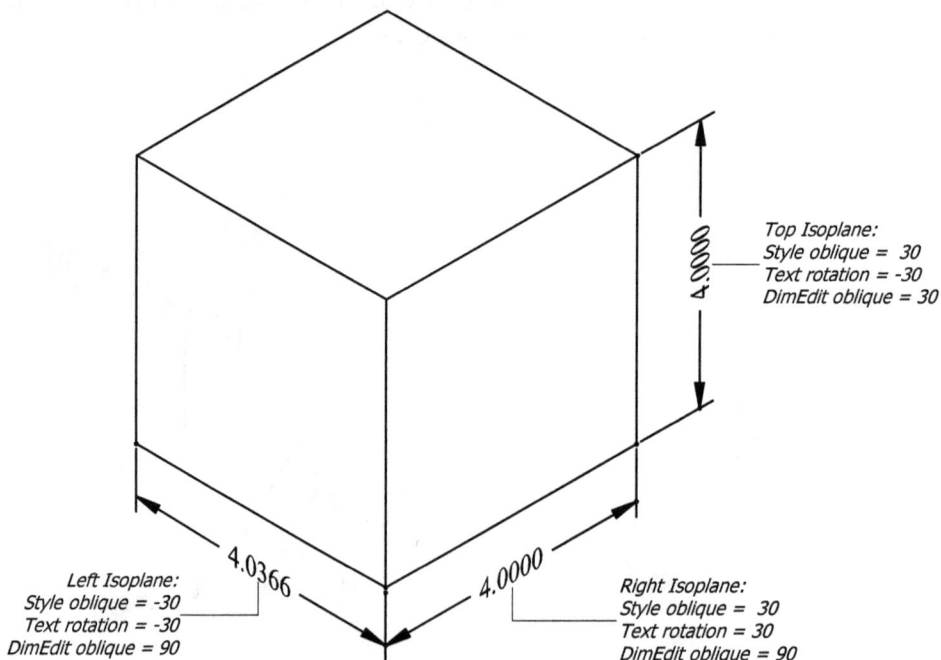

Top Isoplane:
Style oblique = 30
Text rotation = -30
DimEdit oblique = 30

Left Isoplane:
Style oblique = -30
Text rotation = -30
DimEdit oblique = 90

4.0366

4.0000

Right Isoplane:
Style oblique = 30
Text rotation = 30
DimEdit oblique = 90

Dimensions suffer from the same problem: both the text and extension lines need to be adjusted for the three isometric planes. Here the solution is similar: create *dimension styles* and edit them dimensions for a finishing touch.

The previous figure summarizes the angles that need to be applied to dimensions in the three isoplanes. Just two text styles are needed, because the top isoplane uses the right isoplane's text style.

The following table summarizes the angles changed by each command:

Isoplane	Style Name	Style Command: Oblique Angle	Text Command: Rotation Angle	DimEdit Command: Oblique Angle
Left	LeftIso	–30°	–30°	90°
Right	RightIso	30°	30°	90°
Top	RightIso	30°	–30°	30°

Creating Isometric Text Styles

In preparation for creating dimension styles that place correct-looking dimensions, create two text styles with the **Style** command, one for the left isoplane and another for the right and top isoplanes. In each text style, the obliquing angle is set to +30 or –30 degrees.

Later, when placing text in drawings with the **Text** or **MText** commands, you specify a rotation angle of +30 or –30 degrees.

You use the **Style** command to create the text styles, as follows:

1. From the **Format** menu, select **Text Style**. Notice the Text Style dialog box.

2. Click **New**. Notice the New Text Style dialog box.

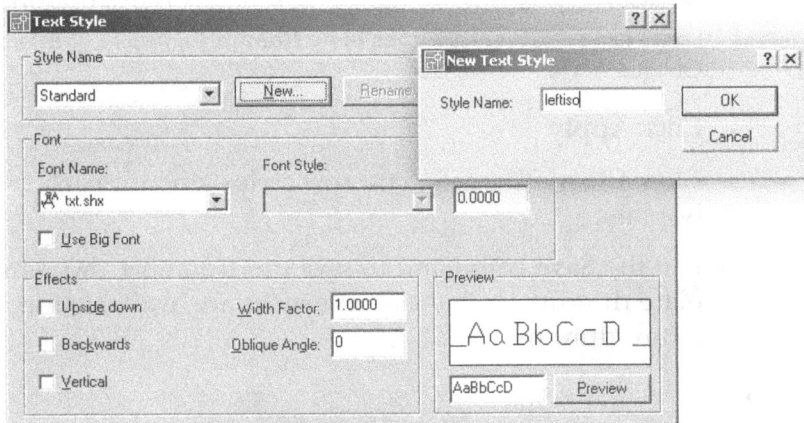

3. In the **Style Name** field, type **leftiso**, and then click **OK**.

4. Back in the Text Style dialog box, set the following options:

Font Name:	**Times New Roman**
	(or any other font that you fancy)
Oblique Angle:	**–30**

    Click **Apply**.

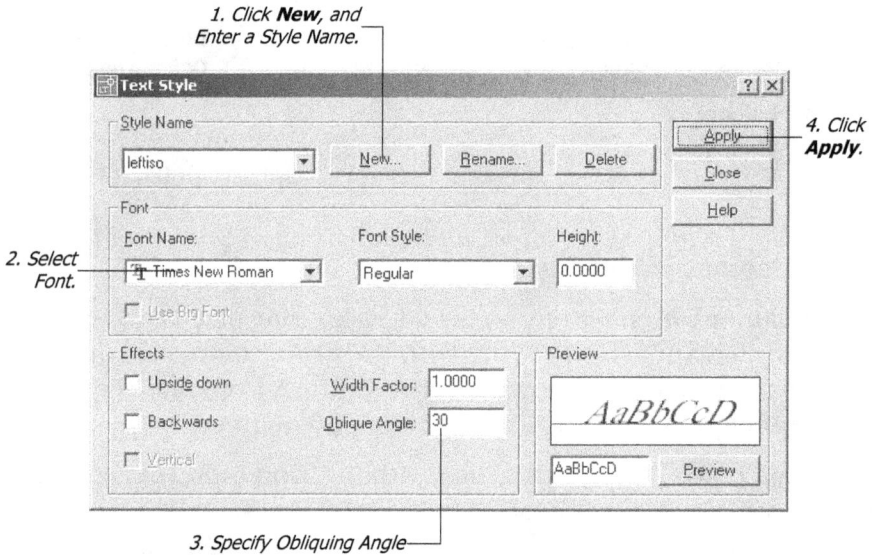

*1. Click **New**, and Enter a Style Name.*

2. Select Font.

3. Specify Obliquing Angle

4. Click Apply.

5. Click **New** to create the other text style. Enter **rightiso** in the **Style Name** field. Click **OK** to exit the New Text Style dialog box.

6. Back in the Text Style dialog box, select these options:

Font Name:	**Times New Roman** *(same font as before)*
Oblique Angle:	**30**

    Click **Apply**.

7. Click **Close**. You now have text styles, one for each isoplane.

8. Use the **Save** command to save the Isometric.dwt template drawing so that the text styles are available for future drawings.

Applying Isometric Text Styles

Practice using the text styles:

1. From the **File** menu, select **New**. (If the Create New Drawing dialog box appears, select **Use a Template**.)

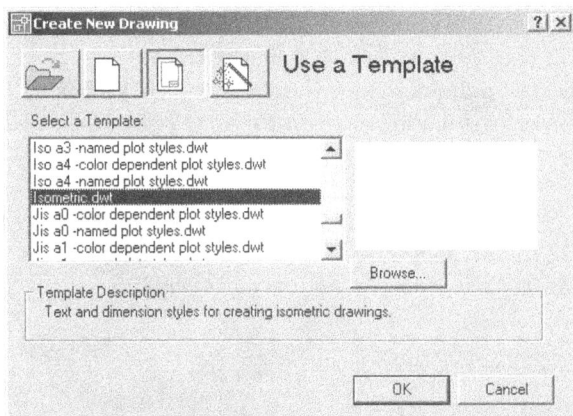

2. In the file list, type **I** to scroll to templates that start with i. Select **Isometric.Dwt**.

> **TIP** Template files with "Iso" in their name have nothing to do with creating isometric drawings! Instead, these templates hold drafting standards decreed by the ISO (International Organization for Standardization).
>
> There is a link between ISO and isometric: the Greek word "iso" means "the same." Standards organizations want everything to be the same, and isometric drawings uses the same angles for the three faces.

3. Use the **Isoplane** command to ensure the left isoplane is set, as follows:

Command: **isoplane**
Current isoplane: Right
Enter isometric plane setting [Left/Top/Right] <Left>: **left**
Current isoplane: Left

4. To help orient yourself, draw an isometric circle using the **Ellipse** command's **Isocircle** option.

5. Place some text with the **Text** command, as follows:

Command: **text**
Current text style: "txt" Text height: 0.2000

6.   Change the style to **LeftIso** with the **Style** option:

Specify start point of text or [Justify/Style]: **s**
Enter style name or [?] <txt>: **leftiso**

7.   Pick the text starting point, and specify a rotation angle of –30 degrees, as follows:

Current text style: "leftiso" Text height: 0.2000
Specify start point of text or [Justify/Style]: *(Pick a point.)*
Specify height <0.2000>: *(Press **Enter** to accept the default.)*
Specify rotation angle of text <0>: **–30**

8.   Now enter the text:

Enter text: **Left Isoplane Text**
Enter text: *(Press **Enter** to exit the command.)*

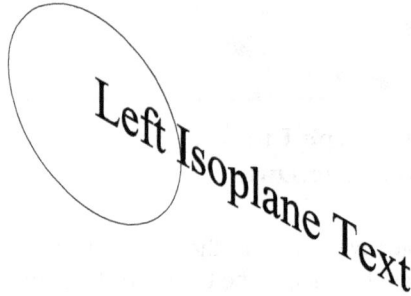

The isometric text looks correct, even though it seems bizarre that it takes an obliquing angle of –30 and a rotation angle of –30 degrees to make it look correct in the left isoplane — but it works!

9.   To place text in the top isoplane, press **F5** to switch to the top isoplane.

Start the **Text** command, and use the **Style** option to select the **rightiso** text style.

Use the **Rotation** option to specify a rotation angle of **–30** degrees. Enter the text **Top Isoplane Text**.

10.   And, to place text in the right isoplane, press **F5** to switch to the right isoplane.

Start the **Text** command, and keep the **rightiso** text style.

Use the **Rotation** option to specify a rotation angle of **30** degrees, and enter the text **Right isoplane text**.

The result is text that looks correct in each isometric plane. The illusion is complete.

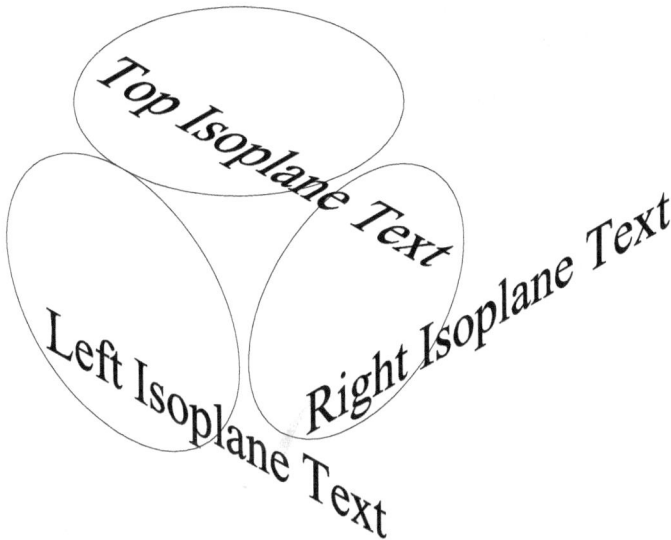

Creating Isometric Dimension Styles

Format | Dimension Style

Similarly, using normal dimension text and extension lines just doesn't look "right" in isometric drawings. The solution is to use the isometric text styles along with the DimOblique command to slant the extension lines.

To summarize, you use the **DimStyle** command to create two dimension styles, one for the left isoplane and another for the right and top isoplanes. Each dimstyle uses the corresponding text style.

Then, after the dimensions are placed in each isoplane, use the **DimEdit** command's **Oblique** option to slant the extension lines, as described in the following table:

Isoplane	Text Style	DimEdit: Oblique
Left	LeftIso	30°
Right	RightIso	–30°
Top	RightIso	–30°

To create dimension style, use the **DimStyle** command. Ensure you are in the Isometric.Dwt drawing. (Select **Isometric.dwt** from the **Window** menu.)

1. From the **Format** menu, select **Dimension Style**. Notice the Dimension Style Manager dialog box.

2. Click **New**. Notice the Create New Dimension Style dialog box.

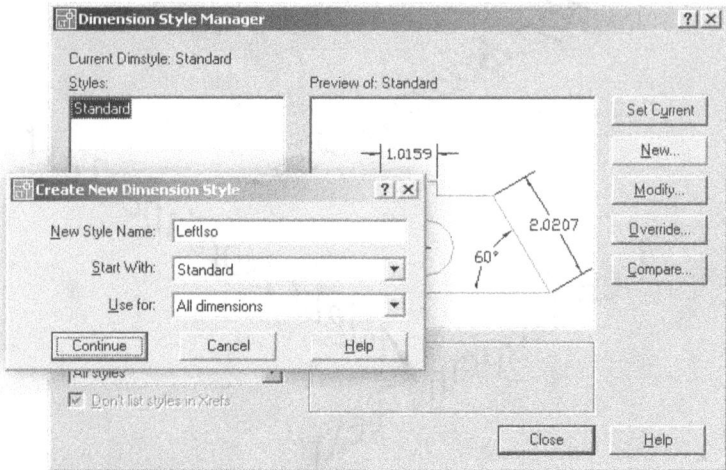

3. Fill in the following data:

New Style Name:	**LeftIso**
Start with:	**Standard**
Use for:	**All dimensions**

   Click **Continue**.

4. Click the **Text** tab of the Dimension Style Manager dialog box, and then fill in the following information:

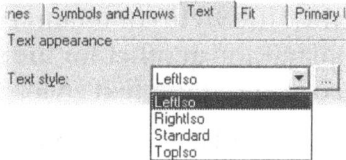

Text style:	**LeftIso**
Text alignment:	**Aligned with dimension line**

5. Click the **Primary Units** tab:

Precision:	**0.0**

   Click **OK**.

6. Repeat for the right isoplane:

   Click **New** to display the Create New Dimension Style dialog box.

New Style Name:	**RightIso**
Start with:	**LeftIso**

7. Click **Continue**. In the Dimension Style dialog box, select the **Text** tab.

Text style:	**RightIso**
Text alignment:	**Aligned with dimension line**

Click **OK**.

(You don't need to specify the precision, because you copied the LeftIso dimension style.)

8. Notice that the **Styles** list contains the original Standard and the two new isometric styles.

(If you like, you can create a TopIso dimension style that uses the LeftIso text style.)

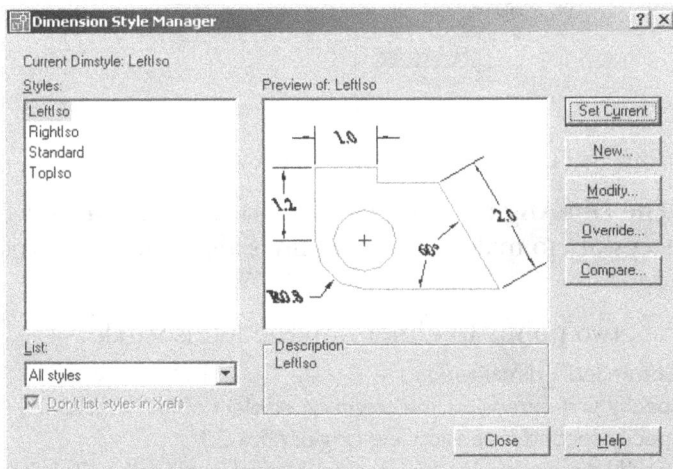

Set the LeftIso dimstyle as current by selecting **LeftIso** and then clicking **Set Current**.

Click **Close**.

9. Once again, it is a good idea to save the Isometric.Dwt template drawing to preserve your hard work. From the **File** menu, select **Save**.

TIP Strictly speaking, isometric arrowheads should be created as well. In practice, they are small enough that the distortion is not noticeable.

Applying Isometric Dimension Styles

Dimension | Aligned
Dimension | Oblique

Let's try using the dimension styles to see what they look like!

1. Start a new drawing using **Isometric.dwt** as the template.

2. Use the **Line** command to draw isometric squares in each of the three isoplanes. Use the **Isoplane** command to ensure the drawing is displaying the left isoplane.

3. From the **Styles** toolbar, select the **LeftIso** dimension style.

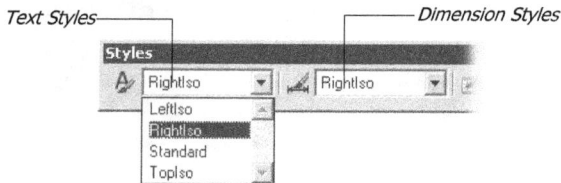

4. From the **Dimension** menu, select **Aligned**.

   (The **DimAligned** command — not **DimLinear** — is necessary to make dimension lines align with isometric edges.)

5. Pick two points to dimension the left isocircle:

   ```
   Command: _dimaligned
   Specify first extension line origin or <select object>: (Pick 1.)
   Specify second extension line origin: (Pick 2.)
   Specify dimension line location or [Mtext/Text/Angle]: (Pick 3.)
   Dimension text = 3.5
   ```

6. Hmm... the dimension looks a bit odd. After the dimensions are placed, you must use the **DimEdit** command to *oblique* the extension lines. For the left isoplane, you apply an obliquing angle of +90 degrees.

   From the **Dimension** menu, select **Oblique**:

   ```
   Command: _dimedit
   Enter type of dimension editing [Home/New/Rotate/Oblique] <Home>: _o
   Select objects: (Pick one or more dimensions.)
   Select objects: (Press Enter to end object selection.)
   Enter obliquing angle (press ENTER for none): 90
   ```

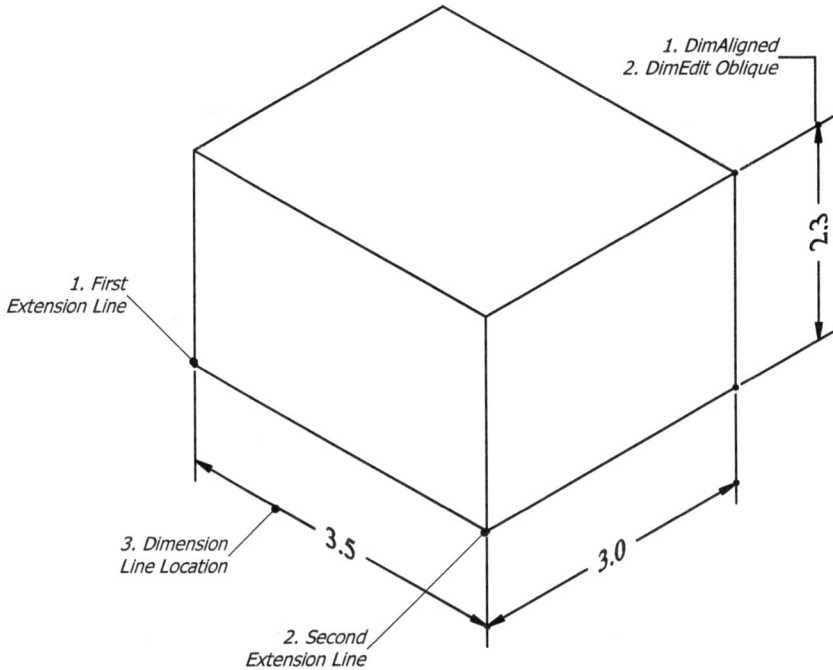

1. DimAligned
2. DimEdit Oblique

1. First
Extension Line

2.3

3. Dimension
Line Location

3.5

3.0

2. Second
Extension Line

Ahh... that's better!

TIP The **DimEdit** command's **Oblique** option works with absolute angles. When you entered **90** for the angle, the extension lines are moved *to* 90 degrees (not *by* 90 degrees).

7. To dimension in the other two isoplanes, you follow this pattern:

   a. Press **F5** to switch to the next isoplane.
   b. Select the dimstyle from the **Styles** toolbar.
   c. Use the **DimAligned** command to place the dimensions.
   d. Use the **Oblique** option of the **DimEdit** command to change the angle of the extension lines. For the right isoplane, specify 90 degrees; for the top isoplane, specify 30 degrees.

Clearly, you want to do as much dimensioning as possible in one isoplane before going on to the next.

Isometric Drafting Tutorial

The first part of this chapter described setting up drawings for isometric drafting. Let's move on to a tutorial on drawing and dimensioning a right-angle clip with a hole.

In general, the approach to creating isometric drawings is to, as much as possible, draw in one isoplane before moving on to the next. It helps to plan the drafting process in advance.

1. Start a new drawing, using **Isometric.dwt** as the template drawing. Toggle these drawing settings:

   Isoplane: **Left**
   Ortho: **On**
   Snap: **On**
   Grid: **On**

2. Use the **Line** command to draw the isometric rectangle shown in the figure. The rectangle is 2 units wide and 0.5 units tall.

   Command: **line**

   Specify first point: *(Pick point 1, shown in the figure below.)*
   Specify next point or [Undo]: *(Pick 2: 2 units away.)*

   Specify next point or [Undo]: *(Pick 3: 0.5 units away.)*
   Specify next point or [Close/Undo]: *(Pick 4: 2 units away.)*

   Specify next point or [Close/Undo]: **c**

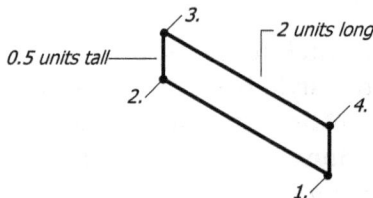

Notice that you have drawn a rhombus, with two corners at 120 degrees and two at 60 degrees. But since this is in isometric mode, it looks like a 2 x 0.5 rectangle with square corners (90 degrees). This shows you that isometric drafting is an illusion!

Note, too, how the ortho and snap modes helped you draw precisely in the isoplane.

3. Switch to the top isoplane, and draw the lines for the next rectangle, which is 1 unit wide.

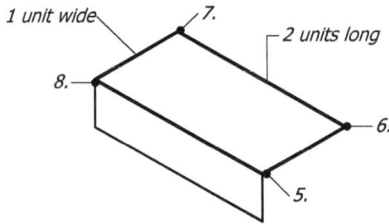

Command: **F5** <Isoplane Top>

Command: **line**
Specify first point: *(Pick 5.)*
Specify next point or [Undo]: *(Pick 6, 1 unit away.)*

Specify next point or [Undo]: *(Pick 7, 2 units away.)*
Specify next point or [Close/Undo]: *(Pick 8, 1 unit away.)*

Specify next point or [Close/Undo]: *(Press **Enter** to end the command.)*

4. Switch back to the left isoplane (press **F5** twice), and then draw the two vertical lines. The two vertical straight lines are 1 unit high.

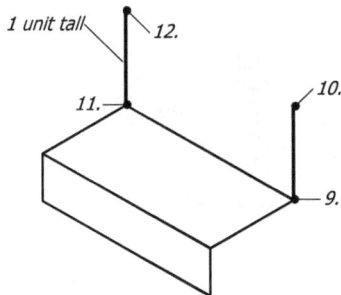

Command: **F5** <Isoplane Right> **F5** <Isoplane Left>

Command: **line**
Specify first point: *(Pick 9.)*

Specify next point or [Undo]: *(Pick 10, 1 unit away.)*
Specify next point or [Undo]: *(Press **Enter**.)*

Command: *(Press Spacebar to repeat the **Line** command.)*
LINE Specify first point: *(Pick 11.)*
Specify next point or [Undo]: *(Pick 12, 1 unit away.)*
Specify next point or [Undo]: *(Press **Enter**.)*

5. Use the **Ellipse** command to draw the 0.5-radius "hole":

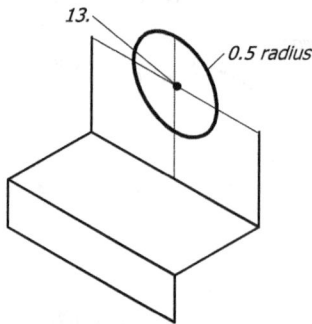

Command: **ellipse**
Specify axis endpoint of ellipse or [Arc/Center/Isocircle]: **i**

Specify center of isocircle: *(Pick 13.)*
Specify radius of isocircle or [Diameter]: **0.5**

6. Repeat the **Ellipse** command to draw the arc, as follows:

Command: *(Press Spacebar to repeat the **Ellipse** command.)*
ELLIPSE Specify axis endpoint of ellipse or [Arc/Center/Isocircle]: **a**
Specify axis endpoint of elliptical arc or [Center/Isocircle]: **i**

Specify center of isocircle: **cen**
of *(Pick isocircle, 13.)*
Specify radius of isocircle or [Diameter]: **1.0**

Specify start angle or [Parameter]: *(Pick 10 again.)*
Specify end angle or [Parameter/Included angle]: *(Pick 12.)*

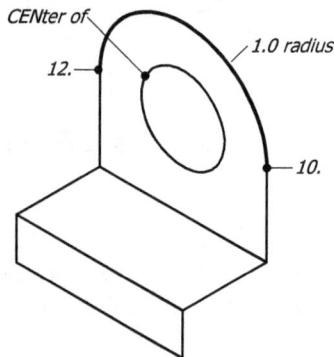

TIP It may seem counterintuitive, but arcs are drawn counterclockwise. Above, the arc is drawn from 10 to 12. If you were to draw it from 12 to 10, you would get the lower half of the arc.

7. Draw the 1.5-unit long line shown below:

    Command: **F5** <Isoplane Top> **F5** <Isoplane Right>
    Command: **line**
    Specify first point: *(Pick 14.)*
    Specify next point or [Undo]: *(Pick 15: 1.5 units away.)*
    Specify next point or [Undo]: *(Press **Enter**.)*

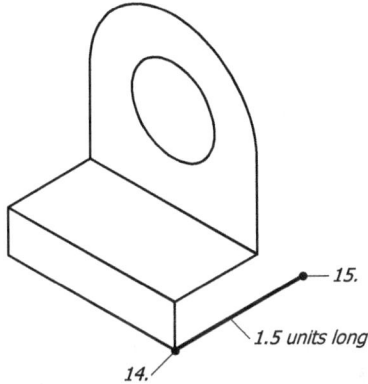

    — 15.

    1.5 units long

    14.

8. The easiest way to create the hole effect is with the **Copy** and **Trim** commands. **Copy** copies the isometric circle, arc, and vertical line. Then, **Trim** cuts the curves, while **Extend** lengthens the line — creating the illusion of hidden-line removal.

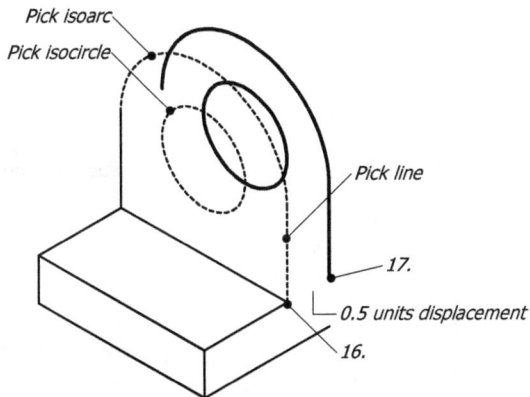

    Pick isoarc
    Pick isocircle

    Pick line

    — 17.

    0.5 units displacement

    16.

    Command: **copy**
    Select objects: *(Pick isocircle.)*
    Select objects: *(Pick isoarc.)*
    Select objects: *(Pick vertical lines.)*
    Select objects: *(Press **Enter** to end object selection.)*
    Specify base point or [Displacement] <Displacement>: *(Pick 16.)*
    Specify second point or
    <use first point as displacement>: *(Pick 17, 0.5 units away.)*

9. Extend the line that connects the copied elements.

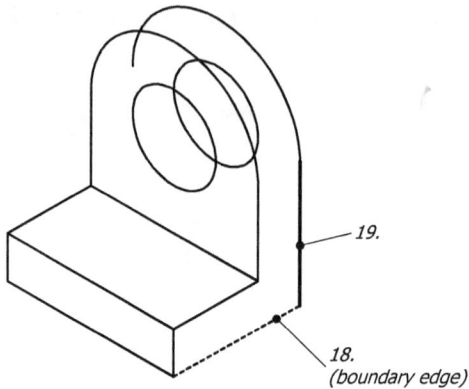

19.

18.
(boundary edge)

Command: **extend**
Current settings: Projection=UCS, Edge=None
Select boundary edges ...
Select objects or <select all>: *(Pick 18.)*
Select objects: *(Press **Enter**.)*

Select object to extend or shift-select to trim or
[Fence/Crossing/Project/Edge/Undo]: *(Pick 18.)*
Select object to extend or shift-select to trim or
[Fence/Crossing/Project/Edge/Undo]: *(Press **Enter** to exit command.)*

10. Now use the **Trim** command to clean up:

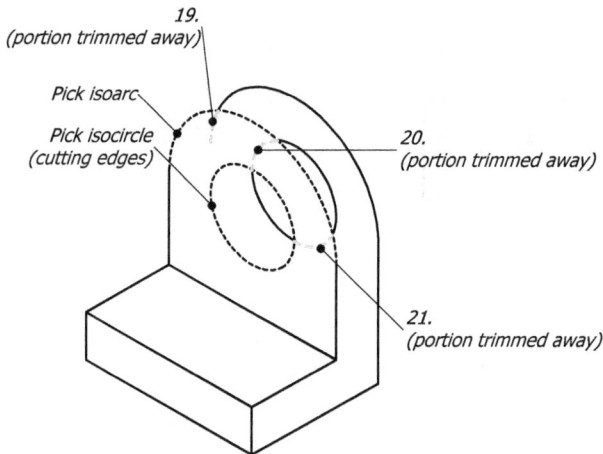

19.
(portion trimmed away)

Pick isoarc

Pick isocircle
(cutting edges)

20.
(portion trimmed away)

21.
(portion trimmed away)

Command: **trim**
Current settings: Projection=UCS, Edge=None
Select cutting edges ...
Select objects or <select all>: *(Pick the isocircle and isoarc.)*
Select objects: *(Press **Enter**.)*

Select object to trim or shift-select to extend or
[Fence/Crossing/Project/Edge/eRase/Undo]: *(Pick end of arc at 19.)*
Select object to trim... *(Pick portion of circle at 20.)*
Select object to trim... *(Pick circle at 21.)*
Select object to trim... *(Press **Enter**.)*

11. Use the **Erase** command to remove the remaining arc:

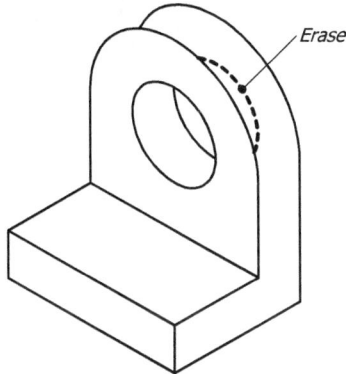

Command: **erase**
Select objects: *(Pick arc.)*
Select objects: *(Press **Enter**.)*

12. Add a line segment to close off the curved part of the clip. Using **QUAdrant** object snap ensures the line is placed correctly between the two arcs.

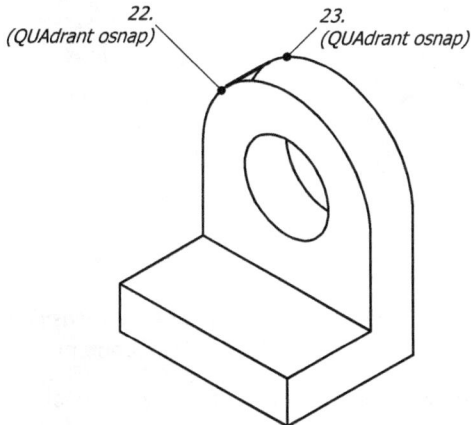

Command: **line**
Specify first point: **qua**
of *(Pick 22.)*
Specify next point or [Undo]: **qua**
of *(Pick 23.)*
Specify next point or [Undo]: *(Press **Enter**.)*

13. The isometric drawing is almost complete! Trim the hangnail, and save your work.

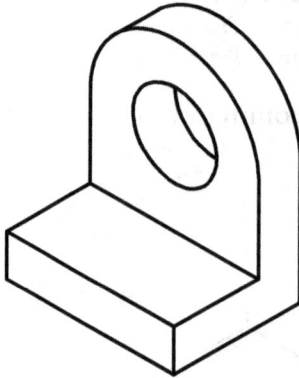

Applying Isometric Dimensions

Earlier in this chapter, you learned how to create text and dimension styles suitable for isometric drawings. Now you will apply aligned and leader dimensions, as illustrated below.

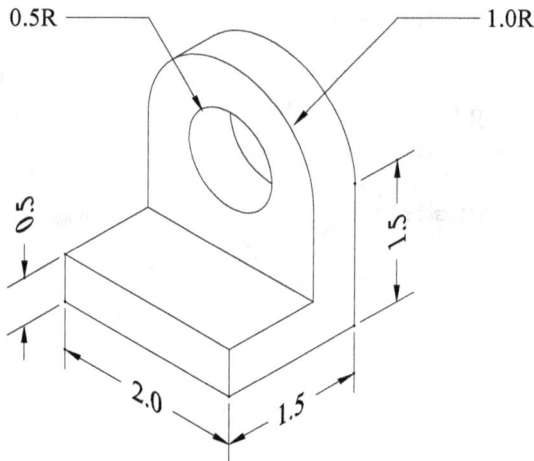

TIPS Use the **QUAdrant** object snap when dimensioning isocircles and arcs. AutoCAD LT correctly snaps to the isometric quadrant point.

The **DimRadius** and **DimDiameter** commands cannot find the center of isometric circles and arcs. Use the **Leader** and **QLeader** commands instead.

Summary

This chapter showed how to create isometric drawings that simulate three dimensions.

Chapter 11

Region Modeling

In This Chapter

- Converting collections of objects into regions
- Using point filters to find coordinates
- Applying Boolean operations to regions
- Finding the mass properties of regions

In this chapter, you learn how to increase your CAD efficiency by work-ing with regions and Boolean operations. These two AutoCAD LT fea-tures let you construct complex 2D shapes, and then analyze them —and AutoCAD LT does this far faster than you would performing the calculations by hand.

Regions

AutoCAD LT has the ability to work with *regions*. Regions are 2D closed areas; regions cannot have intersecting curves.

Creating regions takes two steps:

1. First draw its shape using drawing commands such as **Line**, **Arc**, and **Circle**.

2. Second, convert the shape to a region with the **Region** command.

Key Terms

Booleans — logical operations, such as AND, OR, and NOT
Mass properties — properties of a mass, such as area, centroid, and radius of gyration
Point filter — returns a single coordinate
Regions — closed 2D areas

Abbreviation

.x   X point filter

Commands

Command	Shortcut	Menu Selection
DelObj	...	...
Intersect	in	Modify | Region | Intersect
MassProp	Alt+TYR	Tools | Inquiry | Region/Mass Properties
Region	reg	Draw | Region
Subtract	su	Modify | Region | Subtract
Union	uni	Modify | Region | Union

After conversion, the object looks no different, although it has special properties, which we discuss later. The **Explode** command can be used to change a region back to its original components.

> **TIPS** If the area is hatched, hatch associativity is lost when it is converted to a region. The region must be rehatched.
>
> By default, AutoCAD LT erases the objects after they are converted to a region. To prevent this from happening, turn off the **DelObj** system variable (short for "delete object") by setting it to zero, as follows:
>
> Command: **delobj**
> Enter new value for DELOBJ < I >: **0**

Boolean Operations

When the drawing has two or more regions, you can perform *Boolean operations* on them. These allow you to combine and separate regions.

"Boolean" is a mathematical term describing logical operations named AND, OR, and NOT. AutoCAD LT has three Boolean commands:

> **Union** — joins two or more regions into a single region. In mathematical terms, the Boolean operation returns everything that is in region #1 OR in region #2.
>
> **Intersect** — removes all but the overlapping portions of two or more regions. In math terms, the Boolean operation returns everything that is in region #1 AND in region #2.
>
> **Subtract** — subtracts one region from other regions. Mathematically, the Boolean operation returns everything in region #1 NOT in region #2.

(Region #1 refers to the region you selected first; region #2 is the region selected second. The selection order does not matter for the union and intersect operations, but it does matter for subtract operations.)

In the figure below, the square and circle regions have each Boolean operation applied. Note that there are two possible results for Subtract.

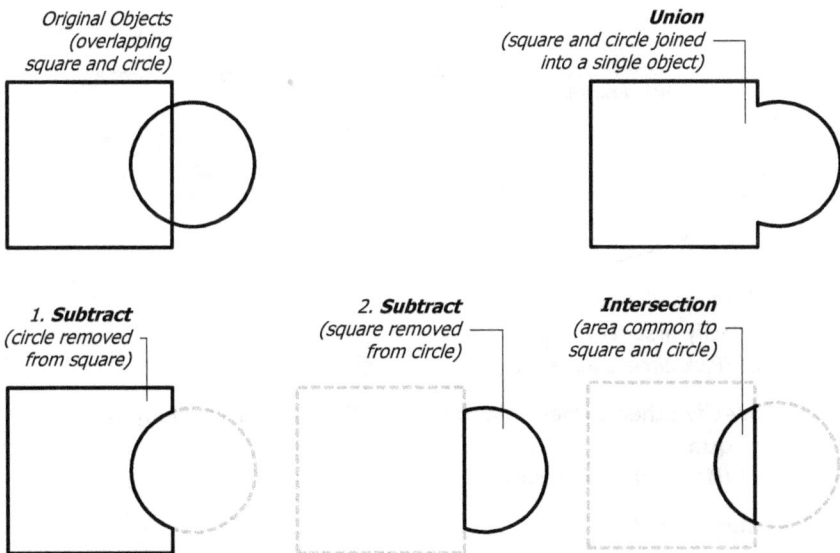

Original Objects
(overlapping
square and circle)

Union
(square and circle joined
into a single object)

1. *Subtract*
(circle removed
from square)

2. *Subtract*
(square removed
from circle)

Intersection
(area common to
square and circle)

The trickiest Boolean operation is Subtract, and so this command is demonstrated in the following tutorial.

Creating Waffle Shapes

Draw | Region
Modify | Region | Subtract

Region and the Boolean operation commands (**Intersect, Subtract**, and **Union**) are useful for making complex shapes. In this tutorial, you create a waffle shape by applying the **Subtract** command to a group of regions, then find the mass properties of the waffle.

1. Start AutoCAD LT with a new drawing, and then draw a circle with a radius of 1.875 inches, as follows:

   Command: **circle**
   Specify center point for circle or [3P/2P/Ttr]: **0,0**
   Specify radius of circle or [Diameter]: **1.875**

2. Draw a rectangle, using object snap and point filters to draw it on the circle, as follows:

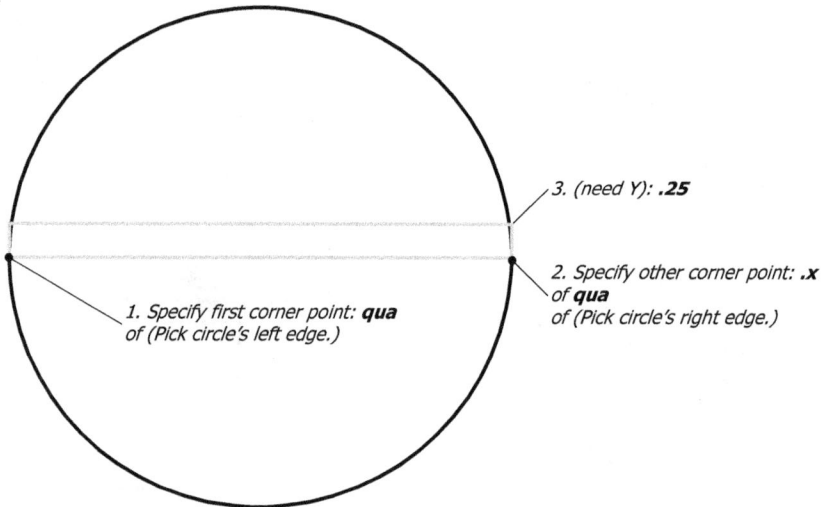

3. (need Y): .25

2. Specify other corner point: .x
of qua
of (Pick circle's right edge.)

1. Specify first corner point: qua
of (Pick circle's left edge.)

   Command: **rectang**
   Specify first corner point: **qua**
   of *(Pick circle's left edge.)*

   Specify other corner point or [Area/Dimensions/Rotation]: **.x**
   of **qua**
   of *(Pick circle's right edge.)*

   (need Y): **.25**

Notice the use of **QUAdrant** object snap, twice, to find precisely the circle's 180- and 0-degree points. The **.x** point filter allows you to pick the location of the x coordinate, then enter the y coordinate (0.25) by hand.

3. Move the rectangle to the bottom of the circle, again using object snap, as follows:

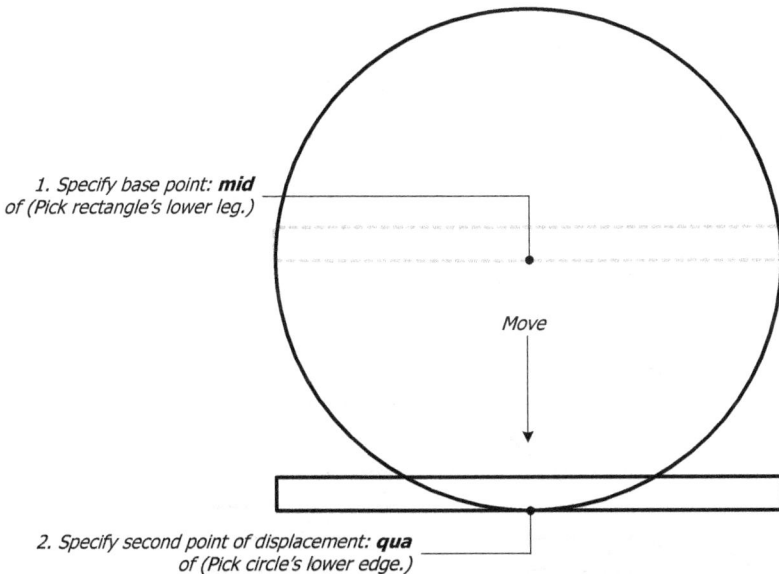

*1. Specify base point: **mid***
of (Pick rectangle's lower leg.)

Move

*2. Specify second point of displacement: **qua***
of (Pick circle's lower edge.)

Command: **move**
Select objects: **l**
Select objects: *(Press **Enter**.)*

Specify base point or displacement: **mid**
of *(Pick rectangle's lower leg.)*

Specify second point of displacement or <use first point as displacement>: **qua**
of *(Pick circle's lower edge.)*

Notice the use of the **L** (last) selection mode to select the last-drawn object visible in the viewport. The **MIDpoint** and **QUAdrant** object snaps are used to ensure precise vertical alignment.

4. The next step is to create copies of the rectangle. While we could use the **Copy** command, it is faster to employ the **Array** command.

The rectangles are arrayed twice. First, use the command-line version of the **-Array** command. (The hyphen forces AutoCAD LT to display the prompts at the command line, rather than use the dialog box.) Later, we use the dialog box version of this command.

Array the rectangle vertically, as follows:

Command: **-array**
Select objects: **1**
Select objects: *(Press **Enter** to end object selection.)*

Enter the type of array [Rectangular/Polar] <R>: *(Press **Enter** to accept default, R)*
Enter the number of rows (---) <1>: **8**
Enter the number of columns (|||) <1>: *(Press **Enter** to accept default, 1)*

Enter the distance between rows or specify unit cell (---): **.5**

Notice that AutoCAD LT instantly creates seven copies of the rectangle.

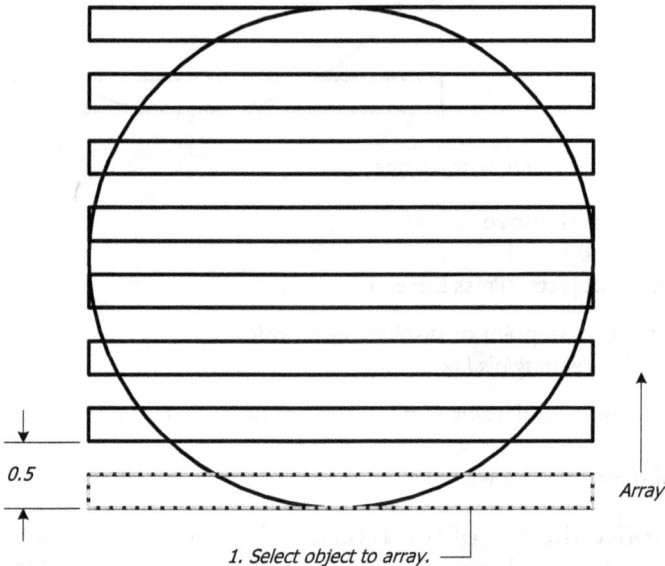

0.5

Array

1. Select object to array.

5. To create the other row of rectangles, mirror one horizontal rectangle, as follows:

Command: **mirror**
Select objects: **p**
Select objects: *(Press **Enter**.)*

Specify first point of mirror line: **0,0**
Specify second point of mirror line: **@1<45**

Delete source objects? [Yes/No] <N>: *(Press **Enter** to accept default, N)*

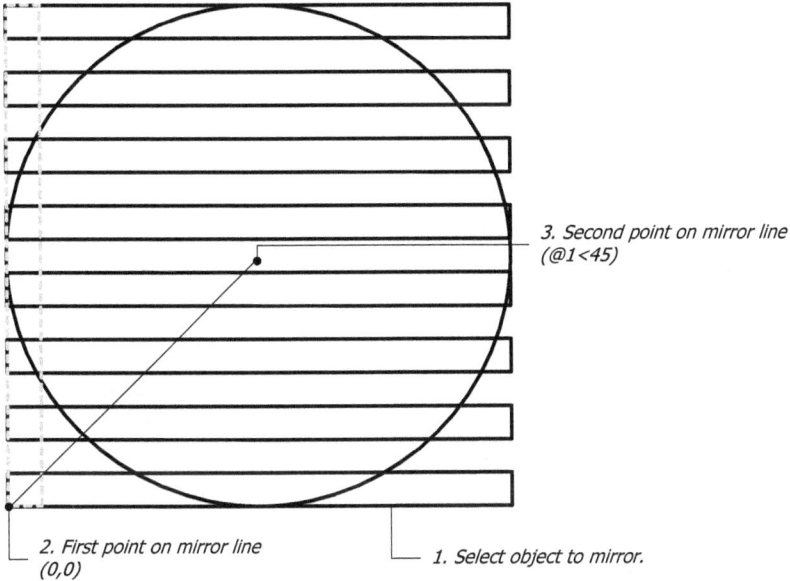

3. Second point on mirror line (@1<45)

2. First point on mirror line (0,0)

1. Select object to mirror.

Notice the use of the **P** (previous) selection set to select the same rectangle as selected for the **Array** command. If you had used **L**, AutoCAD LT would have instead selected the last-drawn object (the final object drawn by the **Array** command).

The placement of the mirror line is not crucial, as long as it is at 45 degrees, hence the use of the relative polar coordinate: **@1<45**.

6. Again, use the **Array** command, this time the dialog box version.

   From the **Modify** menu, select **Array**. Notice that AutoCAD LT displays the Array dialog box.

7. Make the following changes to the dialog box:

Array:	**Rectangular Array**
Rows:	I
Columns:	8
Column offset:	0.5

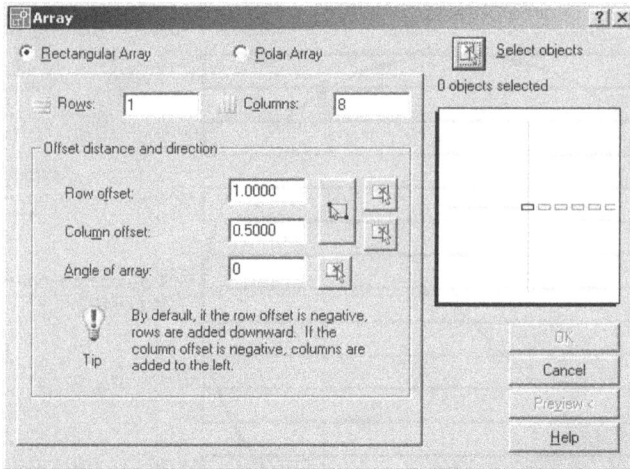

8. Click **Select objects**. Notice that AutoCAD LT removes the dialog box, and prompts you at the command line:

    ```
    Select objects: I
    Select objects: (Press Enter.)
    ```

    Enter **L** to select the last-drawn object (the vertical rectangle), then press **Enter** to return to the Array dialog box.

9. Click **OK**. Notice that AutoCAD LT instantly creates seven copies of the vertical rectangle.

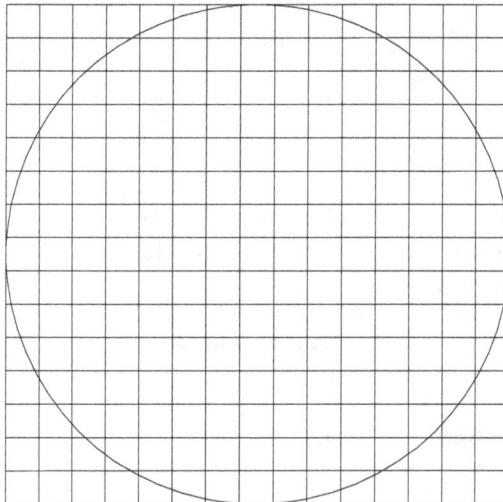

10. Convert the circle and rectangles to region objects with the **Region** command, as follows:

Command: **region**
Select objects: **all**
17 found Select objects: *(Press **Enter**.)*

17 loops extracted.
17 Regions created.

After conversion to regions, the objects look no different. The circle and rectangles are, however, circular and rectangular region objects. (Boolean operations would not work on regular circles and rectangles.)

11. Subtract the rectangular regions from the circular region with the **Subtract** command, as follows:

Command: **subtract**
Select solids and regions to subtract from...
Select objects: *(Pick circle.)*
Select objects: *(Press **Enter**.)*

Select solids and regions to subtract...
Select objects: **all**
Select objects: *(Press **Enter**.)*

To make it faster to pick all the rectangles, use **All** selection mode. The **Region** command ignores the fact that the circle has been picked twice.

Notice the result: the **Subtract** command removes the overlapping regions, producing the waffle effect — yet the 45 parts are really a single object. Those are some of the benefits to working with regions.

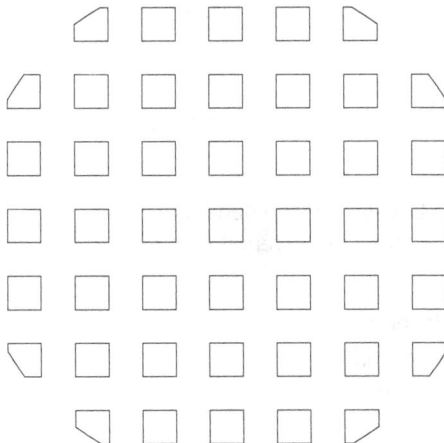

Measuring Regions

MassProp
List
Area

Another benefit to working with regions is determining their properties easily. If the waffle shape were made of regular 2D objects (such as polylines), you would have to find the area of each individual square. In contrast, the waffle shape is a single object.

To find the total area of the waffle pattern, use the **MassProp** command, as follows:

> Command: **massprop**
> Select objects: *(Pick waffle shape.)*
> Select objects: *(Press **Enter**.)*

AutoCAD LT displays the results of the analysis:

```
 AutoCAD LT Text Window - D:\Books\Ultimate Guide LT 05 - Feb 05\CD\RegionTutorial.dwg    _ □ ×
 Edit
Command: massprop

Select objects: 1 found

Select objects:

-----------------       REGIONS    -----------------
Area:                      2.7219
Perimeter:                44.3011
Bounding box:        X:  -1.6250   --   1.6250
                     Y:  -1.6250   --   1.6250
Centroid:            X:   0.0000
                     Y:   0.0000
Moments of inertia:  X:   2.3496
                     Y:   2.3496
Product of inertia:  XY:  0.0000
Radii of gyration:   X:   0.9291
                     Y:   0.9291
Principal moments and X-Y directions about centroid:
                     I:   2.3496 along [0.7071 0.7071]
                     J:   2.3496 along [-0.7071 0.7071]

Write analysis to a file? [Yes/No] <N>:                         ◄ | ►
```

So now you know: The area of the waffle pattern is 2.7219 square units.

> **TIPS**   AutoCAD LT assumes the density of the region is constant, with a value of 1.0. Some of the terms in the report generated by the **MassProp** command may be unfamiliar:
>
> **Bounding box** is the rectangular limit of the region; the coordinate describes the lower-left and upper-right corners of the corners of an imaginary rectangle that tightly encloses the region.
>
> **Centroid** is the center of mass of the region.
>
> **Moments of inertia** is a measure of the region's resistance to angular acceleration.

List, Area, and Properties

Other commands that also report the area and perimeter information of regions are **List**, **Area**, and **Properties**.

The **List** command provides a concise report of the region's area, perimeter, and bounding box.

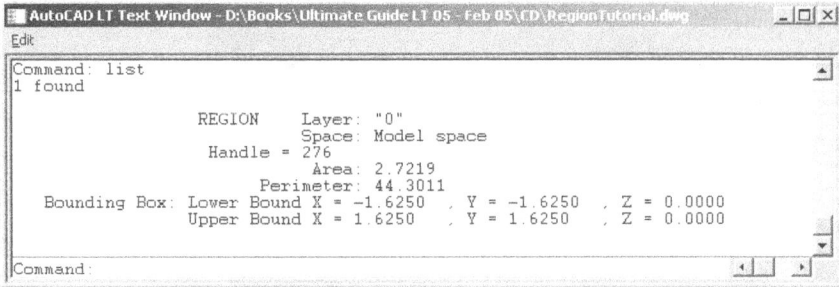

```
AutoCAD LT Text Window - D:\Books\Ultimate Guide LT 05 - Feb 05\CD\RegionTutorial.dwg    _□×
Edit
Command: list
1 found

                    REGION      Layer: "0"
                                Space: Model space
                    Handle = 276
                                 Area: 2.7219
                            Perimeter: 44.3011
    Bounding Box: Lower Bound X = -1.6250   , Y = -1.6250   , Z = 0.0000
                  Upper Bound X = 1.6250    , Y = 1.6250    , Z = 0.0000

Command:
```

The **Area** command displays an even briefer report of just the area and perimeter; use the **Object** option, and select the region:

> Command: **area**
> <First point>/Object/Add/Subtract: **o**
> Select objects: *(Pick.)*
> Area = 2.7219, Perimeter = 44.3011

The **Properties** command displays the area and perimeter in the Properties window.

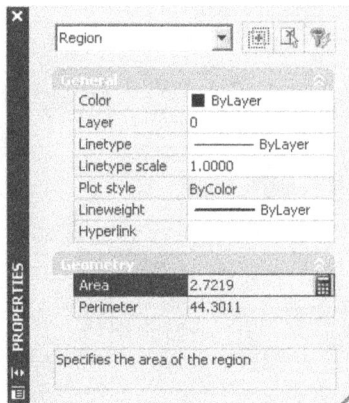

```
×
Region                  ▼  ⊞ ⊠ ▽

General
        Color         ■ ByLayer
        Layer         0
        Linetype      ──────── ByLayer
        Linetype scale 1.0000
        Plot style    ByColor
        Lineweight    ──────── ByLayer
        Hyperlink

Geometry
        Area          2.7219
        Perimeter     44.3011

Specifies the area of the region
```

Summary

This chapter introduced you to regions and Boolean operations. These concepts extend to working with 3D models in AutoCAD and other 3D software packages.

Notes

Part III

Managing
AutoCAD LT

Hand-drafted drawing courtesy Herbert Grabowski

Notes

Chapter 12

Implementing
CAD Management

In This Chapter

- Solving CAD problems, such as budgeting, education, changes to the organization, support staff, file formats, and limited resources
- Creating CAD standards and procedures
- Archival longevity

A student once asked, "What are the *disadvantages* to using CAD?" As editor of *upFront.eZine*, a weekly email newsletter for CAD users, I sometimes am asked for help from college students working on their papers.

The student said he could find plenty of information about the advantages to using CAD, but not the disadvantages. So, I posed the question to my readership, and received several replies, including one from Malaysia:

> Most CAD operators seem to use AutoCAD as a tracing machine. They use the Line, Trim, Extend, and Erase commands as if they were mimicking manual drafting. Their multi-color drawings are created on a single layer!
>
> The result is that other CAD operators cannot continue with the drawing. Because the drawing is not organized, they would rather start over than attempt to edit the drawing.

Key Terms

Proxy objects — custom AutoCAD objects defined by ObjectARX programming
Simplex — AutoCAD LT font that looks like Leroy lettering
Styles — define parameters of text and dimensions
Template drawings — define settings of new drawings; a.k.a. prototype drawing in older releases of AutoCAD LT
Third-party software — software from vendors other than Autodesk and yourself

---

Abbreviations

ACIS	Spatial Technology's Andy, Charles, Ian's System
AIA	American Institute of Architects
ARX	AutoCAD Runtime eXtension
CAD	computer-aided design or computer-aided drafting
CD-ROM	compact disc read-only memory
CPU	central processing unit; the primary chip in a computer
CSI	Construction Specifications Institute
DGN	MicroStation design file
DWG	AutoCAD drawing file
DXF	Autodesk drawing interchange format
IGES	Initial Graphics Exchange Specification
WMF	Windows Metafile Format

Part of the fault lies with their drafting departments, which have failed to implement strict CAD layering and procedures. Part of the fault lies with the engineers and architects, who just want plotted 2D drawings, which are submitted to authorities for approval.

One solution is for CAD managers to implement strict drafting standards. Another solution is for authorities to insist on the DWG file, and reject those drawings that do not meet standards."

For any office with more than one copy of AutoCAD LT, you need to think about managing the CAD software and drawings. Even if you are a sole proprietor with a single copy of AutoCAD LT, you may need to exchange drawings with clients, and therefore need to manage CAD.

It may seem negative to say it this way, but CAD management involves problem solving. The problems that need solving include budgeting, ongoing education, and drawing compatibility. Let's look at some of these.

Solving CAD Problems

After setting up the computers on the desks of drafters, you as the CAD manager need to work on the problems created by the introduction of computer-aided drafting. Knowing about the problems in advance lets you create plans for solving them.

Ongoing Budgeting

CAD is more expensive than manual drafting. Your firm spends money on hardware and software before seeing improved productivity. After the initial purchase, your firm faces maintenance costs and, in a few years, the cost of adding more CAD stations, replacing obsolete and broken hardware, and upgrading software.

After justifying the initial purchase, your toughest job will be justifying the additional expenditures for computer-aided drafting on a continuing basis. Here are some tips:

- To justify the expense, keep a record of increases in drafting productivity.
- Purchase hardware with warranties that match the economic life of the product (three years for computers, longer for CD-ROMs and other add-on components). Typically, I wait for CPU speeds to triple before purchasing new computers. Today's CPUs seem to have leveled off at 3 to 4GHz.
- To offset the cost of new replacement hardware, upgrade just the motherboard (or CPU, if it is upgradeable). Many other components, such as graphics boards and network cards, can be reused in new computers.
- Before purchasing software upgrades, check the new and improved features: are they ones that your firm can use? Just because the software vendor's marketing department has "counted" 250 new features doesn't mean that (1) there are 250 features that are new; and (2) the features are useful. Some firms, for example, skip every second software upgrade.
- Keep in mind that the cost of upgrading is more than the price of the software. Your drafters will lose productive time

learning the new features and, in some cases, the new user interface. Your hardware may need to be upgraded or replaced, and the operating system upgraded to Windows 2000 or XP.

Continuing Education

You should establish an ongoing training program for your CAD operators. Through training, drafters become more efficient, completing more drawings in less time.

Training, however, has three costs associated with it: (1) the invoiced cost of training, (2) the salary paid while in training, and (3) the loss of productive work while training.

Before installing AutoCAD, make sure the firm's principals understand that CAD requires ongoing training. Expect that drafters will be less efficient for the first three to six months; it usually takes that long to get up to speed with CAD.

Arrange for two-hour formal training sessions once every few days, rather than a single, long training period. This lets drafters exercise their newly learned skills between training sessions.

In addition to training drafters, the firm's principals and clients may need training in the ways of CAD, because they should be aware of what AutoCAD LT can and cannot deliver. For example:

AutoCAD LT can...	AutoCAD LT cannot...
Create 2D drawings	Create advanced 3D drawings or renderings
Display ACIS solid models	Create and edit ACIS solid models
Display proxy objects	Create and edit proxy objects defined by ARX
Be customized	Be programmed or linked to databases
Work with some add-on software	Work with most add-ons designed for AutoCAD

Conduct upgrade training during lunchtime; supply the lunch to encourage participation.

Organizational Changes

CAD forces firms to re-engineer themselves, because it changes the lines of communication and areas of responsibility. Here are some of the changes you could expect:

- Engineers become drafters, because they are able to create high-quality drawings themselves.
- Managers can no longer easily "look over the shoulder" to see the progress of the whole drawing.

- Instead of scheduling time with the drafting department, CAD operators need to schedule time with the plotter.
- Because CAD drawings are stored in easily copied electronic formats, your firm needs to determine how to designate the "original drawing."

To more smoothly integrate these changes you should be prepared to do the following:

- Upgrade drafters to technicians and network minders.
- Employ DWG viewing software over the network to let managers look at the projects' progress.
- Purchase one or more plotters that are fast enough to keep up with your firm's output.
- "Lock" the original drawing on a specific folder on the file server or stamp drawings with LT's time-date macro.

You can implement these procedures yourself, or you can license software that manages drawings, plotting, and filing.

Standardizing File Formats

Switching from manual to software drafting can create compatibility problems in file formats.

(There is no problem when everyone uses the same version of the same software. And in having selected AutoCAD LT, you are fortunate that AutoCAD's DWG format has become a de facto standard for CAD drawings.)

Problems arise when you have to work with drawing files created by different releases of AutoCAD or other CAD packages. Your firm needs to understand DXF, DWG, DWF, and other translation formats, as well as the issues in drawing translation. In addition, your firm will be working together with clients to solve mutual translation problems.

To eliminate the problem of drawing translation, use the CAD package your client uses. This may sound heretical in a book about AutoCAD LT, but if your client uses MicroStation, for example, you should consider deploying MicroStation to eliminate drawing translation problems.

If that is not possible, create an experimental drawing that contains all objects, fonts, layer names, linetypes, hatch patterns, and blocks used in the project. Experiment with translating the drawing and check which objects create problems. In particular, look for merged layers, exploded blocks, missing objects, and misaligned text. More details on this subject can be found in Chapter 17, "Translating AutoCAD LT Drawings."

Dealing with Finite Resources

Money may become scarce for acquiring additional CAD resources. After the initial CAD installation, be aware that management may become delighted to find AutoCAD LT paying for itself, and decide to divert parts of your budget to other pet priorities.

From the beginning, include an annual budget item (a.k.a. rainy-day fund) for upgrading the CAD system. Upgrades include networking, larger online storage, additional output devices, and third-party software.

In some cases, you can justify the cost of new additions. For instance, discipline-specific software, such as structural design and mechanical analysis, can generate additional revenue.

By knowing the potential roadblocks introduced after CAD is adopted, you are able to anticipate solutions to these problems.

Creating CAD Standards

The easy way to make AutoCAD LT more efficient is to create a CAD standard. The *CAD standard* (typically) consists of a three-ring binder that describes how to work with CAD.

The standard includes specifications for naming layers and blocks, drawing text and dimensions correctly, archiving drawing files, and other topics. In addition to the three-ring binder, standards are stored in one or more template drawings, as described later in this section.

There are several ways to write the standard. You can make it up from existing practices or borrow it from other firms. In some cases, your firm may be required to follow the standards specified by clients.

Layer Names

No international standard exists for naming layers, because the needs of drawings and the abilities of CAD packages vary widely.

Nevertheless, some disciplines have suggested layer naming standards. One, for example, is the American Institute of Architects' suggestion called the CAD Layer Guidelines. An example of an AIA layer name is ETLIGHT-EMER-xxxx, which has the following meaning:

E	Construction category, "Electrical"
T	Modifier, "Temporary"
LIGHT	Major group name, "Lighting"
EMER	Minor group name, "Emergency"
xxxx	Optional user-definable field

Other firms use a standard based on the CSI (Construction Specifications Institute), or ASCAD for civil engineering. Internationally, several countries have standards for drawings created for their countries.

Circumstances might determine the layer naming convention for your drawings. Consider these scenarios:

- As a minimum, simple drawings should have layers that separate text, hatching, and dimensions from each other. These layers can be frozen during editing to minimize the redraw and regeneration time.
- Some CAD users find that a system that maps layers to plotter pens is adequate for their purposes. Layers are given names that match the pen sizes, such as "000" or "35."
- A more complex layer naming system can be based on logical elements found in drawings your office creates. For example, civil drawings could contain layers named "STREET," "EXISTING," "DEMOLISH," "ROW," and others.

Block Names

Anything drawn twice should be turned into a block. Blocks are stored in AutoCAD LT drawings or as individual DWG files on disk. AutoCAD LT's DesignCenter is very useful for managing libraries of blocks. Feel free to make use of all 255 characters for naming blocks descriptively.

Always use logical names for blocks that segregate them by categories and types. One possible naming system is a "discipline-part-increment" name, such as Elec-LightSwitch-0203:

Discipline designator such as Elec for electrical, Arch for architectural, and Title for title blocks

Part designator such as LightSwitch

Increment number defines different models of the same part, such as 0203 for a two-pole, three-way switch

Once you have created and named symbols as blocks in the drawing, you can store them on disk with the **WBlock** command or share them with other drawings via the DesignCenter. (In older versions of AutoCAD LT, use the Content Explorer, or the **Block** option of the **XBind** command.)

Text Styles

Although AutoCAD LT can make use of any of the thousands of free TrueType fonts, it is best to limit text in drawings to a few predefined text styles based on common text fonts. All Windows computers, for example, have the Arial, Courier New, and Times New Roman fonts. You cannot assume that another computer might have any other font.

The clearest font for AutoCAD LT is Simplex, also called "RomanS," which mimics the Leroy lettering commonly used in hand-drafted drawings.

Style names can be based on the size of text, as follows:

Style Name	Text Height
SMALL	3/32"
NOTES	1/8"
SUBTITLE	5/32"
TITLE	7/32"

You use the values listed above when drawing in layout mode (known as "paper space" in older versions of AutoCAD LT). For text placed in model space, you must scale the text size using the following formula:

$$\text{Model space height} = \frac{\text{Text height (layout mode)}}{\text{Plot scale}}$$

If the plot scale is 1:500, then the text should be drawn with a height of 62.5" in order to plot 1/8" high.

$$\text{Model space height} = \frac{0.125"}{1/500} = 62.5"$$

You cannot save text styles to a file on disk, but you can share text styles via DesignCenter (in older versions of AutoCAD LT, use the **XBind** command's **Style** option).

Dimension Styles

AutoCAD LT includes international dimensioning standards, such as ISO (international), DIN (German), ANSI (American), JIS (Japanese), and Gb (Chinese). These are found in the template drawings stored in the \template folder. For example, all template drawing file names that begin with "DIN" are set up with German standards.

In addition, AutoCAD LT allows you to create *dimension styles*. Styles affect almost every aspect of dimensions: arrowheads, colors, placement of dimension text, and so on. AutoCAD LT stores the style information via system variables in the drawing.

You can specify the look and feel of dimensions with the **DimStyle** command. Like text styles, you can transfer dimension styles between drawings through DesignCenter.

Creating Template Drawings

Once you have layer names set up, assigned blocks, and created text and dimension styles, it is time to save the drawing as a template with the **SaveAs** command. (Older versions of AutoCAD LT call this the "prototype" drawing.) Give the template drawing a meaningful name, then make backup copies.

You may find yourself creating a series of template drawings, one for each discipline in your office.

To use a template drawing, use the **New** command. When the dialog box appears, select **Use a Template**, then choose the name of the previously saved template drawing.

AutoCAD includes a large number of template drawings in the \Template folder. All of them contain a title block and border drawn to standard.

TIPS A-size (imperial) is the rough equivalent of A4-size (metric); E-size is roughly equivalent to A1-size.

You can easily memorize the size of plotter media sizes: double the smaller dimension. Starting with the well-known A-size (also called "letter size") dimensions of $8^1/_2$" x 11", double the smaller dimension to arrive at B-size: 17" x 11".

Architectural-size paper is slightly larger than the engineering media sizes (listed above), and starts with a 9" x 12" sheet for A-size. The same "double the smaller dimension" rule applies:

Architectural (Imperial)		Metric	
A	9" x 12"	A4	210 x 297mm
B	12" x 18"	A3	297 x 420mm
C	18" x 24"	A2	420 x 594mm
D	24" x 36"	A1	594 x 841mm
E	36" x 48"	A0	841 x 1198mm

There are additional sizes of paper designed for long plots to accommodate the aircraft industry. These are named F through K.

Archival Longevity

When projects are complete, you need to consider how to *archive* the drawings. When I worked in the engineering office of a large aluminum smelter company, I was amazed at the yellowed paper drawings that were just 40 years old. We handled them gingerly, if at all.

Digital media doesn't suffer from turning yellow. But don't feel smug about the longevity of digital. Archived files sitting in a bank safe are not immune from damage. Over time, magnetic media, such as diskettes and tape, fail in their ability to retain information. What happens is that the magnetic flux loses its strength. Recently, I tried to install an older, DOS-based version of AutoCAD. (I needed a screen grab to illustrate AutoCAD's old user interface for the book I was writing.) Although the diskettes were just eight years old, I could not complete the installation: DOS kept complaining it could not read one of the diskettes (more than one diskette needed to be read to complete the installation).

Even optical media, such as CDs and DVDs, are suspect. There is great controversy over the life of the discs. Some experts say that compact discs last just ten years, with an even shorter shelf life for CD-R and DVD+Rs you create yourself; other experts say the discs can last 100 years. I supposed only time will tell.

Note that there is a difference between computer data and music or photographs. *All* computer data on discs and tapes is ruined when critical portions of the file structure are damaged; music tracks and digital photographs can still be accessed, even when the media has suffered some damage.

Media Obsolescence

Another concern is *media obsolescence*. Years from now, your computer might not be able to read today's commonly used media. For example, how many computers do you have that read 8" floppy diskettes or reel-to-reel computer tapes? None, probably.

I outfitted one of my computers with a $5^1/_4$" diskette drive to read old floppy disks — just in case. I foresee CD-ROM discs becoming rare at some point in the future, being replaced by DVD discs with ever increasing capacity. Fortunately, all DVD drives are backward compatible and can read CDs.

Over the years, a number of vendors of tape drives and disk cartridges have gone out of business. If they made their product to a standard (such as QIC), then you can use products from competitors.

In other cases, the product is proprietary, and you may have difficulty obtaining replacement parts. For example, SyQuest used to make a popular format of removable disk cartridges in the 1980s and 1990s. The cartridges were proprietary, and the company went out of business in 1999; no other vendor makes drives that can read their cartridge.

More recently, Iomega created a number of proprietary formats of removable discs, with names like Zip, Jaz, and Clic — and I've used them all. Even through the company licensed the production of drives and discs to other manufacturers, the formats can no longer compete in terms of capacity and have become obsolete.

File Format Changes

File formats sometimes suffer a similar fate. In many cases, however, file formats are *backward compatible*. This means that newer versions of software can read older versions of the file format. For example, AutoCAD LT 2006 can read drawings created by AutoCAD LT Release 1.

AutoCAD LT is forward compatible for three releases at a time. This means that some older releases can read newer files. For example, AutoCAD LT 2004 can read drawings saved by LT 2006. The limit is three release numbers; Release 1 cannot read DWG files created by LT 2006.

In some cases, software vendors go out of business. You can continue to use their software until technology forces you to change to software from a vendor still in business. While competitive software often reads (and less often writes) a variety of file formats, none might be able to read the now-defunct format — or might make mistakes in reading the files.

TIPS To guard against media obsolescence and long-term disintegration, a solution is to re-archive drawings: every five or ten years, copy the DWG files (and related support files) from old media to new media.

To guard against file format obsolescence, you might want to consider saving DWG files in an exchange format, such as DXF or IGES.

Using Drawings Beyond Projects

Increasingly, digital drawing data is being used for more than just creating the project. For example, your client may request your original AutoCAD LT drawings for use in FM (facilities management). FM is used to manage the facilities, such as help employees move offices; determine the location of capital assets (desks, computers, etc.); and help design new network wiring.

Indeed, the STEP/PDES committee is attempting to create a standard that would document the project from initial concept to final demolition.

Summary

In this chapter, you received a crash course in CAD management. You learned solutions to some of the issues involved in implementing computer-aided design software in your office. This chapter also provided you with some ways to set up CAD standards and how to deal with the archiving of drawing files.

In the next chapter, you learn how to keep your drawing safe by making regular backups and protecting against virus attack.

Chapter 13

Practicing
Safe Computing

━━━━━━━━━━

In This Chapter

- Knowing the pros and cons of different kinds of backup media
- Action items for creating a backup system
- Implementing real-time anti-virus software with regular updates
- Understanding firewalls and malware

In this chapter, you learn how to practice safe computing. Specifically, you learn the ways of creating backup copies of your valuable drawing files. You also learn the best way to protect your computer against attacks with real-time anti-malware and firewall software that updates regularly. The lessons of this chapter apply to all files, not just AutoCAD LT drawings.

Backing Up Is Easy to Do

Have you ever worked out the value of drawings?

Say your drafters are paid $25 per hour, and it takes an average of ten hours to produce one drawing. A set of construction drawings might contain 25 drawings. The total works out to more than $6,000.

Now consider the loss of drawing sets — for any reason: hard disk crash, flood, fire, disgruntled or accident-prone employees. For a fraction of the cost of a single drawing set, you can set up systems that automatically back up files.

Key Terms

Boot diskettes — diskettes with enough of the operating system to start the computer when the hard drive is broken

Defragment — reorders data on drives so that programs and data load faster

Differential backup — backs up files changed since the last full backup

Disk arrays — two or more drives that computers write to at the same time

Firewall — software that prevents unauthorized access through networks

Full backup — backs up all files on computers

Hot swap — drives that can be replaced while computers are running

Incremental backup — backs up files changed since the last incremental backup

Macro viruses — viruses written using VBA and attached to Microsoft documents

Malware — any software whose purpose is destruction or dishonesty

Mirrored drives — two or more disks that write data simultaneously

Recordable — CDs and DVDs that record data once

Rewritable — CDs and DVDs that record and erase data more than once

Abbreviations

CD-R	compact disc-recordable
CD-ROM	compact disc read-only memory
CD-RW	compact disc-rewritable
DAT	digital audio tape; also used by video cameras
DLT	digital linear tape
DOS	disk operating system
DVD	digital versatile disc
DVD-R	digital versatile disc-recordable (also DVD+R)
DVD-RW	digital versatile disc-rewritable (also DVD+RW)
GB	gigabyte = 1,024 megabytes
QIC	quarter-inch cartridge

Backup Media

To make backup copies of computer data, you have a choice of media: tapes, CD/DVD discs, and removable drives. Each has its benefits and drawbacks.

Perhaps the most important difference between media types is their capacity, typically measured in *gigabytes*. DVDs, for instance, have a capacity of 4.7GB. One gigabyte is 1,024MB (megabytes); one megabyte is 1,024KB (kilobytes); one kilobyte is 1,024 bytes.

Typical AutoCAD LT drawings take up less than a megabyte, which means that you can store more than 4,000 drawings files on a DVD.

Tape

Tape has been traditionally the most popular form of backup media, because it is the cheapest media. When priced by the gigabyte, tape costs less than 50 cents per GB.

Tape was also popular because until recently it had the largest capacity of any backup media. While the capacity of some tape formats has exceeded 100GB, the capacity of external hard drives now exceeds 200GB. The advantage of the large capacity is that you are less likely to need to swap tapes to perform a complete backup.

The drawback to tape is that it is the slowest of all media, particularly when searching for a specific file; think of looking for songs on cassette tapes. Another disadvantage is that tape comes in a variety of sizes and formats, which means that tapes are not as interchangeable as other backup media.

Tape is more susceptible to damage than other media from heat, magnetic fields, and mechanical stress.

Acronyms for formats include:

- **QIC** — 250GB quarter-inch cartridge, the original format for backing up personal computers
- **DLT** — 110GB digital linear tape
- **DAT** — 40GB digital audio tape, also used by video cameras

To use tape for backup, you install an internal or external tape drive with your computer.

CD and DVD

Over the last decade, the plunging price of CDs and DVDs has made them the cheapest forms of backup media when priced by the megabyte.

For backup purposes, these discs comes in two other formats:

Determining Disk Capacity Accurately

Storage capacity of media can be smaller or larger than you expect:

Smaller: Although 1 gigabyte is 1,073,742 kilobytes, all vendors of storage hardware cheat by interpreting 1GB as *one billion bytes*. I have to admit, though, that the fine print in advertising and on product boxes notes that a gigabyte has been reinterpreted as one billion.

For instance, Maxtor advertises that one of its hard drives has a capacity of 250GB; the actual capacity is 233GB — a shortfall of 7%. To find the true capacity of media, right-click the drive letter in Windows Explorer. From the shortcut menu, select **Properties**.

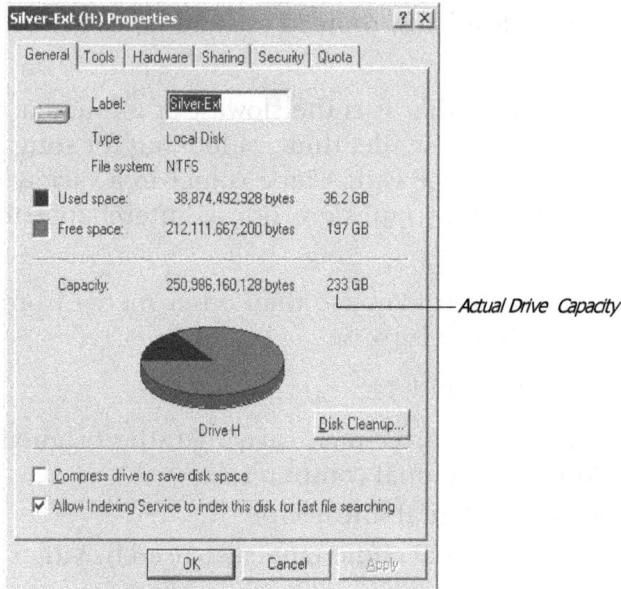

The drive's Properties dialog box reports its true capacity.

The dialog box does the following calculation:

Used Space + Free Space = Capacity

The exceptions are CDs and DVDs, which report the used space only, and not the free space or capacity.

Larger: On the plus side, most backup software compresses data, which fits about 30% more data on the media. Marketing claims may state compression rates of 2x — 100% more. The actual increase depends on the files being compressed; when backing up my entire drive, the compression ratio is 1.3x.

CD-R and **DVD-R** are discs that can be written to once; this is good for archival purposes, because the data cannot be erased or written over. The "R" is short for "recordable."

CD-RW and **DVD-RW** are discs that can be written to more than once; data can be erased and rewritten about a hundred times. This is the preferred format for backups. "RW" is short for "rewritable."

The advantage to CDs and DVDs is that they are universal. Almost every computer today has a CD/DVD drive and so can read the disc.

Another advantage is that CDs and DVDs appear to have the longest shelf life and are more rugged than most other backup media. There is controversy, however: some studies suggest CDs can last at least 100 years, while other studies suggest just 10 years.

Also, there is some question as to how reliable data is when written at high speed. Although today's CD recorders can write as fast as 50x speed, slower write speeds are recommended for accuracy, with the trade-off that the backup takes longer. For example, at 1x speed, CD "burners" write 650MB in 74 minutes, and 16x in 4.5 minutes (just over 2MB per minute). You need to double those times for the data verification stage.

(Note that CD and DVD players rev up to their high speeds on the outermost tracks only. They slow down for the inner tracks, and read/write at 1x speed on the innermost tracks. This means that the average speed is much less than the 50x boasted by advertising.)

The drawback to CDs is their small capacity, which may be too small for backup purposes — just 650 to 700MB. That means that the average disk drive needs dozens of compact discs for full backups.

To write data to CD and DVD discs, you need to install a CD/DVD recorder in your computer. The recording software included with the unit tries to find the optimal recording speed. Even so, expect to toss some CDs into the garbage when they fail to record correctly.

DVDs

While DVD discs store 7x more data than do CDs, the drawback is that among the discs and burners there are three incompatible standards: DVD+R, DVD-R, and DVD-RAM. The compatibility issues are fading as most burners now handle both the +R and -R standards, and the more expensive RAM standard is disappearing from the marketplace. Just make sure, however, that you purchase the correct type of recordable DVD disc for the burner type.

Just as the +R/-R standards war comes to an uneasy truce, a new one arises as 27GB DVDs enter the marketplace. One standard is called "Blu-ray" after the blue-colored laser beam that reads and writes the discs; the other standard is called "HD-DVD," short for "high density." At the time of writing, both sides are lining up as many supporters as possible.

Once high-density DVDs become affordable, you could put on one disc:

- 8 hours of video from your digital camcorder, or
- 6,200 songs in MP3 format, or
- 24,000 AutoCAD LT drawing files, or
- 42,000 digital camera photographs

CD and DVD Rot

CDs and DVDs are made of layers of plastic and aluminum. The aluminum layer is stamped with the data, which is read by the laser in the CD/DVD player. The aluminum is protected by a relatively thick layer of plastic, but the top (or label) side is covered by a thin layer of lacquer more delicate than the bottom (or data) side's plastic.

When the top lacquer layer is scratched, oxygen in the atmosphere oxidizes the aluminum, forming holes that corrupt the data. (Having grown up in Kitimat, "The Aluminum City" of northern Canada, I learned that aluminum metal has a dull finish because of the layer of oxidation that forms almost instantly.) Writing on the label with a ballpoint pen can tear through the lacquer and aluminum, creating a see-through CD — one that doesn't work.

DVDs are tougher, with a layer of plastic on the top and bottom. But the glue holding the two halves together can sometimes fail. Bending DVDs may cause them to fail sooner.

CD-R and DVD-R (recordable) discs are thought to have a shorter lifespan than CDs and DVDs because their heat-sensitive layer decays faster than does the aluminum. Keep the discs out of hot areas, and protect them from physical damage.

One solution to the worry of disc rot is to make multiple backups. For example, I keep one copy of valuable data files on a 250GB external hard drive and another copy on DVDs stored off-site.

Removable Drives

The most expensive backup media is the removable drive, such as the 2GB Jaz drive from Iomega. The capacity is moderate. The advantage is speed. When hooked up to a SCSI interface, a Jaz drive backs up data at 140MB/minute — about 140 times faster than the fastest CD-R drive.

The primary drawback is the high cost; removable discs are the most expensive of all forms of backup media. The secondary drawback is incompatibility; vendors create their own format for the cartridge. Even within a vendor's line, the product can be incompatible. For example, older 1GB Jaz drives cannot read the newer 2GB cartridges.

To use removable drives for backup, you will need to install the drive in your computer specific to a particular cartridge format.

External Hard Drives

You might be surprised that I suggest using hard drives for data backup — especially after I admit to having a hard drive go "bad" nearly every year on every computer I've used. But external drives are becoming common and, with their common FireWire or USB 2 interfaces, can be instantly attached to any other computer.

I use two 160GB external drives for archiving and backup. Because FireWire connections can be daisy-chained (one drive connected to the next), only one FireWire port is needed on the computer to handle the two drives and DVD burner.

Advanced Hard Drive Usage

In some advanced installations, an *array* of hard drives is used. Data is not stored to just one drive (as is traditional) but is *mirrored* to other drives. If one drive fails, the next drive contains an up-to-date copy of your data. Software is needed to make the operating system generate disk mirroring.

A disadvantge to data mirroring is that when bad data is written to one drive, the same bad data is written to the other drives.

When hard drives fail, some models have the ability to be *hot swapped*. This means the broken hard drive can be removed while the computer is still running, and the new drive installed.

USB Keys

Flash memory is memory that doesn't forget, unlike the RAM memory used inside of computers. Flash memory is slower than RAM, however. But for purposes like USB (short for "universal serial drive") keys and digital cameras, flash memory is fast enough.

USB keys are about the size of pocketknives, and consist only of memory and a connector that fits USB ports on computers. When plugged into the computer, the USB key looks like another disk drive. Files can be dragged to and from the key device. USB keys range in capacity from 32MB to over 1GB. The drawback is that flash memory is the most expensive form of backup.

As an alternative to flash memory, miniature hard drives (smaller than one inch in diameter) provide larger capacity at lower cost. Some USB keys are now actually hard drives.

Other devices can act like USB keys because they also appear as a hard drive when connected to the USB ports of computers. These devices include MP3 players, digital cameras, and portable multimedia devices.

Comparing Backup Media Costs

One way to compare the cost of backup media is to ask, "How much does it cost to store a gigabyte of data?" The following table calculates the cost per GB for the devices discussed in this chapter.

Implementing Backup Strategies

You know that you *should* back up the data stored on your department's computers. In many cases, unfortunately, implementing the backup strategy is a job left for another day. That day is usually the first time that data becomes corrupted.

As one person put it, "Doing regular data backups is like brushing your teeth. It's not fun or exciting, but you must do it if you want to keep your data (and your teeth) safe."

Cost Comparison of Backup Media

Media	Capacity[1]	Price Each[2]	Cost per GB	Backup/ Restore Speed[3]	Ruggedness/ Archival[4]
Tape					
DLT Tape	110GB	$100.00	$0.90	Slow/Slow	Med/Med
DAT Tape	40GB	$10.00	$0.25	Slow/Slow	Med/Med
Discs					
CD-R	700MB	$0.50	$0.40	Slow/Fast	High/Long
CD-RW	700MB	$1.00	$1.40	Slow/Fast	High/Long
DVD-/+R	4.7GB	$0.50	$0.10	Slow/Fast	High/Long
DVD-/+RW	4.7GB	$2.60	$1.80	Slow/Fast	High/Long
DVD-RAM	9.4GB	$12.00	$1.30	Slow/Fast	High/Long
Other					
Hard Drive	250GB	$250.00	$1.00	Fast/Fast	Low/Med
Jaz Cartridge	2GB	$60.00	$30.00	Fast/Fast	Med/Med
USB Key	1GB	$150.00	$150.00	Fast/Fast	High/Long

[1] Representative capacity; capacity may increase over time as technology improves.
[2] Representative price researched in January 2005. Actual prices will vary, and may fall over time.
[3] *Backup/Restore Speed* refers to the time it takes to create a backup copy and the time to restore the data.
[4] *Ruggedness/Archival* refers to the ruggedness of the media (how well it withstands physical and electromagnetic damage) and the longevity of the data on the media.

Portions of the following backup strategies are reprinted by permission of Enhanced Software Technologies, now defunct.

1. Do Backups on a Regular Schedule

As CAD manager, you must create a schedule for backing up data. If the number of files is small, it is easiest to perform a *full backup* every day. If the total bytes or files to be backed up is large or exceeds the size of your backup media, then perform a *partial backup* every day, and do a full backup every week or month. Some backup software automatically performs a full backup after every tenth partial backup.

There are two types of partial backup:

Incremental backups — back up the files changed since the last incremental backup. An incremental backup is faster, but the restore takes longer. If you have one full backup and a week's worth of incremental backups, a complete restore consists of the full backup plus all seven incremental backups.

Differential backups — back up all files changed since the last full backup. The differential backup takes longer, but the restore is much faster. To perform a complete restore, you need the full backup plus just the most recent differential backup.

The best way to make sure that backups are done regularly is to let the backup software do it automatically. Set it up to run at a regular time every day. In most cases, it's best to schedule backups for the middle of the night, when the computer is not busy.

When you let the computer do most of the work, you remove the drudgery from the important job of doing a backup.

Backup systems sometimes include simple backup software, or you can download such from the Internet. Full-featured backup software is not expensive.

2. Maintain Physical Security for the Backup Media

The backup media — whether discs or tapes or flash memory — contain valuable data about your company. They should be stored in a secure location. Anyone (a competitor or maybe a disgruntled employee) can steal tapes and discs carelessly left lying around on desks. This can do more damage than any computer virus or hacker.

It's a good idea to maintain a copy of your important data in a separate location (or in a fireproof cabinet). For example, one trusted employee could take a copy of the backup tape home each night. If backup copies are not stored off-site, then disasters such as fire and flooding could destroy your computer (source of the original data) and the backup data. When I go on vacation, I take along a full backup on a Jaz cartridge, which takes up almost no room in the luggage.

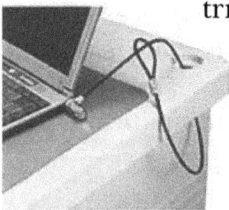

Also vulnerable are notebook computers, which are easily transportable (i.e., stolen) and usually contain gigabytes of data on the hard drive. I have heard of a thief who, acting like a courier (not all couriers wear uniforms), walked into a manager's office and left with a notebook computer. The alarm was not raised until an employee noticed the "courier" riding off on a bicycle, notebook computer under arm. Notebook computers are also stolen from cars and homes. Locking devices are available for notebook computers, which look like a thinner version of antitheft bicycle cables.

3. Rotate Your Backup Media

Some managers think they save money by using a single tape (or other media) to hold all daily backups — data from Monday through Friday is overwritten to one tape. Their computer writes today's backup data on top of yesterday's data.

Imagine the problem if that single tape went bad, failing while doing the unattended backup. Don't think it can't happen — Murphy's law says it will. All it takes is a power surge, static electricity, a misentered command, or almost anything else. This advice is especially true for media that hold hundreds of gigabytes of data.

As a minimum, you should have two sets of backup tapes, called "Set A" and "Set B." Always alternate your backups between the sets. Write one day's backup to Set A, the next day's to Set B, and so on.

It's better to have five backup tapes, one for each day of the week. If one set fails during a backup, you will still have the previous day's backup data that is good.

When you use more than one set of media for backups, you get more than just redundancy. It also saves wear and tear on the media. Retire your old media before they wear out and become unreliable.

A story I heard many years ago told of a backup drive that itself was faulty, physically damaging the backup media. The CAD manager accidentally destroyed two sets of backup media before realizing where the problem lay. Fortunately, he had a third set. Similarly, Zip drives from Iomega have been found to stop working correctly — a problem that was called "the click of death."

Don't try to save money on backup media. Even the most expensive tape is a hundred bucks — your data is worth more than that!

4. Create a Boot Diskette

When your hard drive crashes, you need another way to reboot. Without a boot diskette, you're "dead in the water."

Microsoft prompts you to create the boot diskette during installation of the system — misleadingly calling it the "Windows Startup Diskette." If you have ever tried it, you will have found that it doesn't start up Windows; instead, it starts the computer with a bare-bones version of DOS.

The workaround is to create your own boot diskette. Actually, it shouldn't be a diskette, since the capacity of a diskette (1.44MB typical; 2.44MB maximum) is minuscule compared to the dozens of megabytes needed by the Windows operating system.

You have a couple of options. One is to create a diskette that boots DOS, then starts up Windows from another device, such as a removable hard disk. This is a complicated process for most people, so software is available that creates the bootable diskette and copies the system files to the removable drive. In addition, the software monitors your computer and alerts you to update the discs when system files change. For a while, I used Norton System Doctor SE, since it came free with the Iomega Zip drive.

The other option is to boot directly from the removable hard disk. The BIOS of almost all of today's computers allows you to boot from a drive other than A: (diskette drive) or C: (primary hard drive). For example, I can instruct my computer to boot from the CD-ROM drive, a Zip drive, or another drive.

5. Make a Copy of the Restore Utility

This seems obvious, but people forget to include their restore software when creating the boot diskette. (You did create a boot diskette, didn't you?)

It's a good idea to make at least two copies of your boot diskette (who knows what can happen!). Like your backup data, keep the restore and boot diskettes secure, and keep a copy off-site.

6. Verify the Backup Data

Your backup data isn't valid unless it's correct. Some free backup utilities are notoriously unreliable when writing data to a tape. If an error occurs, your data could be lost, without any kind of error message or warning.

Verifying the backup is the best way to make sure that the data is correct. Ensure that the backup software has this feature. While this doubles the

time it takes to create the backup, time isn't an issue if the backup happens overnight. There are several types of verification:

Filename check — is the simplest verification that simply re-reads the file names. It does not check the data.

Checksum verification — scans for errors by reading the data that was just written. A checksum verification is done for each block of data. This is a quick check (only a few minutes for a 60MB tape) that immediately detects most kinds of failures.

Inspection mode — verifies data by using error-detecting checksums, which check the integrity of the data. If there are errors, the backup software lists the file names and the location of the problem. Backup tapes can be inspected at any time — it is not necessary to compare the data to the original.

Differences mode — is the most comprehensive verification where the backup software checks for differences in file size, changes in the data, date changes, status changes, and link changes. If there are any differences between the data on the disk and the data on the media, the software points them out.

7. Keep a Backup Log

Keeping backup logs saves you time and trouble. There are two kinds of logs you should keep: a file information log and an error log. Backup software generally generates a file that contains both logs.

The **file information log** contains a list of files that were backed up, the date of each file, and the label of the media containing the files. If you need to restore a file, the file information log will make it much easier to find the proper media.

The **error log** records the errors that may occur during the backup process. This is especially important when you run backups automatically.

Always monitor your log files to make sure that each backup was done successfully. Check each log for messages that might indicate a problem.

8. Label the Backup Media

Not labeling the backup media is not fatal, but it causes confusion when you're trying to find the tape or disc you need. Some managers set up a media management system and keep a database containing the media labels and information about the archive.

Even if you have a management database, it's still a good idea to label each tape or disc in case the database crashes. You should label each tape or disc with:

- Date of the backup
- Backup level (full, differential, or incremental)
- Any other important information

To reduce some of the problems associated with keeping track of media, backup software often allows you to electronically label each tape or disc.

9. Practice Restoration

It is no good backing up data if you do not know how to restore it. While restoring data following the disaster is not the time to find out that the restoration system does not work — or you don't know how to work it.

Malware Protection

As virus writers become more clever, the antivirus companies try to keep up with the "game" (as virus writers think of their craft). Today's antivirus software updates itself every day and operates in *real time*: when you open a file or email, the software instantly checks the file for danger.

You must have antivirus software for two reasons: (1) to protect your own computers from viruses, and (2) to protect the computers of your clients, in case you accidentally send them a virus.

I mention email because most virus attacks against computers now come through email. In some cases, I've received email that included a Word document (often a press release) with a macro virus. Each sender was embarrassed to find out that they had sent me a virus; clearly, none had real-time antivirus software running on their computer. How would you feel if you unknowingly sent your most valued client a malicious virus?

Other viruses carried by email read your list of email addresses, then send a copy of itself to each one. Viruses can be transported over local networks, too. Several years ago, one such virus began attacking another computer connected to mine over the local area network. I was puzzled by the sudden amount of disk activity (the virus was hunting for DOC files). I got worried and turned off the computer. Fortunately, I had backups of the couple of crucial files that had been erased by the virus.

The virus epidemic is primarily the fault of Microsoft, when the company made the foolish decision to allow VBA (Visual Basic for Applications) macros to be included in otherwise benign document files and automatically installed ActiveX components in Web pages. In the minds of Microsoft managers responsible for software design, convenience trumps security. It is convenient to remove the front door of your house; it is security to leave the door in place and to require visitors to negotiate with the deadbolt lock.

(Other operating systems, such as Unix, Linux, and Mac OS X, can be attacked by malware. In these cases, however, the operating systems were designed with security in mind, and so are far less susceptible.)

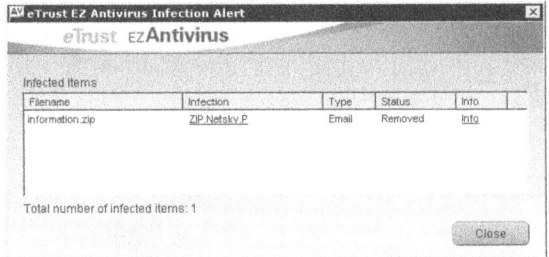

There are two lessons to be learned: (1) install real-time antivirus software that checks every file as it is used, and (2) regularly download updates from the antivirus vendors; this is usually done over the Internet and updates your software automatically. Most antivirus vendors update their software every few days.

AutoCAD LT Is Safe, So Far

As of the writing of this book, no viruses have ever been written that specifically target AutoCAD drawing files. I suspect the reason is that Autodesk software has escaped the notice of the virus writers.

In theory, it might be possible. A macro virus was written to attach to Visio drawing files. It was activated when the infected document was opened. The macro virus used with Visio could be used with AutoCAD, because it also runs VBA. AutoCAD LT is immune from macro viruses, however, because it lacks the Visual Basic for Applications programming interface.

Malware and Firewalls

While *malware* refers to any software that acts maliciously, its specific meaning refers to software that hijacks your computer without your knowledge. Malware often appears on computers as a result of using Microsoft's Internet Explorer as the Web browser (I use Opera as my primary Web browser). Certain Web sites you visit contain code that IE downloads automatically. Other Web sites seem to offer you helpful software for free.

In either case, the software is downloaded and installed. It then sends information about your computer back to a collector Web site. It may even collect your usernames and passwords as you visit shopping sites.

The solution is to use free anti-malware software, such as Ad-Aware from www.lavasoft.de. Run this software every week to hunt down and remove malicious code.

Firewalls

Your first line of defense should be the firewall. There are two kinds of firewalls, hardware and software, and you should install both.

Hardware firewalls are built into the routers that connect your computer to the Internet and other local computers. The purpose of hardware firewalls is to hide your computer from all other computers. If a malicious hacker doesn't know your computer exists, it cannot be attacked. Even if you have just one computer, purchase a router to hide it from attack.

Software firewalls protect your computer from transmitting data without your permission. The firewall does not distinguish between legitimate and illegitimate software, so you have to tell it whether the access request is okay. It remembers the names of honest programs, so it bugs you only once for them. I use the free ZoneAlarm software from www.zonealarm.com.

Summary

In this chapter, you learned how to take safety precautions to protect your valuable data against loss and from malware. The backup of data stored on your computer's hard drives can be automated, so that copies are made even when you forget to.

Real-time virus protection protects the files on your computer against damage from viruses, and firewalls protect your computer from inbound and outbound attacks.

Chapter **14**

Introduction to Networking

In This Chapter

- The benefits and drawbacks to networking
- The history of networking
- Today's network standards
- Selecting network options

(If you already understand networking, skip this chapter and continue with the next chapter, "Working with Networked AutoCAD LT.")

Even when your office has as few as two computers, it can benefit from networking. When computers are *networked*, they are connected together so that they can share the files and programs stored on each other's drives, as well as printers, drives, and some other peripherals.

Networking does two things well: share files and share printers. The reason goes back to the days when disk space and printers were expensive. How expensive? An ad in a computer magazine from the mid-1980s priced 20MB hard drives at $2,200 — each. The first laser printer I encountered was a ten-foot long Xerox unit at the University of British Columbia computing center; in 1979, it cost $750,000 and it printed 120 pages a minute.

Key Terms

Access protocols — determine how to handle two or more computers trying to communicate at the same time over the network

Ethernet — most commonly used access protocol among personal computers

Extranet — networks that connect computers in several offices using the Internet

File locking — method of preventing users from working on files edited by others

Internet — network system that lets dissimilar computers communicate with each other using TCP/IP

Intranet — network that connects users within an office using the Internet protocol

Networks — software, hardware, and cables that connect computers to share resources, like files and printers

Packets — "envelopes" of data prefixed by destination addresses

Packet collision — when two computers try to send data at the same time

Revision control — method of managing the revision of drawings and other documents

Sneakernet — sharing files by walking about the office, USB key in hand

Turnkey — vendors who provide complete computer systems, including "turning the key" to start the system

Abbreviations

10Base2	coaxial network cabling with BNC connectors
10BaseT	twisted-pair network cabling with RJ-45 connectors
ARCnet	Attached Resource Computer Network
AUI	attachment unit interface
CSMA/CD	Carrier Sense Multiple Access with Collision Detection
LAN	local area network
MB	megabytes (1,024 kilobytes)
Mb/sec	megabits per second
MS-DOS	Microsoft disk operating system
NIC	network interface card
NLM	network license manager
TCP/IP	Transmission Control Protocol/Internet Protocol
WAN	wide area network

For that reason, networks were designed to allow several computers to share these "scarce" resources. Today, of course, disk drives and printers are cheap like borsch.

Today, the network has become useful for sharing files between users — no matter where in the world they are located — as well as accessing a variety of hardware, such as printers, plotters, and drives.

For example, you might have a laser printer connected to one computer, a color inkjet to another computer, and an E-size plotter connected to a third. When the three computers are networked together, each computer has access to all three printer/plotters.

Software can also be shared. Parts libraries and databases, for example, are instantly available over the network.

This chapter provides an overview of how networks work, placing its emphasis on using AutoCAD LT on a network for a small office. I make no attempt to discuss network issues of a more general nature, such as setting up email servers, employing groupware software, or getting Web servers working.

Benefits of Networking

The weekly flier from the local electronics superstore arrived just now. Its "We Make Networking Easy" feature promotes wireless networking equipment, and the ad copywriter lists these advantages to networking:

Easily transmit information — transmit video files, music, and pictures quickly and easily without losing performance.

Secure your information — protect your network against Internet hackers through added security features.

Save space and money — save time, money, and space by sharing printers, files, music, pictures, and a single Internet connection among several users.

Enjoy interactive games — play online games with multiple players... *oops, how did that one get in here?*

Work from anywhere — transmit data by radio waves, allowing you to work without wires anywhere in the home (assuming a wireless network is installed).

Those are some of the advantages for networked computers at home. If your office is not yet networked, here are some advantages to consider for CAD users:

- Sharing files
- Sharing peripherals
- Easier installation of software
- Working in groups
- Enforcing standards

File Sharing

The primary benefit of networking your computers is sharing files. No longer do you have to walk around the office, diskette or Zip disk in hand, to give your co-worker a copy of your drawing. An AutoCAD LT drawing expects additional information stored in any number of support files, such as text fonts, linetypes, and menu macros. When you carry the drawing file on diskette, it's easy to forget the support files. When the drawing is accessed over the network, the support files are there.

Accessing drawings on a co-worker's computer over the network is as simple as selecting another drive. Every one of AutoCAD LT's file dialog boxes (such as those displayed by the **Open** and **SaveAs** commands) has an item labeled "Network Neighborhood." This lets you connect the drives (hard drives, floppy drives, CD-ROM drives, etc.) on other computers to your computer — provided the owners of those other computers have given permission for their drives to be *shared*.

Revision Control

Being able to access drawings over the network is a great time-saver, although it leads to less exercise for employees. More seriously though, network-wide access of drawing files leads to the problem of *revision control*. Consider this example:

> I open a drawing located on *Heidi's* computer. I work on the drawing, and save it to *my* computer.
>
> There are now two copies of the drawing: an older copy (the original, actually) is on Heidi's computer, and a newer copy is on mine.
>
> At some point, Heidi will edit her now-older drawing, and then your office will be in an uproar. Who is at fault for having created multiple copies of the drawing — each copy a different version?

It is then that the value of project management software becomes apparent. This class of software:

- Forces CAD operators to work with a single copy of each drawing
- Forces drawings to be stored in a single folder (except for backup copies)
- Places read/write/edit restrictions on each drawing
- Allows everyone to see who has currently checked out drawings
- Allows quick viewing and redlining of drawings

Peripheral Sharing

Networking lets you share peripherals without having to roll them from cubicle to cubicle. Sharing an expensive peripheral, like an E-size color inkjet printer, among several users helps justify the cost of networking — and the printer.

Sharing peripherals, like printers and DVD burners, is similar to accessing drives over the network. Each computer must give its permission before any other computer can access it.

Installation Ease

Application software has become aware of networks. As the network administrator or CAD manager, you might want to install the software from your computer onto the other users' computers over the network.

Even when the setup software is not designed for installation over a network, you can still go from computer to computer, running the Setup program remotely from the CD drive located back at your computer.

Floating Software Licenses

Because networks make it easy for everyone to share a single copy of software, programmers have thought up a variety of ways to keep this software "theft" from occurring.

AutoCAD (not LT) is available with a network license manager (NLM) that permits "floating software licenses." The NLM software keeps track of the number of users launching copies of AutoCAD from the central file server. If your firm is licensed for 20 users, for instance, then the NLM allows up to 20 copies of AutoCAD launched over the network.

When user 21 tries to start AutoCAD, he gets a message asking him to wait until another user ends a session of AutoCAD. To increase the number of authorized users, you pay an additional licensing fee and obtain a new authorization number that permits more users.

An NLM, however, is no longer available for AutoCAD LT. Autodesk says, "Although AutoCAD LT is no longer available with a network version or license manager, it works with other license management utilities."

Workgroup Capability

By networking your firm's computers together, you and your co-workers can begin to collaborate on projects. AutoCAD LT's **Xref** command, for example, lets you view other drawing files stored anywhere on the network. Project managers can use DWG and DWF viewer software, such as Volo View and DWF Viewer, to review and redline all drawings belonging to their project, no matter which CAD operator has the drawing.

Software is available from Autodesk that lets you collaborate on designs with other designers connected to the Internet — with the individual parts stored on computers anywhere in the world.

Autodesk Vault software tracks work in progress with Inventor Series, AutoCAD Mechanical, and Electrical. The software watches for poor design reuse and version control.

Autodesk Streamline software provides collaboration with suppliers and customers using email notifications and project reporting. Streamline is *hosted*, which means you access it with a Web browser, and don't need to install the software on your office network.

Autodesk Productstream software automates release management among multiple team members, ensuring that drawings are complete, accurate, approved, and released to manufacturing.

Autodesk Buzzsaw is a Web-based service that allows multiple designers in different locations to collaborate on designs.

Standards Enforcement

When two or more users share AutoCAD and other files, the need suddenly arises for standards. If drawings are not created the same way, then one CAD operator will have difficulty adapting to another's "homegrown" system of layers, naming, colors, and so on.

When files are not stored using a logical system of files and folder names, then one CAD operator will spend too much time looking for drawings created by another.

Disadvantages of Networking

Despite the electronic superstore's promise that "We Make Networking Easy," networks have disadvantages: downtime from broken network links; greater chance of viruses attacking a larger number of computers; more likely that employees accidentally (or deliberately) damage data.

Of all the problems I have with computers, the most time is spent solving network problems. Sometimes I can figure out the problem; other times, the problem solves itself when the computer finally finds the network again after a wait of several days.

A network lets you do some things easily: share files, printers, and broadband Internet connections. Everything else is more difficult to implement. Think about what is included in "everything else": sharing email and faxes, performing network-wide backups, sharing scanners, and so on.

Network-aware Software Costs More

To share email, you need to install "mail server" software on one computer. Its job is to direct email to the correct computer, and allows employees to send email to each other, as well as to destinations on the Internet.

Backup software is included free with Windows and with some backup media but does not work over networks; the software has been hobbled to prevent it from "seeing" networked computers. To back up files over networks, you have to purchase software designed for network-wide backups.

Networks can waste paper, too. I was puzzled why one networked laser printer sometimes spewed out pages of nearly blank paper. The reason: one networked computer had its printers configured incorrectly. The driver for the color inkjet printer had been redirected to the laser printer port, and since the laser printer misunderstood the print codes, it printed one line of text per page until it ran out of paper.

History of Networking

Setting up networks today is trivial. But it was not always so. In the early days of CAD (I'm talking about the 1980s), there were two options: buy a CAD system with networking built-in or buy one without.

The CAD system with networking truly was a *system*. In the 1980s, it was called a "turnkey system" because the vendor did everything, right down to "turning the key" to turn on the system. The vendor, which had a name like Intergraph or Computervision, provided the hardware, the software, the installation, the training, and the customization at a cost of about $100,000 to $150,000 per seat (station). The hardware consisted of everything needed for CAD works: a central file server, several diskless terminals, matching digitizing tablets, a plotter, the workstation furniture, and the networking.

Back then, CAD systems without networking weren't considered a system, because you had to be a handyman who assembled it yourself. You bought the personal computer (called a "microcomputer" in those days) for $4,000 or $10,000 (depending on models and options) from one dealer, and bought the AutoCAD software for $1,000 (yes, AutoCAD was 4x cheaper back then) from the same or maybe another dealer. Later, as the budget allowed, you added the digitizing tablet, a pen plotter, better graphics board and monitor — along with training yourself and doing your own customization. Networking was not available for the personal computer, at least initially.

If your computers didn't have a network, then you used *sneakernet*. This method of sharing files consisted of copying them to diskettes, then walking them to the destination computer. Sharing a laser printer worked the same way: print the files to diskette, then carry the diskette to the computer that had the printer.

Early Networking with PCs

When networking did become available for PCs, it was awful to deal with. There was no single standard, and the terminology was confusing. The hardware and software for networking was expensive. Until v3.0, the MS-DOS operating system didn't have any provisions for networking. The network driver software took too much precious memory away from AutoCAD.

The primary alternative to MS-DOS was Novell NetWare, but it was expensive. AutoCAD itself was not friendly to networking until Release 11 (released in September 1990) introduced *file locking*, which prevented users from working on drawings edited by other users.

I recall the local 3COM office offering to install a network, free, in the office of the CAD magazine I worked for at the time. Printing was the primary task we were interested in having networked; we had little need to share files.

After the crew finishing installing the network and running wires behind computers, we eagerly printed a document to the office's lone laser printer. We waited expectantly for the printed pages to emerge... We waited... And waited...

Some 20 minutes later, the first page emerged. I still recall the perplexed look on the faces of the 3COM techies as they first tried to solve the problem, then reluctantly yanked the network equipment and wiring out of our office.

By the early 1990s, however, networking became a standard feature when Microsoft released Windows for Workgroups. This little-known release bundled Windows v3.1 with two ethernet cards, 25 feet of coaxial network cabling, a screwdriver, and an instructional videotape. It worked, and Windows 95 included networking invisibly — the hardware was left out by Microsoft. Within a few years, network cards were usually standard in new computers, and Windows 98 automatically detected them via plug and play.

The Internet Becomes the Network

A tagline from Sun Microsystems read, "The network is the computer." Nobody really understood what that meant, until the Internet became popular.

By the late 1990s, the Internet became the ultimate network. Computers were no longer restricted to being networked within an office (called a "LAN," or local area network) or within a corporation (called a "WAN," or wide area network). The Internet allowed any computer to connect with any other computer, no matter where they were located. The terminology changed: LANs became "intranets," while WANs became "extranets."

Windows 98 took advantage — some, including the U.S. government, said "unfair advantage" — of the Internet by smudging the line between files located on the computer and those located on the Internet. AutoCAD LT 98 was the first release of LT to take advantage of this, allowing us to open drawing files located anywhere: on our computers, on any local computer connected via network, or from any accessible Web site on the Internet.

Network Standards Today

Today, there are very few decisions to make before setting up networks in small offices. The only decision you need to make is whether the network is to be wired, wireless, or both.

Fortunately, standards have settled to the point that you have no other decisions to make. Any network card you pick up from the local computer superstore works because they are all designed to the ethernet standard. Indeed, if your computers are recent, they probably have the ethernet connector built into the motherboard.

Ethernet

Ethernet is the name of the access protocol that has become standard for networking personal computers. The *access protocol* decides what happens when two or more computers try to communicate at the same time.

Technical Details of Networking

Data is sent over networks in packets. A *packet* is like an envelope; you write the address for its destination on the envelope, and enclose the letter (the data) inside the envelope. The network packet consists of the address of the destination computer, followed by the data.

The speed of networks is measured in Mb/sec — megabits per second. (The lowercase "b" indicates bits; an uppercase B indicates bytes.) Recall that there are 8 bits to the byte, so the typical 100Mb/sec card transmits data at a rate of *up to* 750MB (megabytes) per minute. That's like the contents of an entire CD per minute. For more money, you can install a 1Gb/sec network that transmits data *up to* 10 times faster.

Notice that I emphasize "up to." In practice, networks never reach their rated speed due to constraints and overhead. The *constraints* include how fast the computer can feed data to the network card and receive data from the card, the design of the card, and how busy the network is. (When the network is requested to transmit a lot of data between many computers, the traffic slows down — just like when there are too many cars on a freeway.) The *overhead* includes the headers added to the data to direct it to the correct computer and checksums to ensure the data arrives correctly.

Research shows that most cards rarely do better than 80% of their theoretical potential. For the first edition of this book, I tested the practical speed of my office's 10Mb/sec (75MB/min) network. I copied 500 files between two computers, measuring a speed of 33MB/min from the slower computer to the faster computer; in the other direction (from faster to slower computer), I measured 16MB/min.

Wireless networks are still developing. As a result, you are faced with standard names that look confusingly similar: 802.11 is the overall name, with letters designating different speeds:

Standard	Speed	Comments
802.11**b**	10Mb/sec	The first standard; all wireless products produced today work with this standard.
802.11**g**	54MB/sec	Faster and compatible with b.
802.11**a**	54Mb/sec	More stable than g but not compatible with b.

Wireless is also known as "WiFi" and "WiMax." Expect wireless products with even faster speeds to arrive in the coming years.

Ethernet was developed by a company called 3COM. Ethernet became the most popular since it is cheap, fast, and flexible (works peer-to-peer or with routers). Other access protocols have names like Token Ring (developed by IBM) and ARCnet (developed by Datapoint), and were too expensive or too slow.

Going back to the freeway analogy, a computer network is like a one-way freeway; all the cars drive in one direction at a time. When a computer wants to transmit data, ethernet (or CSMA/CD, as it is known technically) causes the computer to listen for no traffic. When there is no traffic, the computer sends its data to all the other computers on the network. Each computer reads the address on the packet as it goes past; when the address on the packet matches the destination computer's address, the computer reads the data, then sends an acknowledgment of receipt back to the sending computer.

When two computers try to send data at the same time (this is called "packet collision"), both stop sending packets. Each waits for a random amount of time, then tries to send again.

10BaseT Cables and Connectors

Most network cards connect to just one kind of cable: 10BaseT (a.k.a. twisted pair). The 10BaseT cable looks like fat telephone wire, and it uses an RJ-45 connector at both ends, which look like fat telephone connectors.

Inside the insulation, pairs of wires are twisted about one another to help reduce the electromagnetic radiation. Whereas telephone connectors are four wires wide, RJ-45 network connectors are eight wires wide.

Twisted pair has become more common than thin coax, even though it has more disadvantages. Twisted-pair cabling is more susceptible to damage and electrical interference. Twisted-pair cabling requires the use of a *hub*, which adds a hundred dollars to the cost of the network.

The official name of 10BaseT (the T is short for "twisted pair"). Breaking down the name, we get the following meaning:

10 refers to the 10Mb/sec transmission speed (no longer valid, because the cable can also be used for 100Mb/sec networks).

Base refers to the *baseband* method of data transmission, which uses a direct current pulse.

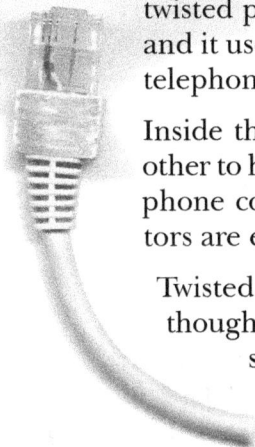

T refers to the maximum length of *T*wo hundred meters between the farthest computers (600 feet).

The *minimum* length of coax cable between two computers, by the way, is 2 meters (6 feet). A box that strengthens the signal, call a *repeater*, is needed for distances longer than 200m.

Other Cables and Connectors

Some network hardware might also work with BNC (bayonet nut connector) and/or AUI (attachment unit interface) connectors. The AUI is a 15-pin D-shape connector designed for transceivers, which are small adapters that permit the connection to thick coax cables.

Thin coax cable (10Base2) looks like the coaxial cable used for wiring cable TV in your home. It is called "coaxial" because it consists of a solid center wire, surrounded by insulation, a braided wire, and more insulation, usually black in color. The braided wire acts as a shield, preventing both the emission of electromagnetic radiation and the network data from being corrupted by external electrical and magnetic influences. It is called "thin" coax because the original specification called for coaxial cabling that was nearly a half-inch thick!

Thin coax cables connect with BNC connectors, which is different from the screw connector used by cable television wiring.

Network Topology

There are two basic ways to string network cabling from computer to computer: star or daisy chain. With today's network, star topology is the most common.

Star Topology

Star topology strings every computer to a central box, called a *hub*. 10BaseT twisted pair cabling is usually used. One end of the cable plugs into the back of the network card, just like plugging a phone into the wall outlet; the other end plugs into the hub.

The advantages to star topology are neater wiring layouts and fewer network breakdowns. This method requires no terminating resistors, and if a break happens, it is isolated to one computer.

The disadvantages are the extra cost of the hub and the lowered resistance to electromagnetic radiation.

Anatomy of Network Cards

Networks cards are available with a variety of capabilities. Indeed, your computers may not need one because the networking chips and connectors are often included on the computer's motherboard.

Illustrated below is a PCI network adapter with two connectors: one is the 10BaseT telephone-like connector, and the other the 10Base2 connector.

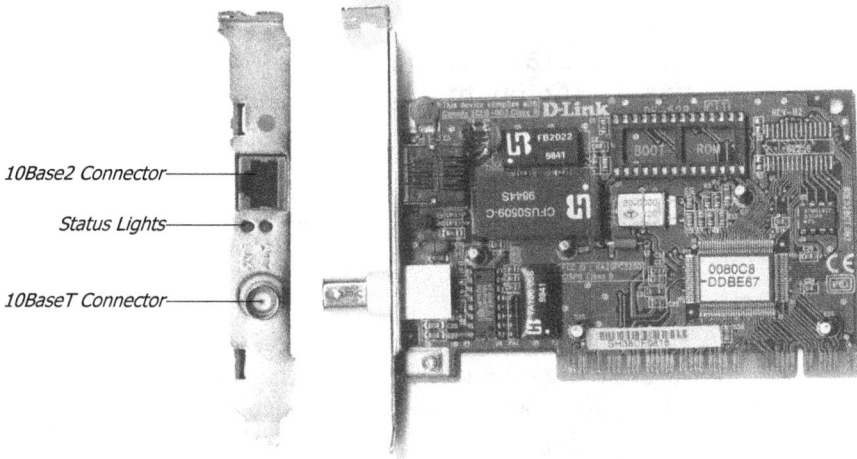

10Base2 Connector

Status Lights

10BaseT Connector

Between the two connectors are the network status lights:

LINK — lights up when the cable connects the card to the hub
ACK — flickers when data is transmitted and received

Wireless cards have an antenna instead of connectors. The figure below illustrates a PC Card network card that plugs into notebook computers.

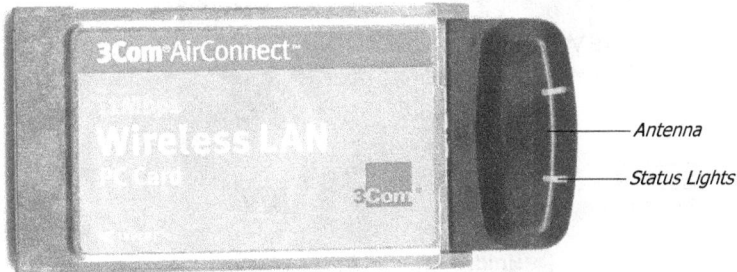

Antenna

Status Lights

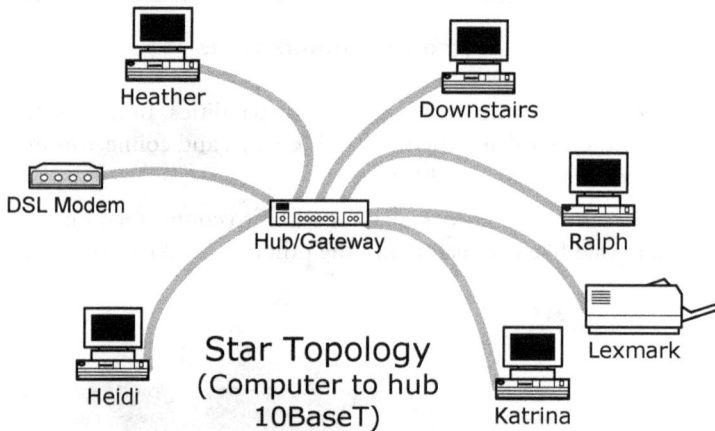

Star Topology
(Computer to hub
10BaseT)

Wireless networks use the equivalent of star topology. Instead of wires, the radio signal from each computer goes back to a *router*, the wireless equivalent to the hub.

Daisy Chain Topology

Daisy chain topology strings the cable from computer to computer (also called *bus* or *sequential topology*). 10Base2 thin coax cabling is usually used. T-connectors are attached to network cards, and two cables are connected to the connectors, each cable going off to the next computer. At the end, a terminating resistor is attached.

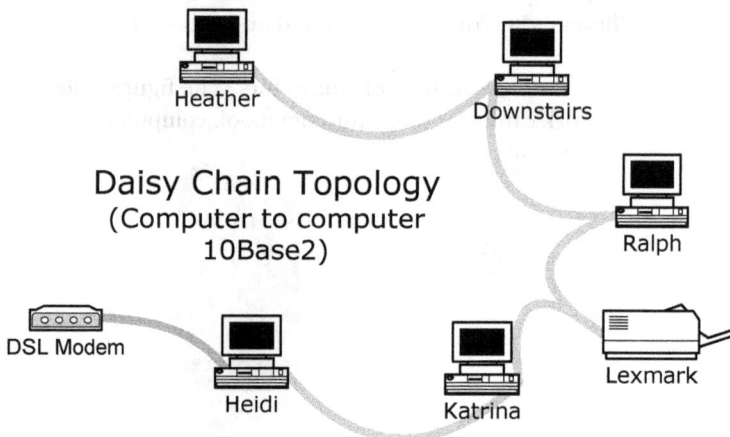

Daisy Chain Topology
(Computer to computer
10Base2)

The advantage to daisy chaining is that this method is easier and cheaper for connecting a small number of computers. The disadvantages are that the wiring is messier, and when the terminating resistor is missing, the network does not work. Similarly, if any part of the connection — either the cable or the connector — breaks, the entire network is down.

Assigning Internet Addresses

Today's networks are all-in-one: they connect computers within the office to each other and to peripherals, and they connect to computers on the Internet.

Computers connected to the Internet use TCP/IP, which requires that every computer (and other device) be assigned a unique identification number. This ID number is called the *IP address*, short for "Internet Protocol address."

Types of IP Addresses

IP addresses look like this:

> 172.31.255.0

It consists of four groups of numbers, separated by a dot. Each group ranges from 0 to 255.

A computer cannot use just any IP address to connect to the Internet. Instead, IP addresses are assigned to specific corporations and agencies. When you sign up to connect to the Internet through a service provider, you are provided either a *static* or *temporary* IP address:

Static — the IP address is permanently assigned to your site (as long as you pay the fees, that is). This option costs more but provides some technical benefits. It is meant for heavy users of the Internet.

Temporary — the IP address assigned to you changes every so often. In practice, you see no difference in operation from static IP addresses.

Private Network Addresses

In addition to the IP address that identifies you to the Internet, there is a range of IP addresses reserved for private networks, such as the computers inside your office. The numbers are:

Class of Network	Maximum Range of IP Addresses	Subnet Mask	Computers
Class A	10.0.0.0 to 10.255.255.255	255.0.0	16 million
Class B	172.16.00 to 172.31.255.255	255.255.0.0	64,000
Class C	192.168.0.0 to 192.168.255.255	255.255.255.0	254

For small and medium size offices, you would select the Class C range of IP addresses, such as 192.168.0.1. This is sufficient for 254 computers, printers, and other network devices.

Planning IP Addresses

You can assign your computers any IP address within the range, with a couple of exceptions, as noted below. For the network in our office, I assigned the following IP addresses:

Name	IP Address
Computers:	
Downstairs	192.168.0.2
Heidi	192.168.0.3
Heather	192.168.0.4
Ralph	192.168.0.5
Katrina	192.168.0.10
Network Printer:	
Lexmark	192.168.0.254

Notice that only the final digit changes. In addition, you need to know about the following:

Workgroup or Community	**Everyone** (the name I chose)
Subnet mask:	**255.255.255.0** (required)
Network IP:	**192.168.0.0** (required)
Gateway:	**192.168.0.1** (recommended)

Microsoft uses the term *workgroup*, which is called "community" in other network environments.

The *subnet mask* is always the same as shown in the table above; it never changes. (Technically, the netmask specifies the local portion of the IP address, so that the address can be logically subdivided for the network.)

There are two IP addresses you reserve for special cases:

- The *network IP* address is the base address for all devices on the network.
- The *gateway* address is for the gateway that lets your network communicate with the Internet.

Assigning IP Addresses

You assign the IP address to each computer running Windows, as follows:

1. From the taskbar select **Start | Settings | Control Panel**.

2. Double-click **Network**. If necessary, add the Microsoft TCP/IP protocol by clicking the **Add** button.

3. Select the TCP/IP network component attached to your computer's network card. It might look like this:

   TCP/IP->PCI Ethernet DEC 21041 Based Adapter

4. Click **Properties**, and select the **Bindings** tab. Ensure the following are turned on:

   Client for Microsoft Networks
   File and printer sharing for Microsoft Networks

5. Select the **IP Address** tab, and select the **Specify an IP address** option. Enter the **IP Address** and **Subnet Mask** numbers.

6. Click **OK** until all dialog boxes are closed. Windows might ask for your Windows installation diskettes or CD-ROM, then ask you to reboot the computer.

Repeat this for every computer. After each computer reboots, use Network Neighborhood to check that you can see the other computers on the network. Refer to your printer's documentation to set it up for TCP/IP; all I can say is that the process is very different from assigning an IP address for your computer.

Wireless Networking

As you can probably imagine, adding network cabling to existing offices is a real pain. When we did some office renovations, we ran some spare network cabling through the walls — just in case we decided to place computers in the rooms.

Wouldn't you know it: when it came time to add a computer to a room, it was a room without a network cable reaching it. For this reason, we instead used *wireless networking*.

Vendors are working on several solutions to the network cabling problem, particularly for the home and home-office markets. One solution makes use of electrical wiring: network connectors are plugged into electrical outlets! Sounds scary, but apparently it works.

The best solution, however, is wireless networking. It has been available for many years but suffered from slow transmission speed and incompatible standards. Early wireless ads boasted of 2Mb/sec — 25 times slower than today.

How Wireless Networking Works

Wireless networking uses radio-like transmissions to send data between computers. Network cards have a small antenna that sticks out the back of desktop computers or from the side of notebook computers.

The network cards transmit data to a *wireless router*, which has a much larger antenna. The router redirects the data to the correct computer.

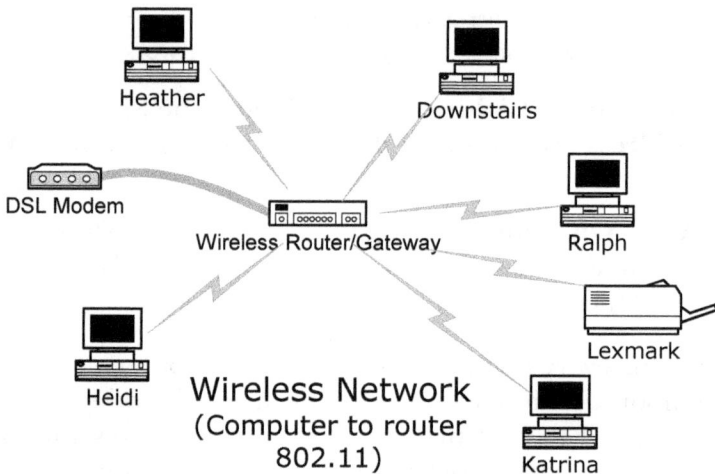

Heather

Downstairs

DSL Modem

Wireless Router/Gateway

Ralph

Lexmark

Heidi

Wireless Network
(Computer to router
802.11)

Katrina

The maximum transmission distance is about 30m (100 feet) in typical homes. The distance is reduced if the home uses metal studs in the walls or if the office is made of concrete or steel construction. In our home-office, the sheet metal of the centrally located furnace reduces the transmission strength between corner locations.

Wireless Security

The drawback to wireless networking is that any computer with wireless capability can connect to your network. "War driving" is the practice of driving around town, looking for unprotected wireless networks.

To protect wireless networks, you must enable encryption, the most common being WEP (Wire Equivalence Protection). Unfortunately, wireless network access points have security turned off; you need to turn it on, using the software included with the device.

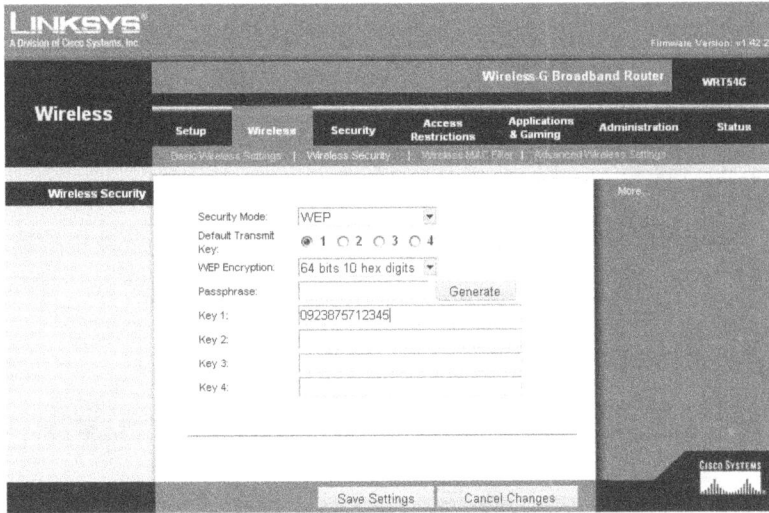

Typically, you enter a long number, similar to a password, as the *key*. Then, you need to go around to every computer using the wireless network and enter the same key. Without the key, rogue computers passing by cannot connect.

Summary

Networking your office makes it easier to share files and hardware, such as printers and CD-ROM drives, and the Internet. The drawbacks are the cost and difficulty of installation (in existing buildings), troubleshooting, and malware, as discussed in the previous chapter.

When installing new networks, you can choose between the cheaper wired networks or the more expensive wireless networks.

In the next chapter, you learn about networking issues specific to AutoCAD LT.

Notes

Chapter 15

Working with Networked AutoCAD LT

In This Chapter

- Working with AutoCAD LT on networks
- Setting up drives and printers for sharing over networks
- Opening and saving files on networks
- Finding files on attached drives

In the last chapter, you were introduced to the pros and cons of networking, the history behind networks, and hardware considerations.

In this chapter, the emphasis is on the software side of networking. With the networking features that are built into Windows and AutoCAD LT, the task of opening and saving files over networks is almost as simple as working with files on your computer. There are some specific techniques for using AutoCAD LT on a network that you need to be aware of, and that is the purpose of this chapter.

Setting Up Windows for the Network

After installing network cards in your computers (and possibly printers/plotters) and stringing the cabling between them all, Windows (usually) automatically detects the presence of the new hardware.

This chapter describes networking with Windows 2000; the directions may differ depending on the version of Windows on your computer.

Key Terms

Bindings — connect network drivers to the operating system
Computer names — names that identify computers to others on the network
Local drives — hard drives located in your computer
Mapping — makes network drives look like local drives
Network drives — hard drives located on other computers and accessible to you through the network
Permissions — the level of access other computers have to shared drives
Shared — drives and printers accessed by other computers over networks
Workgroups — groupings of networked computers

Abbreviations

R/O   read-only
R/W   read-write

Giving Computers Network Names

Every computer on the Windows network needs a unique name and must belong to a workgroup. Later in this chapter, you will see how the name is used.

1. On the Windows desktop, right-click the **My Network Places** icon. Notice the Network and Dial-up Connections window.

    From the shortcut menu, select **Properties**.

2. From the **Advanced** menu, select **Network Identification**. Notice the System Properties dialog box is open to the Network Identification tab.

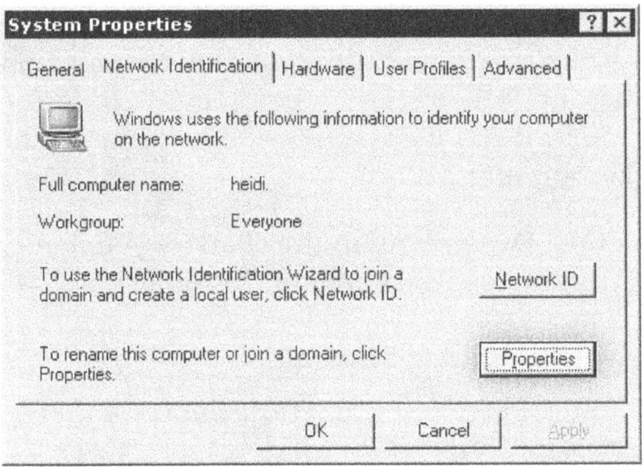
System Properties
General
Network Identification
Hardware
User Profiles
Advanced
Windows uses the following information to identify your computer on the network.
Full computer name: heidi.
Workgroup: Everyone
To use the Network Identification Wizard to join a domain and create a local user, click Network ID.
Network ID
To rename this computer or join a domain, click Properties.
Properties
OK
Cancel
Apply

3. Click **Properties**. Here you give the computers their names.

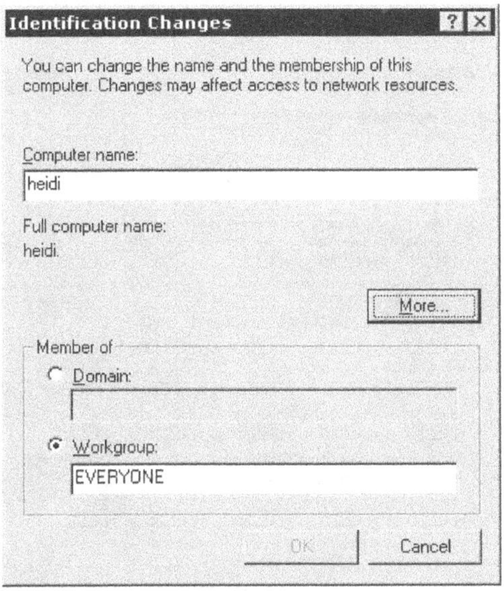
Identification Changes
You can change the name and the membership of this computer. Changes may affect access to network resources.
Computer name:
heidi
Full computer name:
heidi.
More...
Member of
Domain:
Workgroup:
EVERYONE
OK
Cancel

Computer name — identifies the computer to other computers on the network.

Enter a name that is *unique* (no other computer has this name), up to 15 characters long, and has no spaces. I use descriptive names like Upstairs, Heather, and Heidi.

Workgroup — identifies the workgroup that the computer belongs to. A *workgroup* is a way to group a bunch of similar computers together, sort of like folders that group similar files together. Small offices probably have a single workgroup for their computers.

You can enter either the name of an existing workgroup or a new name, which automatically creates a new workgroup. The name can be up to 15 characters long, with no spaces. I use the name "Everyone" as the workgroup in my office.

4. Click **OK**. Depending on the changes you made, Windows might need to reboot at this point.

Turning On Drive and Printer Sharing

To view the software drivers installed on the computers, return to the Network and Dial-up Connections window.

1. From the **Advanced** menu, select **Advanced Settings**.

2. In the **Adapters and Bindings** tab, notice the list of networking drivers.

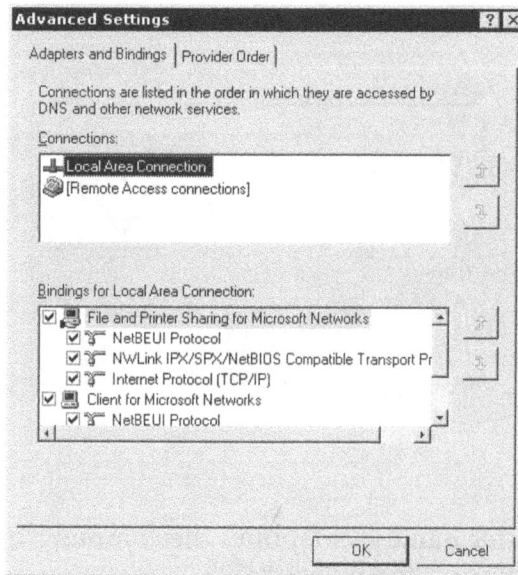

3. Continuing on in the same dialog box, ensure that **File and Printer Sharing** is turned on.

> **NOTE** File and printer sharing allows you to give *share* permission to other users on the network. This is the first step; the second step occurs in the next section, "Sharing Computer Drives and Printers," where you select the drives, folders, and printers of your computer that others may access via the network.

4. Click **OK** to exit the dialog box.

Sharing Computer Drives and Printers

Before other computers can access data on each other's computers, the drives and printers need to be explicitly made available for sharing.

When your computer's drives are shared, other computers can read, copy, and (optionally) write and delete files and folders located on your computer. Because of the danger of others accidentally (or deliberately) erasing files from your computer, Windows allows you to specify passwords to restrict access.

When your computer's printers are shared, then other users can print their documents and drawings on them.

1. In the Windows Explorer (File Manager), right-click any hard drive.

   From the shortcut menu, select **Sharing**. (This menu item appears only when File and Printer Sharing is turned on, as described in the previous section.)

2. Select **Share this Folder**.

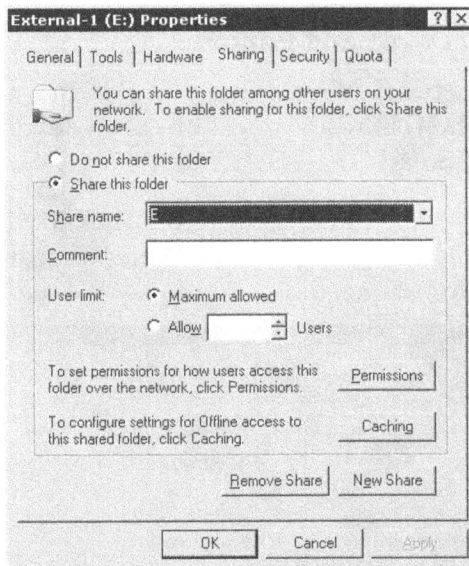

Share Name — provides a name for the shared drive. Users on networked computers will see this as the name of the drive. You can accept the default (the drive letter, such as C), or type another name up to 12 characters long.

Comment — provides a description of the shared drive, such as "CAD Drawing Archive."

3. You can select other options, such as **Permissions** for finer control over who can access and how to access.

   For example, you can limit other users to only reading files from your computer (called "read only").

4. Click **OK** to exit the dialog box.

   Notice that the drive has a hand symbol, indicating it is a shared drive that can be accessed over the network.

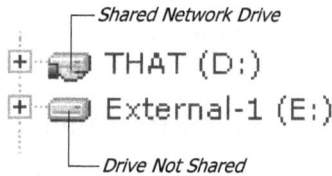

Other users on the network can now access files on your computer. Repeat the above procedure to share other drives and folders on your computer. The icon next to each drive letter tells you its status: the hand means the drive is shared.

Adding Networked Drives and Printers

Windows groups networked computers under the name of "Network Neighborhood." The following procedure provides access to drives and files on other computers:

1. On the Windows desktop, double-click **My Network Places**. There is a delay while Windows searches the network for connected computers.

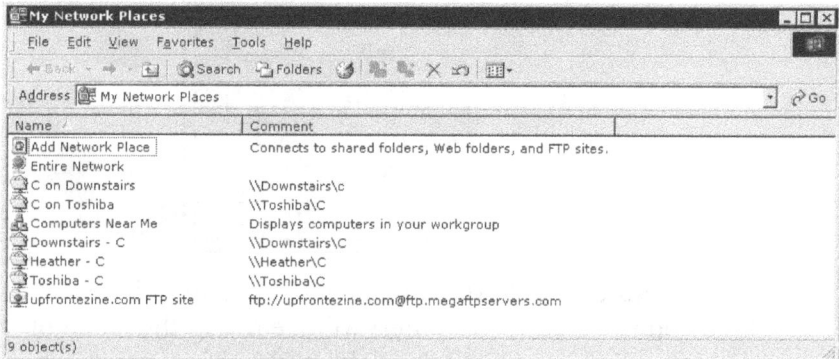

Notice that the connected computers have names like Downstairs and Heather.

Levels of Share Permissions

Full — users can read and write files on this drive.

Read — users can open files located on your computer, and copy files to their computer.

Read-Only — users can read the files on this drive but cannot write files.

Read and Execute — users can read files and run programs.

List Folder Contents — users can only view names of files.

Write (Change) — users can modify and delete both files and folders, and save the changed files back to your computer. Note that write permission includes read permission.

Depends on Password — users who know the password can read and/or write files. Passwords can be any combination of letters, numbers, and punctuation (including spaces) up to eight characters long. Examples include "1234," " " (a single space), and "ralphg."

Read-Only Password — users who enter the password can open and copy files from this drive to their computer.

Full Access Password — users who enter the correct password can read and write files (this password should differ from the read-only password).

> **TIPS** You must gauge the level of security your office requires. In my office, security is not an issue, so I don't use passwords to access other computers. If you decide you need the security of password protection, follow these tips to make it harder for an employee to guess the password:
>
> • Don't use short passwords; use the full eight characters.
>
> • Don't use common words, such as names; use unusual words, such as *zygote*.
>
> • Don't write down the password where it can be found.
>
> For even greater security:
>
> • Do use a random selection of characters, such as 3r9alp5h.
>
> • Do change the password frequently, such as every week.

TIPS Can't find networked computers? Sometimes computer names are not listed in My Network Places. The most common reasons are:

• The computer is turned off. Turn on the computer to see its name in My Network Places.
• The computer has "gone to sleep," commonly known as *suspend* mode or *hibernation*. Move the computer's mouse or press a cursor key on its keyboard to wake up the computer.
• The computer is not running Windows; perhaps the user has exited Windows to MS-DOS or has booted the computer with an operating system that cannot connect to the network.

Or there is a problem with the network hardware. Possible problems are:

• The cable has come loose from the network card.
• The cable is physically broken.
• The network card has come loose from its socket inside the computer.
• The network card has broken down (that's happened to me once).
• With 10Base2 wiring, the terminating resistor has come off.

2. To add networked computers and printers, double-click **Add Network Place**.

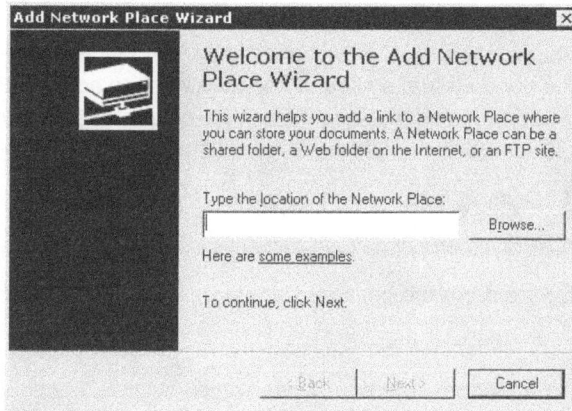

3. Enter the name of a computer or printer in "networkese." The format of the name has to look like this:

    \\ComputerName\Drive\Folder

    For example, if the computer name is Heidi and the drive letter is C:, then enter:

    \\Heidi\C

For access to a specific folder, such as \CAD, use:

\\Heidi\C\CAD

Usually, it is easier (but slower) to click **Browse**, and
then find the computer and drive in the tree:

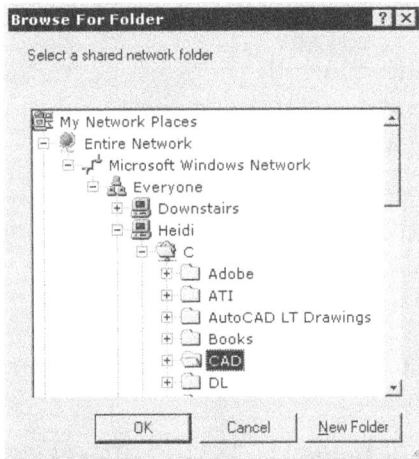

You can now open and copy files from networked computers.

Mapping Network Drives

In most cases, you access network drives via the Network Neighborhood.
For a reason not clear to me, sometimes that doesn't work; the solution
then is to *map* the network drive. This makes networked drives appear
like local drives. To map drives:

1. From the Windows Explorer menu bar, select **Tools |
    Map Network Drive**. Notice the Map Network Drive
    dialog box.

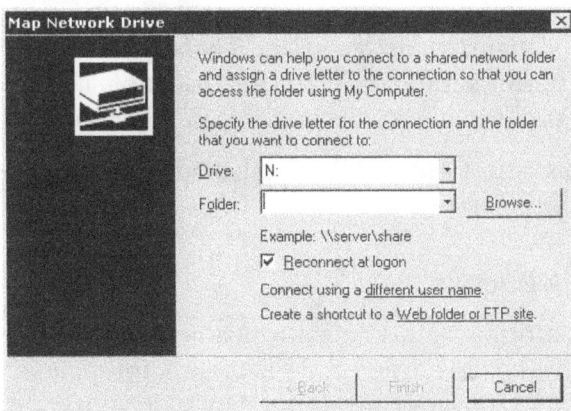

2. The Map Network Drive dialog box has these options:

Drive — specifies the drive letter to assign to the mapped drive. Drive letters range from A: through Z:. (A: and B: are reserved for floppy drives, and C: is usually the first hard drive.)

Windows automatically picks the next available drive letter. In the illustration on the previous page, Windows selected N: as the drive letter.

Folder — specifies the path over the network to the mapped drive. Enter the name of the computer and the drive using the following format:

\\COMPUTER\DRIVE

The **Browse** button lets you browse for the computer and drive names.

Reconnect at logon — specifies that Windows will attempt to map this drive every time it starts up. The disadvantage is that Windows then takes even longer to start. I usually leave this box unchecked.

3. Click **OK**. After a few seconds, the Windows Explorer shows the mapped drive with the "network drive" icon and wording to the effect of:

C on 'DOWNSTAIRS' (N:)

This means that the C: drive on computer Downstairs is now effectively drive N: on your computer.

To disconnect a mapped drive, select **Tools | Disconnect Networked Drive** from Explorer's menu bar. In the Disconnect Network Drive dialog box, select the drive(s) to disconnect and click **OK**.

Later in the "Accessing AutoCAD LT Files on Networks" section, you see how to access files from within AutoCAD LT.

Adding Network Printers

According to Windows' broad definition, a network printer is any printer not connected to your computer. This means the printer is either connected to another computer on the network (local to that computer) or directly connected to the network via its own network card (a true network printer).

You need to know where the printer is located (attached to another computer or attached directly to the network) because that affects how you go about setting it up to be shared:

Attached to another computer — before you can access a printer connected to another computer, it must be set to Shared in a manner similar to sharing drives, as described in "Sharing Computer Drives and Printers." You've got to scoot over to the other computer and turn on sharing, as described below.

Attached directly to the network — network printers are, by definition, shareable. So, there is no need to make a printer "shareable" before you can access it.

Making Local Printers Shareable

1. Go to the computer with the attached printer.

2. From the Windows taskbar, select **Start | Settings | Printers**. Notice the Printers window.

TIPS   Printer icons have subtle differences that indicate the following meanings:

Cable — indicates network printers (printers on other computers), like "BROTHER on GUE."
Hand — indicates shared printers (your computer is available to others), like "HP."
Diskette — printer drivers that print to file, like "Text Print to File."
Check mark — indicates the default printer, which Windows will use unless you select another printer as the default, like "Lexmark Optra."

None of the above means the printer is local, is not shared, is not the default, and doesn't print to disk, like "Lexmark PostScript."

3. Right-click a printer icon. From the shortcut menu, select **Sharing**. Notice the Properties dialog box.

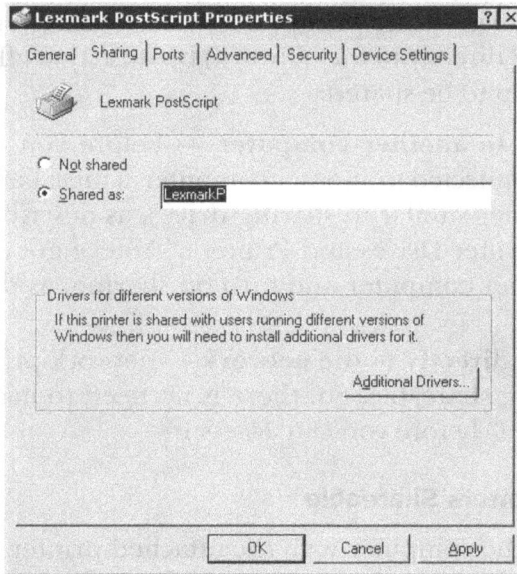

4. Select **Shared As**.

   As with shared drives, the share name provides a name for the shared printer. Users on networked computers see this as the name of the printer. You can accept the default (the printer's name, such as LexmarkP), or type another name up to 12 characters long.

5. Click **OK**.

The local printer is now ready to be accessed by other computers on the network. You still need to install the printer on those other computers, as described in the following section.

Installing Network Printers

Before you can use a printer over the network, you need to install it on your computer (as well as every other computer on the network). Here's how:

1. Go to any computer that is not attached to the printer.

2. From the Windows taskbar, select **Start | Settings | Printers**. Notice the Printers window.

3. Double-click the **Add Printer** icon.

   Notice the Add Printer Wizard. Click **Next**.

4. When asked "How is this printer attached to your computer?", select **Network printer**. Click **Next**.

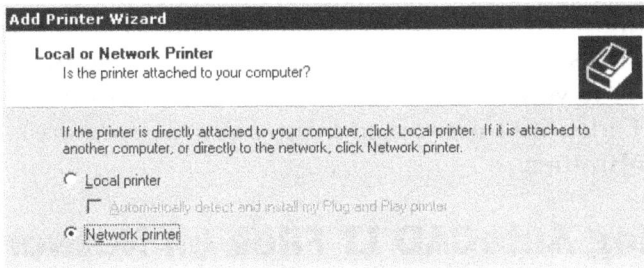

5. In the next step, you may be asked to provide the diskette or CD-ROM for the printer drivers. Insert the disc and follow the instructions.

   The other possibility is that drivers for the printer already exist on the computer. In this case, Windows asks if you want to keep the existing drivers or install new drivers.

6. In the next screen, you are asked for the Network path. Enter the name of the computer and the printer using the following format:

   \\COMPUTER\PRINTER

   Recall that earlier you provided a network name for the computer (such as Downstairs or Heather) and a network name for the printer (such as Epson).

   If you don't know the name of the computer or printer, click the **Browse** button.

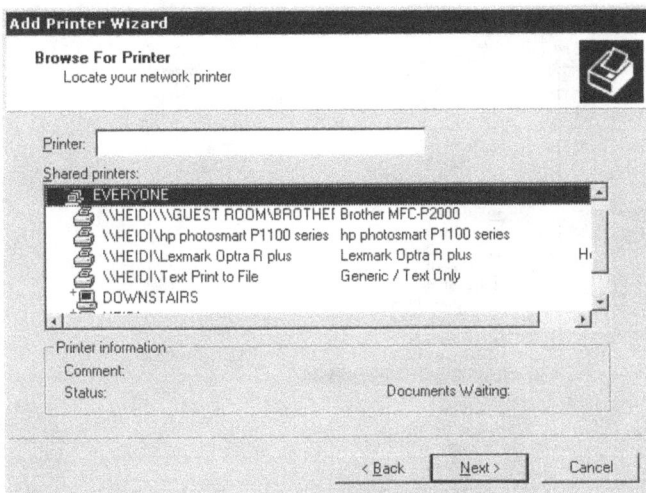

7. In the final step, Windows asks if it can print a test page. Select **Yes** and click **Finish**.

From now on, the network printer appears in the Print dialog box's list of available printers any time you want to print a document. In most cases, it won't matter to you whether you are using a local or networked printer. AutoCAD LT identifies networked printers by their network name, such as \\Heather\Brother.

Accessing AutoCAD LT Files on Networks

There are two ways to access drawing files, depending on whether you know where the files are located:

- When you know the location of drawing files, use the **Open** command.
- When you don't know, use AutoCAD LT's **Find** feature to search for the drawings.

For the following tutorials, start AutoCAD LT.

Opening Drawings on Networks

When you know the names of drawings and their location on the network, select **File | Open** from the menu bar; notice the Select File dialog box — so far, this is identical to opening drawings located on your computer's drives. To open drawings on the drives of other computers, follow these steps:

1. In the Select File dialog box, click the **Look in** list box.

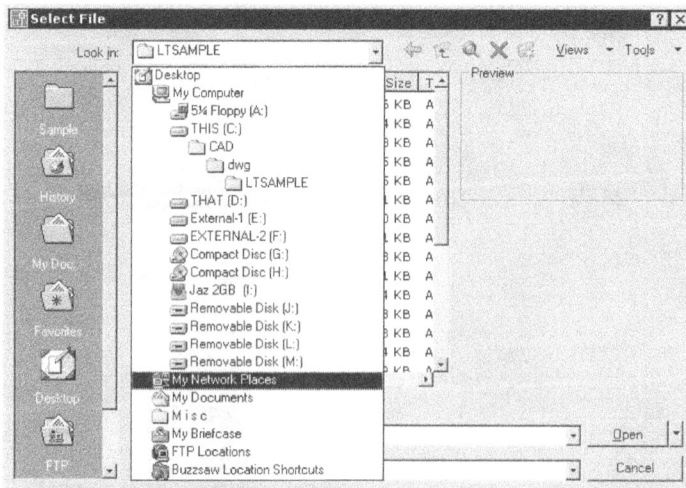

2. Scroll down, and then select **My Network Places**. Notice that the dialog box displays the list of names of computers currently connected to your computer.

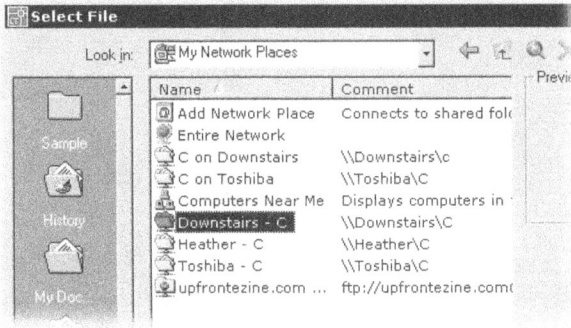

Notice the list of computer and drive names, such as \\Downstairs\C.

> **TIP** If you access a folder frequently, consider dragging it over to the folders pane (shown in dark gray, above). This provides instant access to drawing files and eliminates a lot of clicking and double-clicking to get at files. In the figure above, I dragged the \Sample folder into the folders pane; that gives me quick access to the sample drawings included with AutoCAD LT.

3. Double-click the name of a computer and drive.

4. Again, double-click on the drive and folder names to get to where the drawing file is located.

5. Finally, double-click the DWG name to open the file. Notice that AutoCAD LT opens the drawing exactly as if it were located on your own computer's disk drive.

You use the same technique to load blocks (DWG), externally referenced drawings (DWG), menus (CUI), templates (DWT), linetype definitions (LIN), hyperlinked files, and WMF (Windows Metafile Format) files.

In addition, over the network you can insert OLE objects, specify folders for the **Options | Files** dialog box, recover damaged drawing files, and attach plot style tables (CTB and STB).

Curiously, AutoCAD LT does not let you look for hatch patterns (PAT) or text fonts (SHX and TTF files) on the network via the **BHatch** and **Style** commands.

The AutoCAD DesignCenter

The AutoCAD DesignCenter also allows you to access drawings over the network. The advantage to DesignCenter is that it allows you to access the layer structure, dimension styles, linetypes, and so on of networked drawings.

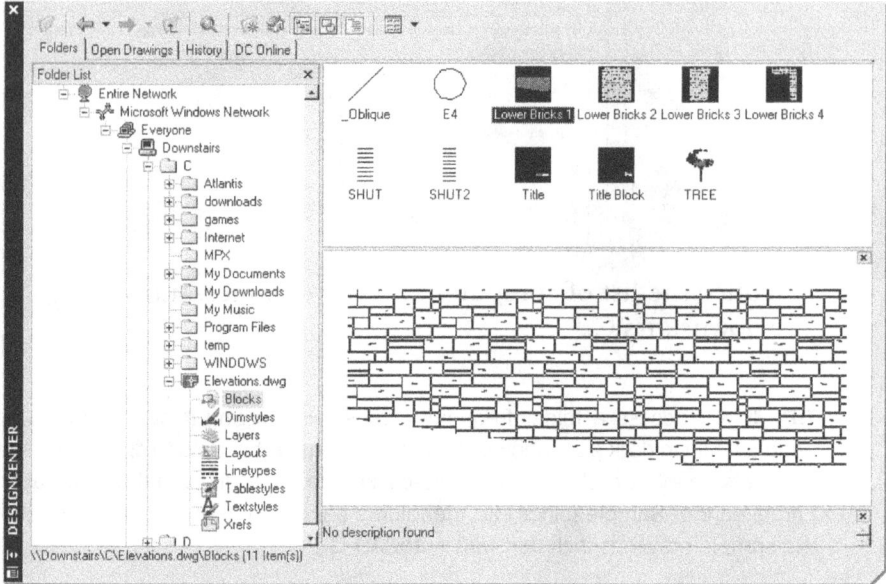

Saving Drawings on Networks

You needn't do anything special to save drawings over networks: click the diskette icon on LT's toolbar, or select **Save** from the **File** menu. AutoCAD LT saves the drawing back to the networked computer from which you opened it.

You use the same technique to export drawings in WMF and DXF formats and extract attributes to files.

To save the drawing to your own computer's hard drive, use the **SaveAs** command to navigate to your own computer's drives and folders.

> **WARNING** Now that you have saved someone else's drawing on your computer, two copies exist: yours and the other. This leads to problems with version control: who has the most recent version of the drawing?

Finding Files on Networks

All of AutoCAD LT's file-related dialog boxes have a command for finding drawing files, accessed through **Tools | Find**.

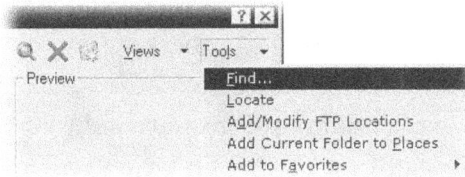

The Find dialog box searches for files on your computer and on computers attached to the network, letting AutoCAD LT search all drives for a particular DWG file.

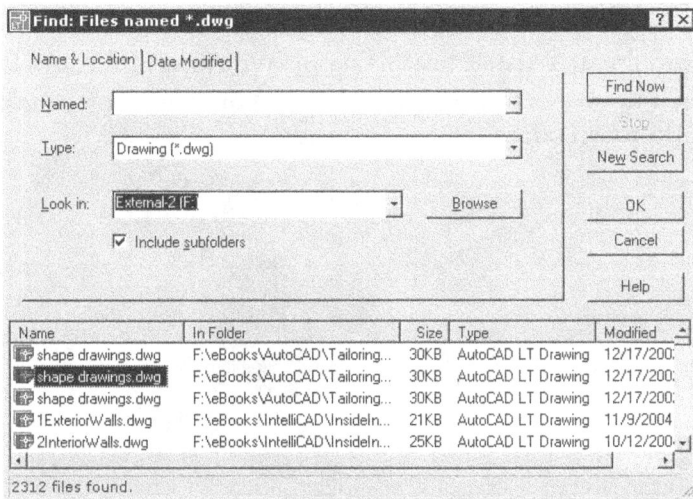

At least that's how it should work. Depending from where you access Find, you can search all drives (local and networked) or just local and mapped drives. For reasons unknown to me, AutoCAD LT cannot search the entire network for files; you have to search each computer or each attached drive, one by one.

Running LT Over a Network

You can run AutoCAD LT over a network. It's best to refer to the *AutoCAD LT Network Administrator's Guide*, which you find in the AutoCAD LT's \Help folder under the name aclt_nag.chm.

Briefly, the steps to deploying AutoCAD LT over the network are:

1. Start the deployment wizard.
2. Create or modify an administrative image.

3. Create or modify a deployment.
4. Specify log file locations.
5. Select a client installation location.
6. Select a client setup type.
7. Enter the product serial number.
8. Enter personal information.
9. Turn on Live Update options (*optional*).
10. Turn on DesignCenter Online (*optional*).
11. Complete registration.
12. Confirm and complete setup.

Summary

In this chapter, you learned how to set up Windows and AutoCAD LT for working on a network. In the next chapter, you learn how to access drawings and other CAD data on the Internet.

Chapter 16

Connecting AutoCAD LT to the Internet

In This Chapter

- Accessing drawings from the Internet
- Understanding the format of hyperlinks
- Starting Web browsers from within AutoCAD LT
- Publishing and transmitting DWF files
- Employing Web-based project management software
- Learning the possibilities of aecXML and LandXML

Over the last two chapters, you learned how to work with AutoCAD LT on networks to share files and other resources. In this chapter, you learn about how AutoCAD LT interacts with the Internet.

Opening Drawings from the Internet

You can access drawings stored on the Internet with the **Open** command. (Previous versions of AutoCAD LT used the **OpenUrl** command.) Instead of selecting a file name, you enter a *hyperlink*.

AutoCAD LT has two ways to enter hyperlinks. One method is to type the hyperlink in the Select File dialog box; the second method uses LT's built-in Web browser to first access a Web site, then specify the file. In the following tutorials, we work through both methods. (To work through the tutorials, your computer must have a connection to the Internet.)

Key Terms

Download — transfer copies of files from Internet sites to your computer
Hyperlinks — reference to other files; when clicked, the files are displayed
Plot files — plots of drawings saved in files on disk
Plug-ins — small software programs that allow Web browsers to display unfamiliar file formats
Upload — transfer copies of files from your computer to Internet sites, usually by FTP
Web browsers — software specifically designed to display Web pages

Abbreviations

DWF	Drawing Web format
FTP	File Transfer Protocol
HTML	Hypertext Markup Language
HTTP	Hypertext Transfer Protocol
ISP	Internet service provider
MIME	Multipurpose Internet Mail Extensions
URL	Uniform Resource Locator
WHIP	Web browser plug-in; short for Windows High Performance

Understanding Hyperlinks

Insert | Hyperlink

AutoCAD LT lets you use hyperlinks in drawings for two purposes: accessing drawings over the Internet and attaching hyperlinks to objects in drawings.

The figure below illustrates a hyperlink attached to the caster of an office chair. Clicking the caster launches the Web browser, which goes to the Web site specified by the hyperlink.

http://www.3ds.com/corporate/investors/earnings
CTRL + click to follow link

Hyperlinks let you locate files just about anywhere, whether stored on your computer or on the Internet. Hyperlinks can point to Web pages, newsgroups, compressed ZIP files, audio clips, and more.

Hyperlinks are more formally known as *URLs*, short for "Uniform Resource Locators." The URL is the universal file naming system of the Internet. You probably are familiar with URLs that look like these:

> http://www.autodesk.com is the Autodesk Web site
> http://www.wordware.com is Wordware Publishing's Web site
> http://www.upfrontezine.com is author Ralph Grabowski's Web site

You usually don't need to type the "http://" prefix, because Web browsers automatically add it. Thus, www.autodesk.com is good enough.

You can add hyperlinks to objects in AutoCAD LT drawings with the **Hyperlink** command. From the **Insert** menu, select **Hyperlink**, or press **Ctrl+K** as the keyboard shortcut.

The hyperlink links the drawing object to files on your computer, or any computer accessible from yours via the network, and to the Internet. (Hyperlinks do not operate when drawings are opened in AutoCAD LT 98 and earlier.)

Accessing Hyperlinks with the Open Command

File | Open

To open drawings using hyperlinks, follow these steps:

1. From the **File** menu, select **Open**. AutoCAD LT displays the Select File dialog box.

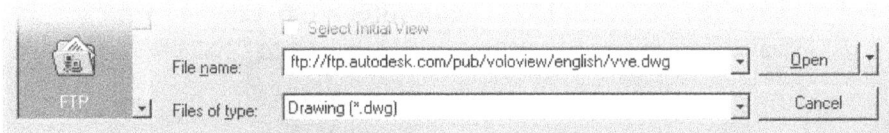

2. In the **File name** field, enter a hyperlink. For this tutorial, enter the following:

    ftp://ftp.autodesk.com/pub/voloview/english/vve.dwg

    This hyperlink accesses a sample drawing file called vve.dwg at Autodesk's FTP (File Transfer Protocol) site.

3. Click **Open**. (If your computer uses dial-up access, Windows displays the Dial-up Connection dialog box; click **Connect**.)

   AutoCAD displays the File Download dialog box, which provides you with a progress report on the file being downloaded to your computer. Depending on the speed of your Internet connection, the drawing can take up to two minutes to download. If you find it necessary to stop the download, click **Cancel**.

4. AutoCAD LT displays the drawing in a new window.

   Save the drawing to the computer's hard drive with the **Save** command.

TIP   The **Open** command doesn't open drawing files directly from the Internet. Rather, AutoCAD LT *caches* the drawing file by this two-step process:

1. AutoCAD LT copies the file from the Internet site to your computer's temporary Internet folder, such as \Windows\Temp, giving the temporary file a system-generated name, such as AC$81E0.dwg.

2. AutoCAD LT loads the drawing file from the hard drive.

Searching the Web

AutoCAD LT includes a simple Web browser that lets you search the Internet. Here's how to use it:

1. To open a drawing using the Web browser, select **Open** from the **File** menu. AutoCAD LT displays the Select File dialog box.

2. Click the **Search the Web** button, the icon of the magnifying glass over the earth.

Notice that the computer connects to the Internet. AutoCAD LT displays its own Web browser, a simplified version of Internet Explorer.

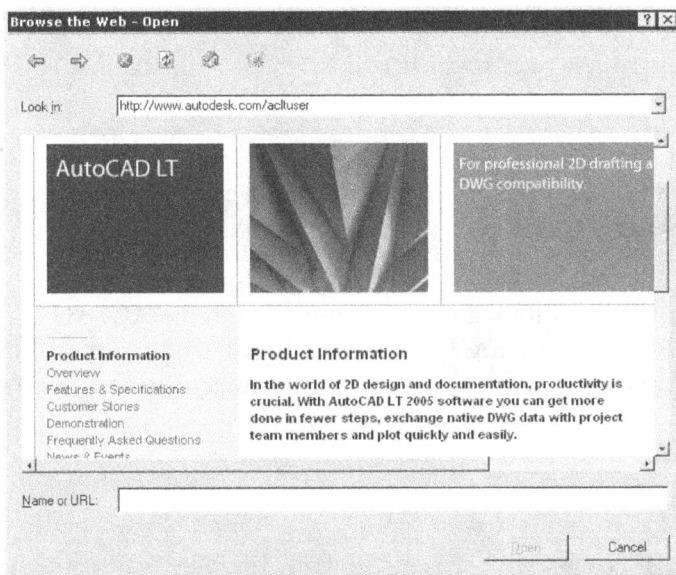

3. The Web browser automatically connects to Autodesk's home page for AutoCAD LT. To stop loading that page, click the **Stop** button (red button with x).

4. In the **Look in** field, type the address of the Web site you wish to access.

    To access a specific file, type its hyperlink in the **Name or URL** field.

Inserting Blocks from the Internet

Insert | Block

The **Insert** command lets you access blocks stored as drawing files at Internet sites. The procedure is very similar to opening drawings, except that you start with the Insert dialog box.

1. From the **Insert** menu, select **Block**. Notice that AutoCAD LT displays the Insert dialog box.

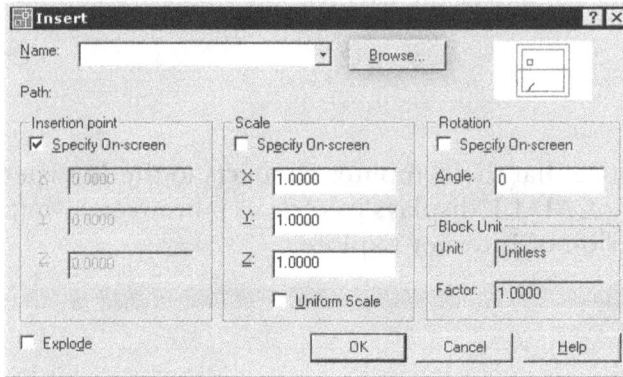

2. Click **Browse**. Notice the Select Drawing File dialog box.

3. Enter a hyperlink in the **File name** field or click the **Search the Web** button.

4. When the download is complete, notice that AutoCAD gives the block a generic name, such as "AC$81E0," in the Insert dialog box's **Name** field. You can then insert the block in the drawing using any traditional method.

Starting Web Browsers

Browser

AutoCAD LT comes with a built-in Web browser. Or you can use your own. To start a Web browser from within AutoCAD LT, use the **Browser** command. Alternatively, you can switch to the Windows desktop and double-click the Web browser's icon.

The **Browser** command launches the default Web browser program installed on your computer — whether Firefox, Opera, or another browser.

1. Type the **Browser** command:

Command: **browser**
Location <http://www.autodesk.com/acltuser>: *(Press **Enter**.)*

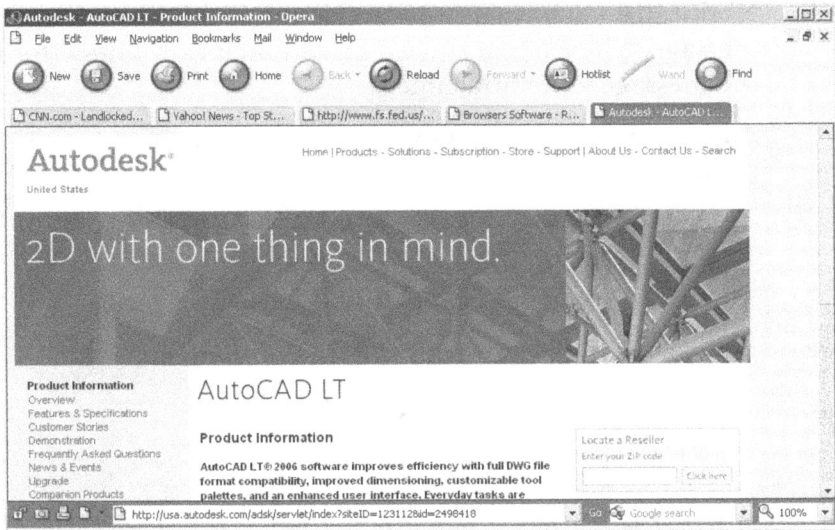

2. AutoCAD prompts you for the Web location. (The default is the AutoCAD LT home page at Autodesk.) Type a hyperlink, and then press **Enter**.

3. AutoCAD LT launches your Web browser, and displays the Web site.

Sending Drawings via the Internet

The Internet has replaced couriers and the post office for sending and receiving drawings and other documents. AutoCAD LT provides several methods of sending drawings through the Internet:

> **Send** — best for sending the current drawing by email
> **eTransmit** — best for sending one or more drawings and their support files by email
> **SaveAs** — best for sending very large files by FTP

Sending Drawings through Email

File | Send

The **Send** command attaches the current drawing to email messages. This method is quick and easy but does not include support files that may be required by the drawing.

1. From the **File** menu, select **Send**.

2. Notice that your email software appears with a new message. The current drawing is automatically added to the message as an attachment.

3. Add the name of the recipient, and send the message on its way.

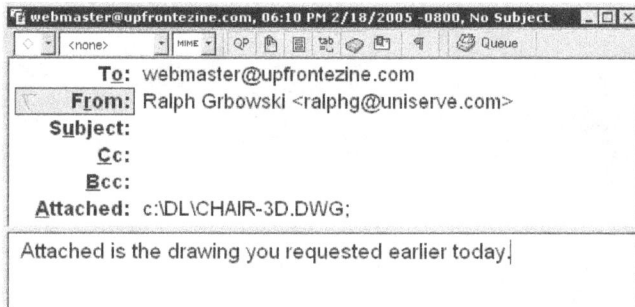

Packaging Drawings and Support Files

File | eTransmit

The **eTransmit** command packages one or more drawings, as well as all required support files. Support files include fonts, hatch patterns, linetypes, external references, and other data not stored in drawing files. This method is best when you need to ensure that the drawing is sent complete.

1. From the **File** menu, select **eTransmit**. If the drawing was modified since being opened, AutoCAD prompt you to save the drawing before proceeding.

2. The Create Transmittal dialog box lists the support files required by the drawing.

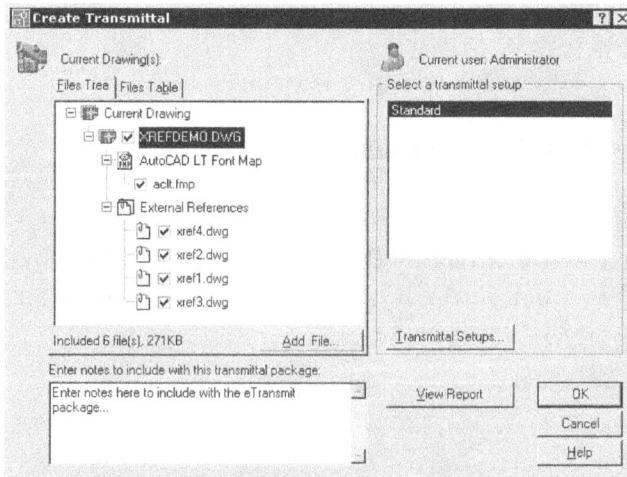

The Notes section is for including a message to the recipient. Text can be copied from other documents using **Ctrl+C** and then pasted here with **Ctrl+V**.

3. To specify the options, click **Transmittal Setups**, and then click **Modify**. The following dialog box appears, filled with options:

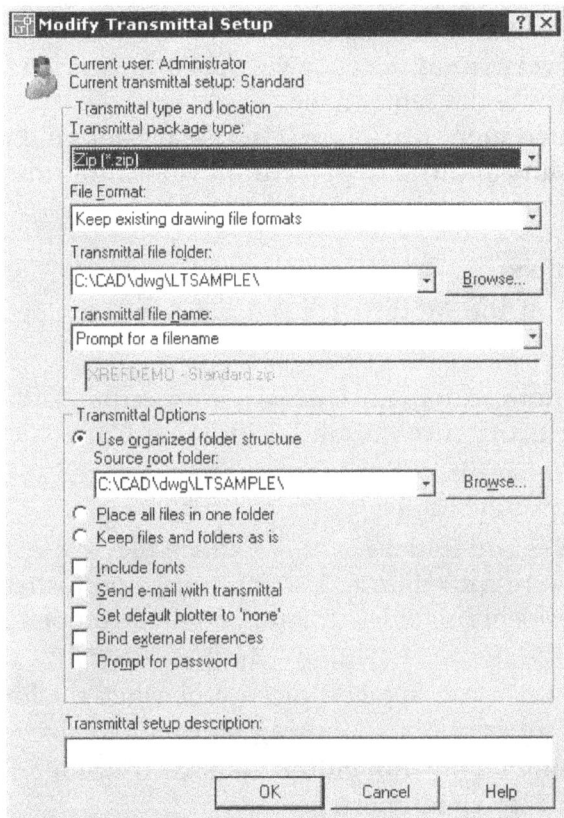

Transmittal Type and Location

The upper half of the Modify Transmittal Setup dialog box has these options:

> **Transmittal package type** — specifies file compression:
> - **Zip (*.zip)** compresses files into a single .zip file. Recipients require PkZip or WinZip to extract (uncompress) files.
> - **Self-extracting executable** compresses file into a single file with the extension .exe. Recipients double-click the file to extract files. Be aware that some email anti-virus systems may reject .exe attachments.

- **Folder (set of files)** stores files in a single folder. Select this option when mailing files on CDs.

File Format — saves drawings in 2004 or 2000 format. (The 2004 format is compatible with AutoCAD LT 2006.)

Transmittal file name — specifies the file name:
- **Prompt for a filename** prompts for a new file name when the transmittal is created.
- **Overwrite if necessary** writes over previous transmittal files of the same name.
- **Increment file name if necessary** adds a digit to the file name in order to prevent previous transmittal files from being overwritten.

Transmittal Options

The lower half of the Modify Transmittal Setup dialog box has these options:

Use organized folder structure — specifies folder in which to place the transmittal files. I find that C:\ is easy to find.

Place all files in one folder — removes paths and stores the files in a single folder.

Keep files and folders as is — extracts files to the same folders as they were copied from. Use this option only when recipients have the identical folder structure on their computers.

Include fonts — determines whether .shx, .pfb, and .ttf font files are included. Turn off this option when the fonts are covered by copyright or if the recipients already have the fonts.

Send e-mail with transmittal — adds transmittal files as attachments to email messages.

Set default plotter to none — removes plotter information from drawings so that it does not conflict with the recipients' plotter setups.

Bind external references — xrefs and images are bound to drawings.

Prompt for password — locks transmittal files with a password. Only those who know the password can open the files.

4. Save the setup and return to the original dialog box.

    The **Add File** button includes additional files with the transmittal, such as documents, spreadsheets, and photographs.

5. Click the **View Report** button. AutoCAD LT generates a report describing the files being sent and other notes.

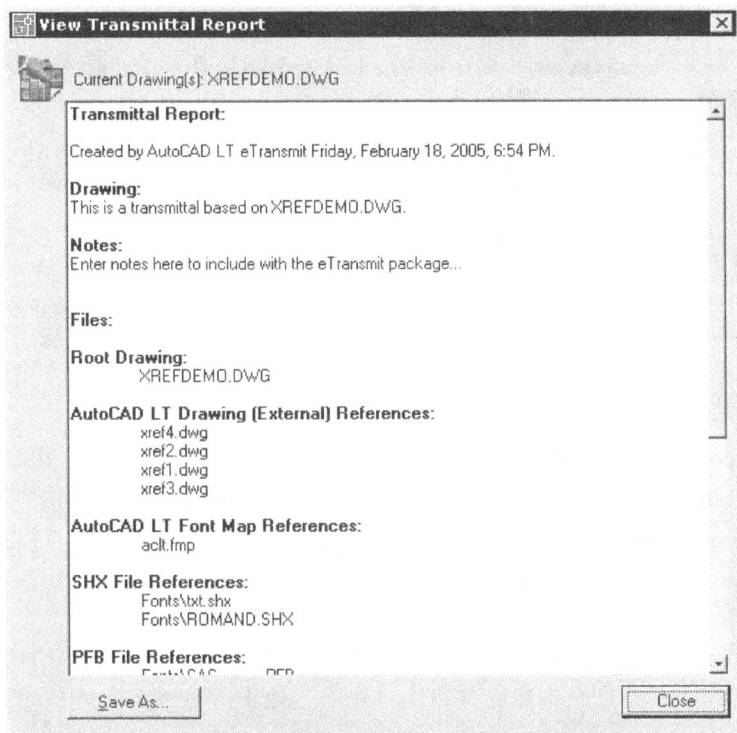

```
View Transmittal Report                                    ×

      Current Drawing(s): XREFDEMO.DWG

  Transmittal Report:

  Created by AutoCAD LT eTransmit Friday, February 18, 2005, 6:54 PM.

  Drawing:
  This is a transmittal based on XREFDEMO.DWG.

  Notes:
  Enter notes here to include with the eTransmit package...

  Files:

  Root Drawing:
        XREFDEMO.DWG

  AutoCAD LT Drawing (External) References:
        xref4.dwg
        xref2.dwg
        xref1.dwg
        xref3.dwg

  AutoCAD LT Font Map References:
        aclt.fmp

  SHX File References:
        Fonts\txt.shx
        Fonts\ROMAND.SHX

  PFB File References:
        Fonts\SAC    DED

         Save As...                              Close
```

6. Click **Close** to return to the original dialog box.

7. Click **OK** to put together the transmittal package.

When done, you can email the file to recipients as email attachments, upload it to Web sites via FTP, or copy the file to CD and then send by courier.

Saving Drawings to the Internet

File | Save As

You can save drawings with FTP (file transfer protocol) to file servers on the Internet using the **SaveAs** command. Here's how:

1. Select **Save As** from the **File** menu. AutoCAD LT displays the Save Drawing As dialog box.

2. Type the hyperlink in the **File name** field.

You must use the ftp:// prefix instead of http://. That's because software cannot write files to a Web site using the HTTP protocol; instead, software uses FTP.

3. Click **Save,** and AutoCAD LT uploads the drawing file to the specified FTP site.

   You must have permission to write to the FTP site; if you do not, AutoCAD LT refuses to upload the file.

Setting Up FTP

You are probably familiar with sending files as attachments through email; the drawback is that email was never designed to handle large files. FTP allows you to send files of any size, even entire CDs and DVDs of files — 1MB, 1GB, and more.

FTP needs to be set up with user names, passwords, and other data. There are two ways to access FTP sites: anonymously and with a password.

   Anonymous sites — accessible by anyone, they are also known as public FTP sites. All that's needed is an email address as the password; usernames are not required.

   Password sites — accessible only when the correct username and password are entered. These are provided by the owner of the FTP site.

AutoCAD LT can be set up to access both anonymous and password-protected sites. Here's how:

1. In the Save Drawing As dialog box, select **Tools | Add/ Modify FTP Locations**. Notice that AutoCAD LT displays the Add/Modify FTP Locations dialog box.

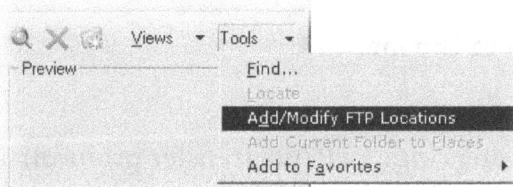

2. Enter data required by the site. For instance, to access Autodesk's public FTP site, enter the following:

Name of FTP site:	**ftp.autodesk.com**
Log on as:	**anonymous**
Password:	**email@email.com**

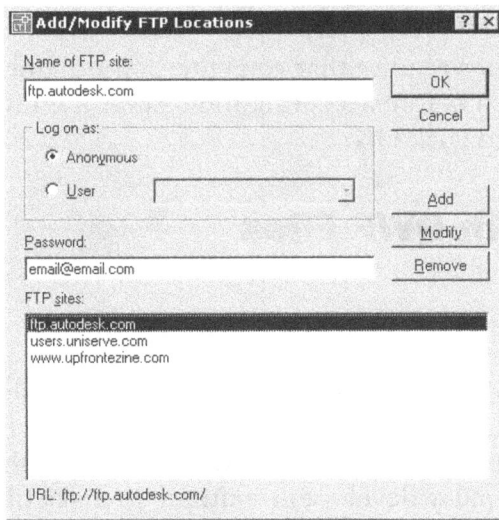

3. Click **Add** to add the site to the list, and then click **OK** to exit the dialog box.

4. Back in the Save Drawing As dialog box, save the drawing by clicking the **FTP** icon in the Folder list.

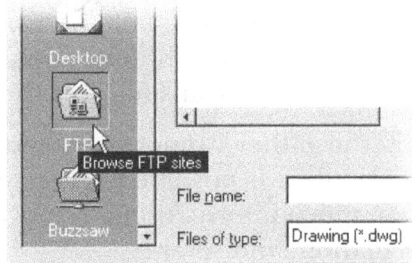

5. Notice the list of FTP sites. Select **ftp.autodesk.com**, and then click **Save**.

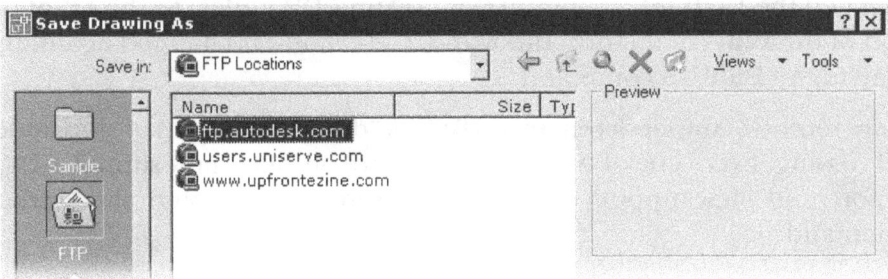

6. Select a folder, and then click **Save**.

7. Some sites require that you enter a username and password before accepting files. Enter the information, and then click **OK**.

Working with DWF Files

File | Publish
File | Publish to Web

Can AutoCAD LT's DWG files be viewed on the Internet? Yes and no. To do so, Web browsers need a *plug-in* that handles DWG files. At one time, Autodesk made such plug-ins freely available (under the name of Volo), and several third-party developers continue to make plug-ins available.

A couple of years ago, however, Autodesk decided we shouldn't be displaying our drawings in Web pages. They switched their emphasis from DWG to DWF.

DWF was first invented by Autodesk during the Internet bubble era of the late 1990s. Short for "drawing Web format," DWF files represented 2D drawing quite well, but were much smaller in file size than the original DWGs. DWF files are as much as eight times smaller than the equivalent DWG file. Smaller means they transmit over the Internet faster.

DWF files are secure, because they cannot be edited in the same way as the original DWG files. While it is possible to reverse-translate the DWF file back to DWG format, much information is removed, such as attribute data, some entity information, and so on.

You can think of DWF as a *plot file*, as when you plot drawings to files on disk instead of to the plotter. Indeed, as of AutoCAD LT 2000, Autodesk changed the **DwfOut** command (for creating DWF files) to the **ePlot** option of the **Plot** command. And with LT 2004, it was changed again, this time to the **Publish** command.

More recently, Autodesk renamed DWF as "design Web format" and added 3D viewing. Every one of Autodesk's software products now supports DWF export, and a few support limited DWF importation through the **Markup** command.

The company has written a range of supporting products, most of which are free (see www.autodesk.com/dwf):

- **DWF Viewer** (free) displays and prints DWF files
- **DWF Composer** views, prints, redlines, and creates DWF files
- **DWF Writer** (free) lets any software output documents in DWF format.
- **DWF Toolkit** (free) provides the API that embeds DWF read/write in other applications.

You should be aware, however, of the drawbacks in using DWF: it takes an extra step to translate drawings in DWF format, and DWF strips out certain information from drawings.

Exporting Drawings in DWF Format

The **Publish** command exports drawings in DWF format. The command also collects multiple drawings into sets. Here are the steps for creating DWF files of drawings:

1. Enter the **Publish** command or select **Publish** from the **File** menu. AutoCAD LT displays the Publish dialog box.

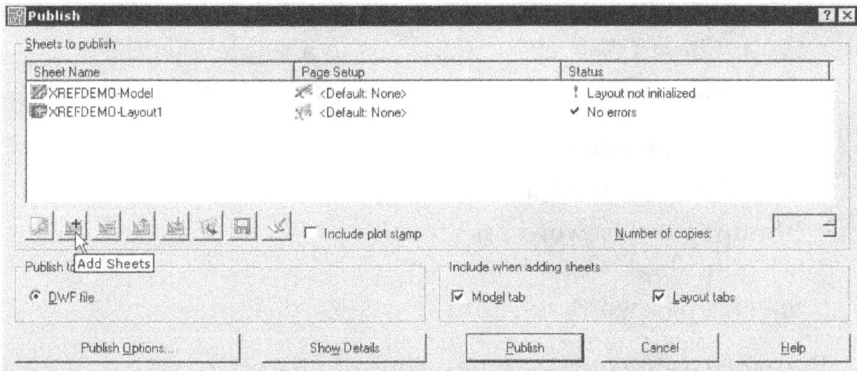

2. To add drawings, click the **Add Sheets** button. Select one or more .dwg files, and then click **Select**.

TIP   Drawing sets are plotted in a specific order. Use the **Move Up** and **Move Down** buttons to change the order of the layouts. Click **Remove** to remove layouts from the list.

3. Click **Publish Options**.

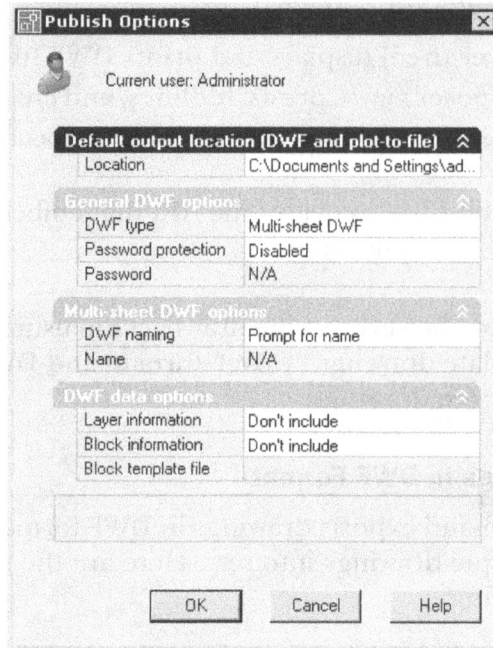

General DWF Options

DWF type — determines how to handle multiple layouts:
- **Multi-sheet DWF** saves all layouts in a single .dwf file
- **Single-sheet DWF** saves each layout to its own .dwf file

Password protection — protects against unauthorized viewing:
- **Disabled** turns off password protection
- **Prompt for password** asks for the password when the DWFs are published
- **Specify password** asks for the password right now

Password — specifies the password (if enabled)

Multi-sheet DWF Options

DWF naming — determines how to name the .dwf file:
- **Prompt for name** asks for the name when DWFs are published
- **Specify name** asks for the file name right now.

Name — specifies the file name (if enabled)

DWF Data Options

> **Layer information** — determines whether layers are included
>
> **Block information** — determines whether blocks and attributes are included
>
> **Block template file** — selects the .blk file that specifies which blocks and attributes are included

4.   Click **OK** to exit the options dialog.

5.   Click **Publish** to save the drawings in DWF format. AutoCAD LT uses background printing to return you to the drawing more quickly. A small plotter icon on the status bar indicates the progress.

When AutoCAD LT is done publishing, a yellow balloon reports whether the job was successful — or not.

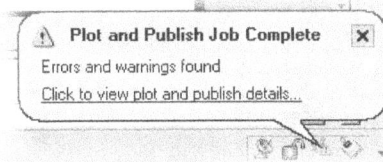

Drawings in Web Pages

The **PublishToWeb** command creates Web pages displaying drawings in DWF or JPEG format. This command is a "wizard" that steps through the processes of creating new Web pages and editing existing Web pages.

1.   From the **File** menu, choose **Publish to Web**.

2.   AutoCAD LT displays the Publish to Web wizard. Select **Create Web Page**, and then click **Next**.

3.   Enter the following data:

Specify the name of your Web page...	**AutoCAD LT Drawings**
Specify the parent directory...	**C:**
Provide a description...	**Example Web page**

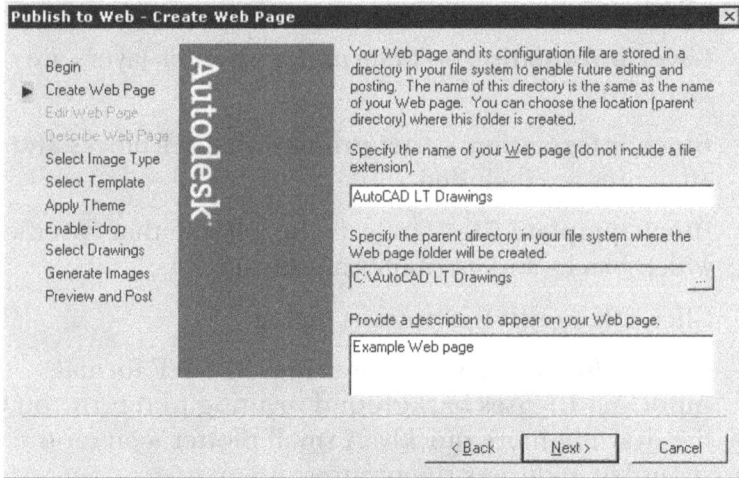

4.   Click **Next,** and then select an image type from the droplist, such as **JPEG.**

TIP   The pros and cons for each image format are:

• **DWF** is a vector format that displays cleanly, and can be zoomed and panned; unfortunately, Web browsers only display DWF images when the appropriate plug-in is installed.

• **JPEG** is a raster format displayed by all Web browsers; unfortunately, it creates *artifacts* (details that don't exist in drawings).

• **PNG** is a raster format that displays cleanly; however, some Web browsers do not display PNG images.

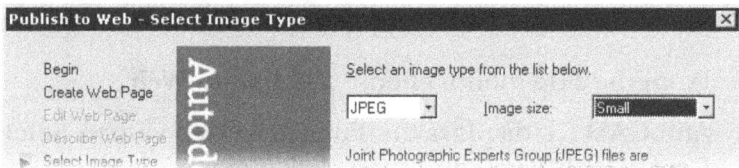

5.   The JPEG and PNG formats have size options. Larger images provide more detail but take longer to transmit.

> **Small** is 789 x 610 resolution
> **Medium** is 1009 x 780
> **Large** is 1302 x 1006
> **Extra Large** is 1576 x 1218

From the Image size droplist, select **Small,** and then click **Next.**

6. The Select Template page provides predesigned Web page formats.

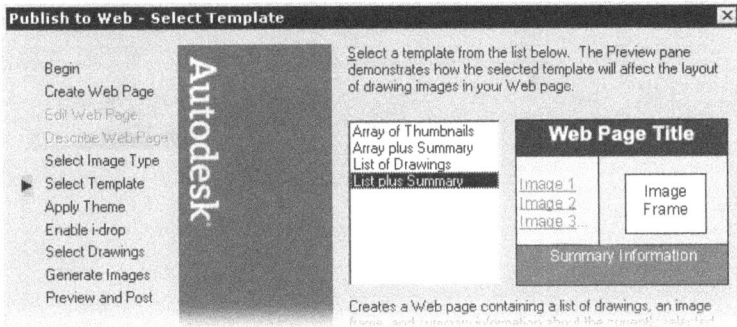

Select **List plus Summary** and then choose **Next**.

7. There are *themes* to apply to Web pages. Themes apply colors and fonts.

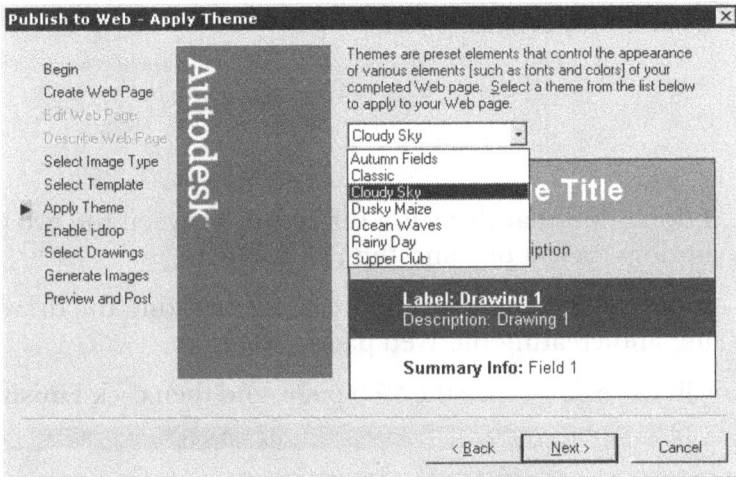

Select **Cloudy Sky** and then click **Next**.

8. As an option, you can enable Autodesk's "i-drop" feature in the Web page. i-drop allows users to drag drawings and blocks from Web pages directly into AutoCAD LT.

For this exercise, leave the **Enable i-drop** option unchecked, and then click **Next**.

9. Select drawing(s) and layouts:

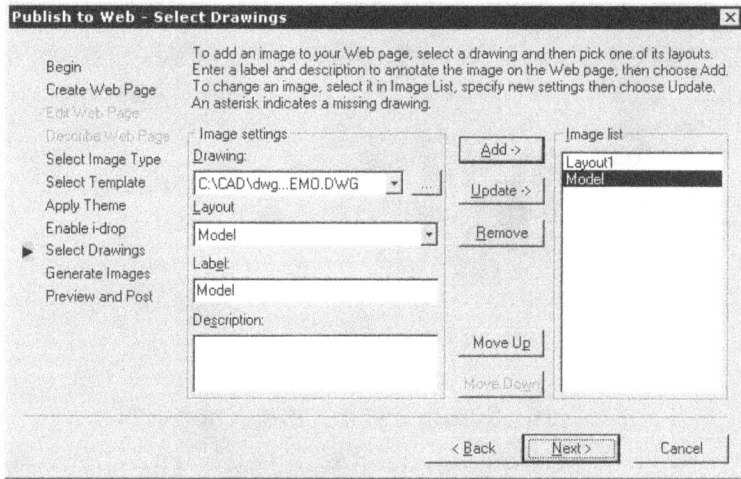

10. Click **Next**. AutoCAD LT regenerates drawings to ensure they are up to date.

I don't find that there is a difference between the two options. Select one and then click **Next**.

AutoCAD LT spends a moment regenerating the drawing and creating the Web page.

11. Click **Preview** to see the Web page, and then click **Finish**.

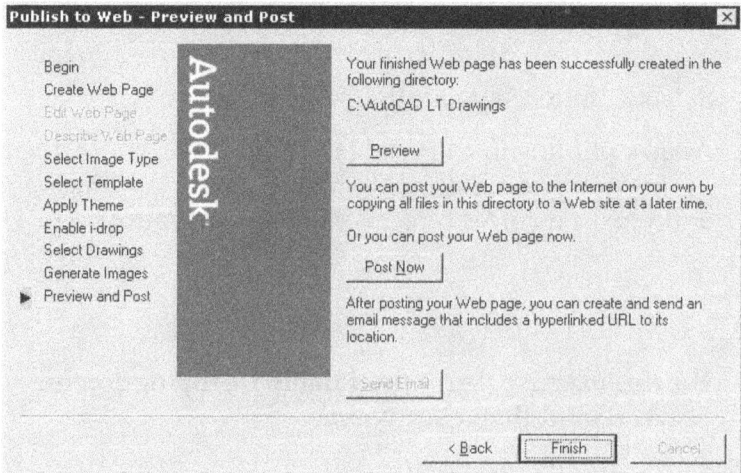

(Click **Back** to make changes if the page is not to your liking.)

TIPS   If you do not see drawings in the Web browser, check (1) whether JavaScript has been turned off; (2) the DWF plug-in is installed; (3) or strict error checking by Internet Explorer requires a download of updated templates from usa.autodesk.com/getdoc/id=DL404058.

The Web page created by AutoCAD LT is named acwebpublish.htm. If it contains DWF images, right-click them to access the shortcut menu of commands, such as Zoom, Pan, and Layers.

The **Post Now** button uploads the Web page files to Web sites. This option works only when FTP has been previously set up correctly.

Viewing DWF Files on the Internet

When DWF files are embedded in Web pages, they can be viewed only when the appropriate plug-in is installed. (Plug-ins allow Web browsers to correctly display any kind of file.) When AutoCAD LT was installed on your computer, the DWF plug-in was also installed in Internet Explorer.

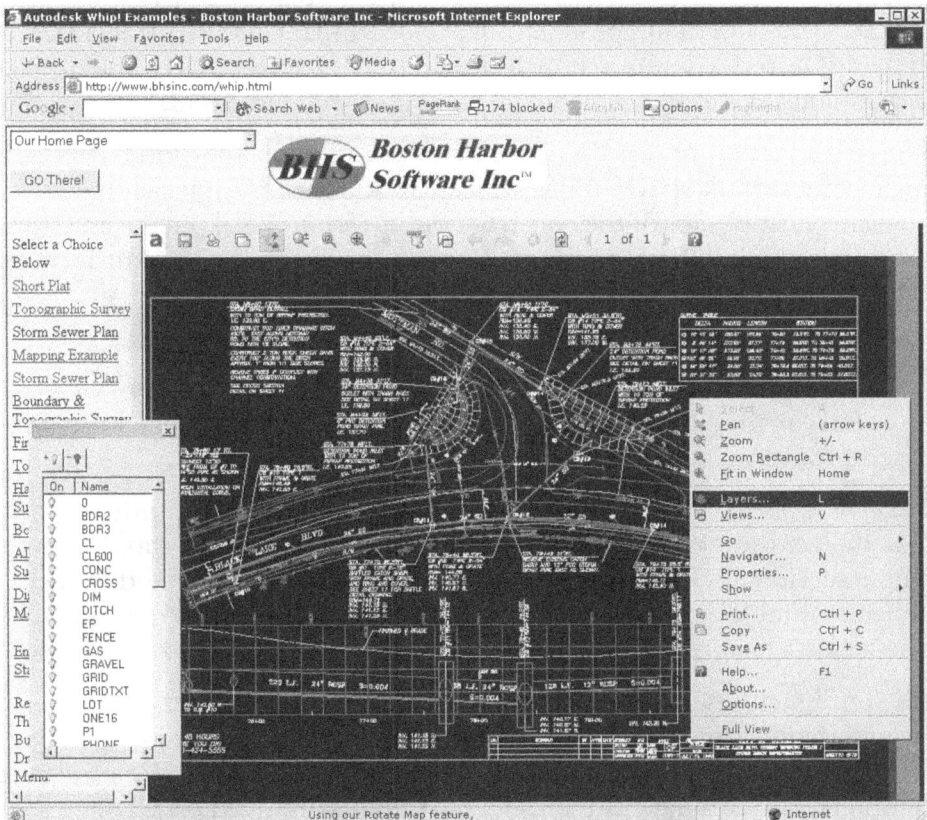

To view samples of DWF being used to display AutoCAD drawings on the Internet, try these Web sites:

> www.dot.co.pima.az.us/gis/maps/maplib/plss/pimatr.dwf — Pima County Department of Transportation Technical Services — GIS database services
>
> www.bhsinc.com/whip.html — Boston Harbor Software; select DWF files from the list on the left-hand side
>
> www.autodesk.com/dwf — Autodesk DWF sample files; select Sample Files from the list on the list-hand side

Online Project Management

With the Internet bubble came all things Internet. A year before the first edition of this book was written in 2000, this section would not have been included. That's because Web-based project management didn't became viable until the second half of 1999.

One of the concepts to survive the popping of the Internet bubble was Web-based project management. These are Web sites that help companies keep track of their construction projects by storing the project's CAD drawings and documents. It also provides a "meeting place" for project participants and keeps a record of all project-related email.

These Web sites are not free anymore. You pay for additional services, such as more disk space, more services, and renting cameras that automatically post photos of the construction site for archival purposes. Other services include: bid management service, facility-management-focused software, 3D model translation, and sharing.

Buzzsaw and ProjectPoint

Autodesk formed a division called buzzsaw.com for its entry into Web-based project management at www.buzzsaw.com.

Buzzsaw calls itself "the building design and construction industry hub that delivers integrated business-to-business collaboration and e-commerce services for everyone in the building industry that needs a faster, more profitable way to work." In other words, buzzsaw.com provides project Web hosting services.

It's simple: choose a site name, add the names of team members, and upload the documents. (A 30-day free trial is available that provides you with space for 20 projects on 1GB of storage space.) After the project is complete, you can have the project documents archived on CDs.

Some of the features include:

> **Portfolio reporting** — tracks status of entire project portfolio
>
> **Portfolio dashboard** — accesses crucial project information instantly
>
> **Approval workflow** — manages design review with predefined rules
>
> **Private discussions** — makes internal communication confidential
>
> **Construction forms** — accesses standard forms for RFIs, submittals, etc.
>
> **Activity log** — views and audits all project and user actions
>
> **Automatic version tracking** — automatically tracks and records changes
>
> **Tiered permissions** — chooses from eight permission levels
>
> **Email notification** — automatically alerts team members to updates

A Look at XML for CAD

Web pages are displayed using HTML (short for "Hypertext Markup Language"), which defines the look of the text, placement of images, colors, and so on. If you have seen HTML code, then you probably recognize that it consists of formatting codes in angle brackets, such as <P>, which indicates the ends of paragraphs.

Programmers have extended HTML to data files, calling the new format XML (short for "Extensible Markup Language"). As you might guess from the term "extensible," XML is a version of HTML designed to be extended. XML is not too much different, except that it contains code defined outside of the standard HTML spec.

XML allows project data to be independent of the authoring software — both between different application software and varying versions of software. This allows data to be archived and accessed more readily on future projects. Any Web browser can display XML. If the Web browser doesn't understand a specific XML code, it simply ignores it.

Over the last several years, several dialects of XML have been developed for CAD. Autodesk briefly flirted with DesignXML, the XML version of DWG drawing files, but quickly abandoned it in favor of DWF, which is not related to XML at all.

What XML Means to CAD Users

You won't see an immediate effect of aecXML and LandXML on your everyday CAD drafting. It takes years for standards to be implemented. First, the vendors (often competitors) take time to agree on how to write the standards. Following this, the standards are usually not implemented until the next release of the software — if at all.

If all goes according to plan, within a couple of years your Web browser, together with AutoCAD LT, will be accessing product data, conducting e-commerce with suppliers and clients, and archiving project data — all seamlessly around the world.

Some of Autodesk's software does support dialects of XML, two of which are aecXML and LandXML.

aecXML for Architecture

A CAD vendor named Bentley Systems took the initiative to develop a dialect of XML for the AEC industry called aecXML (*AEC* is short for "architecture, engineering, construction"). Bentley Systems produces the MicroStation CAD software, which tends to be used by governmental and larger construction organizations.

Members of the group designing aecXML include Autodesk, Primavera Systems, Timberline Software, Blueline Online, and Bidcom. aecXML is part of the IAI (International Alliance for Interoperability). IAI has spent the last several years creating standards for exchanging objects between CAD programs, called IFC (short for "Industry Foundation Classes").

Several committees are working on various aspects of the aecXML sspecification, including plant design; design, specification, schedule, and cost; procurement; construction and project management; and facility management operations and maintenance. The IAI is overseeing the merging of IFC with aecXML and CSI, the construction standards speci-fied by the Construction Specifications Institute. For more information, see www.iai-na.org/aecxml/mission.php.

LandXML for Surveying

Autodesk developed LandXML for CAD users involved in land plan-ning, civil engineering, and surveying. LandXML is based on the EAS-E (short for "Engineering and Survey-Exchange") Initiative, which defines an ASCII data format for highway design projects.

According to Autodesk, "Web-based tools are used to view, edit, and report LandXML data. XSL (short for "Extensible Stylesheet Language") style sheets can be easily created and applied to LandXML data and then run from a project Web page. Examples include XSL style sheets that format raw point data into point tables; and format data to match an organization's internal standards, such as legal descriptions for parcel reports."

Autodesk is developing LandXML in collaboration with other companies, who now serve as the basis for an advisory group. The companies include other CAD vendors, consulting firms, and government agencies: Intergraph; Clough, Harbour and Associates; Florida Department of Transportation; Haestad Methods; Infrasoft; Langan Engineering and Environmental Services; Nebraska Department of Transportation; and Vanasse Hangen Brustlin. For more information on LandXML, see www.landxml.org.

Summary

In this chapter, you learned how AutoCAD interacts with the Internet. The Open and Insert commands open (and insert) drawings from Internet, while the SaveAs command saves a drawing to an FTP site. You also learned to work with DWF files to post your drawings to the Internet in a compact and secure manner.

Web-based project management sites, such as buzzsaw.com, allow you and other team members to manage a CAD (or any other) project from any computer — anywhere in the world — with access to the Internet. The emerging aecXML and LandXML standards may play a role in helping a variety of CAD programs to access data more easily from the Internet.

In the next chapter, you learn about translation and how to exchange drawings with other versions of AutoCAD LT and other Autodesk software products.

Notes

Chapter 17

Translating AutoCAD LT Drawings

In This Chapter

- Differences between drawings from various releases of LT
- Exchanging LT drawings with other Autodesk software
- Translation standards for exchanging drawings with other CAD packages

The last several chapters described how to share drawings with other AutoCAD LT users through office networks (the intranet) and the Internet. In this chapter, you learn about the pitfalls of sharing drawings with other users of Autodesk software, as well as competitor CAD programs. In many cases, drawing translation may be required.

Exchanging Autodesk Drawings

In early versions of AutoCAD LT, Autodesk described it as "the only CAD program that speaks fluent AutoCAD."

Yet even in a pure Autodesk CAD environment, you need to be aware that drawings cannot be casually exchanged between AutoCAD LT, AutoCAD, Inventor, and other software packages.

Key Terms

Custom objects — AutoCAD objects created by ObjectARX programs
Object enablers — software that edits custom objects
Proxy objects — visual representations of custom objects
VDAFS — exchange standard used by German automobile manufacturers

Abbreviations

DWG	drawing file
DXF	drawing interchange format
IAI	Industry Alliance for Interoperability
IFC	Industry Foundation Classes
IGES	Initial Graphics Exchange Specification
LT	LighT
MAI	Mechanical Alliance for Interoperability
PDES	Product Data Exchange Standard
R14	Release 14
STEP	Standard for the Exchange of Product model data
UCS	user-defined coordinate system
VDAFS	Verband der Automobilindustrie Flächenschnittstelle
xref	externally referenced drawings

The reason is that each of Autodesk's software products uses a file format that differs by varying degrees. Perhaps for that reason, the slogan on the AutoCAD LT 2000 box changed to read: "Extending the design team."

How DWG Files Differ

In some cases, the file format is similar between Autodesk's CAD packages but not identical. This is the case for AutoCAD LT and AutoCAD. Both read and write each other's .dwg files. While AutoCAD accurately displays everything you draw in LT, the reverse may not be true. Specifically, AutoCAD LT handles the following objects differently.

Shading Modes

AutoCAD's **ShadeMode** command allows the user to select from seven shading and wireframe viewing options.

AutoCAD LT, however, is limited to five: 256- or 16-color wireframe (with and without edges) and hidden-line removal.

Multiple UCSs

AutoCAD allows the user to create drawings with multiple UCSs (user-defined coordinate systems) in each viewport.

AutoCAD LT, however, is limited to a single UCS per viewport. When you bring a multi-UCS drawing into LT, it recognizes only the current UCS.

Nonrectangular Viewports

AutoCAD allows you to create drawings containing viewports with nonrectangular boundaries; in fact, any object drawn in paper space can be converted to a viewport.

When you bring such a drawing to LT, you can move, copy, and rotate the nonrectangular viewports; you cannot, however, create nonrectangular viewports in AutoCAD LT.

Proxies Represent Custom Objects

In some cases, drawings created by Autodesk CAD software contain one or more *custom objects*. A custom object is created by programming rather than by AutoCAD. Specifically, ObjectARX programs control the creation and editing of custom objects. (ARX is short for "AutoCAD runtime extensions.") Although AutoCAD LT understands ObjectARX, Autodesk chose to not make it available as a programming interface in LT.

Since Release 14, all of Autodesk's software based on AutoCAD, such as Mechanical Desktop, Architectural Desktop, and Land Desktop, makes use of custom objects.

(You can work with custom objects in AutoCAD through the **LsNew** command. This command creates custom objects called landscape objects.)

Object Enablers

For all AutoCAD-based programs (including LT), Autodesk makes available software called Object Enabler. This free software allows you to view and edit custom objects but not create new custom objects. See the complete list at usa.autodesk.com/adsk/servlet/index? siteID=123112&id=2753223&linkID=2475712.

According to the Web page, AutoCAD LT object enablers must be downloaded and installed for Land Desktop and Map 3D. No AutoCAD LT object enablers are available for Building Systems and Civil 3D. AutoCAD LT 2006 includes object enabler support for drawings created by Architectural Desktop.

Proxy Objects

When both the ObjectARX program and the Object Enabler are unavailable — whether in LT or any other AutoCAD-derived software — a "proxy" object is displayed in the place of the custom object. The proxy object looks like the custom object but cannot be edited.

When you open drawings containing custom objects, AutoCAD LT displays a warning dialog box. The dialog box reports the number of proxy objects and their originating ObjectARX application.

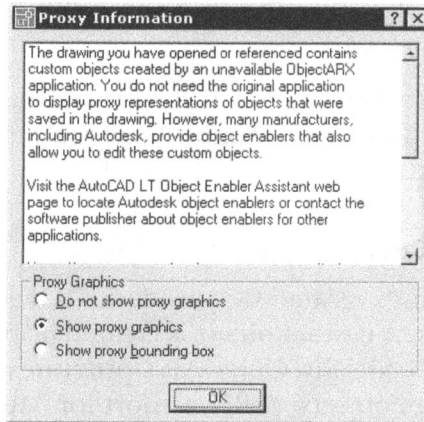

The Proxy Information dialog box provides you with three display options:

Do not show proxy graphics — project objects are not displayed and do not show up in the drawing.

Show proxy graphics — (default) displays a meta-representation of the object.

Show proxy bounding box — displays the object as a rectangular box and provides a brief description of the object.

Use the **Regen** command to redisplay the object in its new form. LT remembers the setting the next time you open a drawing with proxy objects. The following illustration shows the proxy object at left and the bounding box at right.

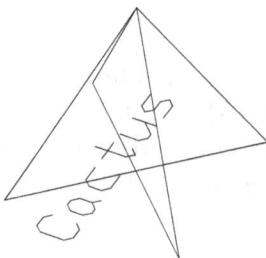

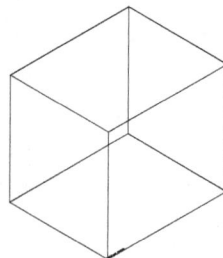

Older Versions of DWG

With each release of AutoCAD LT, Autodesk makes changes to the DWG format. The changes are required so that Autodesk can add new features to the program.

There are two kinds of changes to drawing files: major and minor. Major changes occur every three releases and involve a wholesale overhauling of the file format. The next major change is slated for AutoCAD LT 2007.

Minor changes occur with every new release, and sometimes between releases. For example, AutoCAD LT 2005 introduced the table object. LT 2004 can read drawings with tables, even though it cannot create tables. As long as the table objects are not edited or changed, the drawing is unaffected and can be read by LT 2005.

In general, AutoCAD drawing files are backward-compatible but not forward-compatible:

- **Backward-compatible** means that a newer version of the software can read drawings created by an older version of the software. LT 2006 reads drawings created by LT 98, LT 97, LT 95, LT Release 2, and LT Release 1.
- **Forward-compatible** means that an older version of the software can read drawings created by newer versions of the software. For older versions of LT, this is not possible unless you first use LT 2000 to convert the drawing to the older format.

Saving to Older Versions

File | SaveAs

The **SaveAs** command allows you to convert drawings so that they can be read by older versions of LT. The drawback is that this can have two deleterious effects on your precious drawing: some objects are changed, and some objects are outright erased. The most common example of erasure is new system variables.

To save drawings in a format that can be read by older versions of AutoCAD LT — such as LT 2000 — follow these steps:

1. From the **File** menu, select **Save As**. Notice the Save Drawing As dialog box.

2. In the **Files of type** droplist, select the version of LT to target:

- AutoCAD LT 2000 .dwg
- AutoCAD LT 2000 .dxf
- AutoCAD LT R2 or AutoCAD R12 .dxf

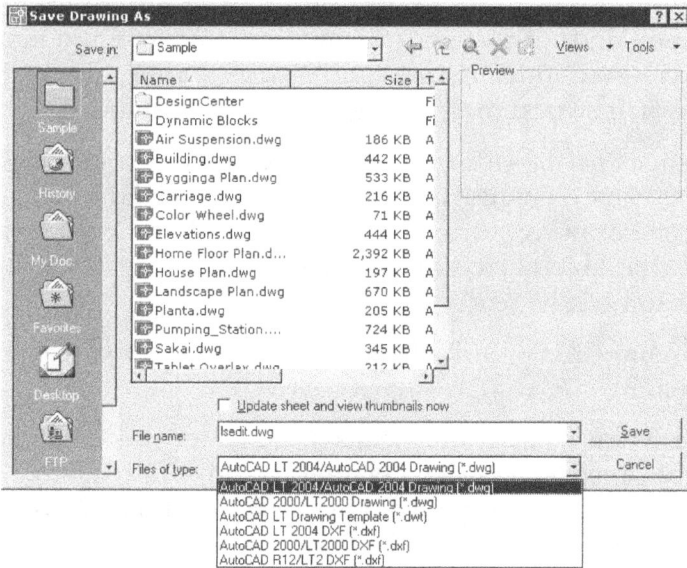

(AutoCAD 2004 format is used by AutoCAD LT 2006.)

3. Select the folder, change the filename (if necessary), and then click **Save**.

TIP Because drawings can change when converted to older versions of AutoCAD LT, it is wise to keep older versions of the program to check the effect of the conversion. You can have AutoCAD LT always save drawings in older formats. In the Save Drawing As dialog box, select **Tools | Options**. In the Saveas Options dialog box, select the format in which to always save drawings.

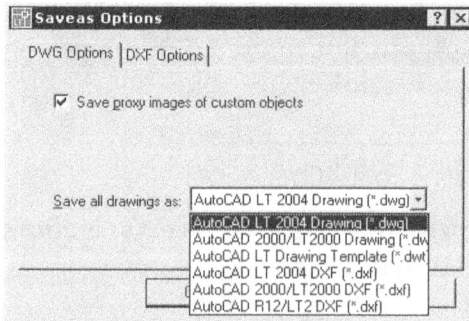

The following table provides the details on what happens to objects in LT 2006 drawings when converted to LT R2 and LT 2000. In the table, *preserved* means that the object is not displayed in the older format but is preserved for its return to LT 2006.

Object	Effect of Conversion to AutoCAD LT Release 2
Dimensions	Additions to the dimstyle table and associated system variables are preserved.
Hyperlinks	Preserved; not active in the drawing.
Layouts	Preserved; the current layout is displayed as paper space.
Lineweights	Preserved; all objects appear to have the same lineweight.
Long names	Truncated to 31 characters.
Plot Style Tables	Preserved; tables no longer available.
Summaries	Preserved; not displayed.
Groups	Group definition is preserved; objects no longer in a group.
Regions	Displayed as a region but cannot be edited.
Revision Clouds	Converted to polyarcs.
Ellipses	Converted to polylines or circles.
Hatches	Associativity is lost.
Leaders	Straight leaders converted to lines; spline leaders converted to polyline. Arrows converted to filled or unfilled polylines, circles, polygons, or solids.
Linetypes	Global linetype scale erased. Shape definitions ignored in complex linetypes.
OLE objects	Erased.
Preview Images	Erased.
Tolerances	Converted to polylines and text.
Xref Overlays	Erased.

When exporting to AutoCAD LT R2, you must export drawings in DXF format. DXF is short for "drawing interchange format"; more details on DXF later.

Autodesk's Incompatible Formats

Some Autodesk software products use file formats completely different from AutoCAD. The most common examples are 3D Studio, Revit, and Inventor. All include DWG translators that import and/or export their drawing in DWG format.

Compatible with DWG

AutoCAD
AutoCAD LT
Buzzsaw
DWF Composer
DWF Viewer
Symbols
Volo View

May Require Object Enablers

Architectural Desktop
AutoCAD Electrical
AutoCAD Mechanical
Building Systems
Civil 3D
Civil Design
Field Survey
Land Desktop
Map 3D
Raster Design
Survey
Utility Design

Requires Translation

AutoSketch
CAiCE Visual Transportation
Crisis Command
Media and Entertainment Products
Envision
GIS Design Server
Inventor
Location-Based Services Products
MapGuide
Mobile Command
OnSite Desktop, Enterprise, View
Pre-Plan
Pre-Plan Command
Productstream
QuickCAD
Revit
Streamline
Vault

Compatible Software Products

Although Autodesk is best known for AutoCAD, the company produces several dozen software products. See the full list at left.

Many programs are based on AutoCAD, and hence use the DWG file format to store their drawings. Although they use this "common" file format, the drawings may not be 100% compatible between programs. Differences may occur due to version numbers, custom objects, and database limitations.

Incompatible Software Products

Other software from Autodesk does not use DWG. Instead, the software uses other file formats.

One reason is that the software was originally developed by another company, which Autodesk subsequently purchased (such as 3ds max and MapGuide).

Another reason is that although the software was developed by Autodesk, the company felt that a different, more efficient file format was better suited (such as for AutoSketch and Inventor). These products include translators for importing and exporting DWG files.

The table lists the Autodesk software products that use DWG as their file format and those that do not.

Drawings from Other CAD Programs

You can get into trouble when trying to read drawings created by non-Autodesk CAD programs. It is possible to successfully read such drawings, but there are pitfalls. Here are some of the most common problems:

- Objects missing
- Blocks in the wrong place
- Colors look incorrect
- Text screwed up

Why do these problems occur? Every CAD product is designed differently. Even Autodesk is forced to create a variety of file formats so that each program can be optimized for its specialization.

Almost every CAD vendor creates its software in deliberate "isolation." The file format is designed for the needs of the CAD program — not the translation needs of its competitors! As a result, CAD programs define objects, file formats, the user interface, the programming interfaces, and even the jargon differently.

For example, AutoCAD has a "point" object, whereas older versions of the MicroStation CAD program represent points by lines with zero length. (MicroStation V8 now includes all DWG objects.)

Similarly, AutoCAD has both "circle" and "ellipse" objects, but older MicroStation had just the ellipse; it represented circles as round ellipses.

AutoCAD allows you to create a tapered polyline (a polyline with varying width), which most other CAD programs cannot replicate. Illustrated below is column.dwg in AutoCAD LT (at left) and the same drawing translated into Visio (at right). The Visio translation makes errors with polylines. (The two drawings are not identical in size due to differences in scale.)

In AutoCAD LT, you can give blocks and layers names of up to 255 characters long. Earlier versions of AutoCAD are limited to names 31 characters long. Some old CAD programs are limited to eight or 12 characters.

AutoCAD LT can have, in theory, an unlimited number of layers and linetypes. Most old CAD programs are limited to 255 layers and a fixed number of linetypes. MicroStation is limited to 63 layers and six linetypes.

Even the terminology changes between CAD programs:

- "Layers" in AutoCAD LT are "levels" in MicroStation.
- "Blocks" in AutoCAD LT are "smartshapes" in Visio Technical are "parts" in CadKey are "symbols" in Visual CADD are "cells" in MicroStation.
- Sometimes, the same word has different meaning. For example, "attributes" in AutoCAD LT are "tags" in MicroStation; when a MicroStation user talks of "attributes," he's referring to "styles" in AutoCAD LT.

There are dozens of other differences between AutoCAD and other CAD programs.

There have been a few efforts to design new CAD programs based on competitor file formats. The best example is IntelliCAD, which was deliberately designed to work with AutoCAD and its DWG files. For more information, see www.intellicad.org.

Drawing Translation

Almost as an afterthought, CAD vendors include some level of drawing translation. Translators convert proprietary file formats into other formats (called "exporting") or convert other file formats into the CAD product's proprietary format (called "importing").

Some CAD vendors provide both export and import; some provide just the one. Some CAD vendors work very hard to provide excellent translation; some provide a barely adequate facility, primarily for marketing purposes.

Writing drawing translators is difficult work, because it takes an in-depth understanding of both CAD programs. This understanding is, unfortunately, one-sided. I recall a CAD vendor proudly asking me to evaluate their AutoCAD translator, which he felt was "pretty good." I did, and found many flaws. When I presented the report to the CAD vendor, he protested at the failings I found, stating that I didn't understand the "philosophy" of their CAD product. They were right, becuase my expertise is in AutoCAD. My point was, however, that if they wanted to attract AutoCAD users, they needed to understand the philosophy of AutoCAD. Because they did not, the translation was poorly handled.

Using the earlier problems as examples, a good translator would know when a MicroStation ellipse should be translated as an AutoCAD LT circle or as an ellipse object. A good translator needs to know how to handle an AutoCAD LT drawing with too many layers (such as more than 63 or 255), and when a layer name is too long.

Even more difficult is round-trip translation. It is one thing to translate a drawing as accurately as possible into another format; it is nearly impossible to turn the translated drawing file back into the original drawing. For example, if an AutoCAD layer name is too long, the translator might truncate the name to 12 characters. Upon the return translation back to AutoCAD format, the truncated layer name should be extended back to its original long name, but it won't be.

Over the last 20 years, various committees and vendors have attempted to create a standard for accurately exchanging data between different CAD software programs. All have had limited success; nevertheless, the effort (which I consider futile) goes on. The standards are known by their acronyms. The most common standards are IGES, PDES/STEP, DXF, and IAI.

IGES

IGES was the first attempt to create an industry-wide translation standard. (IGES is short for "Initial Graphics Exchange Specification.")

IGES was created by committee, and was used commonly among larger CAD systems, such as those used by automotive and aerospace corporations. Today, IGES has been replaced by STEP. More information at www.nist.gov/iges.

PDES/STEP

Like IGES, STEP was created for a translation standard for the entire CAD industry. (PDES is short for "Product Data Exchange Standard'; STEP is short for "Standard for The Exchange of Product model data.") It has been under development since the late 1980s, and like IGES is being created by a committee.

STEP is meant to be powerful enough to handle all aspects of a project, from the initial design through to construction and decommissioning. More info at pdesinc.aticorp.org.

DXF

Autodesk developed DXF in the early days of AutoCAD. (DXF is short for "drawing interchange format.") Because DWG is a proprietary file format that Autodesk does not document, DXF was originally intended as a method for third-party developers to access the data stored in the DWG file.

Over the decades, DXF became popular among smaller CAD systems as a file exchange standard. Today, even Autodesk uses it for drawing translation.

With each release of AutoCAD, the DXF format changes. More recent versions contain encrypted data, defeating its openness. More information at usa.autodesk.com/adsk/servlet/ item?siteID=123112&id=752569.

IAI and MAI

With AutoCAD Release 13, the DWG file format became much more complex. It could contain custom objects, whose properties are defined by programs written using ObjectARX. When DWG files contain custom objects, they are no longer fully compatible with versions of AutoCAD lacking the ObjectARX code (see the discussion on proxy objects earlier in this chapter).

To help overcome this problem, Autodesk helped found the IAI and MAI. (IAI is short for "Industry Alliance for Interoperability"; MAI is short for "Mechanical Alliance for Interoperability.") The purpose of both committees is to develop standards in custom objects. For example, the IAI is working on IFC, short for "Industry Foundation Classes."

Autodesk has since spun off its own IFC development work to an independent company. More information at www.iai-international.org.

Summary

In this chapter, you learned about the methods and pitfalls of sharing drawings between different versions of AutoCAD LT, as well as between Autodesk software products and other CAD programs.

While translation can be perfect in many cases, this chapter made you aware of the changes that can happen to the drawing.

Part IV

Customizing AutoCAD LT

Notes

Chapter 18

Introduction to
Customizing AutoCAD LT

In This Chapter

- Different methods for customizing AutoCAD LT
- Programming available in LT
- Customizing LT's startup

When AutoCAD first came out in the early 1980s, one of its strengths was its ability to be customized. While program customization is taken for granted today, 20 years ago it was a radical departure from the norm. Back then, software simply was not customized — other than perhaps changing the color of the screen. If you wanted something "custom," you programmed it yourself or paid someone a lot of money to do it.

AutoCAD LT can be customized in a number of areas, although not as extensively as AutoCAD, as described in this and following chapters.

Key Terms

Customize — modifies the way that AutoCAD LT acts and looks
Startup switches — specify actions LT performs upon starting

Abbreviations

CHM   Compiled HTML help file
CNT   Contents file
DIESEL Direct Interpretively Evaluated String Expression Language
HTML   Hypertext Markup Language
LISP   List Processing
VBA   Visual Basic for Applications

Customizing LT's Startup

You can add *startup switches* to AutoCAD LT. Startup switches cause LT to perform an action, such as to not display a specified view name or to run a script file.

Startup switches are added to the LT icon's Properties dialog box, found on the Windows desktop. It can have multiple startup switches. And the Windows desktop can have multiple LT icons, each for a different customized configuration.

Adding Command-Line Switches

You add command-line switches as follows:

1. Right-click the AutoCAD LT icon on the Windows desktop. Notice the shortcut menu.

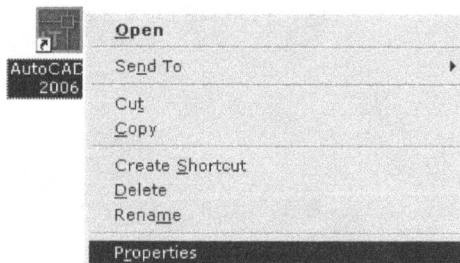

2. From the shortcut menu, select **Properties**. Notice the AutoCAD LT Properties dialog box. Ensure the Shortcut tab is showing.

3. In the AutoCAD LT Properties dialog box, add the startup switch text to the **Target** field.

   Enter the switch (and its parameters, if required) after the closing quotes, as follows:

   "C:\CAD\AutoCAD LT\aclt.exe" /nologo

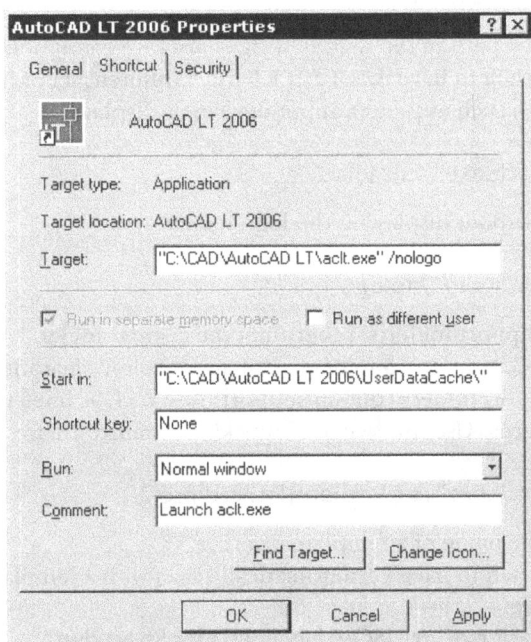

   There must be a space between the closing quote and the / symbol. (The quotes are required when there are spaces in the names of files and folders, such as "AutoCAD LT.")

4. Click **OK**.

   Test the switch by starting AutoCAD LT.

Catalog of Startup Switches

The following startup switches are available to AutoCAD LT. (This list is more complete than that provided by Autodesk.)

Switch	Meaning
/b	Specifies the name of a script file to run once AutoCAD LT starts. Use this switch to have LT perform tasks automatically. For example: "c:\cad\aclt.exe" **/b** purge.scr
/c	Specifies the path to the Aclt2006.cfg (hardware configuration) file. Use this switch to have AutoCAD LT use a different set of hardware peripherals, such as plotter, input device, or display. For example: "c:\cad\aclt.exe" **/c:**\cad\alt
/nologo	Starts LT without displaying the logo screen. For example: "c:\cad\aclt.exe" **/nologo**
/s	Specifies support folder(s) other than the current folder. You can specify up to 15 folders, with a semicolon separating each folder name. Support folders contain support files, such as linetype patterns and hatch patterns. Use this switch to quickly customize LT for different projects. For example: "c:\cad\aclt.exe" **/s** c:\cad\proj1;c:\cad\proj2
/t	Specifies the name of a template drawing. Use this switch to have LT automatically start with a template file. For example: "c:\cad\aclt.exe" **/t** "ISO A1-Named Plot Styles.dwt"
/v	Specifies the name of a saved view. Use this switch to have LT display the view when it opens the drawing. For example: "c:\cad\aclt.exe" **/v** viewname

Technically, the command-line switches do not alter the settings of the Windows registry. The switch settings are valid for the current LT session only.

Programming AutoCAD LT

AutoCAD LT can be programmed to a limited extent only. When the beta version of the very first AutoCAD LT was introduced, it included the AutoLISP programming language. (I still have a copy of it.) When LT was released to the buying public, however, AutoLISP had disappeared. What happened?

Dealers were concerned that the inclusion of the powerful AutoLISP programming language would make LT so popular that it would stunt sales of the more expensive AutoCAD. Under this pressure, Autodesk pulled AutoLISP at the last moment. The dealers were correct, because even without a programming language, LT outsells AutoCAD 3:1.

Before each new release of LT, a rumor circulates that LT will finally include AutoLISP or some other programming interface, such as VBA. With each new release, the rumor is found to be false. That leaves LT as the only CAD program on the market lacking the ability to be programmed. (The exception is a simplistic programming language in LT called DIESEL.)

That hasn't stopped third-party developers, however. As you read in later chapters, clever programmers figured out how to link LT with external programs.

How LT Cannot Be Programmed

As I indicated, AutoCAD LT lacks all programming interfaces found in AutoCAD, with the sole exception of DIESEL. Missing are the following:

Program	Comments
AutoLISP	A simple, yet powerful programming language based on LISP (short for "List Processing")
Visual LISP	AutoLISP with a modern user interface and modern programming constructs
ADS	No longer used in AutoCAD; short for "AutoCAD development system"
DCL	The dialog control language used to create dialog boxes
ASI	The AutoCAD SQL (structured query language) interface, used to link AutoCAD with external databases
ObjectARX	The object-based AutoCAD Runtime Extension, the basis of nearly all third-party add-ons as well as most new features in LT
VBA	Microsoft's Visual Basic for Applications

Perhaps the biggest loss to AutoCAD LT users is that you cannot use Object Enablers. Written in ObjectARX, Object Enablers allow you to view, edit, and plot custom objects created by variants of AutoCAD such as Architectural Desktop and Autodesk Mechanical.

Summary

In this chapter, you learned about how AutoCAD LT can (and cannot) be customized. You also learned how to customize the manner in which LT starts up.

In the next chapter, you learn how to customize LT's command names, use system variables to your advantage, and write script files.

Chapter **19**

Customizing Commands

In This Chapter

- Customizing command names with abbreviations
- Accessing system and environment variables
- Writing script files

Typing commands may seem like an anachronism in this Windows-centric world. If you are familiar with AutoCAD LT's commands, then there is no faster way to draw and edit. AutoCAD LT has a number of alternatives to entering commands. These include:

- Typing command aliases
- Pressing shortcut keys
- Selecting a command from the menu bar
- Selecting a button on a toolbar
- Right-clicking and selecting a command from the shortcut menu
- Selecting a command from the tablet menu

In this chapter, we look at the first two options; the other options are the subject of subsequent chapters.

Key Terms

Aliases — command abbreviations
Environment variables — variables stored in the Windows registry
Scripts — files that execute commands as if they were typed at the keyboard
System variables — store values of variables that determine the state of AutoCAD

Abbreviations

PGP   File extension for program parameters file
SCR   File extension for script files

Command Aliases

Customize | Edit Program Parameters

AutoCAD LT allows command names to be abbreviated. For example, you needn't type the full name of the **Line** command; you could also type simply the letter **L**, as follows:

```
Command: l
LINE Specify first point:
```

Notice that AutoCAD LT reminds you of the meaning of the L by printing the full name of the command, LINE.

Command abbreviations are called *aliases*. AutoCAD LT has over 200 aliases. Most are abbreviations of commands, while others exist for reasons of compatibility.

For example, AutoCAD LT 2004 removed the **DdUcs** command, replacing it with the **UcsMan** command. When you type **dducs**, AutoCAD LT executes the UcsMan command.

AutoCAD LT stores aliases in a file named aclt.pgp. (PGP is short for "program parameters file," but was known in the past as the "pig pen file.")

The aclt.pgp file is stored deep in the bowels of your computer's folder structure, in a hidden folder called C:\Documents and Settings\ <login name> \Application Data\Autodesk\AutoCAD LT 2006\R11\enu\Support.

Because that's too difficult to access, Autodesk makes the file available through a menu pick.

From the **Tools** menu, select **Customize | Edit Program Parameters (aclt.pgp)**. AutoCAD opens the Notepad text editor with the aclt.pgp file displayed.

```
aclt.pgp - Notepad                                          _ □ ✕
File  Edit  Format  Help
;
;
;    Program Parameters File for AutoCAD LT 2006
;    Command Alias Definitions

; Copyright (C) 1997-2005 by Autodesk, Inc.   All Rights Reserved.

; Each time you open a new or existing drawing, AutoCAD LT searches
; the support path and reads the first aclt.pgp file that it finds.

;   -- Command Aliases --
; The Command Aliases section of this file provides default settings for
; AutoCAD LT command shortcuts.  Note: It is not recommended that  you directly
```

The top portion of the file documents how to create aliases; the lower portion contains contain the aliases.

```
XA,        *XATTACH
XB,        *XBIND
-XB,       *-XBIND
XL,        *XLINE
XR,        *XREF
-XR,       *-XREF
Z,         *ZOOM
```

Writing Aliases

The format of the file is ASCII, which makes it easy to add and edit aliases with Notepad.

Here is how the file defines the alias for the **Arc** command:

A, *ARC

"A" is the alias. It is followed by a comma and an asterisk. (Why? I have no idea.) The asterisk is followed by the full command name, Arc.

You can use as many letters as you like for aliases, but by keeping it to three or fewer letters you follow the spirit of *shortening* command names.

The only time many letters are used for aliases is when commands are redefined, such as:

PRINT, *PLOT.

All of AutoCAD LT's aliases are listed in Appendix A.

Using System Variables

GetEnv
SetEnv
SetVar

To complement commands, AutoCAD LT uses system variables to store settings. These settings retain options that you select in commands. They also report on settings in AutoCAD LT and the operating system. AutoCAD LT has several hundred system variables.

Accessing System Variables

For example, when you draw a line with the **Line** command, AutoCAD LT stores the last point you picked in the system variable called **LastPoint**. To see the value of **LastPoint**, enter it at the 'Command:' prompt, as follows:

> Command: **lastpoint**
> Enter new value for LASTPOINT <212.22,127.67,0.00>: *(Press Enter.)*

The last x,y coordinates entered were 212.22,127.67. (The z coordinate reports the elevation.)

You can change the value by entering a new set of coordinates. But when you just press the **Enter** key, you retain the value stored in the variable.

Read-Only Variables

Some system variables cannot be changed. For instance, the **LastAngle** command similarly stores the last angle you picked:

> Command: **lastangle**
> LASTANGLE = 340 (read only)

In this case, the **(read only)** indicates that you cannot change the value of the system variable.

Toggle Variables

Other system variables are called "toggles," because they have just two values:

0 means off.

1 means on.

An example is the **ToolTips** variable. It determines whether tooltips (small yellow tags) are displayed when you pause the cursor over a toolbar button. The value of ToolTips can be 0 (off) or 1 (on).

I find it sometimes easier to change values using system variables than accessing the related command. For example, you could select **Customize | Toolbars** from the **Tools** menu bar, then click **Show ToolTips** on toolbars in the dialog box, then click **OK**. Or, you can use the **ToolTips** system variable to toggle the tooltips more quickly.

TIPS   To see the list of system variables and their current values, enter:

Command: **setvar**
Enter variable name or [?] <LASTANGLE>: **?**
Enter variable(s) to list <*>: *(Press Enter.)*

Notice that there are several hundred system variables.

To see the meaning of system variables, their options, and default values, press **F1**. When the AutoCAD LT Help System window appears, click the **Contents** tab. Navigate to the **System Variables** item. Notice that the variables are listed alphabetically by name.

User Variables

There are 10 system variables for your personal use, five each for storing integer numbers (no decimal point) and real numbers. The storage is, however, temporary; the values are lost when you exit AutoCAD.

System Variable	Meaning
UserI1 – UserI5	Meant to hold integer numbers.
UserR1 – UserR5	Meant to hold real numbers.

(The UserS1 – UserS5 system variables, meant for strings of text, are missing from AutoCAD LT.)

You can access the value of system variables in script files, menu macros, toolbar macros, and DIESEL macros:

Customization	Function for Accessing System Variables
Scripts	Setvar *varname value*
Menu macros	' _Setvar *varname value*
Toolbar macros	' _setvar;*varname*;*value*;
Diesel macros	$(getvar,*varname*)

You learn more about these functions in the following chapters.

Environment Variables

AutoCAD LT has one advantage over AutoCAD with its unique **SetEnv** and **GetEnv** commands. These two commands allow you to directly manipulate values in the Windows registry.

You use **GetEnv** to *get* the value of an environment variable; you use **SetEnv** to *set* (change) the value of an environment variable.

Unlike the **SetVar** command's ? option, these two commands don't provide a handy list of variables for your reference.

Earlier versions of AutoCAD LT used the two commands to access data stored in the aclt.ini file, which no longer exists. At first, the two commands were not even documented by Autodesk; later releases grudgingly admitted the existence of **SetEnv** first, later followed by **GetEnv**. Even in LT's documentation, Autodesk doesn't say much about the commands: "AutoCAD LT system registry variables can be set from within AutoCAD LT with **SetEnv**. The two most likely registry variables to be reset are **MaxArray** and **MaxHatch**." Period.

MaxArray limits the maximum number of objects created by the **Array** command; the default value is 100,000.

MaxHatch similarly limits the maximum number of entities created by the **Hatch** and **BHatch** commands; the default is 10,000.

Since Autodesk mentions the names of two environment variables, let's try them first. Let's find out the value of **MaxArray**:

```
Command: getenv
Enter variable name: MaxArray
100000
```

> **TIP** You must enter the name of environment variables *exactly* as written, with mixed upper- and lowercase letters. If you enter "maxarray", for instance, all you get back from AutoCAD LT is a blank stare. This is different from all other areas of AutoCAD where text in any case — upper, lower, or mixed — is accepted.

Let's now change the value of **MaxArray**:

```
Command: setenv
Enter variable name: MaxArray
Value <100000>: 10000
```

Now use the **Array** command to create an array of more than 10,000 objects, such as an array of 150 by 100 objects. When you click the dialog box's **OK** button, notice the error dialog that AutoCAD LT displays. It warns that the 15,000-member array would exceed the 10,000 limit.

Other Environment Variables

By writing "the two most likely registry variables," Autodesk's documentation writers hint that there may be more environment variables than just two. Finding the names of additional variables is not terribly difficult; it requires that you search the Windows registry.

> **CAUTION** It is too easy to damage the registry, and a damaged registry damages your Windows operating environment. For this reason, I don't provide instructions on how to access the following registry entry. If you already know how, I don't need to tell you; if you don't know how, then you don't need to know.
>
> Before editing the registry, save a copy of the registry data: from the menu bar, select **Registry | Export Registry File**.

Notice the names, like **CmdLine.BackColor** and **CmdLine.FontFace**. These set the colors and fonts for the command-line area of AutoCAD LT.

I don't know why, but some of the variables work with the **Get/SetEnv** duo and some don't. For example, **ToolTips** works but **ShowShortcuts** doesn't. Both are found in the Toolbars section.

Writing Script Files

Script

Scripts were introduced to AutoCAD with version 1.4 back in 1983. A *script* does one thing and one thing only: it mimics what you enter at the keyboard.

Anything that you type that shows up at the 'Command:' prompt can be put into script files. That includes AutoCAD LT commands, their option abbreviations, your responses, and DIESEL statements.

The purpose of scripts is to reduce keystrokes needed to carry out repetitive operations. For instance, a script that draws a line and a circle looks like this:

```
line 1,1 2,2
circle 2,2 1,1
```

Run this as a script, and you don't need to type all those letters, numbers, and punctuation.

About Script Files

Scripts are stored in files that have an extension of .scr.

Script files are written in plain ASCII text. For that reason, don't use a word processor, such as WordPad, Write, or Word, because they add non-ASCII formatting code that chokes up AutoCAD LT.

Instead, use Notepad to write scripts. This simple text editor is included with every copy of Windows. Some third-party developers have written script creation software.

Drawbacks to Scripts

Scripts cannot emulate mouse actions. Examples of mouse actions include clicking a mouse button, selecting a menu item or toolbar button, and selecting objects in the drawing. Nor can the script record mouse movements.

Scripts also do not record some keyboard shortcuts. An example of a keyboard shortcut is holding down the **Alt** key to access the menu bar.

The inability of scripts to deal with dialog boxes has important implications. You can have a script open a dialog box (such as via the **Layer** command), but then the script grinds to a halt because it cannot do anything while the dialog box is open. Nor can it close the dialog box.

(Here's the reason scripts cannot handle mouse-oriented actions: scripting was added to AutoCAD about a half-decade before dialog boxes were invented. Autodesk failed to update scripts to handle subsequent moderizations to AutoCAD's user interface.)

Another limitation is that only one script file can be loaded into AutoCAD LT at a time. That script file can, however, call another script file. Or, you can customize a toolbar or menu item to load (and run) script files with a mouse click.

A further limitation is that scripts stall when they encounter invalid forms of command syntax. You may have to go through the code-debug cycle a few times to get the script correct.

It's useful to have an AutoCAD reference text on hand, such as my own *The Illustrated AutoCAD Quick Reference* (Autodesk Press), which lists all command names and their options.

Methods for Scripts to Call Commands

Because scripts cannot operate dialog boxes, most of AutoCAD LT's commands are also available in non-dialog box versions. AutoCAD LT is inconsistent, however, in how it employs these alternate commands. Here is a summary.

Hyphen Prefix

The hyphen (-) prefix is the most common method to force commands to appear at the 'Command;' prompt instead of in dialog boxes. Hyphenated commands include -Layer, -Linetype, and -MText.

To use these in script files, prefix the hyphen in front of the command name, as follows:

```
; Start the Layer command:
-layer
```

The problem is that not all commands have hyphenated alternatives, as the following sections illustrate.

Prior to AutoCAD LT 2000, the Plot command had its own system variable to turn off its dialog box: CmdDia. Today, you use -Plot.

Some commands have different names for the dialog box version and for the command-line version.

System Variables

Some commands need the **FileDia** system variable turned off (set to 0) to force the command to display the prompts at the command line. Examples include **DxfIn**, **Script**, and **VSlide**, which prompt "Enter name of drawing to open <.>:".

Script files should include the following line to turn off dialog boxes:

```
; Turn off dialog boxes:
filedia 0
```

When **FileDia** is turned off, you can use the tilde (~) character to force the display of the dialog box. For example:

```
Command: script
Script file: ~
```

And AutoCAD LT displays the Select Script File dialog box.

Sometimes, it is more efficient to use system variables than commands in scripts. For example, when a script needs to change layers, use the **CLayer** system variable instead of the **-Layer** command, as follows:

```
; Change layer:
clayer layername
```

No Command-Line Alternative

Some commands have no command-line version. These primarily consist of commands related to OLE (short for "object linking and embedding"), such as **OleLinks** and **PasteSpec**. There is no way to control OLE from a script file.

Script Commands

AutoCAD LT has four commands specific to scripts.

Script

Script performs double-duty: it loads a script file, and then it immediately begins running it. For example:

```
Command: script
Script file: filename
```

The **Script** command can be used in scripts to call other scripts.

RScript

The **RScript** command (short for "repeat script") reruns the script currently loaded in AutoCAD LT. It has no options:

```
Command: rscript
```

This command can be used at the end of scripts to repeat them automatically.

Resume

The **Resume** command resumes paused scripts. You pause scripts by pressing the **Backspace** key. Again, no options:

```
Command: resume
```

This command is not used in scripts themselves.

Delay

The **Delay** command slows down scripts by pausing for a specific number of milliseconds, such as:

```
; Pause script for ten seconds:
delay 10000
```

The minimum delay is 1 millisecond; the maximum is 32767, which is just under 33 seconds.

Special Characters in Scripts

In addition to the four commands, there are characters that have special meaning when used in script files.

Spaces and Returns

The special characters most important in script files are the space character and the return (or end-of-line). They represent you pressing the Spacebar or the **Enter** key. They are interchangeable.

The tricky part is that both are invisible. Some scripts require a bunch of blank spaces, because a command requires that you press the **Enter** key several times in a row:

```
; Edit the attributes one at a time:
attedit   1,2
```

How many spaces are there between "attedit" and the coordinates "1,2"? It is nearly impossible to count them. For this reason, it is better to use returns (one per line) instead of spaces, like this:

```
; Edit the attributes one at a time:
attedit




1,2
```

Now it's easier to count the four spaces, since there is one per blank line.

Semicolons

You may have noticed that the semicolon allows comments in script files. AutoCAD LT ignores anything following semicolons.

```
; This is a comment on The Meaning of Liff.
```

Apostrophes

Scripts can be run transparently during commands. You prefix the **Script** command with an apostrophe to run a script while another command is active.

In the following example, I start the **Line** command, then invoke '**Script**:

> Command: **line**
> From point: **'script**
> >>Script file: **filename**

The double angle brackets **>>** are AutoCAD LT's way of reminding me that there are two commands on the go. All four of AutoCAD LT's script-specific commands are transparent, even **'Delay**.

Asterisks

The asterisk is used in one special case only: prefix the **VSlide** command with the *, and AutoCAD LT preloads the file for faster slide viewing performance:

> *vslide

Preloading was useful in olden days when computers ran slowly. With today's high-speed computers, I doubt that the asterisk is needed any longer.

Backspace

Press the **Backspace** key to pause the script. Use the **Resume** command to continue the script.

Escape

The **Esc** key stops the script file running. Use the **RScript** command to start it again from the beginning.

> **TIPS** If you need to use long file names (more than eight characters) that contain spaces, the filename must be enclosed in double quotes:
>
> **fileopen "a long filename"**
>
> If you run long scripts or use **RScript** to repeat scripts many times, consider turning off undo (through the **Undo Control None** command), as well as the log file (via the **LogFileOff** command).

Examples of Script Files

Here are examples of using scripts in different areas of AutoCAD LT.

Opening Multiple Drawings

This script opens two drawings, called base and demolition plans:

```
; Script to open two drawings.
fileopen base
fileopen "demolition plans"
```

While you can open more than one drawing in AutoCAD LT, you cannot use scripts to switch between them. Use the **Close** command to close the current drawing.

Creating Layers

This script creates three layers in the drawing, named text, dim, and lines:

```
; Script to create three layers.
-layer new text
-layer new dim
-layer new lines


; end of script
```

I added the comment at the end of the script to show the blank line following the last **-Layer** command. The blank line is required to exit the command.

The following modification sets the color for each layer:

```
; Script to create three layers.
-layer new text color red text
-layer new dim color 5 dim
-layer new lines color green lines

; end of script
```

For the first seven colors, you can enter either the color number or name:

Color Name	Color Number
Red	1
Yellow	2
Green	3
Cyan	4
Blue	5
Magenta	6
White (or black)	7

Drawing Boundaries

This script draws the boundary of a lot or property. First, it sets the appropriate units, then it draws the boundary using relative coordinates:

```
; Set the units
-units 3 4 5 4 E N
```

```
; Draw a property boundary
line
0,0
@@116'<S45E
@@80'<N20E
@@116'<N40E
@@80'<N6E
close
```

Saving and Plotting

The following script performs three tasks: zooms to the drawing extents, saves the drawing, and starts the Plot dialog box:

```
; Zoom to extents
zoom extents
; Save the drawing
save
; Start the Plot dialog box
plot
```

Starting AutoCAD LT with Scripts

Startup switches allow AutoCAD LT to perform actions upon starting up, such as running script files, as described in the previous chapter.

To run a script, use the /**b** switch, which specifies the name of the script file to run once AutoCAD LT starts. Use this switch to have AutoCAD LT perform tasks automatically. For example:

```
"c:\cad\aclt.exe" /b purge.scr
```

> **TIP** You can copy and paste scripts into AutoCAD LT. Here's how:
>
> 1. In Notepad, use **Edit | Copy** to copy the script text to the clipboard.
> 2. In AutoCAD LT, click the cursor next to the 'Command:' prompt.
> 3. Press **Ctrl+V**.
>
> The script text is pasted from the clipboard, and AutoCAD LT executes the script.

Summary

In this chapter, you learned how to customize command names, use system and environment variables, and create scripts.

In the next chapter, you learn how to customize AutoCAD LT's menus and shortcut keystrokes.

Chapter **20**

Customizing Menus
and Shortcut Keystrokes

In This Chapter

- The history of menus in AutoCAD
- Customizing menus
- Understanding the menu macro syntax
- Using and creating shortcut keystrokes

AutoCAD has always had a menu system that allows you to select a command rather than having to type commands on the keyboard.

The History of Menus

Nearly all CAD packages of the day (and some to this day) had some sort of menu. Some were located on the right side of the screen; some used a double-column format. Autodesk decided to place AutoCAD's first menu along the left edge of the drawing area.

It was called a "screen menu," because it appeared on the screen, in contrast to the tablet menu. Real CAD users used tablet menus, which consisted of a large piece of cardboard (typically 11" x 17") listing nearly every command, taped to the surface of a digitizing tablet.

Key Terms

Keyboard shortcuts — abbreviated keystrokes that execute commands
Macros — one or more commands combined into a single menu or toolbar item

---

Abbreviations

Alt	Alternate key
^C	Cancels commands in progress
Ctrl	Control key
CUI	Customization user interface files
F	Function keys
XML	Extensible Markup Language

Commands

Command	Shortcut	Menu Selection
Cui	...	Tools | Customize | Interface
CuiLoad	...	...

The earliest versions of AutoCAD had so few commands that they all fit in just two lists of 20 items per screen menu; commands were listed in alphabetical order. Users became adept at manipulating the screen menu using the keyboard. For example, the **Ins** key moved the AutoCAD cursor from the drawing to the screen menu.

As Autodesk added more commands, the screen menu structure was changed to grouping commands by function. Thus, there was the Draw menu, the Edit menu, etc. As even more commands were added, Autodesk needed to create the Draw 1 and Draw 2 menus, and started to leave out less important commands.

The screen menu is still available in AutoCAD. Ever since AutoCAD Release 14, however, the screen menu has been turned off by default, and most users are unaware of its existence. The screen menu was never available in AutoSketch or in AutoCAD LT. The first versions of AutoCAD LT did not support the tablet menu; LT 2000 and on support digitizers and tablet menus.

The Menu Moves from the Side to the Top

In the mid-1980s, the Macintosh's graphical user interface began to have its impact on non-Macintosh software. The Mac boasted the now-common menu bar along the top of the screen. Its menus were called "pull-down" menus because users dragged their mouse downward to open the menus.

Around that time, some of Autodesk's founders — Ben Halpern, Kern Sibbald, and John Walker — took a few months to write a small, new CAD program named AutoSketch. It sported then-new user interface features such as menus and dialog boxes. Unlike the Macintosh, the menus were called "pop-down menus" because they appeared to pop down when users clicked their mouse on them.

Autodesk added menus and dialog boxes to AutoCAD Release 9 in October 1987. The pop-down menus and dialog boxes prototyped by AutoSketch were part of what Autodesk called the "advanced user interface" (AUI).

From the beginning, AutoCAD's status bar had been at the top of the screen, and so Autodesk "hid" the menu bar under the status line. Users moved the cursor up to the status line, which revealed the menu bar. (The status line later moved to the bottom of the drawing area with the first Windows version of AutoCAD; AutoCAD LT has always run under Windows.)

It may seem odd today, but some graphics boards at that time that could not handle the display of menus and dialog boxes. They lacked the **BitBlt** instruction that allowed software to cover up portions of the screen with images of pop-down menus and dialog boxes and then restore them correctly. For this reason, AutoCAD had a read-only system variable named **Popups** that indicated whether the graphics board supported AUI. (The system variable was removed with AutoCAD Release 14.)

Customizing Menus

All along, the menu was customizable — whether on the side of the screen or along the top. AutoCAD LT can customize pull-down menus: the position, wording, and action of nearly every menu item can be changed.

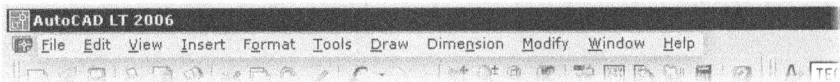

There are some exceptions to which menu items can be changed. The exceptions are items specific to Windows, such as **File | Open** and **Help | About**. These are called *hard-coded*, because they cannot be changed.

To see the hard-coded menu items, use the **CuiUnload** command and unload all menu groups.

The **U** command returns the menus into place.

Menu Groups

CuiLoad
Tools | Customize | Interface

The AutoCAD LT menu system is set up in *groups*. Groups allow you to load individual menu pull-downs, such as those headed by **Draw** and **Modify**. The default menu group is named "ACLT"; third-party software and in-house customization can add their own menu groups.

To have a look at these groups, start the **CuiLoad** command.

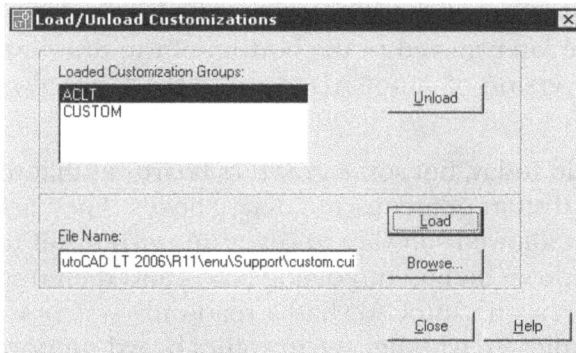

Notice the list under **Loaded Customization Groups**: ACLT and Custom. ACLT controls all the default menus, toolbars, and other customizable aspects of AutoCAD LT; Custom is an extra one that Autodesk throws in for you to play around with, so you don't accidentally on purpose muck up ACLT.

Loading Menu Files

The **Load** and **Unload** buttons add and remove menu groups from AutoCAD LT.

Menus are stored in files with the extension of .cui — short for "custom user interface" — and use a dialect of XML, extensible markup language. (Prior to LT 2006, the file extension was .mnu — short for "menu" — and was written in ASCII.)

In addition to menus, the file contains the definitions of much (but not all) of AutoCAD's user interface:

- Cursor menus (a.k.a. shortcut menus or context-sensitive menus)
- Image tile menus (rarely used; an early form of dialog box)
- Help text (appears on the status line)
- Menus
- Mouse buttons
- Screen menu (not recognized by AutoCAD LT)
- Shortcut keystrokes
- Tablet menus
- Tablet buttons (puck and stylus buttons)
- Toolbars
- Workspaces (new to AutoCAD LT 2006)

The .cui files do not define:

- Aliases (stored in the aclt.pgp file)
- Commands (defined in aclt.exe and .arx files)
- Dialog boxes (stored in .dcl files)
- Hardcoded menu items (defined by Windows)
- Menu and toolbar options (set by the Options dialog box)
- Tool palettes (customized in the Tool Palette window)
- Tool palette groups (customized in the Customize dialog box)

Guided Tour of the CUI

To see the Customize User Interface dialog box, enter the **CUI** command. From the **Tools** menu, select **Customize | Interface**. After a few moments, the dialog box appears.

The dialog box sports three primary areas:

> **Customizations** — lists the areas of AutoCAD LT that can be customized.
>
> **Customization Properties** — makes changes to the selected option.
>
> **Command List** — lists the names of all commands in AutoCAD.

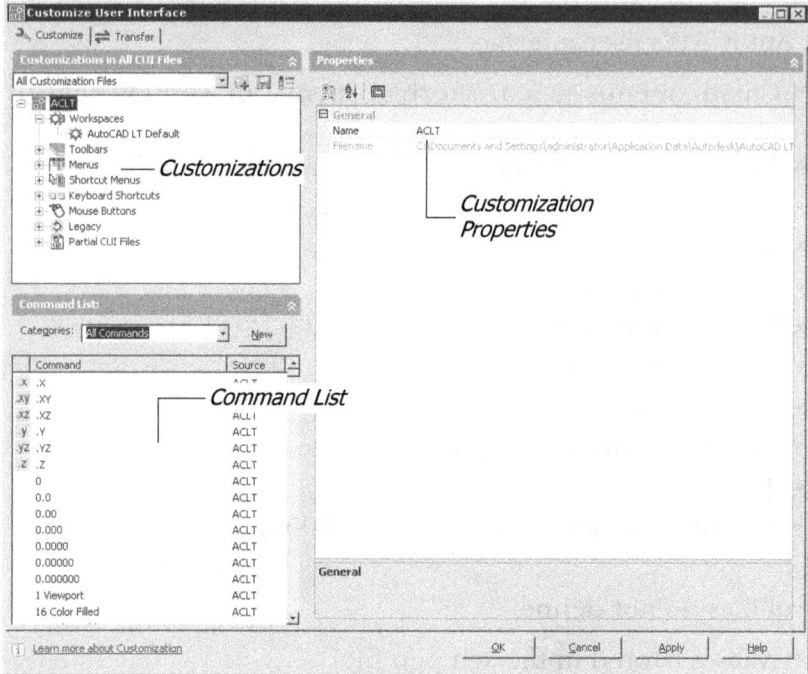

In general, you take these steps to customize some aspect of AutoCAD LT:

1. Select an item from the Customizations list, such as a menu item.

    For example, click the **+** sign next to **Menus**. This lists the menu items, such as File, Edit, and so on.

    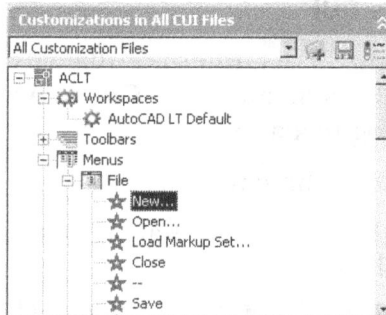

    Click the **+** next to New.

2. Select an option in the Customization Properties area, and then modify it.

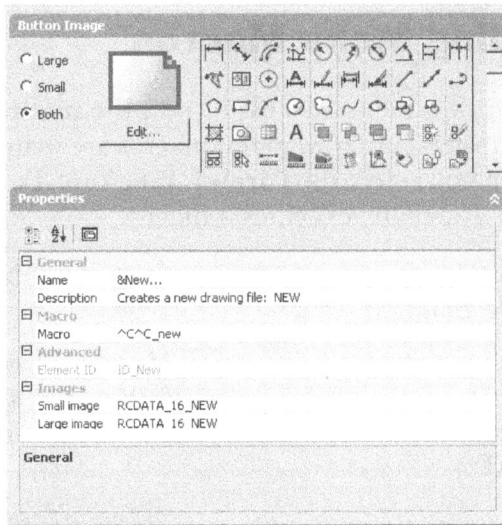

Notice that the Properties area changes to accommodate the item being customized. In this case, you have access to button images and properties. (As of AutoCAD LT 2006, menu items can have images associated with them.)

3. Save the changes by clicking **Apply**.

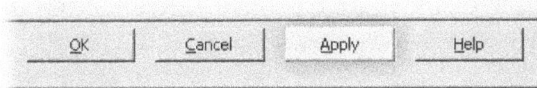

To create a new customization item, right-click an item in the Customizations list, and then select **New** from the shortcut menu.

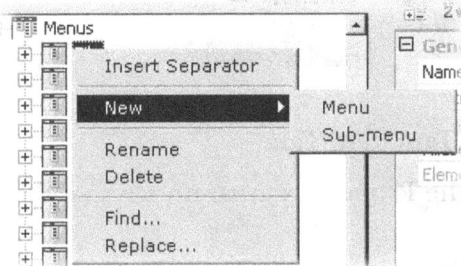

(Prior to AutoCAD LT 2006, users edited .mnu files with a text editor to customize menus, toolbars, and so on.)

Understanding Menu Macros

You can write your own menu macros or edit the macros that come with AutoCAD LT. To understand how menu macros are written, take a look at an example. When you select the **Circle| Tan, Tan, Tan** command from the **Draw** menu, LT actually executes a macro.

1. Use the **CUI** command to open the Customize User Interface dialog box.

2. In the Customizations list, open **Menus**, **Draw**, and **Circle**. (In the figure below, notice how the items in the Customizations list match the menu you see in AutoCAD.)

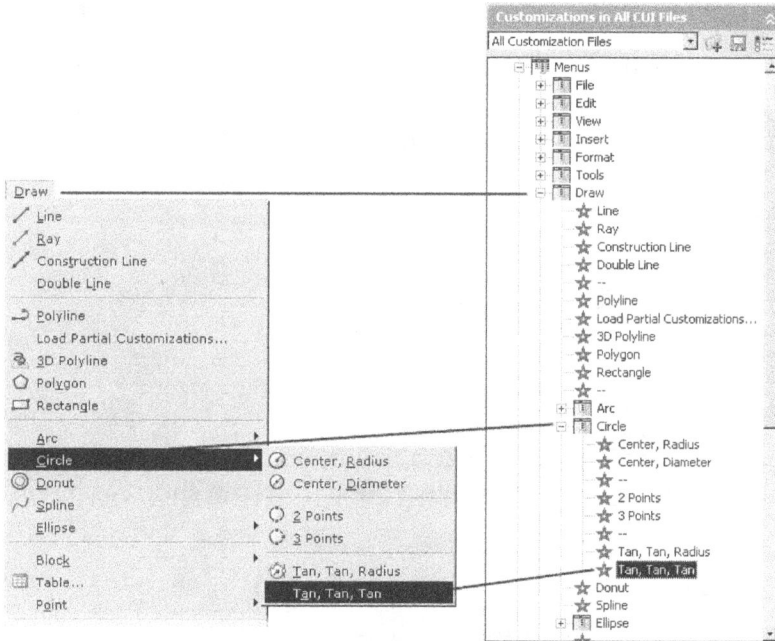

3. Click on **Tan, Tan, Tan**.

   Over in the Properties area, notice that the macro looks like this:

   ```
   ^C^C_circle _3p _tan \_tan \_tan \
   ```

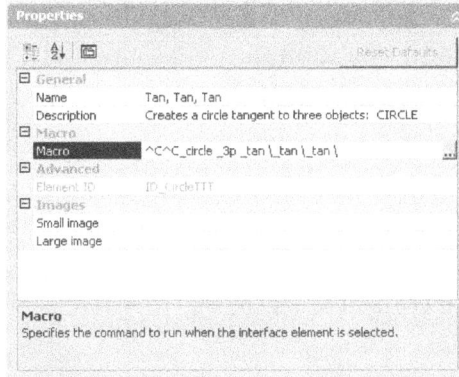

Here is what the characters mean:

^C — The Ctrl+C metacharacter cancels other commands currently active, because the **Circle** command is not a *transparent* command (it cannot run during any other command). This is the equivalent to pressing the **Esc** key. Two ^Cs in a row cancel commands with multiple layers of options, such as the **PEdit** command.

TIP The ^C metacharacter is equivalent to Ctrl+C. In older versions of AutoCAD, Ctrl+C was used to cancel a command; under Microsoft, however, Ctrl+C has come to mean "copy to clipboard." Thus, use ^C to cancel a command in a macro, but use the CopyClip command in a macro to copy to the clipboard.

_ — underscore internationalizes command names. AutoCAD LT is produced in many languages, and the English version of command names is common to all.

circle — Starts the **Circle** command.

(space) — space mimics the pressing of the Spacebar (or **Enter** key) to signal AutoCAD the completion of entering the name of the command or option.

_3p — executes the **Circle** command's **3Point** option.

_tan — TANgent object snap prompts users to locate a circle or arc.

**** — backslash pauses the macro, waiting for user input. AutoCAD waits until the user does something, such as clicking the mouse button or typing coordinates at the keyboard, before continuing with the command.

The three groups of **_tan**(*space*)\ correspond to the three points expected by the Circle command's **3P** option (_tan _tan _tan \ ).

The macro comes to an end simply; there are no "end of macro" markers.

Menu Macro Metacharacters

The metacharacters you saw above are the most important ones. AutoCAD LT allows you to employ many more metacharacters, which it calls "special characters." The complete list is:

Metacharacter	Meaning
; or *space* or ^ M	Equivalent to pressing the Spacebar or Enter key
\	Pauses for user input
$M =	Starts DIESEL macros
^ B	Toggles snap mode
^ C	Cancels commands (equivalent to pressing the Esc key)
^ D	Changes the coordinate display
^ E	Switches to the next isometric plane
^ G	Toggles the grid display
^ H	Equivalent to pressing the Backspace key
^ I	Equivalent to pressing the Tab key
^ K	Displays the Hyperlinks dialog box
^ O	Toggles ortho mode
^ P	Toggles menuecho mode
^ Q	Logs all command text to a file
^ T	Changes tablet modes
^ V	Switches to the next viewport
^ Z	Suppresses blank spaces at the end of macros
_	Internationalizes commands and option names
+	Continues macros on the next line
*	Repeats the macro; equivalent to the Multiple command
~	Disables (grays out) menu items
!.	Prefixes menu items with a check mark
&	Specifies the menu accelerator key
\T	Right-justifies menu labels

(The following metacharacters are no longer needed by AutoCAD LT 2006, because of the new CUI: [,], =*, $, —, ->, and <-.)

Creating Menus

To create a new menu item, follow these steps:

1. Use the **CUI** command to open the Customize User Interface dialog box.

2. In the Customizations tree, right-click **Menus**.

3. From the shortcut menu, select **New | Menu**.

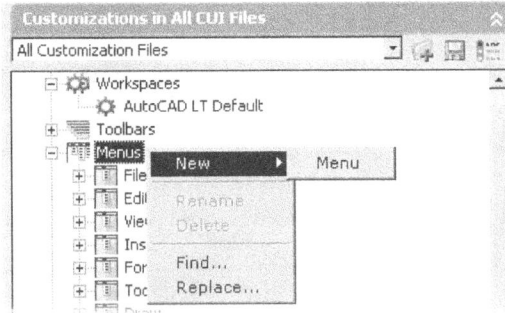

4. Notice that AutoCAD creates a new menu item, naming it "Menu1." It's located at the end of the menu tree.

   To rename it, right-click it, and then select **Rename** from the shortcut menu. For this tutorial, name it **My Menu**.

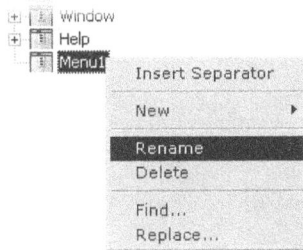

5. The new menu is located at the end of the menu tree, which means it will be placed last on the menu bar. Traditionally, however, the Windows and Help items are the last ones, so it makes sense to relocate My Menu.

Creating Submenus

AutoCAD LT can have menus within menus, called "submenus." There are two ways to create submenus: by dragging items into place or using the **New Submenu** command.

As an example of submenus, take a look at the figure illustrated below by the **Modify | Object | External Reference** sub-submenu:

- **Object** is a submenu to **Modify**
- **External Reference** is a submenu to **Object**

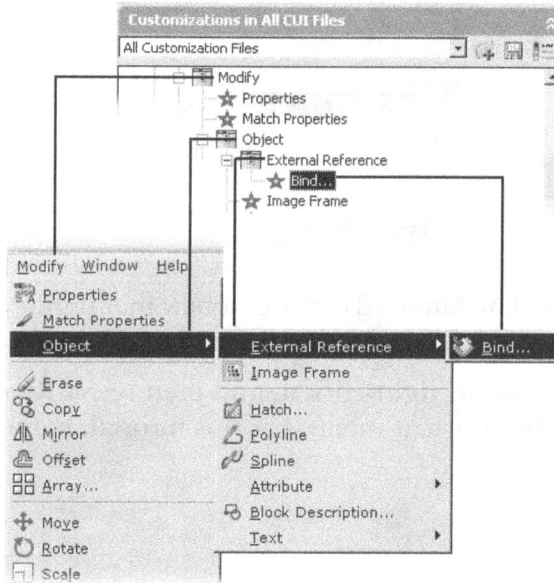

When you pause the dragging motion over a menu item, AutoCAD LT opens the menu tree. If you were to place My Menu "inside" the menu, AutoCAD LT then makes it a submenu.

Right-click a submenu, and then select **New | Sub-menu**. Notice that AutoCAD LT creates a branched submenu named "Menu1." Like menus, submenus can be renamed:

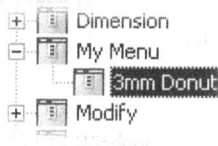

To move menu items, drag them to their new location. A horizontal bar shows you where the item will be located in the tree.

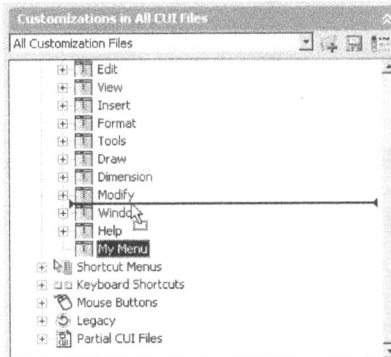

6. So far, all that has been created is the menu title; the menu is empty. To fill the menu item with commands, drag command names from the Command List into the menu.

For this tutorial, drag the **Donut** command up to My Menu.

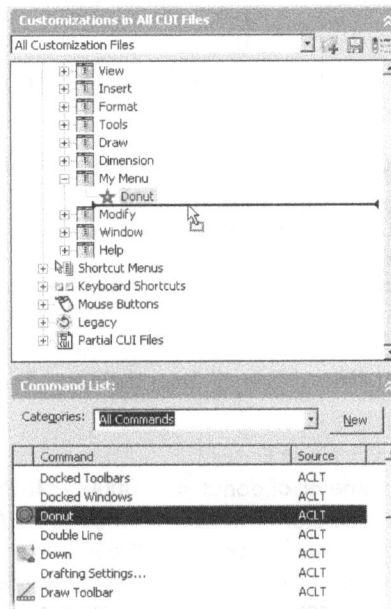

Notice that AutoCAD fills in the Properties area with the command's name, "Donut," as well as:

Description — help text appearing in status bar

Macro — ^ C ^ C_donut

Images — appropriate large and small icons

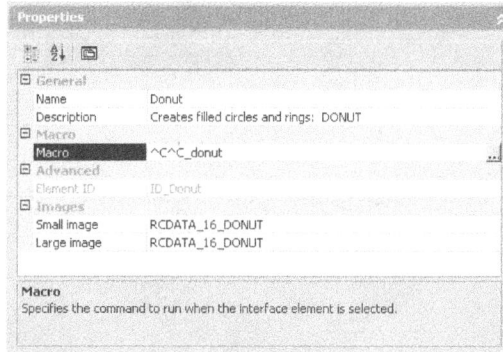

7. Click **Apply** to apply the changes to the menu bar.

    Click **OK** to close the dialog box. Test the menu to see that it works and draws donut objects.

Writing Macros

"Writing macros" is akin to customizing commands.

For example, the Donut command executed by the menu, above, just mimics entering the command at the 'Command:' prompt. There is no value-added, as they say.

Modify the menu macro so that it draws donuts of fixed size: an inner diameter of 1mm and an outer diameter of 3mm. This donut is typical of the copper pads used on printed circuit boards.

Prior to writing the macro, it is helpful to understand the syntax of the **Donut** command.

1. Enter the command, and then answer the prompts, as follows:

    Command: **donut** *(Press **Enter**.)*
    Specify inside diameter of donut <10.0000>: **1** *(Press **Enter**.)*
    Specify outside diameter of donut <20.0000>: **3** *(Press **Enter**.)*
    Specify center of donut or <exit>: *(Pick a point in the screen.)*
    Specify center of donut or <exit>: *(Press **Enter** to exit the command.)*

    On a piece of paper, write out the characters typed above. Use a semicolon (;) each time **Enter** is pressed and a backslash (\) in place of the pick point.

The result should look something like this:

donut;1;3;\^C

2. With the command syntax captured, open the Customize User Interface dialog box with the **CUI** command.

3. Find the **Donut** item in the My Menu menu.

In the Properties area, make the following changes:

Name: **&3mm Pad** *(The ampersand underlines the 3, making it accessible by the keyboard.)*

Description: **Draws 3mm PCB pads with 1mm holes.**
Macro: **^C^C_donut;1;3;\^C**

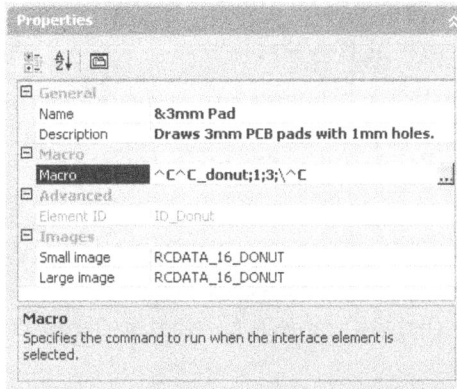

4. To complete the job, click **OK** to close the dialog box.

Test the menu to see that it works by drawing donut objects.

Blast from the Past

Prior to AutoCAD LT 2006, users would have to write the following code with the Notepad text editor, add it to a .mnu file, and then load the file with the **MenuLoad** command.

```
*** MENUGROUP=ADVANCED
***POP1
ID_PcbPads[&PCB Pads]
ID_3mmDonut[&3mm Pad]^C^C_donut;1;3;\^C
***HELPSTRINGS
ID_PcbPads[Pads for PCB work]
ID_3mmDonut[3mm diameter donut with 1mm center]
```

Shortcut Keystrokes

As an alternative to menus and aliases, you can use *shortcut keystrokes* to execute commands. If you like using the keyboard, then shortcut keystrokes, along with aliases, can be the fastest way to draw and edit in AutoCAD LT.

Shortcut keystrokes are used in conjunction with the **Ctrl**, function, and **Alt** keys. Many of them are *transparent*, meaning you can use them during other commands. For example, it's handy to be able to toggle snap mode during commands by pressing **Ctrl+B**.

Customizing Shortcut Keystrokes

You can use the shortcuts defined by Autodesk and create your own. In the old days, prior to AutoCAD LT 2000, the only way to create and edit keyboard shortcuts was to edit the aclt.mnu file with text editing software.

LT 2000 improved on things by allowing users to edit the keystrokes in a dialog box. With LT 2006, Autodesk changed to using a single command (called **CUI**) to provide access to nearly every customization aspect of AutoCAD.

Control Key

Most shortcut keystrokes use the **Ctrl** key. For instance, **Ctrl+A** selects all objects in the drawing: hold down the **Ctrl** key and then press **A**.

Some shortcuts are specific to AutoCAD LT. For instance, **Ctrl+G** toggles the display of the grid dots. Other shortcuts are common to all Windows applications, such as **Ctrl+V**, which pastes objects from the clipboard.

Many shortcut keystrokes are already defined by Autodesk's programmers. But you can add your own and change many of them.

Function Keys

A second system of shortcuts is *function keys*. Function keys are the row of keys along the top of the keyboard.

Again, some keys are specific to AutoCAD LT (press **F5** to change the isoplane), while others are common to Windows (press **F1** for help).

Both control keys and function keys are *transparent*, meaning you can use them anytime, including in the middle of commands.

Alt Key

A third system of keyboard shortcuts involves the use of the **Alt** key. When you press **Alt**, Windows moves the *focus* to the menu bar. You then press the underlined letter that appears in the menus.

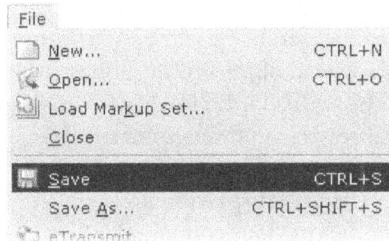

For example, the **File** menu has the **F** underlined, and the **Save** item has the **S** underlined. Thus, one way to save drawings is to rapidly press **Alt**, **F**, **S**. Unlike **Ctrl**-key shortcuts, you don't hold down the **Alt** key.

Again, some of these keyboard shortcuts are common to all Windows programs (such as the **Alt**, **F**, **S** example), while most are specific to AutoCAD LT, such as **Alt**, **D**, **L** to start drawing a line.

Temporary Override Keys

New to AutoCAD LT 2006 are *temporary override* keys. Holding down the keys changes the state of AutoCAD LT until you let go. For example, while drawing lines, holding down the **Shift** key turns on ortho mode — for as long as the key is held down. The reverse also works: after turning on ortho mode, holding down the **Shift** key temporarily turns off ortho mode.

Shortcut Keystrokes: Function and Control Keys

The following shortcut keystrokes are defined by default in AutoCAD LT.
I recommend that you do not change these predefined keys.

Shortcut	Meaning
Alt	Accesses the menu bar
Function Keys	
F1	Displays online help
F2	Toggles between drawing and text window
F3	Toggles object snap mode on and off
F4	Toggles tablet between pointing and digitizing
F5	Cycles through the three isometric drawing planes
F6	Toggles coordinate display
F7	Toggles grid mode on and off
F8	Toggles ortho mode on and off
F9	Toggles snap mode on and off
F10	Toggles polar mode on and off
F12	Toggles dynamic input on and off
Ctrl Keys	
Ctrl+A	Selects all objects in the drawing
Ctrl+B	Toggles snap mode on and off
Ctrl+C	Copies selected objects to the clipboard
Ctrl+D	Cycles through coordinate display modes
Ctrl+E	Cycles through the three isometric drawing planes
Ctrl+F	Toggles object snap mode on and off
Ctrl+G	Toggles the grid display on and off
Ctrl+J	Repeats the previous command
Ctrl+K	Displays the Hyperlinks dialog box
Ctrl+L	Toggles ortho mode on and off
Ctrl+N	Creates new drawing
Ctrl+O	Opens existing drawing
Ctrl+P	Plots current drawing
Ctrl+Q	Toggles the log file on and off
Ctrl+R	Changes focus to the next viewport
Ctrl+S	Saves current drawing
Ctrl+T	Toggles tablet mode
Ctrl+V	Pastes data from the clipboard
Ctrl+X	Cuts selected objects from the drawing to the clipboard
Ctrl+Y	Reverses the effect of the last undo
Ctrl+Z	Undoes the last command
Ctrl+[	Cancels the current command
Ctrl+\	Cancels the current command

Shortcut Keystrokes: Temporary Overrides

The following temporary overrides are defined by default in AutoCAD LT. I recommend that you do not change these predefined keystrokes.

Override Keystrokes		Meaning
Shift		Toggles ortho mode (like F8)
Shift+X	Shift+.	Toggles polar mode (like F10)
Shift+A	Shift+'	Toggles object snap mode (like F3)
Shift+S	Shift+;	Turns on object snap enforcement
Shift+L	Shift+D	Disables all snaps and tracking
Object Snap Overrides		
Shift+E	Shift+P	Endpoint
Shift+V	Shift+M	Midpoint
Shift+C	Shift+,	Center

Well, overrides are not entirely new. Earlier releases had a couple of them, such as pressing the **Ctrl** key to cycle through overlapping items to be selected.

Now, though, AutoCAD LT 2006 introduces a large number of overrides and has given them their own spot in the customization kingdom.

Customizing Keystroke Shortcuts

Keystroke shortcuts are customized with the Customize User Interface dialog box (new to AutoCAD LT 2006). Here are the steps to creating and editing keystroke shortcuts:

1. Use the **CUI** command to open the Customize User Interface dialog box.

   In the Customizations tree, open **Keyboard Shortcuts**, and then open **Shortcut Keys**.

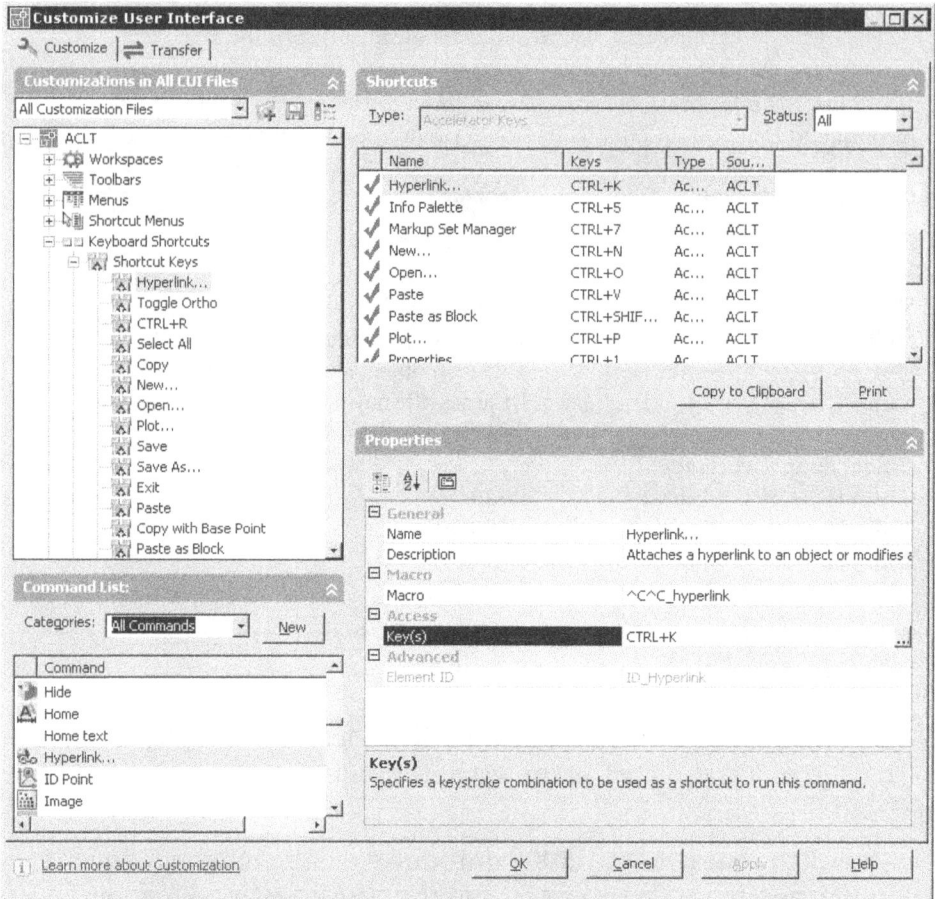

2. Select a shortcut, such as **Hyperlink**. On the right side of the dialog box, notice the Shortcuts and Properties areas.

   In the Properties area, the Key(s) item reports the shortcut keystroke for executing the Hyperlink command: Ctrl+K.

3. You cannot change the keystroke combination directly. Instead, click the **...** button to display the Shortcut Keys dialog box.

   Current Keys — list shortcut assigned to the command

   Press new shortcut key — enter new shortcut here

```
Shortcut Keys

Current Keys:
┌─────────────────────┐
│ CTRL+K              │      Assign
│                     │
│                     │
│                     │      Remove
└─────────────────────┘

Press new shortcut key:
┌─────────────────────┐
│                     │      Cancel
└─────────────────────┘
Currently assigned to:
[unassigned]                 ┌──────────┐
                             │   OK     │
                             └──────────┘
```

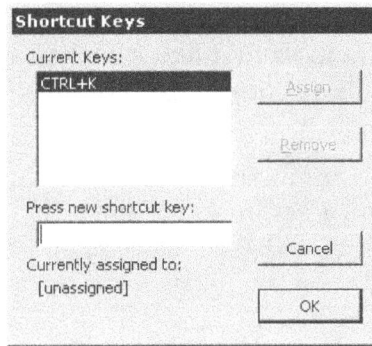

TIP   The shortcut key must follow one of these combinations (this list is more complete than found in the LT documentation):

> **Ctrl**+*key*
> **Ctrl**+**Shift**+*key*
> **Ctrl**+**Alt**+*key*
> **Ctrl**+**Alt**+**Shift**+*key*
> **Ctrl**+**F***n*
> **Shift**+**F***n*
> **Ctrl**+**Alt**+**F***n*
> **Ctrl**+**Shift**+**F***n*
> **Ctrl**+**Alt**+**Shift**+**F***n*

The *key* can be one of the letters A through Z, plus numbers 0 through 9; punctuation cannot be used. **F***n* is any function key, F1 through F12.

4.   Click **Assign** to assign. (Even though it appears that you could assign more than one shortcut to a command, only one is possible.)

Click **OK** to exit the dialog box.

Creating Keystroke Shortcuts

With that overview of how shortcut keystrokes are handled in the customization dialog box, create a new shortcut. Assign **Ctrl+Shift+F** to the **Find** command.

1.   Use the **CUI** command to open the Customize User Interface dialog box.

In the Customizations tree, open **Keyboard Shortcuts**, and then open **Shortcut Keys**.

2.   In the Command List area, select the **Find** command.

(Here's a quick way to get to a command: press the key corresponding to its first letter, such as **F**. AutoCAD LT immediately jumps to the first command starting with F — Face.)

3.   Drag the Find command up into the Customization area's Shortcut Keys item.

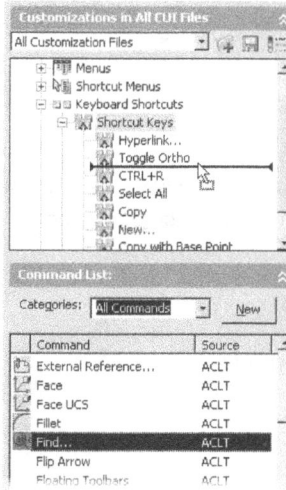

4.   Move your attention to the Properties area.

Under Access, notice that **Key(s)** is blank. Click the **...** button, and then assign **Ctrl+Shift+F** as the shortcut.

5.   Click **OK** to exit the customization dialog box.

Press **Ctrl+Shift+F** to ensure the Find and Replace dialog box appears. If it does, then the new keystroke shortcut works!

Summary

In this chapter, you learned about the history of menus in AutoCAD. You also learned how to customize the look of the menu, and to create and load menu groups, as well as how to use the menu macro syntax.

In the next chapter, you learn how to customize the remainder of the .cui file.

Chapter 21

Customizing Toolbars and Workspaces

In This Chapter

- Creating new toolbars
- Customizing toolbar button icons
- Writing toolbar macros
- Understanding workspaces

AutoCAD LT represents many of its commands through icons on buttons collected into toolbars. Click a button, and AutoCAD executes the underlying command (and sometimes two or more commands) known as a *macro*. When you pause the cursor over the button's icon, it displays a *tooltip*, which briefly explains the icon's purpose. At the same time, the status line displays a sentence-long description of the button's purpose.

AutoCAD LT lets you change just about anything related to the toolbars:

- The macros (commands) executed by buttons
- The look of buttons' icons
- The toolbars to which buttons belong
- The names of toolbars
- The tooltips displayed by the buttons
- The help text displayed on the status line

The **CUI** command does all this.

Key Terms

Icons — images on toolbar buttons
Toolbars — collection of buttons
Tooltips — descriptive text for buttons
Workspaces — customized user interfaces

Changing Toolbar Properties

Tools | Options

While the **CUI** command customizes toolbars, it is the **Options** command that changes the properties of toolbars. (Prior to AutoCAD LT 2006, these options were found in the **Customize** command.)

1. From the **Tools** menu, select **Options**. If necessary, select the **Display** tab.

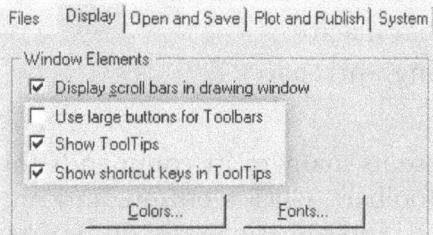

2. In the upper-left corner is the Window Elements area. Three options apply to toolbars:

    Use large buttons for Toolbars — when off, "normal" buttons are shown; when on, larger buttons are displayed.

    Show ToolTips — toggles the display of the helpful tooltips that clue you in to the meaning of buttons.

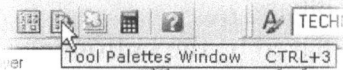

    Show shortcut keys in ToolTips — toggles whether shortcut keystrokes are displayed, for those commands that have 'em, such as **Ctrl+3** for ToolPalettes.

3. Make changes to the options, and then click **OK**.

Further Changes to Toolbar Properties

The properties in the Options dialog box affect all toolbars equally. A further set of properties is found in the Customize User Interface dialog box. These properties affect each toolbar independently of the others.

1. Use the **CUI** command to open the Customize User Interface dialog box.

   In the Customizations tree, open **Toolbars**, and then open a toolbar, such as **Dimension**.

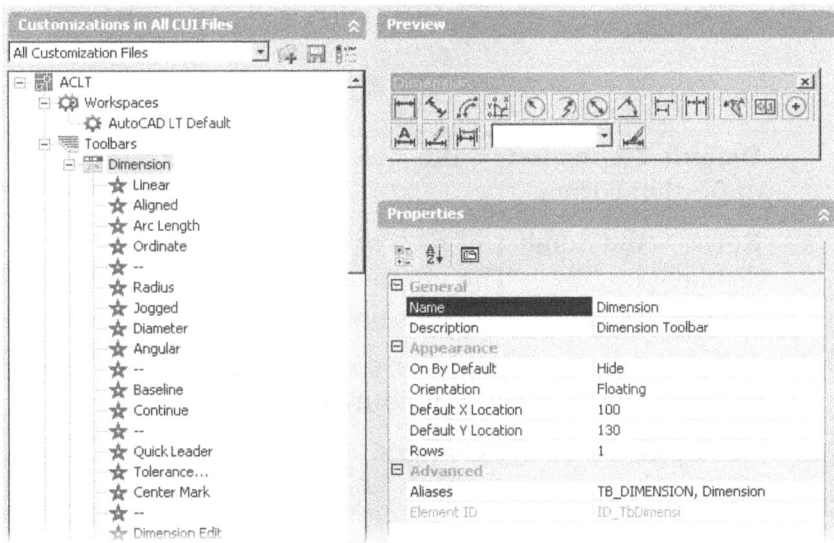

2. Notice that the Preview area illustrates the toolbar, albeit statically. (When the cursor is moved over the buttons, they appear to move, but nothing happens when clicked.) As well, the image of the toolbar does not reflect all the properties listed below it.

3. The Properties area lists a number of properties that can be modified:

   Name — specifies the name on the toolbar's title bar, shortcut menus, and so on. The title bar is seen only on floating toolbars.

   Description — specifies the help text displayed on the status bar.

   On By Default — toggles the toolbar's default display, Hide or Show.

Orientation — determines default location of the toolbar, either floating or docked along an edge of the AutoCAD LT window: Top, Bottom, Left, or Right.

Default X Location — the x coordinate of the toolbar's upper-left corner, relative to the Windows screen. The x and y locations apply only to floating toolbars and specify their initial location.

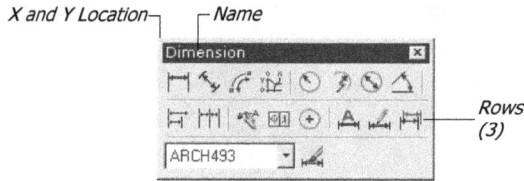

Default Y Location — the y coordinate of the toolbar's upper-left corner.

Rows — the number of rows of buttons the toolbar displays, usually 1. The number of rows applies only to floating toolbars.

Aliases — unique names for the toolbar, which are used by software programs to identify the toolbar.

4. Click **OK** to save the changes.

TIPS To quickly display toolbars, right-click any toolbar. From the shortcut menu, select the name of a toolbar. (Those with check marks are already displayed.)

The **Lock Location** item locks toolbars, preventing them from being moved accidentally.

The **Customize** item displays the Customize User Interface dialog box, opened to the toolbar that was right-clicked.

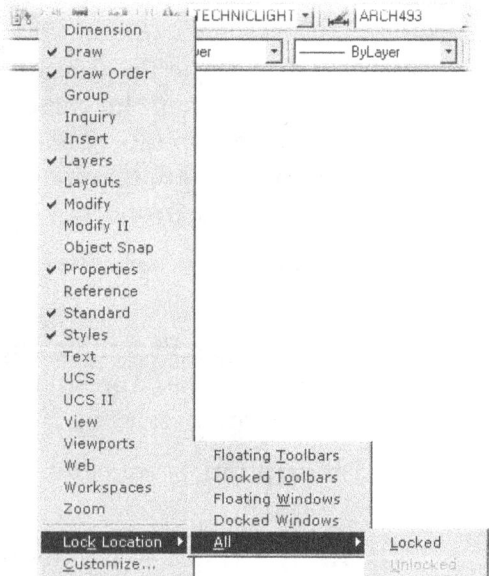

Customizing Toolbars

The steps in customizing toolbars are similar to that for menus. You can use the **CUI** command to open the Customize User Interface dialog box, but here is a shortcut:

1. Right-click the **Draw** toolbar, found along the left edge of the AutoCAD LT window.

2. From the shortcut menu, select **Customize**. Notice that the Customize User Interface dialog box shows the **Toolbars | Draw** item already open.

Adding Buttons to Toolbars

The Draw toolbar contains many, but not all 2D drawing commands. While the **Leader** command is found on the Dimension toolbar, it might be used often enough to warrant placing it on the Draw toolbar, as well.

1. In the Command List area, click on the first command and then press **L** on the keyboard. This moves quickly down the list (of over 500 commands) to those commands starting with "L."

   Scroll further until you reach the Leader command.

2. Drag the **Leader** command up into the Customizations area, dropping it just below the **Revision Cloud** command.

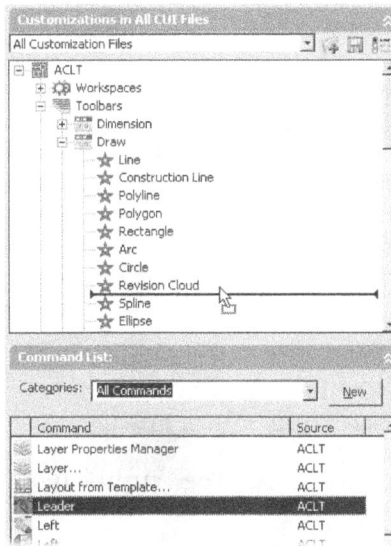

Notice that the Leader button appears in the Preview toolbar. (Later, when you exit the customization dialog box, the Leader button will also appear on the Draw toolbar in AutoCAD LT.)

It's that easy to add buttons to toolbars.

Adding Separator Lines between Buttons

Separator lines are used to separate subgroups of buttons within toolbars.

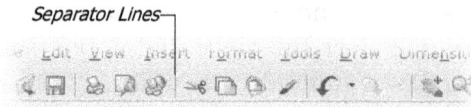

Separator Lines

1. To add the lines, right-click the toolbar button name *above* (before) where the line should go.

2. From the shortcut menu, select **Insert Separator**. AutoCAD adds the separator, shown as two dashes (--).

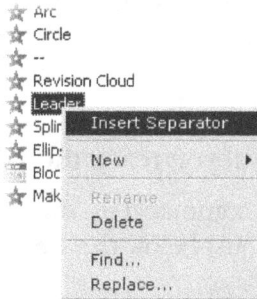

Adding Flyouts to Toolbars

Flyouts are like submenus: they are toolbars that emerge from buttons.

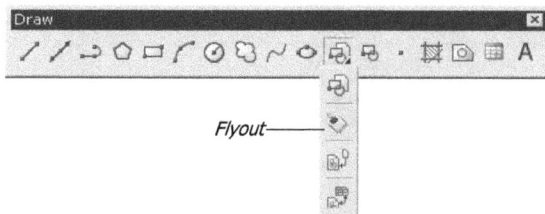

Flyout

Creating flyouts is like creating submenus:

1. In the Customizations tree, right-click the name of a toolbar.

2. From the shortcut menu, select **New | Flyout**.

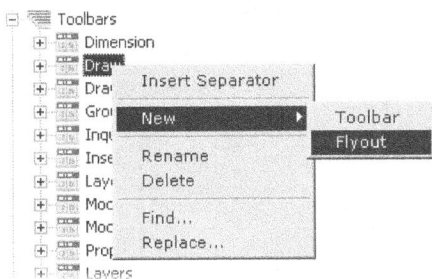

3. Notice that AutoCAD LT gives it the generic name "Toolbar1." Rename the flyout to something more meaningful.

4. Populate the flyout with buttons.

Creating and Editing Icons for Buttons

Not all of the more than 500 commands have icons associated with them; many are blank. When icon-less commands are added to toolbars, AutoCAD LT displays them with a clouded question-mark icon, as illustrated below.

AutoCAD LT provides a way for you to create custom icons, as well as to edit existing icons. Icons can be created using AutoCAD LT's built-in icon editor or copied from .bmp, .rle, and .dib files. (Icons created by third parties are often provided in BMP format.)

Make an icon for **0**, the first command in the Command List without an icon.

1. In the Command List, select **0**. Notice that its icon is blank.

2. In the Button Image area, click **Edit**. Notice the Button Editor.

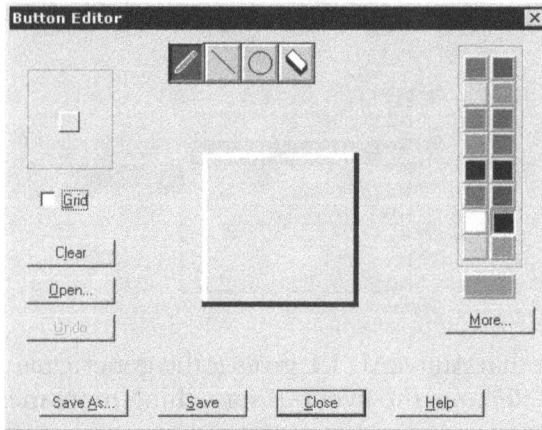

The tools in the Button Editor let you design and save 16 x 16-pixel icons. From left to right, these are:

- Color individual pixels.
- Draw straight lines.
- Draw circles and ellipses.
- Change pixels to gray (erase).
- **Grid** displays a grid as an aid to drawing.
- **Clear** erases the image from the button.
- **Open** button allows you to insert any .bmp (bitmap) file as the icon.
- **Undo** undoes the last action only.
- **More** displays the Select Color dialog box for access to more of AutoCAD LT's colors.
- **Save** and **Save As** save icons to disk as .bmp files.
- **Close** exits the Button Editor.

3. Draw an icon, and then click **Close**.

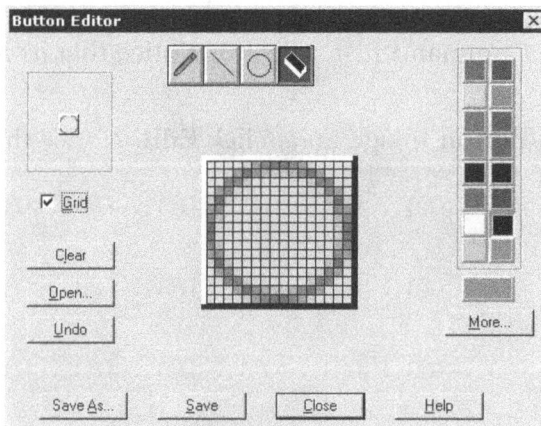

> **TIP** Make a mess of customizing toolbars, buttons, macros, icons, and so on? Fortunately, Autodesk included an oops-fixer.
>
> In the Command List, right-click the command that you want corrected back to its original state. From the shortcut menu, select **Reset to Default**. This sets its properties back to the out-of-the-box state.

Removing Buttons from Toolbars

To remove buttons:

1. Right-click a name in the Customizations list, and then select **Delete** from the shortcut menu.

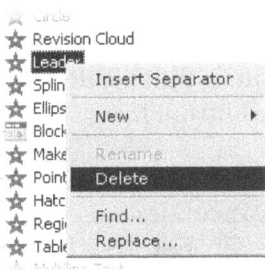

2. AutoCAD LT asks, "Do you really want to delete this element?" Click **Yes** to delete or **No** to keep.

In addition to removing buttons, you can remove entire toolbars from AutoCAD LT. In the Customizations tree, right-click the name of a toolbar, and then select **Delete**.

I don't recommend you remove any toolbars provided with AutoCAD LT.

Writing Toolbar Macros

The purpose of using toolbars is to access commands with single clicks on buttons. The action of clicking buttons executes commands.

For example, click the **Line** button on the **Draw** toolbar, and AutoCAD LT starts the **Line** command, as follows:

    Command: _line Specify first point:

Buttons can execute multiple commands, like script files and menu macros. You specify the command(s) that buttons should carry out at the **Macro** field. (A *macro* is one or more commands that are executed like a single command.) The only limitation is the number of characters that can fit: 410.

TIP To edit very long macros, click the **...** button in the Customize User Interface dialog box's Macro field. This brings up the Long String Editor. Enter the macro, or copy it from another source, and paste it here. Click **OK** when done.

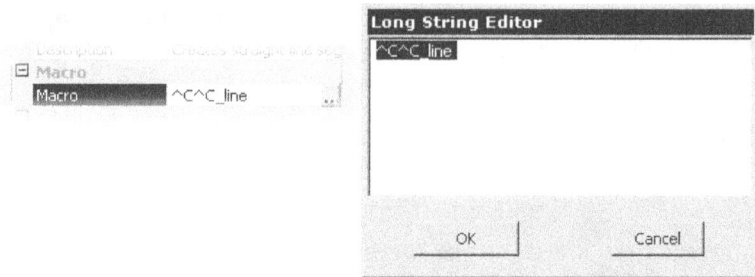

Toolbar Macro Syntax

Toolbar macros use the same syntax as do menu macros, as described in an earlier chapter. The **Line** button, for example, uses the following macro:

    ^C^C_line

Recall that the ^C means cancel. It cancels any existing command and is the equivalent of pressing the **Esc** key. If no command is in progress, AutoCAD LT ignores the ^C. Two ^Cs in a row cancel commands that have nested options, such as the **PEdit** command.

The underscore (_) is a prefix that ensures that any language of AutoCAD LT can execute the command. AutoCAD LT is available in several languages, such as English, German, and French. By using the underscore, your friend with his German-language version of AutoCAD LT can use your macro.

When there is an apostrophe ('), this makes the command *transparent*, meaning it can run during another command. Note that the apostrophe can only be used with commands that can operate transparently. (Commands meant to be transparent should not be prefixed by the ^C character.)

The special characters recognized by AutoCAD LT in toolbar macros are shown in the following table.

TIP To add pauses to toolbar macros, use the backslash (\). This forces the macro to pause for user input.

Toolbar Macro Metacharacters

The following metacharacters can be used in toolbar macros:

Character	Meaning
(*space*)	Equivalent to pressing the Enter key
^ A	Switches between group selection and single-object selection
^ B	Turns snap on and off
^ C	Cancels the current command
^ D	Changes the coordinate display
^ E	Changes to the next isometric plane: left, top, right
^ F	Turns running object snap on and off
^ G	Turns grid display on and off
^ H	Backspace
^ J	Repeats previous command
^ M	Repeats last command
^ O	Turns ortho mode on and off
^ T	Toggles tablet mode (if a tablet is configured)
^ V	Changes to the next viewport
^ X	Cancels current input
^ [	Cancels current command

Macro Options

Toolbar buttons can execute more than just a single command. They can execute command options, as well. For example, click the **Zoom Window** button, and AutoCAD LT starts the **Zoom** command with the **Window** option.

You can use full names of commands and options (zoom and window) or mix command aliases with option abbreviations (z and w). Using the full words, however, results in a macro that is easier to read than one with many one- and two-letter abbreviations. Autodesk sometimes changes the abbreviations of commands and options with new releases of AutoCAD LT, which could cause the macro to fail.

You can string together several commands. For example, a useful command sequence is to save the file, zoom all the drawing, and then plot it. With the fragile state of Windows, it is important to save your work before printing; zooming lets you see the entire drawing.

The commands you would type in are:

> Command: **qsave** *(Press **Enter**.)*
> Command: **zoom a** *(Press **Enter**.)*
> Command: **plot** *(Press **Enter**.)*

That's 18 keystrokes. You can use aliases and keyboard shortcuts:

> Command: *(Press **Ctrl**)* **s**
> Command: **z a** *(Press **Enter**.)*
> Command: *(Press **Ctrl**)* **p**

That's still eight keystrokes. When you pick commands from the menu bar, you would select:

> File | Save
> View | Zoom | All
> File | Print

Add them up: that's seven menu picks.

To combine the 18 (or eight) keystrokes (or seven menu picks) into a single macro, write down the keys you press in order, as follows:

> qsave
> zoom a
> plot

The keystroke syntax is important since AutoCAD LT does not tolerate incorrect keystrokes. Supplying the wrong character in the macro stalls the command.

Recall that commands must be separated by spaces. Also, it is useful to prefix macros with the cancel sequence (^C^C) and the internationalization character (_). Thus, the macro looks like this:

> \^C^C_qsave _zoom a _plot

Attach this macro to a toolbar, as described earlier.

TIP For this macro to work correctly, the drawing must already have been saved at least once. If not, the **QSave** command displays a dialog box that requires you to give the drawing a name before saving it.

Workspaces

Window | Workspaces

In this and previous chapters, you've seen how to customize the look of AutoCAD LT and how to customize user interface elements, such as menus and toolbars.

New to AutoCAD LT 2006 is the ability to save the state of the user interface for future use. For example, you might prefer one set of toolbars when editing drawings and a different set of toolbars when marking up drawings.

Saving the State of the User Interface

The state of the user interface is saved in *workspaces*. The workspace simply saves the location and types of menus, toolbars, and dockable windows. (Dockable windows include Properties, Tool Palette, and Design Center.)

As well, workspaces can save variations of menus and toolbars. For example, the Draw toolbar might contain a different set of buttons for creating drawings than when redlining drawings.

As with menus and toolbars, workspaces are created and edited in the omnibus Customize User Interface dialog box.

Configuring Workspaces

To configure workspaces, use the **CUI** command to open the Customize User Interface dialog box. In the Customizations tree, select **Workspaces**.

AutoCAD LT includes a default workspace, which defines the look of AutoCAD LT the first time it runs after installation. (See illustration at right.)

You can change and create workspaces:

- To edit existing workspaces, click the **Customize Workspace** button.
- A better idea is to first duplicate an existing workspace and then customize it: right-click the workspace name,

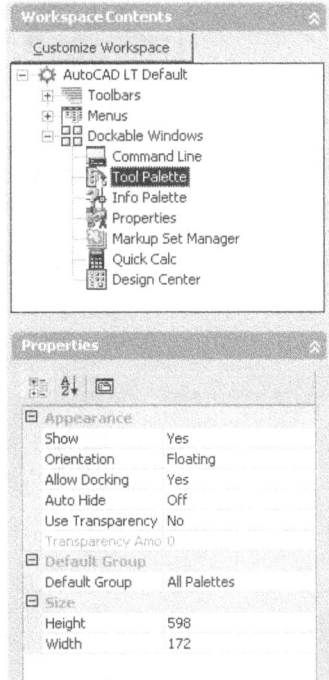

and then select **Duplicate Workspace** from the shortcut menu.

- To create new workspaces, right-click **Workspaces** and then select **New | Workspace** from the shortcut menu. Rename the workspace, if you wish.

You can then add and remove items from the list of toolbars, menus, and dockable windows. When done, click **OK**.

To switch between workspaces, select **Workspaces** from the **Window** menu.

Summary

In this chapter, you learned how to create a new toolbar and customize the look of toolbar icons. You also learned how to write a toolbar macro and the meaning of the special characters used by macros.

Chapter 22

Customizing Buttons, Shortcut Menus, and Tablets

In This Chapter
- Changing button definitions
- Customizing shortcut menus
- Digitizing tablet menus

After covering menus, shortcut keystrokes, toolbars, and workspaces, all that's left in the Customize User Interface dialog box are buttons, shortcut menus, and tablet menus.

Customizing Mouse Buttons

Most mice have two, three, or more buttons. In AutoCAD LT, different buttons perform different functions — and almost all of them can be redefined. The *left* button (called Button1 by AutoCAD LT) is always the pick button and cannot be redefined. Pucks used with digitizing tablets have as many as 16 buttons.

Buttons are customized by the Customize User Interface dialog box's Mouse Buttons section.

Key Terms

Parsing — breaking apart programming code for easier reading
AUX — defines functions of auxiliary input devices
$P0 — specifies the default shortcut menu

The default functions of mouse and tablet buttons are listed in the table below.

Button	Function	Macro
1	Pick	*none*
2	Grips menu	$M=$(if,$(eq,$(substr,$(getvar,cmdnames),1,5),GRIP_), $P0=ACLT.GRIPS $P0=*);
3	Snap menu	$P0=SNAP $p0=*
4	Cancel	^C^C
5	Toggle snap	^B
6	Toggle ortho	^O
7	Toggle grid	^G
8	Toggle coords	^D
9	Toggle isoplane	^E
10	Toggle tablet	^T
11		*no default function*
12		*no default function*
13		*no default function*
14		*no default function*
15		*no default function*

AutoCAD LT 2006 renames the AUX section as "Mouse Buttons." AUX was originally meant for "auxiliary" input devices, such as button boxes, an input device with many buttons that executes commands.

Since AutoCAD LT 2000, the AUX section defined mouse buttons, while all other pointing devices, such as digitizing pucks, used the BUTTONS section, which seems backwards to me. AUX continues to exist as the alias for the mouse buttons:

Button	Alias
click	Aux1
Shift+click	Aux2
Ctrl+click	Aux3
Shift+**Ctrl**+click	Aux4

Understanding the Button2 Macro

The first button definition (Button2) consists of the following definition:

$M=$(if,$(eq,$(substr,$(getvar,cmdnames),1,5),GRIP_),$P0=ACLT.GRIPS $P0=*);

It defines what happens when users click the right mouse button. This code causes AutoCAD LT to display the Grips shortcut menu when an object is selected. Otherwise, it displays the regular shortcut menu.

The $M= hints that the function consists of DIESEL code, as described in the next chapter. To read the code more easily, it helps to *parse* it (break it apart) at the parentheses:

```
$M=
  $(if,
    $(eq,
      $(substr,
        $(getvar,cmdnames),
      1,5),
    GRIP_),
    $P0=ACLT.GRIPS $P0=*);
```

AutoCAD reads the code starting with the innermost parentheses.

$(getvar,cmdnames) — *get*s the value of the **CmdNames** system *var*iable. This variable holds the name of the most recently entered command name.

($substr ... 1,5) — reads the first (*sub*) five (*5*) characters (*str*ing), starting at the first character (*1*).

$(eq ... GRIP_) — checks whether the five characters *eq*ual "GRIP_".

$(if ... $P0=ACLT.GRIPS $P0=*) — *if* CmdNames equals "GRIP_", then display (*$P0=*) the *GRIPS* shortcut menu of the *Aclt* group. But if CmdNames is anything else, then display the default shortcut menu (*$P0=*).

Autodesk fails to document a fact important to this macro being able to work: when users select objects, the **CmdNames** system variable takes on the value of "GRIP_STRETCH".

As users cycle through the grips options, the system variable changes, too:

Grip Action	Value of CmdNames
Stretch	GRIP_STRETCH
Move	GRIP_MOVE
Rotate	GRIP_ROTATE
Scale	GRIP_SCALE
Mirror	GRIP_MIRROR

The first five characters remains the same, which is why the macro checkes for the string "GRIP_".

Second Button Macro

The second mouse button under Click defines the action for the middle mouse button:

```
$P0=SNAP $p0=*
```

The characters in the code have the following meanings:

$ — indicates that a different menu should be displayed.

P0 — specifies that a menu in the Shortcut Menus section should be displayed.

=SNAP — displays the shortcut menu given the SNAP alias. In this case, the shortcut menu displays the object snap shortcut menu.

$p0=* — displays the default shortcut menu.

> **TIP** In some mice, the middle button is missing. In this case, AutoCAD LT defines the other Click sections to be equivalent to the center button. For example, under Shift+Click:
>
> ```
> $P0=SNAP $p0=*
> ```
>
> This means that users can display the object snap shortcut menu by holding down the **Shift** key and pressing the right mouse button.

Other Button Macros

The remaining buttons execute the following functions:

Button 4: ^C^C — equivalent to pressing the **Esc** key twice

Button 5: ^B — snap toggle

Button 6: ^O — ortho toggle

Button 7: ^G — grid toggle

Button 8: ^D — coordinate display toggle

Button 9: ^E — isoplane toggle

Button 10: ^T — tablet toggle

Buttons 11 through 15 have no functions preassigned by AutoCAD LT.

Shortcut Menus

You may be wondering about the strange code fragments, like $P0=*. They come from the early days of customization, when .mnu files defined menus, buttons, toolbars, and so on. The "P" is short for "popup" menu, which is what the shortcut menu was first called in AutoCAD.

This menu is displayed at the cursor location, typically when users right-click. The menu is also called the "cursor menu," "context menu," "context-sensitive menu," or the "right-click menu."

The $P0= code is an instruction for the macro to jump to a shortcut menu. The asterisk (*) is the generic name for the default shortcut menu, the one displayed when no objects are selected and no commands active.

The $P0=ACLT.GRIPS code jumps to the shortcut menu with the GRIPS alias. You can see the alias names by going to the **Shortcut Menus** section of the Customize User Interface dialog box, and then opening the **Grips Cursor Menu**. Notice that its aliases are POP500 and GRIPS, as illustrated below.

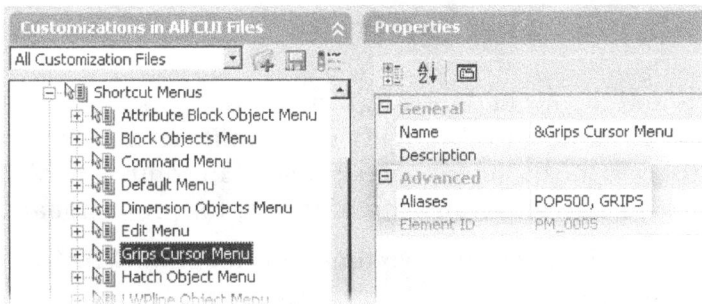

The reason that the Grips shortcut menu has two aliases is that older versions of AutoCAD LT identified shortcut menus by numbers. In addition to POP0, shortcut menus are assigned numbers POP500 through POP999. For compatibility reasons, the old numbering system still exists today.

Shortcut Menu Codes

POPn	ACLT.Name	Action
POP0	SNAP	Object snap mode *(Default shortcut menu.)*
POP500	GRIPS	Grips mode
POP501	CMDEFAULT	Default cursor menu
POP502	CMEDIT	Editing mode
POP503	CMCOMMAND	Command mode
POP504	OBJECTS_DIMENSION	Dimension mode
POP505	OBJECT_VIEWPORT	Viewport selected
POP506	OBJECTS_XREF	Xref selected
POP507	OBJECT_MTEXT	Mtext selected
POP508	OBJECT_TEXT	Text selected
POP509	OBJECT_HATCH	Hatch selected
POP510	OBJECT_LWPOLYLINE	Polyline selected
POP511	OBJECT_SPLINE	Spline selected
POP512	OBJECTS_VIEWPORT	Viewports selected
POP513	OBJECT_MAXVP	Maximized viewport
POP514	OBJECT_MINVP	Non-maximized viewport
POP515	OBJECT_BLOCKREF	Block reference selected
POP516	OBJECT_ATTBLOCKREF	Attributed block selected

Each shortcut menu can have 499 items — even though no display can handle that many items. For typical 1024 x 768-resolution displays, the practical maximum is 36 menu items.

Tablet Menus and Buttons

The buttons and menus of digitizing tablets are defined in a section with a rather rude term, "Legacy." (Legacy is the polite term used by the computing industry to mean "just about obsolete.") In contrast to being legacy items, tablets are still important input devices for professional drafters.

The digitizing tablet performs two functions for AutoCAD LT:

- Selecting commands and accessing the AutoCAD LT user interface
- Drawing, such as tracing paper drawings

Under the Legacy item are three entries:

Tablet Menus — define menus used by digitizing tablets, as illustrated on the next page.

Tablet Buttons — define the buttons on the pucks and styluses used by digitizing tablets.

Image Tile Menus — define an early form of dialog box no longer used in AutoCAD LT. (AutoCAD still uses an image tile menu for the **3D** command.)

Tablet Menus

AutoCAD LT supports numerous menu areas on tablets. They are named Tablet Menu 1, and so on. The four areas are illustrated in the figure on the next page. There is a fifth area, usually in the center, that provides access to AutoCAD LT's user interface, such as screen pointing, toolbars, and menus.

Each tablet menu is subdivided into rows and columns. If you look closely at the figure, you see numbers 1, 2, 3... along the top. These are the column numbers. On the side are letters A, B, C.... These are the row letters.

The Customize User Interface dialog box references the macro for each square on the tablet menu by its row letter, followed by the column number.

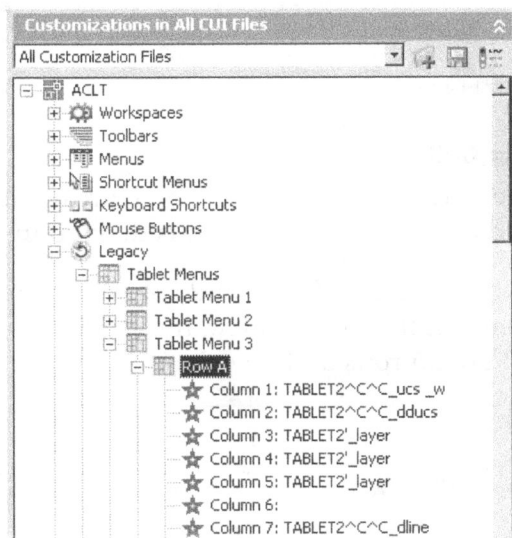

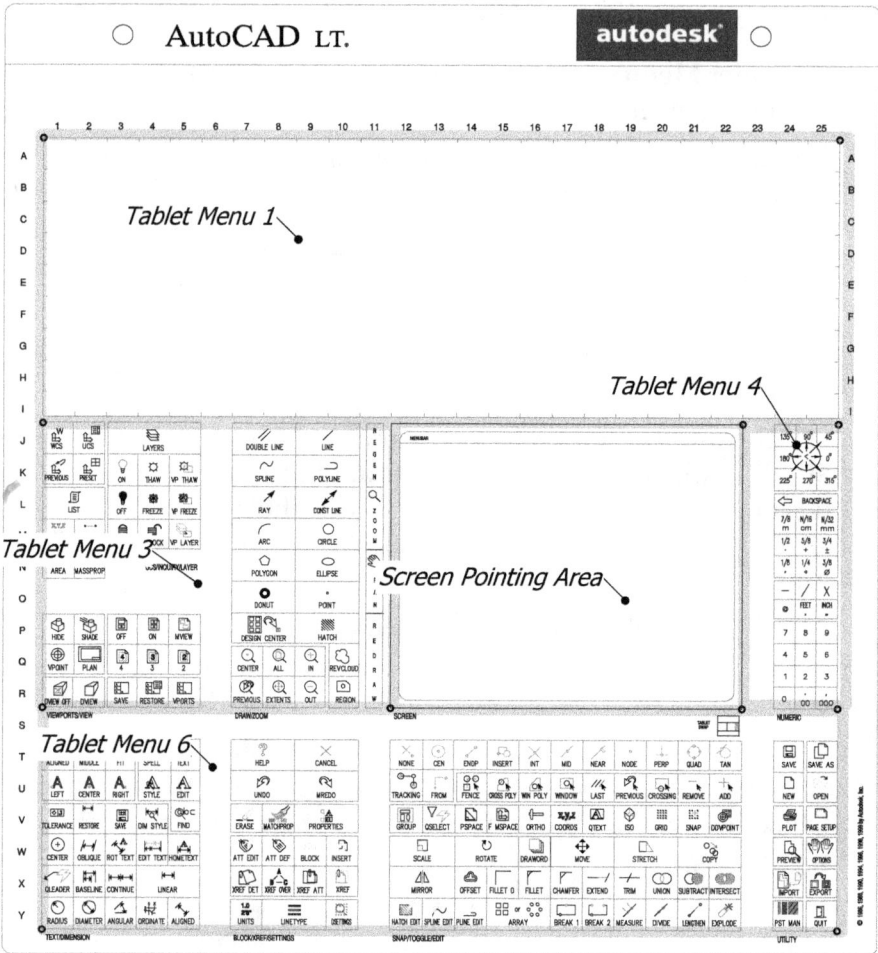

Rows x Columns = Cells

As hinted to by the figure above, the basic structure of tablet menus is the matrix of rows and columns. A menu area is defined in two steps:

1. Specify the number of rows and columns with the **CUI** command. In the figure below, the properties of **Tablet Menu 3** are 25 rows and 25 columns.

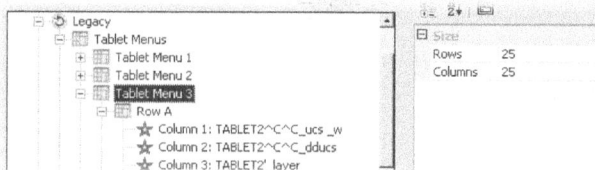

2. Define the rectangular area belonging to the menu with the the **Table Cfg** command.

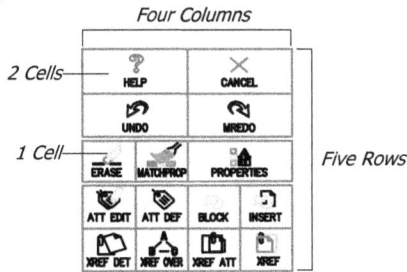

Rows and columns define *cells*. There doesn't need to be one macro per cell; the above figure of the tablet overlay portion shows some double-width cells, such as Help and Cancel. For these cells, there needs to be two identical macros, one for the first cell and another for the adjacent cell.

Tablet Menu 1

The area for Tablet Menu 1 is blank, because it is meant for users to customize. For this reason, the entire Tablet Menu 1 section in the Customize User Interface dialog box is blank, as illustrated below.

Other Tablet Menu Areas

Some of the remaining tablet areas contain AutoCAD LT commands. Tablet macros use the same format as menu macros.

Tablet Buttons

Buttons for digitizer pucks are customized identically to mouse buttons. The only difference is that their name is **Buttons*n*** instead of **Aux*n***.

Name	Keystroke-Button Combinations
BUTTONS1	Button
BUTTONS2	Shift+button
BUTTONS3	Ctrl+button
BUTTONS4	Ctrl+Shift+button

Image Tile Menus

The Image Tile Menus section is used to define *image tile menus* (a.k.a. palette menus). The name replaces the ***IMAGE and ***ICON sections used in older releases of AutoCAD LT, because the menus were named "icon menus" at one time.

Image tile menus are displayed like dialog boxes and don't look like menus at all! The images are generated from slide images, and dialog boxes hold up to 20 images. If there are more than 20, AutoCAD LT automatically displays **Next** and **Previous** buttons.

The figure below illustrating an image tile menu is from AutoCAD's **Draw | Surfaces | 3D Surfaces** command.

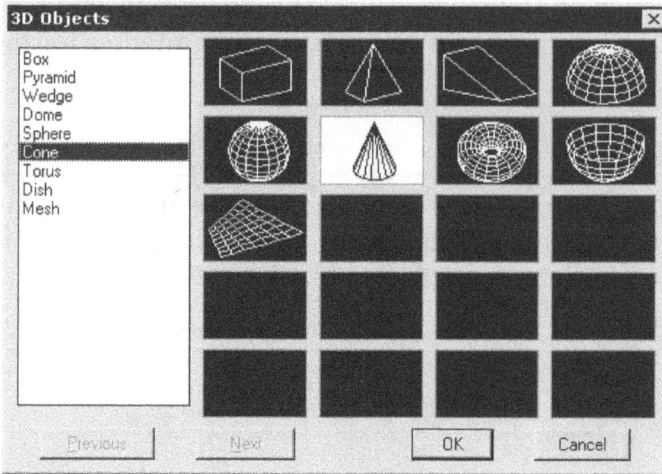

There are no commands that use image tiles in AutoCAD LT. Early versions of AutoCAD LT used image tiles for the **BHatch** command to display samples of hatch patterns.

Summary

In this chapter, you learned how to create accelerators, change mouse button definitions, and create custom shortcut menus, toolbars, and tablet menus. In addition, you learned about the format of the .cui file.

In the next chapter, you learn about advanced customization techniques, including programming with DIESEL and third-party software.

Advanced
Programming Issues

The previous chapters showed you how to customize many aspects of AutoCAD LT. Where LT falls short, however, is in its inability to be programmed. Unlike most other applications software available today, AutoCAD LT cannot be programmed — with two exceptions.

DIESEL is a simple programming language that allows minimal customization. Third-party developers have figured out how to make VBA, AutoLISP, and ObjectARX work. You learn about both in this chapter.

DIESEL

The purpose of DIESEL is to customize the status line. In addition, it is used to add simple programming code to menu and toolbar macros, such as changing the value of system variables. Third-party developers have used DIESEL to extend the programmability of AutoCAD LT.

Abbreviations

API	application programming interface
ARX	AutoCAD runtime extension; also known as ObjectARX
DCL	dialog control language
DIESEL	Direct Interpretively Evaluated String Expression Language
DOS	disk operating system
DXF	drawing interchange format
VB	Visual Basic
VBA	Visual Basic for Applications
VC++	Visual C++ programming language

Commands

Command	Shortcut	Menu Selection
modemacro	...	...
macrotrace	...	...

The History of DIESEL

In the days when AutoCAD ran on DOS and Unix, the status line displayed the letter **O** (to indicate that ortho mode is on), **S** (snap is on), **T** (tablet is on), **P** (paper space is on), the x,y coordinates, the layer name, and the current color. For a dozen years, the status line of AutoCAD remained unchanged. Sometimes, the display driver allowed users to customize the status line to some extent.

For some AutoCAD users, those indicators were not enough. They wanted more information, such as the z coordinate. The official Autodesk response was along the lines of, "We wouldn't be able to add more without missing out on what some other user wants, so it's best we do nothing."

✔ Cursor coordinate values (F6)
✔ Snap (F9)
✔ Grid (F7)
✔ Ortho (F8)
✔ Polar (F10)
✔ OSnap (F3)
✔ Dynamic Input (F12)
✔ Lineweight
✔ Paper/Model
Tray Settings...

Command:

36.5939. 25.9234   SNAP GRID ORTHO |POLAR |OSNAP |DYN LWT |MODEL

With AutoCAD Release 12 for DOS, however, Autodesk did add the fully customizable status line, which continues to be available today in AutoCAD LT. You can select some status line options from a shortcut menu. In addition, you can add more information with a programming language called DIESEL.

DIESEL is short for "Direct Interpretively Evaluated String Expression Language." The programming logic of DIESEL is, unfortunately, as clear as the acronym's meaning. Despite the use of the word "string," DIESEL mostly operates on numbers, not strings.

While its purpose was to customize the status line, DIESEL has became the most powerful programming environment available in AutoCAD LT — and that's not saying a lot, because it is the *only* programming environment provided by Autodesk. European programmers have done some amazing things in third-party software with DIESEL's limited facilities.

The illustration shows AutoCAD LT's standard status line (top) and the status line modified by a DIESEL macro (bottom):

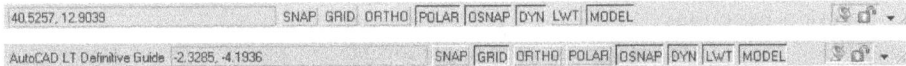

Notice that the status line now displays some text. The DIESEL-generated information is placed to the left of the x,y coordinate display.

DIESEL Programming

Is DIESEL a true programming language? For me, the line of demarcation between macros and programming languages is whether logical functions exist. *Logical functions* make it possible for the program to make decisions. Examples include If, While, and GreaterThan. DIESEL has logical functions, so that makes it a programming language.

Although DIESEL allows you to change AutoCAD LT's status line, there is a limitation: the longer the text displayed by DIESEL, the more the other status information is truncated. On my computer's 1280 x 1024 screen, LT can show about 200 characters on the status line.

In addition to modifying the status line, DIESEL can be used in menu and toolbar macros to perform useful functions that would otherwise not be possible in AutoCAD LT.

Library of DIESEL Functions

DIESEL Function   Meaning

System Functions

edtime	Displays the system time
eval	Passes strings to DIESEL
getenv	Gets the value of variables from the Windows registry
getvar	Gets the value of AutoCAD LT system variables
linelen	Returns the length of the display

String Functions

index	Extracts one element from a comma-separated series
nth	Extracts the nth element from one or more items
strlen	Returns the number of characters of the string
substr	Returns a portion of the string
upper	Converts text string to uppercase characters

Conversion Functions

angtos	Converts numbers to angle format
fix	Converts real numbers to integers
rtos	Converts numbers to units format

Math Functions

+	Performs addition on up to nine values
–	Performs subtraction on up to nine values
*	Performs multiplication on up to nine values
/	Performs division on up to nine values

Logical Functions

=	Equal
<	Less than
>	Greater than
!=	Not equal
<=	Less than or equal
>=	Greater than or equal
and	Logical bitwise AND
eq	Determines if all items are equal
if	If-then
or	Logical bitwise OR
xor	Logical bitwise XOR

DIESEL Code Basics

DIESEL has an unusual format for its macro language. Every function begins with the dollar sign and a parenthesis, as follows:

$(*function,variable*)

The purpose of the $ sign is to alert the AutoCAD LT command processor that a DIESEL expression is on the way.

You use the **ModeMacro** system variable to place text in the status line. When it encounters the $(it begins evaluating the macro.

(I have found that the maximum length of a DIESEL macro is approximately 460 characters, although some third-party programmers say LT can crash if the DIESEL macro is longer than 200 characters.)

The opening and closing parentheses signal the beginning and end of the function. The parentheses allow DIESEL to work on more than one variable at a time. This allows DIESEL functions to be nested, where the variable to one function is another function.

DIESEL works with 28 function names shown in the table on the page opposite. All DIESEL functions take at least one variable; some take as many as nine variables. A comma always separates the function name and the variable(s). DIESEL tolerates no spaces.

> **TIPS**   To display quotation marks on the status line, use double quotation marks:
>
>   " "AutoCAD LT" "
>
> To prevent DIESEL from evaluating macros, use quotation marks around the macro:
>
>   "$(+,I)"

Writing Simple DIESEL Macros

Jump right in and put DIESEL's customizable status line feature to work.

1.   Start AutoCAD LT.

   Use the **ModeMacro** system variable to type something:
   Command: **modemacro**
   Enter new value for MODEMACRO, or . for none <"">: **AutoCAD LT**

   Notice that the words "AutoCAD LT" appear on the status line to the left of the coordinate display:

   AutoCAD LT 13.3854, 4.4650   S∣

2. To restore the status line, enter **ModeMacro** again and then press the Spacebar, as follows:

    Command: **modemacro**
    Enter new value for MODEMACRO, or . for none <"AutoCAD LT">: *(Press Spacebar.)*

    The status line returns to its original state.

3. To display the value of any AutoCAD LT system variable, use the **$(getvar** function. This function *get*s the value of a system *var*iable and then displays its value on the status line.

    AutoCAD LT does not display the z coordinate (elevation). You can fix that ommission by using DIESEL to add the current elevation, as follows:

    Command: **modemacro**
    New value for MODEMACRO, or . for none <"">: **$(getvar,elevation)**

    Notice that AutoCAD LT displays 0, or something similar, on the status line.

4. The lonely zero is not very informative. Add some explanatory text:

    Command: **modemacro**
    New value for MODEMACRO, or . for none <"">: **Elevation = $(getvar,elevation)**

    Notice that the status line now displays **Elevation = 0**.

    Elevation = 0 20.3646, 19.6847   S

5. To prove to yourself that this macro is indeed useful, change the elevation to that of Mount Everest, as follows:

    Command: **elevation**
    Enter new value for ELEVATION <0.0000>: **29035**

    Notice that the value is immediately updated on the status line.

    Elevation = 29035 37.2920, 25.8111   S

Accessing Environmental Variables

In addition to (**$getvar** accessing system varaiables, the (**$getenv** function is designed to *get* the value of variables stored in the Windows registry (also known as *env*ironment variables).

Autodesk documents just two environmental variables: **MaxArray** and **MaxHatch**. They set the default value of 10,000 elements for arrays and hatch patterns, respectively. But there are more variables in the registry accessible by (**$getenv**. Some are listed below:

Environment Variable	Meaning
ANSIHatch	Name of the default ANSI hatch pattern
ANSILinetype	Name of the default ANSI linetype
CustomDictionary	Name of the custom spelling dictionary
EmergencyFont	Name of the font to use when a font is missing
FontMappingFile	Name of the file that maps fonts
ISOHatch	Name of the default ISO hatch pattern
ISOLinetype	Name of the default ISO linetype
LogFilePath	Path to the log file
MainDictionary	Name of the main spelling dictionary
Measureinit	Default measurement units
MenuFile	Name of the default menu file
MtextEditor	Name of the Mtext editor
NetLocation	Default location used by the Browser command
PlotSpoolerDirectory	Location of the folder for output of the plot spooler
SaveFilePath	Default location for saving DWG files
TempDirectory	Location of the folder for holding temporary files
XrefLoadPath	Default path for loading xref'ed drawing files

To find more environment variables that work with AutoCAD LT, search the Windows registry.

To use these variables with DIESEL, enter the variable's name in mixed case, as shown:

Enter new value for MODEMACRO, or . for none <"">: **Plot Spooler Directory = $(getenv,PlotSpoolerDirectory)**

This displays the location of the plot spooler folder (directory) on the status line.

Plot Spooler Directory = C:\Documents and Settings\administrator\Local Settings\Temp\ 17.0100, 4.!

Using DIESEL in Menus

You can use DIESEL code in menus to automate some tasks. Autodesk, for example, uses DIESEL in menu files to turn check marks on and off in the pull-down menus.

For instance, when you select **Display | Attribute Display** from the **View** menu, there are three options: **Normal**, **On**, and **Off**. In the figure below, **Normal** is prefixed by a check mark.

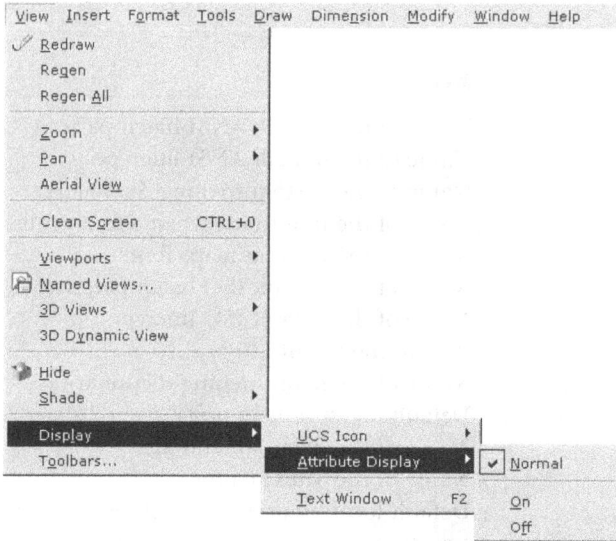

Select one of the other two, and it gets the check mark. Behind the scenes, AutoCAD LT changes the value of the **AttMode** system variable from 1 (normal) to 2 (on) or 0 (off).

The **AttMode** system variable holds the value of the **AttDisp** command:

AttDisp Command	AttMode System Variable
Off	0
Normal	1
On	2

It is trivial to display check marks in menus: prefix the word with the **!.** metacharacter. Turning on and off the display of check marks, however, is not as simple. It requires DIESEL programming. The macros below show how Autodesk programmers accomplished this:

- Normal:
  $(if,$(eq,$(getvar,**attmode**),1),!.)&**Normal**
- On:
  $(if,$(eq,$(getvar,**attmode**),2),!.)&**On**

- Off:

  $(if,$(eq,$(getvar,**attmode**),**0**),!.)**O&ff**

When the value of **AttMode** equals 0, 1, or 2, then the check mark is displayed next to the appropriate menu item. You can read the code:

$(if,$(eq,$(getvar,**attmode**),**1**),!.)**&Normal**

as "**If** the value of system variable **AttMode equals 1**, then display **check mark** in front of Normal." Let's parse the functions in this code:

> **$(if,)** — DIESEL macro starts with the **$(if** function to test the expression following. Read it this way: *If* the expression is true, *then* apply the next expression.
>
> Recall that commas separate expressions and values in a DIESEL statement. No spaces allowed!
>
> **$(eq, ,1)** — the **$(eq** function compares two values. If the value of **AttMode** (see below) is **1**, then **$(eq** returns **1** (which means *true*).
>
> - **True** means the value is 1.
> - **False** means the value is 0 (zero).
>
> The **$(eq** function is *nested*, which means it is within another function; in this macro, it is nested within the **$(if** function.
>
> **$(getvar,**attmode**)** — the **$(getvar** function gets the value of the **AttMode** system variable, which has three possible values: **0, 1,** and **2**. This is another nested DIESEL expression; because it is the innermost nested function, DIESEL evaluates it first.
>
> **!.** — this metacharacter is interpreted by AutoCAD's menu system to mean "display a check mark." In this macro, the check mark is displayed when **AttMode** equals **1**; the check mark is not displayed if **AttMode** has any other value.
>
> **&Normal** — the ampersand metacharacter underlines the letter following, in this case <u>N</u>ormal.

The sole purpose of this DIESEL code is to turn the check mark on and off in the menu. It takes this piece of macro code to change the value of **AttDisp**:

```
'_attdisp _n
```

TIP You can reuse the code for all kinds of toggle situations. (*Toggle* means to turn on or off, like a light switch.) There are many toggle commands in AutoCAD LT, such as **Grid**, **Snap**, **Ortho**, and **UcsIcon**.

Go though the list of system variables; those with a value of 0 or 1 (or On or Off) are toggles. To reuse this code for other toggles, simply replace the appropriate parts.

For example, below is the code that turns on the check mark for the **UscIcon** command:

```
$(if,$(and,$(getvar,ucsicon),1),!.)&On
```

DIESEL Error Messages

To go along with its obscure syntax, DIESEL has an equally bizarre set of error messages — all four of them. The cryptic error messages are printed by DIESEL on the status line, as shown by **$(IF,??)** below:

```
$(IF,??) 9.2210, 4.5035                              S
```

Here's what they mean, along with an example of how the error can occur. Keep an eye on the question mark: it points out the location of the error.

$? — right parenthesis left out. For example, here the closing parenthesis is missing:

$(+,1,2

The error message could also mean that the left quotation mark is missing. For example, here the left quotation mark is missing from in front of To:

$(eq,To")

$(func)?? — wrong name entered for function. For example, here the **strlen** function is misspelled as "stringlenth":

$(stringlenth, ...)

$(func,??) — incorrect number of arguments included with function. For example, the **if** function needs at least two arguments, but here is has none:

$(if,)

$(++) — output string is too long.

TIP The most common error is allowing spaces in the DIESEL macro. Each DIESEL argument must be separated by a comma; there must be no spaces within the expression.

Tracing Bugs in DIESEL

To help track down bugs in DIESEL macros, turn on the **MacroTrace** system variable, as follows:

    Command: **macrotrace**
    New value for MACROTRACE <0>: **l**

When **MacroTrace** is turned on, AutoCAD LT displays step-by-step evaluations of DIESEL macros in the Text window. Here's how it works for the following macro, which converts the value of the fillet radius to metric:

    Command: **modemacro**
    New value for MODEMACRO, or . for none <"">:
    $(*,2.54,$(getvar,filletrad))

AutoCAD displays the following:

    Eval: $(*, 2.54, $(getvar,filletrad))
    Eval: $(GETVAR, filletrad)
    ===> 0.5
    ===> 1.27

The innermost function is evaluated first (resulting in 0.5), and then subsequent functions are evaluated (resulting in 1.27).

CAUTION You cannot access help while typing DIESEL macros during the **ModeMacro** command. When you press **F1**, AutoCAD LT doesn't display help; instead, it adds '**_help** to the macro:

    Enter new value for MODEMACRO, or . for none <" ">: **$(getenv'_help**

Other Programming Interfaces

Although DIESEL is the only programming approved by Autodesk for LT, full-grown AutoCAD has many programming interfaces. They go by the names of AutoLISP, Visual LISP, DCL, ARx, DBx, and VBA. Autodesk has disabled these in LT, but third-party developers have managed to implement them regardless.

AutoLISP

Introduced in 1985, AutoCAD's first programming language is known as AutoLISP. It lets you create programs that manipulate nearly every aspect of AutoCAD and the drawing.

Autodesk originally included AutoLISP in the beta version of AutoCAD LT Release 1, but then yanked out the code in the final days before the software began shipping to dealers, who worried that AutoCAD LT with AutoLISP would outsell the more profitable AutoCAD.

They needn't have worried: even without AutoLISP, AutoCAD LT outsells AutoCAD by a margin of nearly 3:1, even after Autodesk nearly doubled the price of AutoCAD LT.

AutoLISP is used in AutoCAD at the command line or loaded from text files with the .lsp extension. When you try to use AutoLISP in AutoCAD LT, however, the program responds: "LISP command not available."

Visual LISP

Autodesk added Visual LISP to AutoCAD Release 14. It provides a visual programming environment for AutoLISP, such as using colors to show nesting of functions.

Visual LISP is not available for AutoCAD LT.

DCL

To create dialog boxes, AutoCAD uses DCL, short for "dialog control language." DCL defines the layout of dialog boxes, and then AutoLISP is used to activate the buttons, sliders, list boxes, text entry fields, and other elements of dialog boxes.

DCL is used by AutoCAD LT; look for DCL files in the \support folder. But you cannot access DCL, because AutoLISP is not available.

Making AutoLISP and DCL Work in LT

drcauto provided this description of how its software allows AutoLISP applications to work with AutoCAD LT:

The LT Toolkit 2006 (with LISP) from drcauto allows AutoCAD LT 2006 to run AutoLISP and Visual LISP programs. It includes the code for handling DCL files.

Our toolkit also works with encrypted LISP files created with Protect, Kelvinator, and Loklisp. In addition to the LISP interface, the LT Toolkit adds functions and commands for layer manipulation, extended keyboard control, fast input of 3D viewpoints, text editing, and extended move and copy commands.

LT Toolkit allows LISP routines to be loaded using a dialog box interface (via the **AppLoad** command) or at the command line using:

> (load filename [on-error])

LISP files can be loaded automatically when AutoCAD LT is first started, and when each drawing is opened. Use toolkit.lsp and toolkitdoc.lsp where acad.lsp and acaddoc.lsp would be used in AutoCAD 2006.

For more information, contact drcauto sales manager Hugh Fox through email hughf@drcauto.com or visit www.drcauto.com.

VBA

Microsoft invented VBA (short for "Visual Basic for Applications") as a common programming language loosely based on Visual Basic.

(Microsoft got its start as a company when Bill Gates and his partner adapted BASIC for the very first personal computer in the 1970s. VBA shares nothing with BASIC, except for part of the name.)

Although VBA is available in AutoCAD, Word, Excel, and low-cost CAD applications, it is not available in AutoCAD LT.

ARX

AutoCAD's most powerful programming interface is known as ARX (short for "AutoCAD runtime extension"). It is "merely" an interface; you have to buy additional programming tools (read: $$$) and have an in-depth knowledge of advanced programming methodology.

The primary advantage to using ARX is speed; these programs run code as much as 100 times faster than AutoLISP. Autodesk uses ARX applications to add features to LT; look for file names ending in .arx.

ARX programming is not available for AutoCAD LT.

Making ARX Work in LT

Gary D'Arcy of drcauto describes some of the issues involved in getting ARX and AutoLISP applications to work with AutoCAD LT:

Autodesk had a backdoor function in AutoCAD LT 97/98 that no longer exists in AutoCAD LT 2006. In LT 97/98, there were four companies that figured out a method to access one or more APIs. AutoCAD LT 2006 is much more difficult, and some of these companies have ceased development.

There are a number of possible methods to enable other applications to work in conjunction with AutoCAD LT. The things that need to be taken care of include:

- Command input via command line, menu, and toolbars
- Selection sets
- Writing to and retrieving from the drawing database
- Returning messages to the command prompt
- Connection(s) between LT and the third-party application

Generally, ARX applications are written by high-end developers with a thorough knowledge of VC++. For this reason, ARX applications are for sale for commercial gain. drcauto provides several products that work with AutoCAD LT 2006 including:

!slingshot — a base level product that brings back missing commands like Xref Clip, Image Attach, and so on

Supertools — generic tools for layer manipulation, block counting, and attribute editing

LToolkit — generic LISP interpreter that runs .lsp files in AutoCAD LT

LToolkitMax — generic LISP interpreter that runs .lsp and .arx files

SmartArchitect — powerful architectural application

AccuRender LT — popular rendering program from Robert McNeal running inside LT. (All applications are !slingshot based)

LT Toolkit 2006 (with LISP) — enables the LISP API

To our knowledge, about 95% or more of existing AutoLISP routines that work in AutoCAD will work in AutoCAD LT 2006 with little or no modification. While many commercial programs are still written in AutoLISP, most AutoLISP routines are used by end users for noncommercial purposes. Our LISP enabler excludes Visual LISP functions that require the (vl-load-com) function and reactor functions, but most other VLISP functions work.

For more information, contact drcauto managing director Gary D'Arcy, email garyd@drcauto.com or visit www.drcauto.com.

Writing ARX Applications for LT

Owen Wengerd of ManuSoft provides this description of how he gets ARX applications to work with AutoCAD LT:

There are two basic ingredients necessary:

- The ARX must be loaded into the LT process
- Functions and services not available in LT must be provided for the ARX to function

The first ingredient is the easiest. While there are several different ways of achieving it, my solution involves using a *tee* driver to hook into the printer driver in AutoCAD LT 97 and 98 or the display driver in more recent versions. I chose this solution because tee drivers can be installed merely by modifying a file (for AutoCAD LT 97 and 98) or a key in the registry (for AutoCAD LT 2000 and after).

The LTX tee driver is loaded by AutoCAD LT when it starts. It then loads the real printer or display driver and passes all driver calls through to the real driver. In addition, it loads the ARX applications into the AutoCAD LT process space. If multiple LTX-enabled applications are installed, there is a chain of tee drivers, one for each application.

There is more to it, however. Because an ARX application is implicitly linked to AutoCAD's Acad.exe, the operating system resolves many imported functions called through API functions exported from Acad.exe. Therefore, before an ARX can be loaded, it must be rebound so that it links to equivalent functions exported from AutoCAD LT.

LTX uses a proprietary method to reroute such functions, either to equivalent functions in AutoCAD LT or to functions in LTX when AutoCAD LT does not provide equivalent functions. A lot must be done behind the scenes to make this seamless from the point of view of the ARX applications. LTX performs all these acrobatics in real time as ARX application calls into API functions and vice versa.

To make the ARX seamless from the point of view of the user, LTX also processes command-line input and calls the appropriate ARX commands when the user enters commands defined in ARX modules. This portion of LTX requires the use of proprietary hooking techniques, which cannot be revealed.

What I have described above is the basic process. I might add that the process is much too difficult to benefit the casual user or developer. The tee driver technique, however, is relatively simple to implement and might be useful for add-on utilities that only use Windows API functions and services to perform their function.

For more information, contact ManuSoft president Owen Wengerd at owenw@manusoft.com or check out the LTX page at www.manusoft.com/Software/LTX/Index.stm.

The DWG and DXF Formats

AutoCAD LT drawings are stored in files that have an extension of .dwg. For that reason, the file format has become known as "DWG."

In the early 1980s, Autodesk did something no other CAD vendor had ever done: it published the format of its DXF files (short for "drawing interchange format"). Autodesk invented DXF as a way to allow users and outside programmers access to the data stored in the DWG file. Since then, DXF has become a format used to exchange drawings between different CAD programs.

Even though Autodesk continues to keep the DWG file format proprietary, a number of third-party programmers around the world have reverse-engineered the DWG file format. Companies that have done this include Cyco International (Netherlands) and Cimmetry Systems (Canada). They used this information to create software programs that don't need AutoCAD to read and write DWG files. Examples include file viewers, drawing management software, and file translators.

Some of these third-party vendors released their knowledge of the DWG format in the form of APIs (short for "application programming interfaces"), which then allowed other CAD software to read and write AutoCAD's DWG files.

The first CAD package to do this was Bentley Systems' MicroStation v4.1, using the API from MarComp. As a result, MarComp's API became the most commonly used by other CAD vendors.

The OpenDWG Alliance

Early in 1998, Visio Corp. purchased MarComp. At first, the other CAD vendors were worried that Visio would cut off access to the MarComp API. Quite the opposite occurred: Visio created the OpenDWG Alliance, which made the MarComp API freely available from www.opendwg. org. (The alliance has since renamed itself Open Design Alliance.)

Autodesk itself has not joined the alliance, saying that DWG is meant to be a compressed, secure, fast-loading file format. Instead, Autodesk supports these other data exchange standards:

DXF (drawing interchange format)

IGES (Initial Graphics Exchange Specification)

IAI (International Alliance for Interoperability)

IFC (Industry Foundation Classes)

DBX (access to the DWG files)

PDES (product definition specification)

STEP (Standard for the Exchange of Product data)

DWF (drawing Web format)

OGC (Open GIC Consortium)

LandXML (extensible markup language for survey data)

Documenting DWG

Autodesk has never documented (for outsiders) the DWG format. For this reason, the Open Design Alliance has instead done the job as best it can. You can read it at www.opendesign.com/downloads/guest.htm.

A word of caution: no one has ever fully documented the DWG format. Even the alliance's documentation has areas labeled "Unknown Section." Part of the difficulty stems from Autodesk changing the DWG format with every release of AutoCAD, and often between releases as well.

You may be wondering what the DWG format looks like. It is a binary file, which means it is easily understood by computers but is gibberish to humans. The following illustration shows a "hex viewer" program displaying a DWG file.

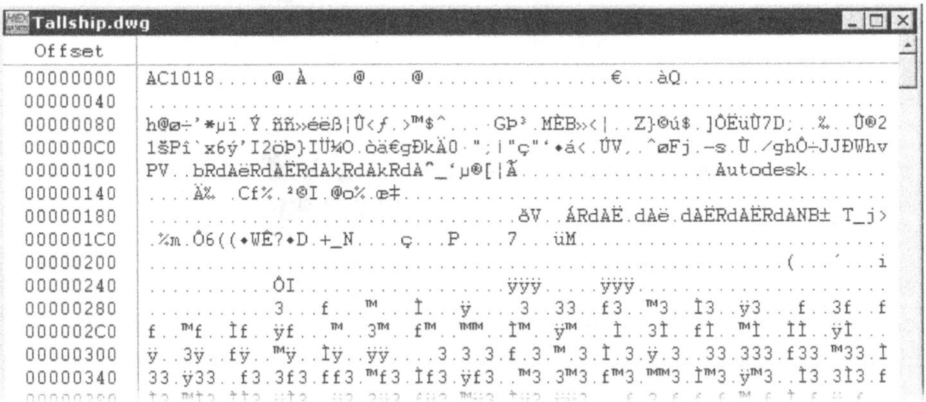

The Alliance's *AutoCAD DWG File Specification* describes the arrangement of data in DWG files as follows:

> Header
> > File Header
> > DWG Header Variables
> > CRC
>
> Class Definitions
> Padding (R13c3 and later)
> Image Data (pre-R13c3)
> Object Data
> > All entities, table entries, dictionary
> > entries, etc., go in this section.
>
> Object Map
> Unknown Section (R13c3 and later)
> Second Header
> > Image Data (R13c3 and later)

```
 Tallship.dxf - Notepad
File  Edit  Format  Help
  0
SECTION
  2
HEADER
  9
$ACADVER
  1
AC1018
  9
$ACADMAINTVER
 70
     72
  9
$DWGCODEPAGE
  3
ANSI_1252
  9
$LASTSAVEDBY
  1
Autodesk
  9
$INSBASE
 10
0.0
 20
0.0
 30
0.0
  9
$EXTMIN
 10
2.749999999999999
 20
5.75
 30
0.0
  9
$EXTMAX
 10
370.3056073224096
 20
272.0
 30
0.0
  9
$LIMMIN
 10
```

DXF Documentation

The purpose of DXF, as explained by AutoCAD LT 's documentation, is "to share drawing data between applications." DXF files are (usually) written in plain ASCII, which means you can "easily" read it.

The illustration at right shows the first several lines of a DXF file output by AutoCAD LT using the **File | Save As** command's **DXF** option.

Not all drawing data is, however, stored in the DXF file: OLE objects and application-generated objects are not stored in DXF; ACIS data is encrypted in DXF. The Autodesk documentation for DXF is at www.autodesk.com/techpubs/autocad/acad2000/dxf/index.htm.

Summary

In this chapter, you learned how to write "programs" using DIESEL. DIESEL can be used to customize the status line and to provide simple programming of toolbar and menu macros.

You learned about some of the attempts of third-party programmers to provide advanced programming capabilities to AutoCAD LT. You were introduced to the DWG and DXF file formats and also learned about the attempts to open up the DWG file format.

AutoCAD LT
Command Reference

This appendix contains the complete list of commands found in AutoCAD LT, along with several methods of accessing the commands:

Command Name — type command names at the 'Command:' prompt

Menu Selection — select commands from the menu

Shortcut — press shortcut keystrokes, such as **Ctrl+C**

Alias — enter one- or two-letter aliases

Rel — this appendix notes when commands were added to AutoCAD LT:

LT97	AutoCAD LT 97
LT98	AutoCAD LT 98
LT2K	AutoCAD LT 2000 (there was no "LT 99")
LT2i	AutoCAD LT 2000i (no "LT 2001")
LT02	AutoCAD LT 2002
LT04	AutoCAD LT 2004 (no "LT 2003")
LT05	AutoCAD LT 2005
LT06	AutoCAD LT 2006

A blank entry means the command was added with AutoCAD LT Release 1, Release 2, or 95 (there was no "LT 96").

A ~~strikethrough~~ means the command was removed from AutoCAD LT.

Command Name — lists the names of commands that are entered at the 'Command:' prompt. Some commands use the following prefixes:

- ' Transparent command; can be invoked in the middle of another command
- - Forces the command-line version

Menu Selection — indicates when commands can be selected from the menu bar. The | symbol (vertical bar) separates menu picks. For example, **Help | About AutoCAD LT** means to select **Help** from the menu bar, then select **About AutoCAD LT** from the drop-down menu. You can create customized menus with the **CUI** command.

Shortcut — indicates commands that have keystroke shortcuts, such as function keys and the **Ctrl** key. A bolded uppercase entry, such as **SNAP**, indicates the shortcut is on the status bar. You can create other shortcuts with the **CUI** command.

Alias — indicates commands with aliases, which allow you to specify the command without entering the full name. For example, instead of typing "adcenter" to open the AutoCAD DesignCenter window, type just "adc" to save you a few keystrokes.

Some aliases are included by Autodesk for compatibility reasons. For example, the "ce" and "content" aliases open the AutoCAD DesignCenter window, which replaced the old Content Explorer found in AutoCAD LT 98. You can create aliases in the acad.pgp file (**Tools | Customize | Edit Program Parameters**).

Rel	Command Name	Menu Selection	Shortcut	Alias
A				
	'About	Help | About AutoCAD LT	...	...
LT2K	AdcClose	Tools | AutoCAD DesignCenter	Ctrl+2	...
LT2K	AdCenter	Tools | AutoCAD DesignCenter	Ctrl+2	ce, content, dcenter
LT2K	AdcNavigate	...	...	...
	Aperture	...	...	...
	Arc	Draw | Arc	...	a
	Area	Tools | Inquiry | Area	...	aa
	Array	Modify | Array	...	ar
LT98	-Array	...	...	-ar
LT2i	Assist	Help | Info Palette	Ctrl+5	...
LT2i	AssistClose	Help | Info Palette	Ctrl+5	...
LT97	AttachUrl	...	...	...
	AttDef	Draw | Block | Define Attributes	...	at, att, dad, ddattdef
LT2K	-AttDef	...	...	-at, -att
	AttDisp	View | Display | Attribute Display | On	...	ad
	AttEdit	Modify | Object | Attribute | Global	...	ae, ate, ddatte
LT2K	-AttEdit	...	...	-ate, atte
	AttExt	Tools | Attribute Extraction	...	ax, ddattext
	Audit	File | Drawing Utilities | Audit	...	...
B				
	'Base	Draw | Block | Base	...	ba
	BHatch	Draw | Hatch	...	bh, h
	-BHatch	...	...	...
	'Blipmode	...	...	bm
	Block	Insert | Block	...	b, bmake, bmod acadblockdialog
LT2K	-Block	...	...	-b
LT2K	BlockIcon	...	...	bupdate
	BmpOut	...	...	...
	Boundary	Draw | Boundary	...	bo, bpoly
	-Boundary	...	...	-bo
	Break	Modify | Break	...	br
LT97	Browser		...	...
~~LT2i~~	~~BuyOnline~~	*Removed; not replaced*		
C				
LTO6	Cal	...	...	...
	Chamfer	Modify | Chamfer	...	cha
	Change	...	...	-ch
	ChProp	...	...	...
	Circle	Draw | Circle	...	c

Rel	Command Name	Menu Selection	Shortcut	Alias
LTO4	CleanScreenOff	View | Clean Screen	Ctrl+O	...
LTO4	CleanScreenOn	View | Clean Screen	Ctrl+O	...
LT2K	Close	File | Close	Ctrl+F4	...
LT2i	CloseAll	Window | Close All	...	...
	Color	...	...	col, ddcolor, colour
	-Color	...	...	...
LTO6	CommandLine	Tools | Command Line	Ctrl+9	cli
LTO6	CommandLineHide	Tools | Command Line	Ctrl+9	...
LT97	Convert	...	...	...
LT2K	ConvertCtb	...	...	...
LT2K	ConvertPStyles	...	...	...
	Copy	Modify | Copy	...	cp, co
LT2K	CopyBase	Edit | Copy with Base Point	...	...
	CopyClip	Edit | Copy	Ctrl+C	...
	CopyHist	*In Text Screen:* Edit | Copy History	...	...
	CopyLink	Edit | Copy Link	...	cl
LTO6	CUI	Tools | Customize | Interface	...	toolbar, to
LTO6	CuiExport	Tools | Customize | Export	...	...
LTO6	CuiImport	Tools | Customize | Import	...	...
LTO6	CuiLoad	...	...	...
LTO6	CuiUnload	...	...	...
LT98	Customize	Tools | Customize | Tool Palettes	...	...
	CutClip	Edit | Cut	Ctrl+X	...

D

Rel	Command Name	Menu Selection	Shortcut	Alias
LT2i	DbClkEdit	...	...	...
	~~DdAttDef~~	*Removed from LT 2000; replaced by AttDef.*		
	~~DdAttE~~	*Removed from LT 2000; replaced by AttEdit.*		
	~~DdAttExt~~	*Removed from LT 2000; replaced by AttExt.*		
	~~DdChProp~~	*Removed from LT 2000; replaced by Properties.*		
	~~DdColor~~	*Removed from LT 2000; replaced by Color.*		
	DdEdit	Modify | Object | Text | Edit	...	ed
	~~Ddemodes~~	*Removed from LT 97; replaced by DSettings.*		
	~~DdGrips~~	*Removed from LT 2000; replaced by DSettings.*		
	~~DDim~~	*Removed from LT 2000; replaced by DimStyle.*		
	~~DdInsert~~	*Removed from LT 2000; replaced by Insert.*		
	~~DdLModes~~	*Removed from LT 97; replaced by Layer.*		
	~~DdLType~~	*Removed from LT 97; replaced by Linetype.*		
	~~DdModify~~	*Removed from LT 2000; replaced by Properties.*		
	~~DdOSnap~~	*Removed from LT 97; replaced by DSettings.*		
	'DdPType	Format | Point Style	...	...
	~~DdRename~~	*Removed from LT 2000; replaced by Rename.*		
	~~DdRModes~~	*Removed from LT 2000; replaced by DSettings.*		
	~~DdSelect~~	*Removed from LT 2000; replaced by Select.*		
	~~Ddstyle~~	*Removed from LT 97; replaced by Style.*		

Rel	Command Name	Menu Selection	Shortcut	Alias
	~~DdUcs~~	*Removed from LT 2000; replaced by UcsMan.*		
	~~DdUcsP~~	*Removed from LT 2000; replaced by UcsMan.*		
	~~DdUnits~~	*Removed from LT 2000; replaced by Units.*		
	~~DdView~~	*Removed from LT 2000; replaced by View.*		
LT2K	DdVPoint	...	...	vp
	'Delay	...	...	...
LT 97	DetachUrl	...	...	...
	'Dist	Tools | Inquiry | Distance	...	di
	Divide	Draw | Point | Divide	...	div
	DLine	Draw | Double Line	...	dl
	Donut	Draw | Donut	...	do, doughnut
LT06	DrawingRecovery	File | Drawing Utilities | Drawing Recovery Manager	...	drm
LT06	DrawingRecoveryHide	...	...	...
LT 97	DrawOrder	Tools | Display Order	...	dr
LT2K	DSettings	Tools | Drafting Settings	...	ds, rm, se, polar, ddrmodes
	DsViewer	View | Aerial View	...	av
	~~DText~~	*Removed from LT 2000; replaced by Text.*		
	DView	View | 3d Dynamic View	...	dv
LT 97	~~DwfOut~~	*Removed from LT 2000; replaced by Plot.*		
LT 97	~~DwfOutD~~	*Removed from LT 2000; replaced by Plot.*		
LT2K	DwgProps	File | Drawing Properties	...	...
	DxfIn	File | Open	...	dn
	DxfOut	File | Save As	...	dx

Dimension

Rel	Command Name	Menu Selection	Shortcut	Alias
	Dim	...	...	...
	Dim1	...	...	d1
	DimAligned	Dimension | Aligned	...	dal
	DimAngular	Dimension | Angular	...	dan
LT06	DimArc	Dimension | Arc Length	...	dar
	DimBaseline	Dimension | Baseline	...	dba
	DimCenter	Dimension | Center Mark	...	dce
	DimContinue	Dimension | Continue	...	dco
	DimDiameter	Dimension | Diameter	...	ddi
LT02	DimDisassociate	...	...	djo, jog
	DimEdit	Dimension | Oblique	...	ded
LT06	DimJogged	Dimension | Jogged	...	...
	DimLinear	Dimension | Linear	...	dli, dimrotated, dimhorizontal, dimvertical
	DimOrdinate	Dimension | Ordinate	...	dor
	DimOverride	...	...	dov
	DimRadius	Dimension | Radius	...	dra
LT02	DimReassociate	Dimension | Reassociate Dimensions	...	dre

Rel	Command Name	Menu Selection	Shortcut	Alias
LTO2	DimRegen	...	...	...
	DimStyle	Dimension | Style	...	dst, d, dm, ddim
	DimTEdit	Dimension | Align Text	...	...

E

Rel	Command Name	Menu Selection	Shortcut	Alias
	Elev	...	...	...
	Ellipse	Draw | Ellipse	...	el
	~~End~~	*Removed from LT 97; replaced by Quit.*		
LT2i	~~EndToday~~	...	...	...
	Erase	Edit | Clear *or* Modify | Erase	Del	e
LTO2	eTransmit	File | eTransmit	...	...
	Explode	Modify | Explode	...	x
	Export	File | Export	...	exp
	Extend	Modify | Extend	...	ex

F

Rel	Command Name	Menu Selection	Shortcut	Alias
	FileOpen	...	...	...
	'Fill	...	...	...
	Fillet	Modify | Fillet	...	f
LT2K	Filter	...	...	...
LT2K	Find	Edit | Find	...	...

G

Rel	Command Name	Menu Selection	Shortcut	Alias
	GetEnv	...	...	...
LTO2	GotoUrl	...	...	...
	'GraphScr	...	F2	...
	'Grid	...	F7	**GRID**
			Ctrl+G	

H

Rel	Command Name	Menu Selection	Shortcut	Alias
	Hatch	...	...	-h, bh
	-Hatch	...	...	-h
	HatchEdit	Modify | Object | Hatch	...	he
	-HatchEdit	...	...	...
	Help	Help | Help	F1	?
	Hide	View | Hide	...	hi
LTO4	HISettings	...	...	...
LT2K	Hyperlink	Insert | Hyperlink	Ctrl+K	...
LT2K	HyperlinkOptions	...	...	...

I

Rel	Command Name	Menu Selection	Shortcut	Alias
	'Id	Tools | Inquiry | ID Point	...	...
LT97	Image	...	...	im
LT97	-Image	...	...	-im
LT97	ImageFrame	...	...	...

Rel	Command Name	Menu Selection	Shortcut	Alias
	Import	Insert | File	...	imp
LT97	~~InetCfg~~	*Removed from LT 2000; not replaced.*		
	Insert	Insert | Block	...	i, ddinsert, inserturl
LT2K	-Insert	...	...	-i
	InsertObj	Insert | OLE Object	...	io
LT97	~~InsertUrl~~	*Removed from LT 2000; replaced by Hyperlink.*		
	Intersect	Modify | Region | Intersect	...	in
	'Isoplane	...	F5 Ctrl+E	Is

J

LT06	Join	Modify | Join	...	j
LT04	JpgOut	...	...	...
LT02	JustifyText	Modify | Object | Text | Justify	...	...

L

	'Layer	Format | Layer	...	la, ddlmodes
	-Layer	...	...	-la
LT2K	Layout	Insert | Layout | New Layout	...	...
LT2K	-Layout	...	...	lo
LT2K	LayoutWizard	Insert | Layout | Layout Wizard	...	...
	Leader	...	...	...
	Lengthen	Modify | Lengthen	...	len
	'Limits	Format | Drawing Limits	...	lm
	Line	Draw | Line	...	l
	'Linetype	Format | Linetype	...	lt, ltype, ddltype
	-Linetype	...	...	-lt, -ltype
	List	Tools | Inquiry | List	...	li, ls
LT97	~~ListUrl~~	*Removed from LT 2000; not replaced.*		
	LogFileOff	...	...	...
	LogFileOn	...	...	...
	'LtScale	...	...	lts
LT2K	LWeight	Format | Lineweight	...	lineweight, lw **LWT**

M

	~~MakePreview~~	*Removed from LT 97; not replaced.*		
LT05	Markup	Tools | Markup Set Manager	Ctrl+7	msm
LT05	MarkupClose	Tools | Markup Set Manager	Ctrl+7	...
LT98	MassProp	Tools | Inquiry | Region/Mass Properties	...	...
LT05	MatchCell	...	...	...
LT2K	MatchProp	Modify | Match Properties	...	ma, painter
	Measure	Draw | Point | Measure	...	me
LT2i	~~MeetNow~~	*Removed; not replaced.*		

Rel	Command Name	Menu Selection	Shortcut	Alias
	MenuLoad	Tools | Customize Menu	...	...
	MenuUnload	...	...	...
	Mirror	Modify | Mirror	...	mi
LT2K	Model	...	...	**MODEL**
	Move	Modify | Move	...	m
LT98	MRedo	...	...	mr
	MSlide	...	...	...
	MSpace	View | Model Space (Floating)	...	ms
	MText	Draw | Text | Multiline Text	...	mt, t
	-MText	...	...	-mt, -t
	MtProp	...	...	mtedit
	Multiple	...	...	...
	MView	View | Floating Viewports	...	mv

N

	New	File | New	Ctrl+N	n

O

	Offset	Modify | Offset	...	o, of
	OleLinks	Edit | OLE Links	...	...
LT2K	OleScale	...	...	...
	Oops	...	...	oo
	Open	File | Open	Ctrl+O	openurl, dxfin
LT05	OpenDwfMarkup	File | Open Markup Set	...	...
LT97	OpenUrl	Removed from LT 2000; replaced by Open.		
LT2K	Options	Tools | Options	...	preferences, gr, op, pr, ddgrips
	'Ortho	Tools | PolarSnap Settings	F8 / Ctrl+L	or / **ORTHO**
	OSnap	Tools | Drafting Settings	F3 / Ctrl+F	os, ddosnap / **OSNAP**
	-OSnap	...	...	-os

P

LT2K	PageSetup	File | Page Setup	...	...
	'Pan	View | Pan | Realtime	...	p, rtpan
	-Pan	View | Pan	...	-p
LT06	PartialCUI	Tools | Customize | Load Partial Customization	...	...
	PasteAsHyperlink	Edit | Paste as Hyperlink	...	...
LT2K	PasteBlock	Edit | Paste as Block	...	...
	PasteClip	Edit | Paste	Ctrl+V	...
LT2K	PasteOrig	Edit | Paste to Original Coordinates	...	...
	PasteSpec	Edit | Paste Special	...	pa
LT2K	PcInWizard	Tools | Wizards | Import AutoCAD Plot Settings	...	...

Rel	Command Name	Menu Selection	Shortcut	Alias
	PEdit	Modify | Object | Polyline	...	pe
LT2K	PkFstGroup	Tools | Group Manager	...	g, group
LT2K	-PkFstGroup	Tools | Group	...	-g, -group
	Plan	View | 3D Viewpoint | Plan View	...	...
	PLine	Draw | Polyline	...	pl
	Plot	File | Plot	Ctrl+P	pp, print, dwfout
LT2i	PlotStamp	...	...	ddplotstamp
LT2i	-PlotStamp	...	...	...
LT2K	PlotStyle	...	...	...
LT2K	PlotterManager	File | Plotter Manager	...	...
LT04	PngOut	...	...	...
	Point	Draw | Point	...	po, pt
LT97	~~Polar~~	*Removed from LT 2000; replaced by DSettings.*		
	Polygon	Draw | Polygon	...	pol
	~~Preferences~~	*Removed from LT 2000; replaced by Options.*		
LT97	Preview	File | Print Preview	...	pre
LT2K	Properties	Tools | Properties	Ctrl+1	ch, mo, props, ddchprop, pr, ddmodify
LT2K	PropertiesClose	Tools | Properties	Ctrl+1	prclose
LT2K	PSetupIn	...	...	...
	PsOut	File | Export | EPS	...	...
	PSpace	View | Paper Space	...	ps, **MODEL**
	~~PsUpdate~~	*Removed from LT 2000; not replaced.*		
LT04	Publish	File | Publish	...	...
LT2i	PublishToWeb	File | Publish to Web	...	ptw
	Purge	File | Drawing Utilities | Purge	...	pu
LT98	-Purge	...	...	-pu

Q

Rel	Command Name	Menu Selection	Shortcut	Alias
LT06	QcClose	Tools | QuickCalc	Ctrl+8	...
LT2K	QkUngroup	Tools | Ungroup	...	...
LT2K	QLeader	Dimension | Leader	...	le
	QSave	File | Save	Ctrl+S	...
LT2K	QSelect	Tools | Quick Select	...	...
	QText	...	...	qt
LT06	QuickCalc	Tools | QuickCalc	Ctrl+8	qc
	Quit	File | Exit	Alt+F4 Ctrl+Q	exit

R

Rel	Command Name	Menu Selection	Shortcut	Alias
LT2K	R14PenWizard	Tools | Wizard | Add Color-Dependent Plot Style Table	...	...
	Ray	Draw | Ray	...	...
	Recover	File | Drawing Utilities | Recover	...	...
	Rectang	Draw | Rectangle	...	rec, rectangle

Rel	Command Name	Menu Selection	Shortcut	Alias
	Redo	Edit | Redo	Ctrl+Y	...
	Redraw	View | Redraw	...	r
	Regen	View | Regen	...	re
LT2K	RegenAll	View | Regen All	...	rea
LT98	Region	Draw | Region	...	reg
	ReInit	...	...	ri
	Rename	...	...	ren, ddrename
LT2K	-Rename	...	...	-ren
	'Resume	...	...	...
LT98	RevCloud	Tools | Revision Cloud	...	rc
	RevDate	Tools | Time And Date Stamp	...	rd, rev
LT2i	~~RmIln~~	*Removed from 2006; replaced by Markup.*		
	Rotate	Modify | Rotate	...	ro
	RScript	...	...	...

S

Rel	Command Name	Menu Selection	Shortcut	Alias
	Save *and* SaveAs	File | Save As	Ctrl+S	sa, dx, dxfout, saveurl
LT97	~~SaveUrl~~	*Removed from LT 2000; replaced by SaveAs.*		
	Scale	Modify | Scale	...	sc
LT06	ScaleListEdit	Format | Scale List	...	...
LT02	ScaleText	Modify | Object | Text | Scale	...	...
	Script	Tools | Run Script	...	scr
LT04	SecurityOptions	...	...	...
	Select	Tools | Selection	...	...
LT97	SelectUrl	...	...	...
	(Send)*	File | Send	...	...
	SetEnv	...	...	...
	'SetVar	...	...	set
	Shade	View | Shade	...	sh, shade
LT2K	ShadeMode	...	...	...
LT04	SigValidate	...	...	...
	Snap	...	F9	sn
			Ctrl+B	**SNAP**
	Solid	...	...	so
LT02	SpaceTrans	...	...	...
	Spell	Tools | Spelling	...	sp
	Spline	Draw | Spline	...	spl
	SplinEdit	Modify | Object | Spline	...	spe
	Stretch	Modify | Stretch	...	s
	Style	Format | Text Style	...	st, ddstyle
	-Style	...	...	...
LT2K	StylesManager	File | Plot Style Manager	...	...
LT98	Subtract	Modify | Region | Subtract	...	su
	SysWindows	Windows	Alt+Enter	...

* Command exists only as a menu choice.

Rel	Command Name	Menu Selection	Shortcut	Alias
T				
LT05	Table	Draw | Table	...	tb
LT05	TablEdit	...	...	...
LT05	TableExport	...	...	...
LT05	TableStyle	Format | Table Style	...	ts
	'Tablet	Tools | Tablet	F4 Ctrl+T	ta
	~~Tbconfig~~	*Removed from LT 97; replaced by Customize.*		
	Text	Draw | Text | Single Line Text	...	tx, dt, dtext
LT2i	-Text	...	...	...
LT05	TextToFront	Tools | Draw Order | Bring Text and Dimensions to Front	...	...
	'TextScr	View | Display | Text Window	F2	...
	Thickness	Format | Thickness	...	th
LT04	TifOut	...	...	...
	Tilemode	...	...	ti, tm
	'Time	Tools | Inquiry | Time	...	...
LT05	TInsert	...	...	...
LT2i	~~Today~~	*Removed; replaced by Startup sysvar.*		
	Tolerance	Dimension | Tolerance	...	tol
	-Toolbar	...	...	...
LT04	ToolPalettes	Tools | Tool Palettes Window	Ctrl+3	tp
LT04	ToolPalettesClose	Tools | Tool Palettes Window	Ctrl+3	...
LT04	TraySettings	...	...	...
	Trim	Modify | Trim	...	tr
U				
	U	Edit | Undo	Ctrl+Z	...
	Ucs	Tools | Ucs	...	...
	UcsIcon	View | Display | UCS Icon	...	...
LT2K	UcsMan	Tools | Named UCS	...	uc, dducs, dducsp
	Undo	Edit | Undo	Ctrl+Z	...
LT98	Union	Modify | Region | Union	...	uni
	'Units	Format | Units	...	un, ddunits
LT2K	-Units	...	...	-un
	~~Unlock~~	*Removed from LT 97; not replaced.*		
LT05	UpdateThumbsNow	...	...	...
V				
	'View	View | Named Views	...	v, ddview
LT2K	-View	...	...	-v
LT05	ViewPlotDetails	File | View Plot and Publish Details	...	...
LT2K	ViewRes	...	...	...
	~~Viewtoolbar~~	*Removed from LT 97; replaced by Customize.*		

Rel	Command Name	Menu Selection	Shortcut	Alias
	VpLayer	...	...	vl
LTO5	VpMax	...	...	...
LTO5	VpMin	...	...	...
	VPoint	View | 3D Viewpoint	...	vp, -vp
	VPorts	View | Tiled Viewports	...	viewports
	VSlide	...	...	vs
LTO6	VtOptions	...	...	...

W

Rel	Command Name	Menu Selection	Shortcut	Alias
	WBlock	...	...	w, acadwblockdwg
LT2K	-WBlock	...	...	-w
LT2K	WhoHas	...	...	...
LTO4	WipeOut	Draw | Wipeout	...	...
	WmfIn	Insert | File | WMF	...	wi
	WmfOpts	Insert | File | WMF | Options	...	...
	WmfOut	File | Export | WMF	...	wo
LTO6	Workspace	...	...	...
LTO6	WsSave	Window | Workspaces | Save Current As	...	...
LTO6	WsSettings	Window | Workspaces | Workspace Settings	...	...

X

Rel	Command Name	Menu Selection	Shortcut	Alias
LT97	XAttach	Insert | External Reference | Attach	...	xa
	XBind	Modify | Object | External Reference Bind	...	xb
	-XBind	...	...	-xb
	XLine	Draw | Construction Line	...	xl
	Xplode	...	...	...
	XRef	Insert | External Reference	...	xr
	-XRef	...	...	-xr

Z

Rel	Command Name	Menu Selection	Shortcut	Alias
	'Zoom	View | Zoom	...	z, rtzoom

3

Rel	Command Name	Menu Selection	Shortcut	Alias
	3dPan	...	...	...
	3dPoly	Draw | 3D Polyline	...	3p
	3dZoom	...	...	...

Rel	Command Name	Menu Selection	Shortcut	Alias

Miscellaneous

	Cancel command	...	Esc	...
	Dynamic input	...	...	**DYN**
	Tracking	...	...	tk, track
	Coordinates	Click coordinates on status bar	F6	...
			Ctrl+D	
	Menu bar	...	Alt	...

Special Commands

The following commands are designed for use by menu and toolbar macros, but can also be typed at the keyboard.

> **TIP** The **-View** command has four hidden options: **swiso, seiso, neiso,** and **nwiso**. These display the southwest isometric view, etc.

Command	Meaning
Ai_Browse	Starts Web browser with a URL.
Ai_Deselect	Removes all objects from the selection set.
Ai_Dim_TextAbove	Moves text above dimension line.
Ai_Dim_TextCenter	Moves text to center position.
Ai_Dim_TextHome	Moves text to dimension line.
AiDimPrec	Sets dimensions to specified decimal places.
AiDimStyle	Saves the properties of the selected dimension in up to six dimension styles.
AiDimTextMove	Moves text with dimension line, leader, or alone.
Ai_DrawOrder	Changes display order of overlapping objects.
Ai_EditCustFile	Starts external applications.
Ai_Fms	Switches to layout mode.
Ai_InvokeNFW	Launches new features workshop.
Ai_Learning_Assistance	Starts the Learning Assistance wizard.
Ai_Molc	Makes the layer of a selected object the current layer.
Ai_Pan	Moves the view: left, right, up, and down.
Ai_Product_Support	Opens a Web page at the pointa.autodesk.com site.
Ai_SelAll	Ctrl+A; selects all objects in the drawing.
Ai_StartApp	Starts an external application.
Ai_Support_Assistance	Displays window with support assistance and tips.
Ai_Tab3	Loads alternate tablet area 3 for metric units.
HyperlinkBack	Navigates to the previous hyperlinked document.
HyperlinkFwd	Navigates to the next hyperlinked document.
HyperlinkStop	Cancels the current navigation selection.

Notes

System Variables

The state of AutoCAD LT is controlled by a large number of system variables — 256 in all. You can change the value of many of these variables, except for the ones marked r/o (short for "read-only"). The following table lists the system variables in alphabetical order, along with default values.

Variable Name	Value
A	
Aflags	0
Angbase	0
Angdir	0
Apbox	0
Aperture	10
Area (r/o)	0.0000
Attdia	0
Attmode	1
Attreq	1
Auditctl	0
Aunits	0
Auprec	0
Autosnap	55
B	
Backz (r/o)	0.0000
Blipmode	0

Variable Name	Value
C	
Cdate (r/o)	20000311.14473487
Cecolor	"BYLAYER"
Celtscale	1.0000
Celtype	"BYLAYER"
Celweight	-1
Chamfera	0.5000
Chamferb	0.5000
Chamferc	1.0000
Chamferd	0
Chammode	0
Circlerad	0.0000
Clayer	"0"
Clipboard (r/o)	5
Cmdactive (r/o)	1
Cmddia	0
Cmdecho	1
Cmdnames (r/o)	"SETVAR"

Variable Name	Value
Coords	0
Cplotstyle	"ByColor"
Ctab	"Model"
Cursorsize	5
Cvport	2

D

Date (r/o)	2451615.61641655
Dbmod (r/o)	4
Dctcust	"*path*\sample.cus"
Dctmain	"enu"
Deflplstyle	"ByColor"
Defplstyle	"ByColor"
Delobj	1
Diastat (r/o)	1

Dimension Variables

Dimadec	0
Dimalt	OFF
Dimaltd	2
Dimaltf	25.4000
Dimaltrnd	0.0000
Dimalttd	2
Dimalttz	0
Dimaltu	2
Dimaltz	0
Dimapost	" "
Dimaso	ON
Dimasz	0.1800
Dimatfit	3
Dimaunit	0
Dimazin	0
Dimblk	" "
Dimblk1	" "
Dimblk2	" "
Dimcen	0.0900
Dimclrd	0
Dimclre	0
Dimclrt	0
Dimdec	4
Dimdle	0.0000
Dimdli	0.3800
Dimdsep	"."
Dimexe	0.1800
Dimexo	0.0625
Dimfit	3

Variable Name	Value
Dimfrac	0
Dimgap	0.0900
Dimjust	0
Dimldrblk	" "
Dimlfac	1.0000
Dimlim	OFF
Dimlunit	2
Dimlwd	-2
Dimlwe	-2
Dimpost	" "
Dimrnd	0.0000
Dimsah	OFF
Dimscale	1.0000
Dimsd1	OFF
Dimsd2	OFF
Dimse1	OFF
Dimse2	OFF
Dimsho	ON
Dimsoxd	OFF
Dimstyle (r/o)	"Standard"
Dimtad	0
Dimtdec	4
Dimtfac	1.0000
Dimtih	ON
Dimtix	OFF
Dimtm	0.0000
Dimtmove	0
Dimtofl	OFF
Dimtoh	ON
Dimtol	OFF
Dimtolj	1
Dimtp	0.0000
Dimtsz	0.0000
Dimtvp	0.0000
Dimtxsty	"Standard"
Dimtxt	0.1800
Dimtzin	0
Dimunit	2
Dimupt	OFF
Dimzin	0
Dispsilh	0
Distance (r/o)	0.0000
Donutid	0.5000
Donutod	1.0000
Dragmode	2

Variable Name	Value	Variable Name	Value
Dragp1	10	Hpname	"ANSI31"
Dragp2	25	Hpscale	1.0000
Dwgcheck	0	Hpspace	1.0000
Dwgcodepage (r/o)	"ANSI_1252"	Hyperlinkbase	" "
Dwgname (r/o)	"Drawing1.dwg"		
Dwgprefix (r/o)	"C:\path\"	**I**	
Dwgtitled	0		
		Imagehlt	0
E		Indexctl	0
		Inetlocation	"www.autodesk.com/acltuser"
Edgemode	0	Insbase	0.0000,0.0000,0.0000
Elevation	0.0000	Insname	" "
Exedir (r/o)	"C:\path\"	Insunits	1
Expert	0	Insunitsdefsource	1
Explmode	1	Insunitsdeftarget	1
Extmax (r/o)	$-1.0E+20,-1.0E+20,$	Isavebak	1
	$-1.0E+20$	Isavepercent	0
Extmin (r/o)	$1.0E+20,1.0E+20,$	Isolines	4
	$1.0E+20$		
Extnames	1	**L**	
		Lastangle (r/o)	0
F		Lastpoint	0.0000,0.0000,0.0000
		Lenslength (r/o)	50.0000
Facetres	0.5000	Limcheck	0
Filedia	1	Limmax	12.0000,9.0000
Filletrad	0.5000	Limmin	0.0000,0.0000
Fillmode	1	Locale (r/o)	"ENC"
Fontalt	"simplex.shx"	Logfilemode	1
Fontmap	"*path*\aclt.fmp"	Logfilename (r/o)	"*path*\Drawing1.log"
Frontz (r/o)	0.0000	Logfilepath	"*path*\"
		Ltscale	1.0000
G		Lunits	2
		Luprec	4
Gridmode	0	Lwdefault	25
Gridunit	0.5000,0.5000	Lwdisplay	OFF
Gripblock	0	Lwunits	1
Gripcolor	5		
Griphot	1	**M**	
Grips	1		
Gripsize	3	Maxactvp	64
		Maxsort	200
H		Mbuttonpan	1
		Measureinit	0
Handles (r/o)	1	Measurement	0
Hideprecision	0	Menuecho	0
Highlight	1	Mirrtext	1
Hpang	0	Modemacro	" "
Hpbound	1	Mtexted	"Internal"
Hpdouble	0		

Variable Name	Value
O	
Offsetdist	1.0000
Olehide	0
Olequality	1
Olestartup	0
Orthomode	0
Osmode	16421
Osnapcoord	2
P	
Paperupdate	0
Pdmode	0
Pdsize	0.0000
Pellipse	0
Perimeter (r/o)	0.0000
Pickadd	1
Pickauto	1
Pickbox	1
Pickdrag	0
Pickfirst	1
Pickstyle	1
Platform (r/o)	varies
Plinegen	0
Plinetype	2
Plinewid	0.0000
Plotid	" "
Plotrotmode	2
Plotter	0
Polaraddang	" "
Polarang	90
Polardist	0.0000
Polarmode	0
Polysides	4
Projmode	1
Proxygraphics	1
Proxynotice	1
Proxyshow	1
Psltscale	1
Psprolog	" "
Pstylemode (r/o)	1
Pstylepolicy	1
Pucsbase	" "

Variable Name	Value
Q	
Qtextmode	0
R	
Rasterpreview	1
Regenmode	1
Rtdisplay	1
S	
Savefile (r/o)	" "
Savefilepath	"C:\WINDOWS\TEMP\"
Savename (r/o)	" "
Savetime	120
Screensize (r/o)	1209.0000,805.0000
Sdi	0
Shadedge	3
Shadedif	70
Shortcutmenu	11
Snapang	0
Snapbase	0.0000,0.0000
Snapisopair	0
Snapmode	0
Snapstyl	0
Snaptype	0
Snapunit	0.5000,0.5000
Sortents	96
Splframe	0
Splinesegs	8
Splinetype	6
Syscodepage (r/o)	"ANSI_1252"
T	
Tabmode	0
Target (r/o)	0.0000,0.0000,0.0000
Tdcreate (r/o)	2451615.61624051
Tdindwg (r/o)	0.00028287
Tducreate (r/o)	2451615.94957384
Tdupdate (r/o)	2451615.61624051
Tdusrtimer (r/o)	0.00028287
Tduupdate (r/o)	2451615.94957384
Texteval	0
Textfill	1
Textqlty	50
Textsize	0.2000
Textstyle	"Standard"

Variable Name	Value
Thickness	0.0000
Tilemode	1
Tooltips	1
Tracewid	0.0500
Trackpath	0
Treedepth	3020
Treemax	10000000
Trimmode	1
Tspacefac	1.0000
Tspacetype	1
Tstackalign	1
Tstacksize	70

U

Variable Name	Value
Ucsaxisang	90
Ucsbase	" "
Ucsfollow	0
Ucsicon	3
Ucsname (r/o)	" "
Ucsorg (r/o)	0.0000,0.0000,0.0000
Ucsortho	1
Ucsview	1
Ucsxdir (r/o)	1.0000,0.0000,0.0000
Ucsydir (r/o)	0.0000,1.0000,0.0000
Undoctl (r/o)	5
Undomarks (r/o)	0
Unitmode	0
Username (r/o)	" "

V

Variable Name	Value
Version (r/o)	"2006"
Viewctr (r/o)	6.7612,4.5000,0.0000
Viewdir (r/o)	0.0000,0.0000,1.0000
Viewmode (r/o)	0
Viewsize (r/o)	9.0000
Viewtwist (r/o)	0
Visretain	1
Vsmax (r/o)	40.5672,27.0,0.0
Vsmin (r/o)	-27.0448,-18.0,0.0

W

Whiparc	0
Wmfbkgnd	ON
Worlducs	1
Worldview	1

X

Xclipframe	0
Xedit	1
Xloadctl	1
Xloadpath	"C:\WINDOWS\TEMP\"
Xrefctl	0

Z

| Zoomfactor | 10 |

Notes

Setting Up
Printers and Plotters

This appendix describes the plotters and printers that AutoCAD LT works with and explains how to create custom configurations for your plotters.

System Printers

After AutoCAD LT is set up on your computer, it prints its drawings to any *system printer*. System printers are any printer that is connected to your computer, whether directly or via networks.

A *direct* connection means the printer is connected directly to your computer via a USB (most common), parallel (less common), serial (rare nowadays), or infrared port.

A *network* connection means the printer is connected indirectly to your computer; you access it over the network. The printer either is connected to another computer (and the computer is connected to the network) or is on the network (the printer contains a network card).

When you use the **Plot** command, AutoCAD LT's Plot dialog box lists the system printers reported to AutoCAD LT by Windows. The list is often similar to the list of printers you see in any other Windows application.

The system printers most commonly found in an office environment include laser printers that produce high-speed, black-white prints; inkjet printers for color prints; and fax "printers" for sending faxes.

Output Devices and Drivers

More general than system printers
are *output devices*, which are anything
to which AutoCAD LT can output
drawings:

- System printers
- Pen plotters (illustrated at right)
- Inkjet plotters
- Laser printers
- Milling machines
- 3D stereolithography devices

To communicate with printers, applications use software called *drivers*.
The drivers translate AutoCAD LT's drawings into the format under-
stood by the printer. For example, many printers manufactured by
Hewlett-Packard use a language known as PCL (short for "printer con-
trol language"). The HP driver translates AutoCAD LT drawings into
PCL format, and then sends the data to the printer.

Plotting to Files

There is one other output device: files. AutoCAD LT can plot drawings to
files on disk, which are then used by other software. For instance, it is
common to plot a drawing to disk in HPGL (Hewlett-Packard Graphics
Language), then import the file into desktop publishing software. More
recently, Autodesk has hit upon plotting to files as a way to generate .dwf
files for its DWF Viewer and DWF Composer software; they call it "eplots,"
or electronic plotting.

All of the plotter listed on the facing page can plot to disk. In addition,
AutoCAD LT include a Raster File Formats driver that plots drawings to
files in these raster formats:

BMP (uncompressed bitmap) — used by Windows

CALS — scanned drawings

JPEG (Joint Photographic Experts Group) — highly compressed raster images on the Internet and in digital cameras

PNG (Portable Network Graphics) — used as a royalty-free
alternative to GIF and lossless-compression alternative to JPEG

TIFF (Tagged Image Format) — desktop publishing

TGA (Targa) — high-end imaging

PCX (PC Paintbrush) — paint programs

A separate driver, the AutoCAD DXB File driver, exports the drawing in DXB (drawing interchange binary) format, a holdover from the mid-1980s.

Autodesk created the simple vector format to import drawings that had been converted from raster scans via its now obsolete CAD\camera software.

The Plotter Manager

The **PlotterManager** command (**File | Plotter Manager**) runs the Add-A-Plotter wizard, which steps you through the process of setting up newly added plotters. The settings are saved in files with the extension PC3 (short for "plotter configuration v3").

After plotter configurations are added to AutoCAD LT, you can use the Plotter Configuration Editor to modify the settings, if necessary.

AutoCAD LT allows you to set up more than one configuration for each plotter. This allows you to plot drawings several different ways — color, grayscale, fax — without needing to select and reset parameters in the Plot dialog box; you simply select the saved configuration.

Plotters Supported by AutoCAD LT

In addition to supporting the hundreds of printer drivers provided with Windows, AutoCAD LT includes drivers for the following brands of printers and plotters:

Adobe

PostScript Level 1
PostScript 1 Plus
PostScript 2

CalComp

Artisan pen plotters
PaceSetter and PaceSetter Classic pen plotters
DesignMate pen plotters
DrawingMaster and DrawingMaster Plus pen plotters
TechJet Color inkjet plotters
Solus LED plotters
Monochrome and color electrostatic plotters

Hewlett-Packard

74xx, 75xx, and 76xx-series pen plotters
DraftMaster and DraftPro pen plotters
DesignJet inkjet plotters
LaserJet laser printers
Any plotter using HPGL or HPGL/2 plotter language

Oce

5xxx and 9xxx-series plotters
TDS series plotters

XESystems (Xerox)

60xx-series plotters
Wide Format Print Systems

Creating Custom Plotter Configurations

To create custom plotter configurations for AutoCAD LT, follow this tutorial that shows how to add an HPGL plotter and then configure it to plot to files.

1. Start AutoCAD LT.

    From the **File** menu, select **Plotter Manager**. Notice that AutoCAD displays the Plotters window.

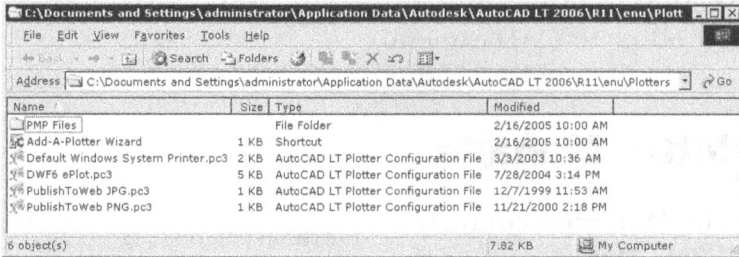

    Double-click the **Add-A-Plotter Wizard** icon to start the wizard program.

    NOTE   You can get to the Add-A-Plotter wizard several different ways. One is to select **Wizards | Add Plotter** from AutoCAD LT's **Tools** menu.

    Another way is to select **Options** from the **Tools** menu. In the Options dialog box, select the **Plotting** tab, then click the **Add or Configure Plotters** button.

    External to LT, you access the wizard from the Windows **Start** button: select **Settings | Control Panel**. In the Control Panel, double-click **Autodesk Plotter Manager**.

    If you have more than one release of AutoCAD LT on your computer, the Autodesk Hardcopy System dialog box asks you to choose one of them. Select **AutoCAD LT 2006**, and then click **Continue**.

2. AutoCAD LT displays the Add Plotter-Introduction Page. Click **Next**.

3. AutoCAD LT displays the Begin page. You can select from three kinds of printers (plotters):

    My Computer — printers that need to be configured specifically for AutoCAD LT

    Network Plotter Server — printers that use network plotter servers, such as Novell and Windows Server

System Printer — for multiple configurations of system printers

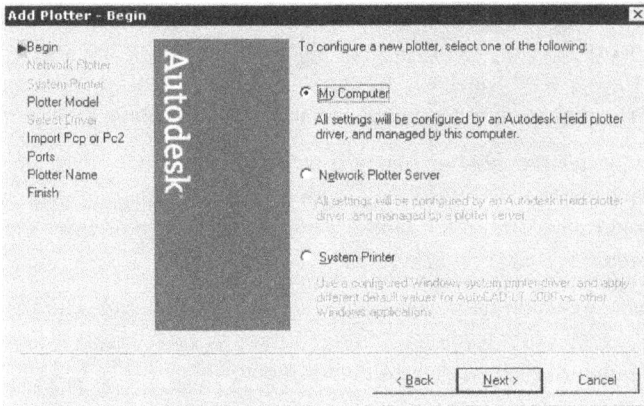

For this tutorial, select **My Computer**, and then click **Next**.

4. In the Plotter Model page, select the manufacturer and the model that matches the plotter or printer.

   For example, if the printer is an HP LaserJet 5, you would select **Hewlett-Packard** from the **Manufacturers** list. Then, scroll down the **Models** list until you see **LaserJet 5**.

   For this tutorial, select:

Manufacturers:	**Hewlett-Packard**
Models:	**7550A**

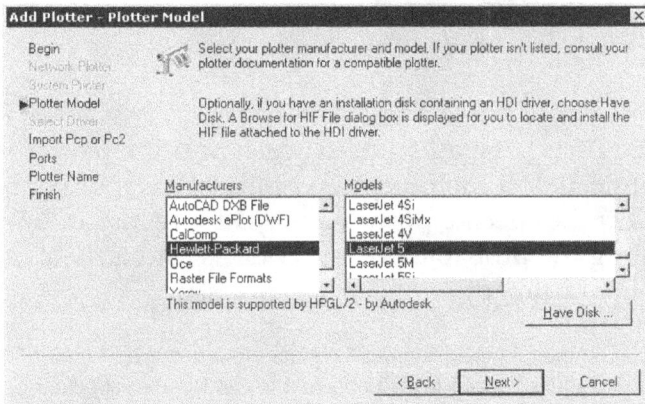

Click **Next**.

NOTE If your plotter's brand name and/or model number don't match any on the two lists, you have a couple of choices:

• The plotter may include a disk or CD containing AutoCAD plotter drivers. The documentation may refer to them as "Heidi" or "HDI" drivers. (You cannot use "ADI" drivers with AutoCAD LT; these are meant for older versions of AutoCAD.) Insert the disk in your computer, and then click the **Have Disk** button.

• The plotter probably emulates a brand name plotter. Most, for example, are compatible with HPGL or HPGL/2. Plotters with the PostScript logo can use Adobe's PostScript driver. Read the plotter's documentation to find out which model(s) it emulates.

Careful! Emulation gets worse each year as manufacturers update their drivers and abandon older formats. Some old devices don't properly support the HPGL specification, which can cause output problems.

5. Unless you have .pcp or .pc2 plotter configuration files from earlier releases of AutoCAD LT, skip the Import Pcp or Pc2 page by clicking **Next**.

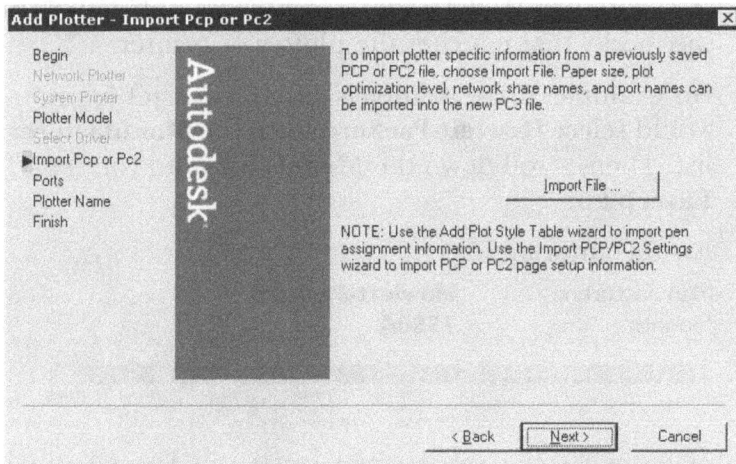

6. The Ports page asks you to which port the plotter is connected. If the plotter is connected to your computer, select the specific port. AutoCAD LT helps out by short-listing the probable ports, as well as listing the names of printers already connected to ports.

NOTE The oldest plotters always connect to a serial port (identified by the COM prefix). Not-quite-as-old laser printers and plotters usually connect to a parallel port (identified by the LPT prefix). Today's printers and plotters connect to the universal serial bus (identified by the USB prefix). Networked printers are identi-fied by a network name and "Network Port."

The other options on this page are:

Plot to File — instead of sending drawings to plotters, AutoCAD LT stores the plot data in files on disk.

AutoSpool — AutoCAD LT sends the plot data to temporary files on disk. Another program, known as a *spooler*, reads the files and sends them to the plotters. This option helps speed up plotting to older plotters with small amounts of memory.

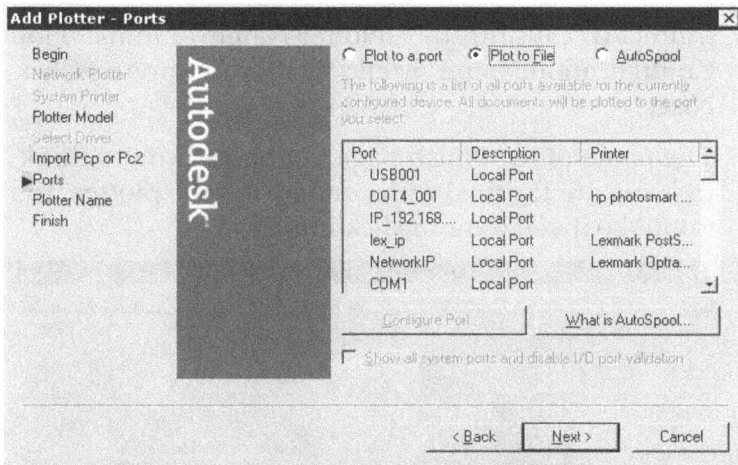

If you do not see the port name that you require, click **Show all system ports and disable I/O port validation**.

For this tutorial, select **Plot to File**, and then click **Next**.

7. In the second-to-last step, give the plotter configuration a name.

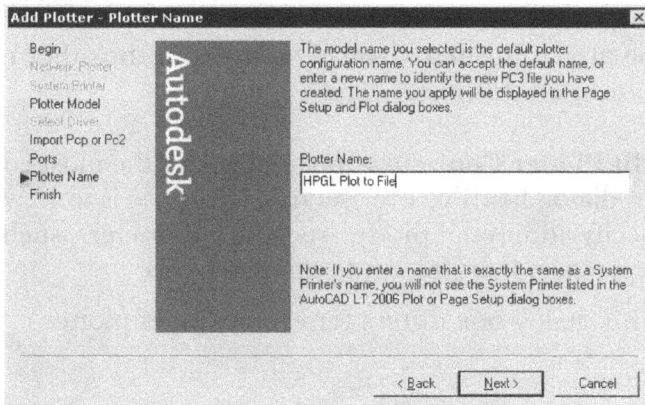

The first time you create the configuration, the name is not that important; AutoCAD offers defaults that might be good enough.

When you create more than one configuration for a single plotter, you will want to make the name more descriptive, such as "Color plots" and "Faxed plots."

For this tutorial, enter:

Plotter Name: **HPGL Plot to File**

(AutoCAD calls this the "Plotter Name"; I think "Plotter Configuration Name" would be more accurate.) Click **Next**.

8. The name of the Finish page might lead you to think that you are finished with configuring the plotter. You would be if you were to click **Finish**.

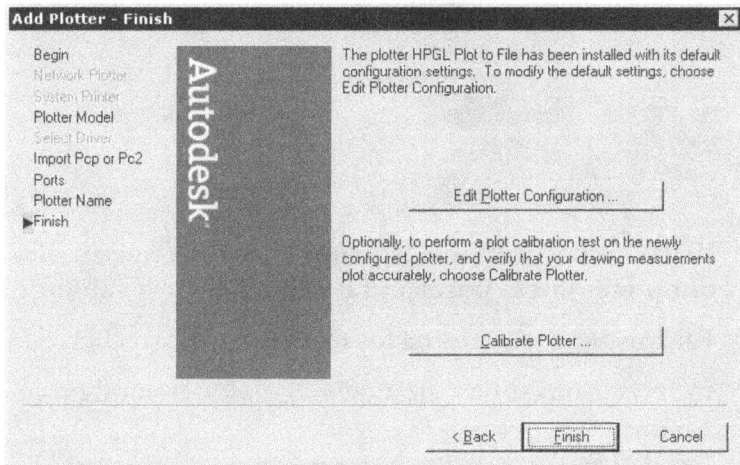

You aren't finished if you click either of the other two buttons on this page:

Edit Plotter Configuration — displays the most confusing dialog box I've ever seen. Its purpose is to let you specify additional plotter-specific parameters, such as paper size, margins, and pen matching.

(This dialog box differs for every type of plotter.)

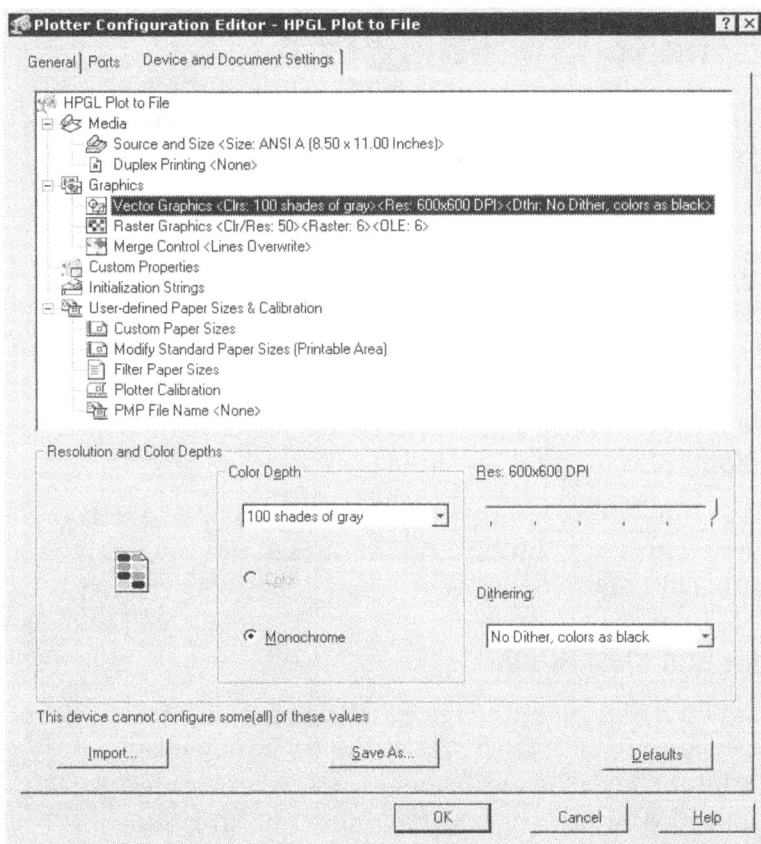

Calibrate Plotter — leads to another wizard that calibrates plotters, which is required for ultra-precise plots; the process ensures that an inch in AutoCAD LT plots as 1.0000000 inches on the plotter.

For this tutorial, click **Finish**.

9. You've completed the plotter configuration. Now try it out. In AutoCAD LT, open a drawing. From the **File** menu, select **Plot**. Notice the Plot dialog box.

   In the Printer/plotter area, click the **Name** list box. Select **HPGL Plot to File**. Notice that the **Plot to File** box is now checked.

   If you wish, click **OK** to plot the current drawing to a file on disk.

Solutions to LT Plotting Problems

Autodesk's support Web site provides these solutions to AutoCAD LT plotting problems reported by users.

Plot Dialog Box Slow to Open

Problem: When opening the Plot or Page Setup dialog boxes, a delay of seconds to minutes can occur before the dialog box opens.

Solution 1: When AutoCAD LT opens these dialog boxes, it attempts to locate CTB files, PC3 files, and system printer devices. The delay is due to the software hunting for the files.

Solution 2: If the delay is very long, it could be due to a network authentication issue involving multiple operating systems or clients are not correctly connected to the network.

DesignJet 600 Slow to Plot

Problem: When plotting with Hewlett-Packard DesignJet 600 plotter and AutoCAD LT's HDI driver, it may take several minutes for plotting to begin. Or, when using the Optimized Windows system driver, the speed is good but the quality is poor.

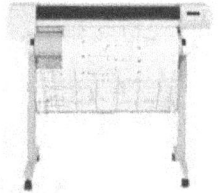

Solution: These problems can often be cured by updating the plotter firmware. Contact Hewlett-Packard to obtain the firmware updates.

"Missing Driver" Error

Problem: While configuring a printer or plotter in the Add-A-Plotter wizard, sometimes these error messages are displayed:

> Warning Missing Driver
> Program Error with the ADDPLWIZ.EXE.

The error occurs when an HDI driver is selected that was designed for a previous release of AutoCAD. HDI drivers for previous releases are not compatible with newer versions.

Solution: Contact the plotter manufacturer for updated HDI drivers or use a Windows system printer driver.

"Requested Resource In Use" Error

Problem: When plotting to local printers attached to a parallel port, the following error message may be displayed:

> Error writing to LPT1: for *application-name*. The requested resource is in use. Do you wish to retry or cancel the job?

Solution 1: Select **Retry** to complete the print job.

Solution 2: Follow these steps:

1. From the Windows **Start** button, select **Settings | Printers**.

2. From the **File** menu, select **Server Properties**.

3. In the dialog box, select the **Ports** tab.

4. Select the appropriate printer port (LPT1, LPT2, or LPT3), and then click **Configure Port**.

5. Set the Transmission Retry value to **90** or greater.

Incorrect Limits Plotted

Problem: When plotting drawings by their limits, the preview and the plot are incorrect. The lower-left corner is located in the center of the plot, so that part of the drawing is missing.

This bug occurs when the **Target** system variable is set to a value other than 0,0,0. (This read-only system variable is set by the **DView** command and cannot by changed by users.)

Solution 1: Reset the **Target** system variable using the **DView** command, as follows:

```
Command: dview
Select objects or <use DVIEWBLOCK>: all
Select objects or <use DVIEWBLOCK>: (Press Enter.)
Enter option [CAmera/TArget/Distance/POints/PAn/Zoom/TWist/CLip/
Hide/Off/Undo]: po
Specify target point <23.0409, 15.1766, 0.0000>: 0,0,0
Specify camera point <23.0409, 15.1766, 1.0000>: 0,0,1
Enter option [CAmera/TArget/Distance/POints/PAn/Zoom/TWist/CLip/
Hide/Off/Undo]: (Press Enter.)
Regenerating model.
```

Perform a **Zoom** to **Extents**, and then use the **Preview** command to check that the problem is solved. If not, then it may be due to another bug.

Solution 2: When objects are too close to the limits of the drawing, the limits calculation snaps to the object and affects the plot. To fix the bug, turn off running object snaps:

1. From the **Tools** menu, select **Drafting Settings**.

2. In the Drafting Settings dialog box, choose the **Object Snap** tab.

3. Click the **Object Snap On** check box to clear it.

4. Exit the dialog box, and then use the **Preview** command to check that the problem is solved.

Dots Plot as Diagonal Dots

Problem: When plotting hatches that use the Dots pattern, bold diagonal dots appear on the paper. This problem occurs with the Dots pattern is plotted with the lineweight set to 0.05, and when the hatching is dense.

Solution: Use a linewight heavier than 0.05.

HPsetup Causes General Protection Fault

Problem: This error message is displayed when installing the Windows-optimized driver for AutoCAD LT:

HPsetup Caused a General Protection Fault in module DDEML.DLL.

Solution: Disable Norton Desktop before the installation.

TIP   If you experience plotting problems, check out these two Autodesk support Web sites:

• AutoCAD discussion groups at discussion.autodesk.com have questions from users and answers from other users and Autodesk employees.

• AutoCAD support at support.autodesk.com lists solutions to bugs reported by users.

Compatibility
with AutoCAD 2006

AutoCAD LT is more compatible with AutoCAD than any other CAD package on the market. There remain, however, some incompatibilities due to missing features and different features.

Both editions of AutoCAD contain features unique to each other. In fact, there are more a hundred commands that AutoCAD and AutoCAD LT don't have in common with each other.

Features Missing from AutoCAD LT

A large number of AutoCAD features not found in AutoCAD LT are summerized in the following sections.

Missing 2D Operations

Multilines are displayed and can be edited using regular editing commands, such as **Move**. But multilines cannot be drawn, because all related commands are missing, including **MLine** and **MlEdit**. *Replacement*: use the **DLine** command.

All shape commands are missing, including **Load** and **Shape**. *Replacement*: use blocks.

Externally referenced drawings can be displayed and controlled with the **XAttach**, **XRef**, and **XBind** commands. But all other xref commands are missing, such as those for in-place editing, clipping, and partial loading.

Raster images can be displayed and controlled with the **Image** and **ImageFrame** commands. But all other image-related commands are missing.

The number of colors is limited to 256; AutoCAD LT does not support 16.7 million colors nor color books.

Gradient fills are displayed for drawings created in AutoCAD, but they cannot be created because the Hatch dialog box is missing the Gradient tab.

All SheetSet commands and operations are missing, including those found in the **View** command.

The **Field** and **FieldEval** commands are missing, as are their application to text, dimensions, tables, and attributes. You can enter formulas with the **MText** command.

Missing 3D Operations

Most 3D editing commands, such as **Mirror3D**, are missing.

3D surfaces are displayed, and they can edited by standard editing commands, such as **Rotate** and **Explode**. But All 3D surface primitives and surface construction commands, such as **Ai_Box** and **RevSurf**, are missing.

3D solid models can be viewed and manipulated with standard editing commands, such as **Copy** and **Erase**. But all 3D surface modeling and editing commands, such as **Sphere** and **SolidEdit** are missing.

All landscape commands, such as **LsEdit**, are missing.

All high-quality rendering commands, such as **Render** and **MatLib**, are mssing. *Replacement*: use the **Hide** and **Shade** commands.

Other Missing Operations

The collection of Express Tools, which rely on AutoLISP, are not included with AutoCAD LT.

All commands related to CAD management, layer previous, and enhanced attribute editing and extraction are missing.

All external database commands, such as **dbConnect**, are missing.

All AutoLISP, Visual LISP, DCL, VBA, DBX, and ARX programming interfaces are missing. *Replacement*: use DIESEL and macros.

AutoCAD LT imports and exports fewer formats. Drawings cannot be exported in SAT, STL, 3DS, or DWS formats.

Specific Commands Missing from LT

In addition to the groups of missing commands listed above, the following AutoCAD commands are not found in AutoCAD LT:

Command	Meaning
AppLoad	Loads AutoLISP, Visual LISP, VBA, and ObjectARX routines
DbList	Lists all objects in drawings
DxbIn	Imports DXB files
LayTrans	Translates layer names between drawings
MInsert	Inserts blocks as arrays
MvSetup	Multiple viewpoint setups
PsFill	Hatches areas with PostScript fill patterns
Redefine	Returns command names to their default definitions
RegenAuto	Controls when AutoCAD executes automatic regenerations
Shell	Runs programs external to AutoCAD
Sketch	Sketches in real time
Status	Reports the status about drawings and AutoCAD
Trace	Draws wide lines
TreeStat	Controls the memory structure of drawings
Undefine	Temporarily removes the definitions of command names
VpClip	Clips the display of viewports
XClip	Clips the displayable area of externally referenced drawings
3dOrbit	Allows interactive viewing of 3D models

Features Unique to LT

The following AutoCAD LT commands are not found in AutoCAD:

Command Name	Meaning
DLine	Draws parallel (double) lines
GetEnv	Gets the values of environment variables from the Windows registry
PsFstGroup	Displays the Group Manager window
QkUngroup	Removes the group definition
RevDate	Inserts and revises user name, company name, drawing name, date, and time on the TITLE_BLOCK layer
SetEnv	Sets the values of environment variables in the Windows registry

Differences in User Interface

The user interfaces of AutoCAD and AutoCAD LT seem indentical to the untrained eye. The structure of the menus and toolbars differs between AutoCAD LT and AutoCAD, because AutoCAD has fewer commands and, in some cases, different commands.

The most dramatic difference is with the **Insert** menu. The following illustration highlights the differences between AutoCAD LT 2006 (left) and AutoCAD 2006 (right):

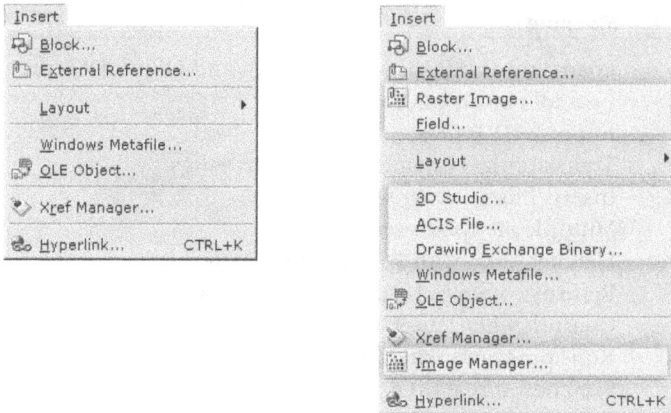

Other Differences in User Interface

Other user interface differences include the items detailed below.

In AutoCAD LT, the status line displays 2D x,y coordinates, rather than the 3D x,y,z coordinates displayed by AutoCAD. *Workaround*: add the z coordinate with the **ModeMacro** command and appropriate DIESEL code.

AutoCAD allows multiple UCSs per viewport; AutoCAD LT is restricted to a single UCS per viewport.

AutoCAD has seven options for the **ShadeMode** command; fewer are available in AutoCAD LT.

In AutoCAD LT, the **Export** command exports only WMF and DWG (Wblock), although the **PsOut** command also exports drawings in EPS format; the **Import** command is limited to WMF. AutoCAD also exports ACIS, STL, DXX Extract, BMP, and 3D Studio formats.

AutoCAD LT's **Open** and **SaveAs** commands lack the DWS format (drawing standard) found in AutoCAD, because AutoCAD LT does not have the commands related to enforcing CAD standards.

AutoCAD LT's **Group** command displays the *non-modal* Group Manager window; in AutoCAD, the **Group** command displays the *modal* Object Grouping dialog box (see the following illustrations).

Modal means that the dialog box must be dismissed before you can continue editing the drawing; non-modal means the window can stay open.

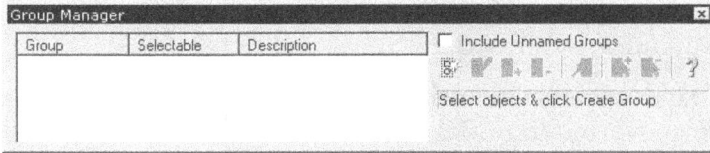

AutoCAD LT's Group Manager window is non-modal

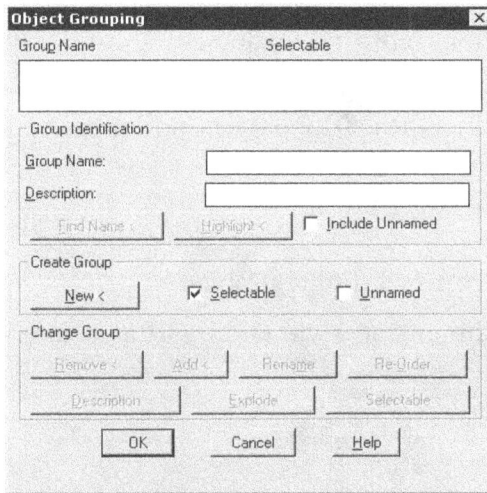

AutoCAD's Object Grouping dialog box is modal

DWG File Compatibility

For the most part, AutoCAD LT and AutoCAD can read each other's DWG files accurately, with some exceptions.

AutoCAD LT displays — but cannot create — xref clipping paths, images, 3D surface and solid models, and landscape objects.

AutoCAD LT does not display multiple user-defined coordinate systems in a single drawing file; or 2D and 3D solid object shading.

Compatibility with Earlier AutoCAD Versions

Objects specific to AutoCAD LT 2004, 2005, and 2006 are erased or converted to a format compatible with earlier releases of AutoCAD LT:

LT 2000 and Earlier

The Model tab and the current layout tab are saved, but multiple layouts and layout names are erased.

Names of layers, views, and other objects are truncated to 32 characters. Spaces are converted to underscores.

Lightweight polylines and hatch patterns are converted to Release 12 polylines and hatch patterns.

Solids, bodies, regions, ellipses, leaders, multilines, rays, tolerances, and xlines are converted to similar-looking lines, arcs, and circles.

Groups, complex linetypes, OLE objects, and preview images are not displayed.

LT 98 and Earlier

Dimension text is converted to text objects.

Additions to the dimension style table and associated system variables are ignored.

New system variables are erased.

LT 97 and Earlier

Groups listed by the List command.

Regions identified as regions but cannot be manipulated.

Revision cloud converted to a series of polylines.

LT 95 and Earlier

Ellipse converted to a series of polyline arcs or a circle.

Hatch pattern associativity lost.

LT Release 2 and Earlier

Xline converted to a line, cut off at the drawing extents.

Ray converted to a line, cut off at the drawing extents.

Spline converted to a series of polylines.

TrueType fonts converted to txt.shx font.

Mtext (paragraph text) converted to multiple text objects; individual formatting may be lost.

> **NOTE**   To use drawings with AutoCAD LT Release 2, save them using the **SaveAs** command's AutoCAD R12/LT2 DXF option.

LT Release 1

Leader converted to lines or polylines; arrows are converted to filled or unfilled circles, polygons, or polylines.

Global linetype scale ignored.

Shape definitions in complex linetypes ignored.

OLE objects ignored.

Overlays ignored.

Preview image ignored.

Tolerance converted to polylines and text.

Notes

Index

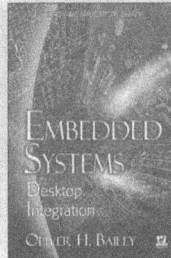

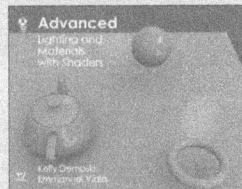